U0023394

觀察・類推・條理化 上冊
分析性的英語語法

湯廷池──編著 許淑慎──監修

SYNTAX

ENGLISH GRAMMAR

元華文創

〈永世夫妻〉

青梅竹馬，笑開懷於寒冬中。

新竹高中與新竹女中教書時，嬉戲於竹中操場。

兒子一家人返臺探親，歡樂於新竹照相館。

與學生共度 80 歲生日，悲喜交織於臺北餐聚。

〈教學相長〉

以「誤人子弟，天誅地滅」互勉，切磋於竹中宿舍。

與學生參加國際研討會，留影於中研院蓮花池。

〈有你真好〉

湯廷池老師生前熱愛慢跑，經常帶著學生在新竹十八尖山跑步，
亦師亦友，輔導課業與生活於綠意盎然小徑中。

清華大學語言學研究所追思網址

https://ling.site.nthu.edu.tw/p/406-1400-187636,r5972.php?Lang=zh-tw

http://ling.hss.nthu.edu.tw/tingchitang/

http://140.114.116.1/tingchitang/

編著者自序

湯廷池：新竹中學 1951 年第四屆畢業

摘　自：新竹中學 1961 年第十四屆畢業生《2011 年五十週年同學會紀念冊》

　　我並不是一個十分用功的學生，只是喜歡靠自己讀書，尤其是喜歡靠自己觀察、分析、思考、推論。我對於教育這個工作懷有深厚的使命感，臺大法律系畢業以後，就與臺大外文系畢業的妻子，分別回到母校新竹高中與新竹女中擔任英文教員。我們時常以「誤人子弟，天誅地滅」互勉，幾乎課本裡的每一個生字都查詢家裡的每一部英文辭典，不但準備了非常詳盡的教案，還在家裡預演如何上課。1963 年與 1971 年我前後兩次出國，都在極短時間內順利獲得學位歸國。這樣的表現並非由於我特別的聰明或用功，而是來自平時的「教學相長」，是學生對我的期望與我對學生的責任感造就了今天的我。

　　我的專業領域是語言學，特別是華語、英語、日語的語法理論與分析，而我今生的志願則是把現代語言學的理論與方法傳授給學生，好讓現代語言學在國內生根茁壯。教學生涯已五十五年，五十五年如一日，一直樂在其中，不改其樂。教學為的是回報，著書為的是薪傳。活到老學到老，人盡其才而物盡其用。無論自己的年紀多大，都願意把自己當做資源回收與廢物利用的對象來繼續努力，一直到最後回歸大地為止。

編著者介紹

　　湯廷池，臺灣苗栗縣通霄人，一九三一年生，一九五七年與畢業於臺灣大學外文系的青梅竹馬許淑慎小姐共結連理。臺灣大學法學學士、美國德州大學奧斯汀分校語言學碩士、美國德州大學奧斯汀分校語言學博士。曾任臺灣師範大學英語學系與研究所教授、清華大學外國語文學系教授兼創系主任與語言學研究所教授、輔仁大學語言學研究所兼任教授、東吳大學日本語文學系兼任教授、元智大學應用外語系教授兼創系主任、輔仁大學翻譯學研究所兼任教授、交通大學語言與文化研究所兼任教授、新竹教育大學臺灣語言與語言教育研究所兼任教授、東吳大學日本語文學系所客座教授、輔仁大學外語學院野聲講座教授、輔仁大學跨文化研究所兼任教授。二〇二〇年九月二十一日與愛妻一起長眠於家鄉通霄。

　　曾獲得「行政院圖書出版金鼎獎」、「教育部六藝獎章」、「中華民國語文獎章」、「行政院國家科學委員會傑出研究獎」、「行政院國家科學委員會優等研究獎」、「行政院國家科學委員會特約研究人員」、「中華民國英語教師學會終身貢獻獎」、「傑出人才發展基金會傑出人才講座」、「中華民國私立教育事業協會大仁獎章」、「教育部教育文化獎章」、「元智大學績敘獎勵研究特優獎」、「元智大學第七屆研究獎傑出教授獎助一等獎」、「臺灣語言學學會終身成就獎」等獎勵。著有五十多本專書，以及數百篇期刊論文與會議論文。

主要專書

1968.（與楊景邁共編）《如何教英語》臺北：東華書局。

1969a. *A Transformational Analysis of Japanese Verbs and Verb Phrases.* 臺北：海國書局。

1969b. *A Transformational Approach to Teaching English Sentence Patterns.* 臺北：海國書局。

1972a.《國語格變語法試論》臺北：海國書局。

1972b. (with co-editors C. H. Tung and Y. T. Wu) Papers in linguistics in honor of A. A. Hill. 臺北：臺灣虹橋書店。

1973.（與許淑慎共編）《現代高中英文：社會組》臺北：海國書局。

1974.（與許淑慎共編）《現代高中英文：自然組》臺北：海國書局。

1973-1976.《實用高級英語語法》（共六冊）臺北：海國書局。

1975.《國語格變語法動詞的分類研究》臺北：海國書局。

1977a.《國語變形語法研究第一集：移位變形》臺北：臺灣學生書局。

1977b.《英語教學論集》臺北：臺灣學生書局。

1978. (with co-editors R. L. Cheng and Y.-C. Li) Proceedings of Symposium on Chinese Linguistics. (1977 Linguistic Institute of the Linguistic Society of America). 臺北：臺灣學生書局。

1978-1979.《最新實用高級英語語法》（共兩冊）臺北：海國書局。

1979a.《國語語法研究論集》臺北：臺灣學生書局。

1979b. (with co-editors F. F. Tsao and I. Li) Proceeding of 1979 Asian and Pacific Conference on Linguistics and Language Teaching, August 24-26. 臺北：臺灣學生書局。

1980. 主編《一九七九年亞太地區語言教學研討會論集》臺北：臺灣學生書局。

1981.《語言學與語文教學》臺北：臺灣學生書局。

1984a.《英語語法修辭十二講：從傳統到現代》臺北：臺灣學生書局。

1984b.《英語語言分析入門：英語語法教學問答》臺北：臺灣學生書局。

1985.《最新實用高級英語語法（修訂本）》（共兩冊）臺北：海國書局。

1988a.《英語認知語法：結構、意義與功用（上集）》臺北：臺灣學生書局。

1988b.《漢語詞法句法論集》臺北：臺灣學生書局。

1989a.《漢語詞法句法續集》臺北：臺灣學生書局。

1989b.《國中英語教學指引》臺北：臺灣學生書局。

1992a.《英語認知語法：結構、意義與功用（中集）》臺北：臺灣學生書局。

1992b.《漢語詞法句法三集》臺北：臺灣學生書局。

1992c.《漢語詞法句法四集》臺北：臺灣學生書局。

1994a.《英語認知語法：結構、意義與功用（下集）》臺北：臺灣學生書局。

1994b.《漢語詞法句法五集》臺北：臺灣學生書局。

1999a.《日語語法與日語教學》臺北：臺灣學生書局。

1999b.《閩南語語法研究試論》臺北：臺灣學生書局。

2000a.《極小主義分析導論：基本概念與原則》臺北：金字塔出版社。

2000b.《漢語詞法論集》臺北：金字塔出版社。

2000c.《漢語語法論集》臺北：金字塔出版社。

2000d.《英語語法論集》臺北：金字塔出版社。

2002a.（與姚榮松等共編）《古典散文選》（共三冊）臺北：國立編譯館出版。

2002b.（與姚榮松等共編）《古典散文選・教師手冊》（共三冊）臺北：國立編譯館出版。

2010a.（許淑慎監修）《語言學、語言分析與語言教學（上冊）》臺北：致良出版社。

2010b.（許淑慎監修）《語言學、語言分析與語言教學（下冊）》臺北：致良出版社。

2012a.（許淑慎監修）《日語形容詞研究入門（上冊）》臺北：致良出版社。

2012b.（許淑慎監修）《日語形容詞研究入門（下冊）》臺北：致良出版社。

2014a.（許淑慎監修）《英語應用語言學研究入門（上冊）》臺北：致良出版社。

2014b.（許淑慎監修）《英語應用語言學研究入門（下冊）》臺北：致良出版社。

2014c.（許淑慎監修）《英語語法研究入門》臺北：致良出版社。

2014d.（許淑慎監修）《華語詞法研究入門（上冊）》臺北：致良出版社。

2015a.（許淑慎監修）《對比分析研究入門（上冊）》臺北：致良出版社。

2015b.（許淑慎監修）《對比分析研究入門（下冊）》臺北：致良出版社。

2015c.（許淑慎監修）《華語詞法研究入門（中冊）》臺北：致良出版社。

2015d.（許淑慎監修）《華語詞法研究入門（下冊）》臺北：致良出版社。

2016.（許淑慎監修）《華語語言分析入門》臺北：致良出版社。

2018a.（許淑慎監修）《河洛語語法研究入門（上冊）》臺北：致良出版社。

2018b.（許淑慎監修）《河洛語語法研究入門（下冊）》臺北：致良出版社。

2019a.（許淑慎監修）《英語形式句法分析導論（上冊）》臺北：致良出版社。

2019b.（許淑慎監修）《英語形式句法分析導論（中冊）》臺北：致良出版社。

2019c.（許淑慎監修）《英語形式句法分析導論（下冊）》臺北：致良出版社。

2019d.（許淑慎監修）《語言學 英、日、華 術語對照與簡介（上冊）》臺北：致良出版社。

2019e.（許淑慎監修）《語言學 英、日、華 術語對照與簡介（下冊）》臺北：致良出版社。

2021a.（許淑慎監修）《日本語言語学研究入門（上）》臺北：致良出版社。

2021b.（許淑慎監修）《日本語言語学研究入門（中）》臺北：致良出版社。

2021c.（許淑慎監修）《日本語言語学研究入門（下）》臺北：致良出版社。

推薦序一

《觀察 ‧ 類推 ‧ 條理化：分析性的英語語法》
——傳授顯性語言知識的一個典範

　　英語教學一直存在兩種不同的觀點：一種觀點認為，傳授語法知識是重要的，不僅需要讓學生在使用英語的時候符合語法規則，而且還要讓學生了解語言形式背後所蘊含的規則，就是說學生需要具備顯性語言知識；另一種觀點則認為，教授英語應該以有效的練習和強化方法，讓學生培養聽說讀寫能力，在日常交際中運用自如。能做到這點，就表示已經掌握了語法規則，至於是否了解英語語法規則，並不重要。湯廷池教授 30 多年前出版的《最新實用高級英語語法》(修訂本)，是傳授顯性語言知識的一個典範，至今仍然有極大的參考價值。舊版的檔案雖然早已遺失，幸好隨著科技的進步，掃描舊版原書後，更名為《觀察‧類推‧條理化：分析性的英語語法》，由元華文創重新編排，分成上下兩冊出版。

　　《最新實用高級英語語法（修訂本）》成書於 1985 年，正是英語教學熱衷於宣揚傳意語言教學（communicative language teaching）的年代（Wilkins 1976; Widdowson 1978; Johnson 1982）。在這之前的 1950-1960 年代，英語教學法受美國行為主義影響，盛行機械式口語練習（oral drills），認為通過強化某些句式，口語能力就能得到顯著提高，這種客觀的語言能力提升是對學員最大的鼓勵，其激勵作用不亞於有趣生動的課堂教學（Lado 1964）。這種強調句式操練的教學法，過分突出語法形式而忽略語意和語境，很快就顯示其弱點。學員們往往死記硬背了許多語法規則和句子結構，也難以真正把結構掌握好；由於脫離語境，不一定能用得上，或者用在不恰當的場景。因此，自 1970 年中期開始，就有許多應用語言學專家提倡，語言教學法應以語意和傳意為基礎，認為學員只要能在特定語境準確使用恰當的語句，就意味著他 / 她們掌握了傳意語法（communicative grammar）。

　　在 1970 年代當英語老師的時候，有一位資深英國老師就跟我推薦一種實用的傳意語言教學觀點，認為針對一種情景（例如問候，問路、或者承諾）只需要學一

兩種恰當而管用的固定句式，能夠在相關情景下運用自如，這樣就足夠了，不需要學那麼多不同的句法形式。我們的確常遇到一種情況：學員上課時學了各種不同句式，但碰到特定的情景，如問候、問路、承諾等，就要思索該用哪種形式，反而變得結結巴巴，說不出口，達不到語言溝通的基本功能。傳意語言教學法以交際互動、語言功能為基礎，對英語學習者來說似乎很管用，用這種方法很快就能用英語來實現某種傳意功能，滿足交際需要。

　　然而，對二語學習者來說，傳意教學法的局限也是顯而易見的。任何一個語言都有豐富的詞彙，裡面的名詞、動詞、形容詞都有著複雜的內容，儘管普遍語法規定了人類語言的普遍通則，讓我們對句法形式和語意的搭配有一些基本的認識，但畢竟語言之間具有許多差異，每個語言都存在著一定的獨特個性和偏離常規的例外，這些都需要我們對語法形式反覆推敲，對語言細微之處有所體會，否則是無法提高到高級水平層次的。例如，高級英語學習者在用關於「建議、推薦、要求」等動詞的時候，常會犯如（1a-1c）裡面的錯誤。英語中 *suggest, recommend, demand* 等動詞後面的子句，需要用假設法現在式（subjunctive mood，上冊第 7 章），而不是用不定詞動詞（infinitive –to）。就是說，必須使用光杆動詞原形 "V" 或者用 "should +V" 這種格式，如（2a-2c）所示。

（1）　a. *John suggested us to invite our teacher to the party.

　　　　b. *The artist recommended us to design a poster for the event.

　　　　c. *The residents demanded the mayor to build a bridge.

（2）　a. John suggested that we invite our teacher to the party.

　　　　　John suggested that we should invite our teacher to the party.

　　　　b. The artist recommended that we design a poster for the event.

　　　　　The artist recommended that we should design a poster for the event.

　　　　c. The residents demanded that the mayor build a bridge.

　　　　　The residents demanded that the mayor should build a bridge.

　　為何英語需要用假設語氣來表達子句所表述的未然情況，而不用普通的不定詞 "to VP" 子句結構，這涉及英語本身一些特殊情況，學習英語時需要特加注意，否則會不斷犯錯而不察覺，強化了這種錯誤。

　　為何連英語程度不錯的學員也會犯這種錯誤？因為在一定程度上，用 "to VP" 格式來表達「建議、推薦、要求」等言語行為的物件，是符合語法規律的。原因有二：首先，"to VP" 這個形式一般表達未然情況或事件，而相對於表達「建議、推薦、要求」等言語行為來說，子句所表達的都屬於尚未發生的行動或情況。第二，許多語義上跟 "suggest, recommend, demand" 近似的動詞，如 "request, advise, require" 等動詞，卻容許帶 "to VP" 作為子句補語，從（3a-3c）例句可見。如果學員們用類比（analogy）推算就很容易認為，既然（3）裡面的例子成立，例子（1）裡面的句子應該也符合語法。這些與英語具體動詞相關的細節，需要學習者仔細掌握。對於高階英語學員來說，關於英語語法的顯性知識（explicit knowledge）是必須具備的，否則難以糾正自己常犯的語法錯誤，無法自我提升英語水平。

（3）a. John requested us to invite our teacher to the party.

　　　b. The artist advised us to design a poster for the event.

　　　c. The law requires us to put on our seat belt while driving.

　　湯廷池教授的《觀察 ‧ 類推 ‧ 條理化：分析性的英語語法》正是一本弘揚顯性語法知識的典範英語語法參考書，具有以下幾個特點，值得讀者注意。

（一）定義清晰；清楚區分形式與語義

　　本書以簡單清晰的語言來定義語法術語，並把一些容易混淆的概念清楚界定。例如，Time（時間）和 tense（時式）的區分，以及可數名詞與不可數名詞的區分，對初次接觸英語語法的讀者來說，都是容易混淆的概念。本參考語法把這些基本語法概念都梳理得非常清楚，把語言形式及其所表達的語意加以嚴格區分。

‧ 時間（time）和 時式（tense）的區分

　　第三章「十二種動詞時變式」對時式和時間的區分就有以下說明：「英語的動詞只有兩種『時式』（tense）：現在式（present）與過去式（past）」。「我們必須區別時式與時間（time）這兩個不同的概念。時間指過去、現在、未來所有的時間；時式卻指動詞的形式。我們用各種不同的時式來表示各種不同的時間，但是現在式不一定表示現在時間，過去式也不一定代表過去時間。」既然英語只有現在式和過去式，而沒有未來時式，如何表達未來時間，書中就有詳細的討論，和更進一

步的複習，鞏固讀者對這個區別的認識。

· 可數名詞與不可數名詞的區分

有些傳統英語語法著作，把可數名詞和不可數名詞用語義標準加以區分，認為可數名詞指向可以數數的物體（如 *person*「人」、*table*「桌子」、*car*「汽車」、*computer*「電腦」等名詞），而不可數名詞則描述不可數的物質（如 *water*「水」、*milk*「牛奶」、*meat*「肉」、*air*「空氣」等名詞）。語言學家很早就指出，以語意區分可數與不可數名詞是站不住腳的（Gleason 1965），這個語法區別只能用形式分佈來加以定義。本書上冊第 11 章就是以形式和分佈對這個區分進行說明的。

「名詞如果可以有『單數形』（singular）與『複數形』（plural），就叫做可數名詞（count nouns）」。「可數名詞的單數形，必須加上冠詞 *a*（*an*），*the* 或其他『限定詞』（如 *this, that* 等）」。「僅有單數形、不能有複數形的名詞叫做不可數名詞（noncount nouns）」；「不可數名詞不能加上 *a*（*an*），但是可以加上 some, the, this, that 等。」按照這個清晰的標準，*person, table, car, computer* 都是可數名詞，因為既有單數形，也有複數形 *persons, tables, cars, computers*。而 *water, milk, meat, air* 則只有單數形，而且不能在名詞前面加不定冠詞 *a*（*n*），因此屬不可數名詞。[1]

· 助動詞的詞類定義

本書對助動詞這個詞類的定義，也是嚴格用語言形式來界定的。上冊第 1 章就開宗明義說，英語的句型按照動詞可以劃分為三種；含有 *be* 的句型；含有助動詞的句型；以及含有 *be* 和助動詞以外的動詞。英語助動詞不多，就以列舉定義，包括 *will, would; shall, should; can, could; may, might; must; have, has, had; ought to*。當然，在談到助動詞特點的時候，會介紹各個助動詞所表達的語意，但關鍵是在定義這個詞類時，只列出形式準則，沒有用語意標準。

1　這幾個詞如果加了 -s，變成 *waters, milks, meats, airs*，當然也符合語法，但就不是原來名詞的涵義了。

（二）本參考語法介紹了大量的語法規則細節，主要不是用抽象的符號
　　　規則或語言學課上常用的樹形圖，而是通過示範和大量的例句。
　　　在介紹規則的時候，也注重詞彙的個性和例外。

　　以下用五個實例來說明湯教授參考語法的豐富內容。

‧ 假設法（subjunctive mood）的使用

　　本書第 7 章在介紹假設法（subjunctive mood）的使用時，清楚列舉哪些動詞
和形容詞需要用上這種句型。

　　「在表示『提議』、『請求』或『命令』的動詞（如 suggest, request, order 等）
後面的子句，常用動詞的基本式（「假設法現在」）：

The doctor suggested that the patient stop smoking.

We requested that he give us another chance.

The judge ordered that the prisoner be set free.

She demanded that she be given a fair trial.」

　　所選的子句都用第三人稱單數作為主語，因為這樣才能顯示假設法現在式的語
法特點。還進一步說明，如果子句為否定句，否定詞 not 應該放在什麼位置；並指
出，除了用動詞基本式（即動詞原形）外，還可以用 "should" 與動詞的基本式來
代替假設法現在式。

　　此外，本書還指出，假設法現在式的使用並不限於動詞，有些形容詞也需要
用這種句式：「在表示『重要』、『需要』或『適當』的形容詞（如 important,
necessary, proper 等）後面的子句，也常用動詞的基本式。這是一般英語語法書極
少會談到的細節。

It is important that he follow the doctor's directions.

It is necessary the he be there by noon.

It is essential that I not be disturbed before I finish my letter.」

‧ *Tough-* 前移句型

　　英語有些句式，涉及主賓語位置的互換，有一種句型將不定式子句（infinitival
clause）的賓語前移到主句的主語位置，英語語法書常稱作「*tough-* 前移句型」。

本書下冊第 15 章對此句型做了以下介紹：

「拿『不定詞子句』做主語，因此也可以改成『It is ＋ 形容詞 ＋ 不定詞子句』的句型：

For them to solve the question is difficult.

It is difficult for them to solve the question.

這種句型，不定詞的賓語可以取代句首的 it 而變成主句的主語：

The question is difficult for them to solve.」

書上接著指出，能否有「*tough-* 前移句型」要看動詞和述語而定。例如，impossible 可以容納這種句型，但 possible 就不行，如下列句子所示。事實上，如 "He is possible to reason with" 這樣的句子，正是高階英語學習者常犯的錯誤。本書一方面詳細介紹語法規則細節，也同時關注一些具體特例，兩方面都兼顧。

<u>It</u> is impossible to reason with <u>him</u>.

<u>He</u> is impossible to reason with.

<u>It</u> is possible to reason with <u>him</u>.

*<u>He</u> is possible to reason with.

・助動詞的使用

上冊第五章介紹表示情態的助動詞，指出這些助動詞在屈折形式形態上的特點。「助動詞與主動詞不同，不因為主語的身與數而變化。因此助動詞只有現在式（can, may, will, shall, must）與過去式（could, might, would, should, must），沒有第三身單數現在式（V-s），也沒有現在分詞式（V-ing）或過去分詞式（V-en）」。除了描述典型的助動詞外，還談到 ought to, need, dare, used to 等比較特別的助動詞的用法。在介紹 need 的時候，指出這個詞可以當主動詞用，也可以當助動詞用，但當助動詞用的時候，「只限於否定句與帶有否定意味的問句裡。」

（主動詞用法）

He needs to work so late.

Does he need to work so late?

He doesn't need to work so late, does he?

（助動詞用法）

Need he work so late?

He needn't work so late, need he?

在介紹 used to 作為助動詞的時候，則指出 used 的否定式與問句式，美式英語多用 did not use to 於 did...use to 這些句型。

He didn't use to talk much.

Did he use to play tennis?

You used to play tennis, didn't you?

・關係代詞 whose 的使用問題

對高階英語語法學習者來說，如何處理所有格關係代詞 whose 是令人困惑的問題，何時能用，何時不能用，如何界定？關於這個細節，本書下冊第 17 章解釋如下：

「關係代名詞 whose 用來代替名詞（或代名詞）的所有格。這個名詞主要的是表示人的名詞，但是偶爾也可能是表示物或動物的名詞。注意：這個時候 whose 後面的名詞也要一起提前放在關係子句的句首。」

You bought the man's car./

（I met）the man whose car you bought.

The editor of the newspaper was fired./

（Have you read）the newspaper whose editor was fired?

The windows of the house are broken./

（Can you see）the house whose windows are broken?

（Can you see）the house of which the windows are broken?

作者一方面指出所有格關係代詞可以代替無生名詞，但從修辭效果考慮則主張避免使用，建議改用其他句式來表達同樣意思：「無生名詞的所有格，一般都避免用關係代名詞 whose 或 of which 來代替，而改用由 with 引導的介詞片語。

Can you see the house whose windows/of which the windows are broken?（欠通順）

Can you see the house with broken windows?（較通順）」

‧ 關係代詞和「介詞流落」（preposition stranding）

英語關係子句中當關係代詞為介詞的賓語的時候，介詞與關係代詞一起前移，還是讓介詞留在動詞後面，這是一個「介詞流落」（preposition stranding）的語法現象。本書下冊第 17 章對何時介詞留在動詞後頭，何時不能，都有詳細描述。對不同的關係代詞和介詞出現的語法環境都有明確規定，讓讀者一目了然。

「當關係代名詞 whom 是介詞賓語的時候，介詞可以放在關係代名詞的前面，也可以放在關係子句的句尾：

the man with whom you dined（較文的說法）

the man who（m）you dined with（口語的說法）」

「在下列情況中，介詞只能放在關係子句的後面。」

（a）當關係代名詞被省略的時候：

This is the house we have been invited to.

（b）當關係代名詞是 that, as 或 but 的時候：

This is the very book that I am looking for.

There is no one but he can find fault with.

（c）當關係代名詞同時做兩個以上介詞的賓語的時候：

What is the subject（that）you have seen an increasing interest in and controversy over?

「在下列的情形，介詞常放在關係代名詞（whom, which）的前面。」

（a）連接關係子句：

George, with whom I used to go to school, is now a well-known novelist.

（b）關係代名詞前面有「數量詞」all, both, some, many, none, neither, one 等。

I have two friends, both of whom are on holiday at the moment.

（c）介詞與關係代名詞 which 所代替的名詞形成一種固定的狀態副詞片語：

the courage with which he faced the enemy

（d）beyond, around, opposite, besides, than, as to, outside, except, during, considering 等介詞，一般都放在關係代名詞的前面。

the man opposite whom I'm sitting

the fountain around which they are standing

高階英語學習者在掌握上述假設式子句、*tough* 子句賓語前提、典型與非典型助動詞、以及關係代詞等虛詞和句式特點的時候，既需要掌握規律，也需要瞭解常規之外的情況，需要學習許多句式和虛詞的獨特性，否則學不好英文。由於這些虛詞和句式的特點和限制，對一般二語學員來說，不一定出現在平日接觸到的語料裡面，因此只能靠顯性知識去掌握。湯教授的參考語法提供了豐富的參考指引。

（三）本書雖然強調語法形式的重要性，沒有依循傳意語法的路子，但卻對詞彙之間的細微差異以及句式和語意的搭配非常重視，因為語言形式之間的語意和語用差別，是學員所必須掌握的。以下也用五個實例來說明本書這個特點。

·內動詞和外動詞的區別

英語的表達聽覺和視覺具備兩套動詞，一套表達積極的知覺模態，即個體行動者主動地、有意識地去注意一些現象，如 look at, listen to；還有一套描述非積極的知覺模態，即由於外部環境的感知或外部因素而得到了某種知覺或產生了某種變化，如 see, hear。這種積極與非積極模態的區別也體現在其他動詞的差別上，如 look for 和 find 的差別，前者表達積極的尋找，而後者表示「找到了」，達到了目的。本書把前者稱為「外動詞」（public verbs），把後者稱為「內動詞」（privative verbs），在上冊第 4 章有詳細的列舉。

"I *see* him now.（「看見、看到」：內動詞）

I *am looking at* him now.（「看」：外動詞）

I *hear* the music now.（「聽見、聽到」：內動詞）

I *am listening to* the music now.（「聽」：外動詞）

·追問句的語調

語法和語調的相互作用，對英語學習者來說是不好掌握的，這方面具備語法和語用知識，懂得其中規律，會有很大的幫助。本書上冊第 1 章對追問句（tag question）的語調特點有很好的說明，指出如 "He's an American, isn't he?" 這樣的句子，如果尾部追問部分 "isn't he?" 是降調，表示說話者對所說的話相當有把握；

如果尾部追問部分是升調，則表示說話者對所說的話沒有多大把握。同樣一串詞語和句式，如果語調不一樣，問句的預設將會截然不同。這種句法與語調的複雜界面現象，對於英語學習者來說，是非常重要的資訊。

以下的例子更能說明，本書對語法與語意之間的關係非常重視，而且所提出的描述分析，是其他英語參考語法不一定提到的。書中下冊第 16 章，對英語動詞的過去分詞兩種用法，有如下介紹：

· 動詞過去分詞作為形容詞

「動詞的『過去分詞』或『en 式動詞』也可以放在名詞的前面做修飾語。這個時候，及物動詞的過去分詞含有『被動（被……的）』的意思；不及物動詞的過去分詞含有「完成（已經……的）」意思。」

文中還提醒讀者注意，過去分詞作為形容詞，放在名詞前作為修飾語和放在系動詞後面作為補語，意思是不一樣的。例如，"the broken cup" 的涵義是「被打破的杯子」而 "the cup is broken" 描述一種靜態的狀況「那個杯子是破的」。同樣的，"a wounded soldier" 涵義是「一個受傷的士兵」；而 "a soldier was wounded"，除了可以表示「有一個士兵被打傷了」這個意思外，還可以描述有一個過去的狀態，即「有一個士兵曾經是受過傷的」，目前這個狀態已不再存在。另外，如 "fall" 這樣的非及物動詞，"a fallen leaf" 描述一片已經墜落在地上的樹葉，但 "a leaf has fallen" 可以描述一片正在墜落的樹葉。

the broken cup（比較：The cup is broken.）

a wounded soldier（比較：A soldier was wounded.）

a fallen leaf（比較：A leaf has fallen.）

書中還進一步指出，不是所有動詞的過去分詞都可以作為形容詞的，有些過去分詞具有形容詞特點，可以出現在名詞前作為修飾語，被加強詞修飾，也可以作補語，如 *tired, surprised, pleased* 等過去分詞。但也有一些過去分詞並不是形容詞，不能被加強詞（如 very）修飾而出現在名詞前或者系詞後面，如 *wounded, punished, beaten*。[2] 這些細緻的差別，是高級英語學習者不一定能察覺到的，通過

2　對於什麼動詞的過去分詞能充當形容詞，後來的語法著作有更詳細的二語習得分析，請參看 Wang and Lee（1999）.

語法書來掌握相關知識，是有效的途徑。

The boy was very tired/surprised/pleased.

*The boy was very wounded/punished/beaten.

·動名詞

本書對動名詞（gerundive nominal）一些形式及語意上的差別，也有詳細解說。例如，"I don't like your coming late" 和 "I don't like you coming late"，或者 "I hate Bob's borrowing money from me" 和 "I hate Bob borrowing money from me"，前者用了所有格 's，後者則只是賓格，到底有什麼差別？這種問題是高階英語學習者常有的疑惑。下冊第 43 頁詳細列出哪些動詞可以帶動名詞 V-ing 形式（gerund）作為賓語，並區分兩種動名詞，一種如 like, prefer, fancy, hate, dislike, detest, mind, dread, fear, regret, understand, remember 等動詞，可以出現在「主語＋動詞＋所有格（代）名詞＋V-ing…」句型，而另一種如 finish, avoid, advise, suggest, deny, begin, continue, postpone, need, want 等動詞，則只出現在「主語＋動詞＋V-ing…」句型。書中並指出「主語＋動詞＋所有格（代）名詞＋V-ing…」可以變成「主語＋動詞＋賓格（代）名詞＋V-ing…」，但兩者有細微的語義差別：「在日常口語中常把所有格（代）名詞改為賓格，以表示所強調的是引起事件的人而非事件本身。」

·時間介詞的特點

作者對語意的重視，從對動詞的分類可見。上冊第 4 章就提出，表示瞬間的動詞和表示持續時段的動詞，其搭配情況是不一樣的，需要區分。「根據能否有表示時間長短的副詞，英語的動詞可以分為兩種。『持續性動詞』（如 live, stay, wait, sit, stand, sleep, lie, work, study, read, write, listen 等）可以有由 for, till, until 引導的期間副詞。」因此可以說以下句子：

They waited for a long time.

He slept till/until nine o'clock.

「『瞬間性動詞』（如 come, go, leave, start, arrive, die, appear, disappear 等）不可以有由 for, till, until 引導的期間副詞。」因此不能說以下句子：

*They came for a long while.

*He left till/until nine o'clock.

書中同時指出，持續性的動詞可以出現在由 while 引導的副詞子句中，而瞬間性的動詞卻不能。因此可以說 The band was playing while I waited；但不能說 *The band was playing while I left。相反地，持續性動詞不能出現在由 when 引導的副詞子句中，而瞬間性的動詞卻能。因此不能說 *The band was playing when I waited; 但可以說 The band was playing when I left。

書中對時間介詞一些細微的差別，有精確的描述。例如，下冊第 19 章對 for 和 during 的時間特點有以下補充：「for 一般表示『不特定的期間』；during 表示『特定的期間』。」例如，在下列句子，for 都是跟表不定時間段的短語搭配，如 for two weeks, for several months；而 during 則跟特定時間段搭配，如 during the summer, during the vacation 等短語。這些精細而重要的語義差別，在書中處處可見，讓讀者常有驚喜。

We waited for a week/two weeks/several months.

I hope to see you some time during the week/the summer/ the vacation.

He was in Japan for the month of May. 「整個五月都在日本」

He was in Japan during May. 「不一定整個五月都在日本」

（四）本書的第四個特點，在於書中所描述的許多語法細節，吸收了當代語言學（尤其是生成語法學）1960-1980 年代的最新研究成果，從書中的參考書目可見作者的研究素養和功力。

‧動詞的補語子句

在 1970 年代生成語法對動詞補語子句有深入的分析，將動詞按照子句類型的不同，加以分類，並以此作為基礎揭示各種語法現象，讓人能對複雜句結構有一個通盤的認識（Bresnan 1972; Grimshaw 1979）。本書下冊第十五章將動詞的補語子句稱為「名詞子句」，指出有四種名詞子句：[that- 子句]、[wh- 子句]、[不定詞 -子句]、[動名詞子句]，並舉例說明：

I know that he has arrived. （ [that- 子句]）

I know when we should start. （[wh- 子句]）

It is easy for us to study English. （ [不定詞子句]）

Nobody knows my going to Japan.（[動名詞子句]）

該章節詳細列出，哪些動詞和形容詞可以接受 [that- 子句] 做為賓語，哪些接受 [wh- 子句] 做為賓語。及後更指出，有些動詞可以容許子句中的 wh- 詞提前移到句首，有些動詞卻不可以。同時提醒讀者，疑問句中子句中的 wh- 詞，移到兩個位置，表達兩種不同的語義；wh- 詞在句首表達一個特指問句；wh- 詞在子句之首，則表達是非問句。名詞子句（即補語子句 complement clause）中的 wh- 詞，與主句動詞和句子語義之間的關係，生成語法對 wh- 結構的深入研究，在一定程度上反映在書中對名詞子句的詳細論述。

Do you know <u>when</u> he will come?（yes/no 問句）

<u>When</u> do you think he will come?（wh- 問句）

·關係子句的限制和非限制用法

語法學家在 1970 年代對關係子句的限制和非限制用法，在句法形式和語意特點的分析上，都有不少研究（Peranteau, Levi and Phares 1972; Stockwell, Schachter and Partee 1973），也反映在本書對關係子句的描寫。下冊第 17 章對這兩種關係子句的語義區別有非常簡要準確的說明：

「關係子句在性質上是一個形容詞子句，其功用在修飾前面的名詞。例如在下面的句子裡，關係子句 that was nearest to his house 修飾前面的名詞 the garage，即從眾多的修車廠裡面特地指出離他家最近的那一家修理廠來。

He walked to the garage that was nearest to his house.

『他走到離家最近的修車廠。』

這種用法就叫做關係子句限制的用法（the restrictive use），因為這個時候關係子句的功用在修飾或限制前面的名詞。

另外有些關係子句，其功用並不在修飾前面的名詞，而在連接這個關係子句，以便接著繼續把話說下去。例如在下面的句子裡，我們已經知道他去的是最近的一家修車廠，用不著再用關係子句來告訴我們究竟指的是哪一家。所以這裡關係子句 which was a mile away 的主要目的是，補充說明或者順便提一提這家修車廠座落在一里遠的地方。

He walked to the nearest garage, which was a mile away.

『他走到最近的一家修車廠，而這家修車廠離他家有一里之遠。』

這種用法就叫做連接的用法（the continuative use）。」

本書對關係子句的非限制性用法稱為「連接的用法」，更能帶出這種用法的實質特點，因為這種用法就是針對所修飾的名詞作出補充說明。

· 子句的時式

本書對一些語意現象的描述，也反映了當時語言學界對相關現象的研究成果。如何表達子句裡面的時式（tense），是令高階英語學習者困惑的問題。上冊第 4 章對間接陳述句的時式問題，通過下列例句作出概括。

I said, "I am tired" → I said that I was tired.

He said that honesty is the best policy.

She said that she takes a walk in the park every morning.

「如果傳達動詞是過去式的話，那麼按照時式一致的原則，間接引句裡面的動詞也要改為過去式」。「但是如果間接引句的內容時表示普遍的真理、常習的動作或歷史的事實的話，那麼就不一定要改成過去式或過去完成式。」上面的概括，基本上與語言學家對時式序列（sequence of tenses）所總結的規律一致（Comrie 1985）。

· 論元結構的承襲（argument structure inheritance）

一個動詞具有論元結構，例如在句子 John refused to help 中，及物動詞 refuse「拒絕」有兩個論元，一個是作為施事的主語 John，另一個是作為客體的不定名詞子句 to help。問題是假如這個動詞名詞化了之後，它的論元結構是否仍然存在，是否為衍生的名詞所承襲？就是說，在 refuse 變成名詞 refusal 後，能否說 "John's refusal to help"？這種語法問題在生成語法著作裡面有所討論（Lees 1963; Grimshaw 1990），但在一般參考語法書中極少涉及。本書下冊第 15 章有以下描述，指出一些動詞在名詞化後仍然保留了原來的論元結構和補語特點，有些動詞卻不能：

「含有動詞（如 need, desire, tend, fail, hesitate, guarantee, plan, arrange, agree, request, refuse, promise, decide, threaten, intend, advise, invite, remind 等）與不定詞的

子句可以直接把動詞改為名詞（need, desire, tendency, failure, hesitation, guarantee, plan, arrangement, agreement, request, refusal, promise, decision, threat, intention, advice, invitation, reminder）以後當名片語用。這個時候動詞的主語要用所有格。」

He failed to get the job.

His failure to get the job（made her very unhappy）.

They agreed to help him.

（They forgot all about）their agreement to help him.

有些動詞（如 need, like, prefer）改為名詞（need, liking, preference）以後還要把後面的不定詞改為 for+ V-ing.

→ His preference for eating alone（is quite well known）.

·有定冠詞 *the* 語義的描述

由於漢語是一種沒有冠詞的語言，對母語為漢語的英語學習者來說，英語的冠詞是很難掌握的一個系統，何時該用不定冠詞 a（n），何時用有定冠詞 the，高級學習者也會常犯這方面的錯誤。為何冠詞系統如此難以掌握，其中困難之處在於長久以來對冠詞的句法語意分析，尚未總結出較全面的規律，對冠詞所涉及的各種指稱涵義，也缺乏清晰的界定。這個局面在 1960 年後有了許多突破。例如，Baker（1966）關於定指和不定指的研究引進了 specific/ non-specific（實指 / 虛指）這組指稱概念。Hawkins（1978）的專著比較全面地描述了英語中定指和不定指（definite/ indefinite）的表達方式，從聆聽者的角度，分析了含有定冠詞的名詞短語「the + 名詞」的各種使用情況；有時候 the N 在前文有明顯的先行語，即其所指向的物體，前文已經提過；有時候 the + 名詞可以直接指向語境中的特定物體；但有時候它和前文的連接是比較間接的，需要說話者利用對客觀世界的認識來建立。本書上冊第 12 章對有定冠詞 the 的用法，提出四條規律：

「（1）『後指』：指在前文裡已經出現過的名詞。注意，這些名詞前後用不同的冠詞。」書中並不是孤立看有定冠詞，而是對比不定冠詞 *a*（*n*）和有定冠詞 *the* 的用法。在以下例子，前者 *a cat* 引進一個話語對象，後者 *the cat* 回指先行語 *a cat* 已經引進的對象。

I saw *a cat* in the tree this morning, but when I looked again this afternoon, *the cat* was gone.

「（2）『明指』：名詞的前後有修飾語，足以認定某一個特定的人或物。」在以下例子，「the + 名詞」直接指向語境中的一些物體，是一種直指或明指（deictic）的情況。

Hand me *the longer piece of chalk* on the desk, please.

This is *the book* I have been looking for.

「（3）『暗指』：名詞的前後雖然沒有修飾語，但是從生活經驗或語言情況中仍可以判定所指的是一個特定的人或物。」在下列書中例子，聽話者聽到 the post office，可以憑生活經驗和話語語境判斷，就是指常去的那個郵政局；至於聽到 the letter 也可以憑生活經驗判斷為一般去郵政局時投寄的信件。

He went to *the post office* to mail *the letter*.

「（4）『泛指』：用在單數可數名詞之前，以表示一類的所有分子。」書中指出，定冠詞表類指，有一定的限制，例如只限於單數可數名詞。

The horse is a noble animal.

總的來說，本書關於英語有定冠詞用法的說明，反映了 1960-1970 年代語言學研究這方面取得的成果，從聆聽者的角度來總結有定／無定名詞的使用規律，描述的相當精確。表達指稱概念所採用的中文術語有些也屬作者原創，跟後來語言學研究者常用的一些術語互相輝映。例如，書中用「後指」來代表 anaphora，而不用「回指」；用「明指」來涵蓋一些 deixis（直指）的情況；以「暗指」來代表一種常被稱為 associative use 的有定冠詞用法。這些術語「望文生義」，有助讀者把握術語背後的含義。

如上所述，湯廷池教授的《觀察 · 類推 · 條理化：分析性的英語語法》是一本弘揚顯性語法知識的典範英語語法參考書，對語法規則以及各種虛詞和句型的語意特點都有詳細精要的描述，充分反映現代語言學界的研究成果，許多討論都是一般語法參考書所不會涉及的。湯教授基於多年英語教學的經驗，在介紹相關語法結構的時候，避開抽象的符號，而用具體示範和豐富事例來說明，書中在不同章節都提供了大量的練習，以便讀者鞏固對相關句型結構的理解。英語的語法規則，有

些基本適用與某個語法範疇的所有成員（例如，動詞第三身單數屈折形式 -s）；另外有些規則適用與某個語法範疇的大部分成員，但仍然有不少例外的情況（例如複數標記 -s 加在可數名詞後面）；還有許多其他語法規則（如假設法 subjunctive mood，或者 tough- 前移規則），都只適用與某些動詞。這些都是需要英語學習者特加注意，用詞彙學習的方法去掌握的。作者除了介紹語法規律，還花了大量篇幅討論詞彙獨特的情況，這是本書一大特色。

此書是一本適合英語老師和高階英語學習者參考的中文著作，如果將之跟同時代一些流行的英文著作相比，例如 Michael Swan 的 *A Practical English Usage*（Swan 1980），絲毫不會遜色，而且處處顯示作者的心得和心血。用中文來講解英文語法，對母語為漢語的學習者更有針對性，所強調的主題和選擇的題材更能照顧學習者的需要。用中文向華語讀者介紹最前沿的語言學概念和研究成果，是湯廷池教授畢生信奉的寫作原則，這本英語參考語法體現了湯教授這種學術理念，也是他留給英語教學界的重要貢獻。

李行德

香港中文大學語言學及現代語言系榮休教授

大學通識教育部主任

2022.04.08

References

Baker, C. L. (1966). *Definiteness and Indefiniteness in English*. Master Thesis. University of Illinois. Reproduced by the Indiana University Linguistics Club.

Bresnan, Joan. 1979 [1972]. *Theory of complementation in English syntax*. New York: Garland.

Comrie, Bernard. 1985. *Tense*. Cambridge: Cambridge University Press.

Gleason, H. A. 1965. *Linguistics and English grammar*. New York: Holt, Rinehart and Winston.

Grimshaw, Jane. 1985 [1977]. *English Wh-constructions and the theory of grammar*. New York: Garland.

Grimshaw, Jane. 1990. *Argument structure*. Cambridge, MA: MIT Press.

Hawkins, John. 1978. *Definiteness and indefiniteness: a study in reference and grammatical prediction.* London: Croom Helm.

Johnson, Keith. 1982. *Communicative syllabus design and methodology*. New York: Pergamon.

Lado, Robert. 1964. *Language teaching: a scientific approach*. New York: McGraw Hill.

Lees, Robert. 1968. [1963]. *The grammar of English nominalizations*. The Hague: Mouton.

Peranteau, Paul, J. Levi and G. Phares. eds. 1972. *The Chicago which hunt: papers from the Relative Clause Festival.* Chicago: Chicago Linguistic Society.

Stockwell, Robert, P. Schachter and B. Partee. 1973. *The major syntactic structures of English.* New York: Holt, Rinehart, and Winston.

Swan, Michael. 1980. *A practical English usage*. Oxford: Oxford University Press.

Wang, Chuming and Thomas H.-T. Lee. 1999. L2 acquisition of conflation classes of prenominal adjectival participles. *Language Learning* 49(1), 1-36.

Widdowson, H. 1978. *Teaching language as communication*. Oxford: Oxford University Press.

Wilkins, David. 1976. *Notional syllabuses: a taxonomy and its relevance to foreign language curriculum development.* Oxford: Oxford University Press.

推薦序二

最體貼的經師與人師

　　個人追隨湯師二十多年，是老師從清華大學退休之後的追隨者之一。我們這群號稱「湯家班」也獲得老師首肯認證的小團體，從老師退休後在東吳大學博士班任教以來，長年追隨老師的成員多數是日文專業背景。由於老師英日語左右逢源，日文造詣更勝母語者，故在授課之際總是鼓勵我們為學宜廣宜深，並能英日語並用。我也就不知不覺深受感召，聽從老師的教導，十餘年來逐步涉獵英語並開啟探索英美社會文化的興趣。

　　而本書正是老師推薦我研讀的英語文法書。可惜，我當時上網買來的，和這本書的格式、編排都大不相同。如果不是如今有機會翻閱這個版本，恐怕始終不知自己當年讀來著實吃力的內容，原來跟原始版本竟有如此巨大的差異！

　　從本書的版面、圖式、簡表，乃至例句對比、編排順序等，都可以看出老師為學習者投注的貼心設想。這些設計環節都是他認為需要熟記的內容，因而透過視覺化的認知途徑，盡可能地減輕學習者負擔的巧思。同時，他以語言學者的知識高度，卻要求自己不輕易使用學術語言；舉重若輕的行文表達，做的正是他自己知行合一、奉行多年的寫作心法──「把輕鬆理解留給讀者，苦心煎熬留給自己」。

　　本書為了高三生英語總複習而設計了直截淺白、有效易懂等有助認知記憶的表達形式之外，老師身為語言學者的嚴謹自是如影隨形。例如，他引述了所有的語料來源，並強調本書例句採集自英語母語者的原則。此外，從三個重要句型、十個基本句型、十二種動詞時變式，再到各種變式的用途等，一路由淺入深的「華麗」展開，處處透露出一位巨人般的語言學者，俯身對待小朋友的溫柔用心。

　　甚至，他還照顧到英語課堂上的老師，指出後續的練習方式，可以透過口頭問答，取代習題的書寫。這也反映了老師一向不喜書呆子式的苦讀之道，而「靈活權變、與書對話」，則是他認為不會被書讀死的康莊大道。而之所以匯集了豐富的習題，則是為了讓學習者透過實踐熟能生巧。個人有幸聽聞老師曾經提起本書匯集眾

多語料與習題的緣由，披露於此或可供讀者或外語教師印證所學與經驗。

　　感謝志真與志永老師重新出版此書，不僅對老師思念甚深的學生受惠，如今為學英語不得其門而入的莘莘學子必定獲益良多。重展此書，環顧現今的學術環境，願為高中生寫語法書的語言學者恐怕將成絕響了。更何況，以湯師在語言學上無人能及的洞見與博學，能夠惠澤青年學生的基礎教育，當是所有讀者難能可貴的緣分與福分！

楊承淑

輔仁大學學術特聘教授

於 2021 年 9 月 28 日教師節

悼念恩師

推薦序三

勤練習是內化文法規則的不二法門

　　六月時收到湯志真轉寄來信告知，在新竹中學圖書館黃大展主任和退休蔡肇慶老師的協尋下，臺南女中圖書館劉文明主任和新竹中學退休曾義興老師，分別收藏了一套湯廷池老師 1985 年由海國書局出版的絕版文法書《最新實用高級英語語法（修訂本）》和習題解答本，書況還算不錯，決定由元華文創重新出版這上下兩冊為一套的文法書，並定名為《觀察・類推・條理化：分析性的英語語法》以追思湯老師，我很高興這套文法書能重新出版並為在天上最敬愛的湯老師寫一序文。

　　元華文創李欣芳主編寄來當時由海國書局出版的原始文法書電子掃描檔後，我翻著一頁頁泛黃並有著斑點的 PDF 文件，不知不覺地時光回到過去，一幕幕老師站在講臺上教我如何觀察、分析、思考、推論的容顏又浮上腦海，同時也讓我想起 35 年前在清華大學讀語言學研究所時和這套文法書的因緣。研究所二年級時，我為了家教一高中生英文，就是跟湯老師借這套文法書來當教材使用。當時就覺得這是一部與眾不同的文法書，好學又好記。此番重讀，依然覺得這文法書有其獨特之處，是一部值得時常查閱並終生收藏的好文法書。

　　這套文法書共二十二章，第一章到第十四章分為上冊，第十五到第二十二章為下冊，兩冊近 1100 頁，專供高中三年英語教學之用，現重新出版，依然保留原始章節安排，但開本加大，以方便空白處作筆記。看到近 1100 頁的頁數，很多人也許會嚇壞了，免不了懷疑這怎麼讀得完？背得起來嗎？要回答這個問題之前，我說說一個我個人的小故事。在大四那年還是讀研究所時的暑假，我想提升自己的英文實力，但單字是個門檻，能主動使用的詞彙有限。後來在報上看到有人建議單字其實不用背，最好的方法是大量閱讀，閱讀中不懂的字因為會重複出現而自動記憶。所以那年暑假我跟圖書館借了多本英文著名小說，從早讀到晚。除了被小說故事吸引外，發現許多不懂的單字真的會重複出現，而且只需第一、二次查一下字典或猜意思，那個字就記起來了，因而那個暑假我學會也記得了許多新單字。

　　上面那個學單字的方法，和湯老師文法書上所體現的教學方法其實有異曲同工之妙。老師的文法書雖然看似有 1100 頁之多，但真正的文字敘述只佔據了很小一部份。湯老師把大部分的文法，特別是需要熟記的部分，都整理歸納成簡單的句型或圖表，並有例外規則的參考說明，以方便記憶。但更重要的是文法書上的所有規則及句型都有豐富的例句演示，並且提供大量由簡到難的不同練習題來反覆操作。這些練習的目的就是要透過次數來強化牢固規則的記憶，其道理就和單字不用死記死背是一樣的，只要同一個單字重複地出現，腦中就容易記得那個單字的意思和用法。同理，重複地利用不同的句子來練習同一種句型，想不記得那個句型也難。人家常說，同樣一件事，能做一百次，就會成為那件事的專家，我相信勤練習也是在學習英文時內化其文法規則的不二法門。湯老師的文法書正是希望所有讀者都能成為文法專家，所以練習題佔據了很大的空間，而不是文字說明。

　　大學上湯老師課時，他常說他是個不喜歡死記死背的人，他喜歡用自己的推理推論來獲得規則。但就如同他文法書上所說，學習語言不能完全離開熟記，而熟記的最有效方法就是用多次練習來強化記憶。湯老師的文法書在這方面真的是下足了一番功夫，所以不怕你學不會，記不來，只怕你不練習，肯練習就一定記得住。我在此序文向所有想學好英文文法的人大力推薦，一定要在案頭擺上湯老師的這套文法書，相信你將因此終生受用。

林若望

中央研究院語言學研究所所長

2021.09.28

推薦序四

書香飄兩岸，桃李念師恩

　　2011 年，兩岸實現高等教育學歷互認，首批大陸學生赴臺灣就讀大學和研究所，這是兩岸教育合作史上的一個里程碑。受益於這項政策，我得以於 2017 年從北京跨越海峽到輔仁大學攻讀口譯研究博士，並在輔仁大學有幸成為湯廷池先生的學生。

　　最早聽說先生名號是在我的博士生導師楊承淑教授（2010）的一本專著序言裡。她提及曾拜師於湯廷池先生門下，以學徒的方式學習語言學長達 20 年之久。楊教授是在兩岸四地都很有影響力的口譯研究學者，我斷定，能吸引她追隨學習如此之久的湯先生，必定是一位品格高潔的飽學之士。

　　自新竹清華大學退休後，湯先生長期在輔仁大學擔任講座教授，為研究生講授語言學課程。為了方便先生授課，學校專門就近先生住所在臺北大安森林公園附近租賃了教室。從新莊輔大校園去上課不免舟車勞頓，卻擋不住同學們的學習熱情，先生課上總是有很多人。

　　先生當時已經年逾八旬，講話緩慢但有力，思路特別清晰。艱深抽象的語言學理論，在先生的口中變得深入淺出。在先生的課堂上，我頓悟了不少曾經百思不得其解的生成語法的概念。除了學習知識外，從先生的言傳身教中，更是學到寶貴的為學之道，燃起了對學術研究的熱愛。

　　先生在生活中隨身攜帶小筆記本，隨時記錄自己看到和聽到的新詞或特別的語言現象，拿到課堂上與同學們一起進行語言分析。我在先生課上交的第一篇作業題目是《語法「三品說」評述》。先生對我的作業給予了鼓勵，作業紙上卻留下密密麻麻的紅筆批註。

　　先生改作業時，不僅要看行文結構和學術觀點，任何遣詞造句甚至標點使用的不當之處都難逃他的「金睛火眼」。先生一直諄諄教誨我們，要建立起「觀察」、「類推」和「條理化」的思維，才能透過現象看本質，做好學問。

　　我是那一期語言學班上唯一的陸生。知道我來自遙遠的北京後，先生給予了我特別的關照。在課堂上給我更多回答問題的機會，在課堂外對我在臺灣的生活也關心有加。他告訴我，看到大陸地區近些年在各個領域的快速發展，他的內心充滿了喜悅。他鼓勵我多做一些促進兩岸學術交流的事。

　　湯先生 1992 年曾主編過一套由臺灣學生書局出版的《現代語言學論叢》。在先生的推動下，該叢書中包含了一本大陸學者石毓智的專著，他親筆為該書作序。該書應該是那個時期大陸語言研究者在臺出版的第一本新書。在該書序文中，湯先生表示，出版一本大陸學者的書所花的心血與時間，遠超出版臺灣學者的十本書，但是他覺得有責任來努力縮短海峽兩岸在學術空間上的人為距離。1997 年，先生曾訪問北京大學。據那次訪問的北大對接人趙楊教授回憶，先生就美國語言學發展、認知語法等主題與北大教師開展了對話。訪問期間，先生還非常興奮地登上了長城。

　　除了做好語言研究，先生的另一個宏願是幫助更多學子學好英語。我的臺灣同學告訴我，先生曾經擔任臺灣高中英文教科書的編輯委員長，他編寫的《最新實用高級英語語法（修訂本）》曾經是幾代臺灣人英語學習的啟蒙。大陸《語言文字週報》有篇文章對先生在生成語法的推廣與普及方面所做的貢獻給予了高度的評價，稱先生「善於將高深的理論用淺顯的語言表述出來」（丁健，2017）。《最新實用高級英語語法（修訂本）》就是這樣一本在高深理論指導下編寫而成的淺顯易懂的語法書。

　　聽聞此書在臺灣的影響力後，大陸地區的不少英語學子紛紛在網路上的豆瓣、知乎等平臺表達對此書的濃厚興趣，同時也因找不到此書而抱憾。先生的女兒湯志真也是一位語言學教授，退休前在臺灣中研院語言所就職。我從她那裡得知，她不時也會收到一些大陸地區學子表達類似訴求的郵件，讀者的熱情期盼是促成此書得以再版的最重要的力量之一。

　　新技術賦予了圖書更強大的生命力。此書將以「電子書＋紙質書」的組合形式再版，讀者可以獲得更加豐富的閱讀經驗。乘著新技術的翅膀，這部經典之作還將跨越地域限制，惠及兩岸乃至全球更多的讀者。

　　我在臺灣於 2021 年取得博士學位後，來到北京第二外國語學院任教。作為一名教師，我相信此書會給大陸地區的英語學子帶來不同的學習視角；作為湯先生的

學生，我希望他的更多著作能得到再版，讓更多學子受益；而作為兩岸教育合作與
交流的受益者，我盼望未來兩岸在學術領域能有更多類似的建設性互動。

齊濤雲

北京第二外國語學院 副教授

2021 年 9 月北京

編 輯 大 意

一、本書根據教育部頒高級中學英語課程標準編輯，分上、下兩冊，專供高級中學三年英語語法教學之用。

二、語法說明力求淺顯，以冀學生能自行閱讀。同時附有許多圖式、例句與比較，以幫助學生了解。

三、語法術語力求簡化，並盡量採用語言學上最近通用的術語。凡是不必要的定義，無意義的分類，都一概刪去。

四、學習語言不能完全離開熟記，因此需要學生熟記的部分都列成簡單的表式，以幫助記憶。

五、有關參考資料如用字、發音以及比較瑣碎的語法問題都列在參考裡，排列的次序大致是由重要到次要。老師們可以視實際需要做適當的取捨，不必全部教授。

六、練習的分量不少，每一種練習的安排大致是由易到難。其目的在供給老師充足的補充教材，以免除蒐集的麻煩。同時，每一位老師的教授對象不同，程度有差異，老師們可以自行斟酌選擇適量的習題。如果學生的程度較高，則簡易習題可以省略不做。或者可以採用口頭練習，回答正確，習題即可算做完。老師們不必擔心習題過多，負擔過重。

七、本書的英語，無論是例句與習題，都盡量採用參考資料中英美人士所實際使用的句子，盡量避免自己造句。

目　次

第*1*章
三個重要的句型

1-1. 三個重要的句型

英語有三個很重要的句型，一個是含有 **Be 動詞**（am, are, is, was, were）的句型；另外一個是含有**助動詞**（will, would; shall, should; can, could; may, might; must; have, has, had; ought to）的句型；最後一個是只含有上述 Be 動詞與助動詞以外的動詞（例如 work, works, worked; study, studies, studied; go, goes, went）的句型。如果用 **Be** 來代表 Be 動詞，用 **AV** 來代表助動詞，用 **V** 來代表一般動詞的話，這三個句型可以用下面的圖式表示出來。

> **Subj Be …**

John *is* a nice boy.

You *are* very kind.

I *am* studying English right now.

> **Subj AV V …**

John *will* leave tomorrow.

They *can* speak French very well.

I *should* have finished my work yesterday.

> **Subj V …**

John *works* very hard.

We *went* to the zoo last week.

She *told* us a story about China.

這三種句型的區別非常重要，英語裡有很多句式的變化都要看這三種句型而定。

習　題　1

用 **Be, AV, V** 注出三個不同的句型。

Examples:　　My cousin is a fool. (**Be**)

I gave him some books. (**V**)

Nobody has seen him before. (**AV V**)

1. There are seven days in a week.

2. The sun shines every day.

3. We all must work hard.

4. It is raining outside.

5. I always carry a handkerchief.

6. Spring is the first season of the year.

7. We will bring some fruit and a lunch basket.

8. She came home before her stepmother and sister.

9. She was the happiest woman in the world.

10. We can do a lot of things with money.

1-2. 否定句

英語的否定句是在肯定句裡加 not 而成的。

(1) 含有 Be 動詞的句型，在 Be 動詞後面加 not。

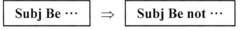

$$\boxed{\textbf{Subj Be} \cdots} \quad \Rightarrow \quad \boxed{\textbf{Subj Be not} \cdots}$$

He is busy. → He is *not* busy.

They were at home. → They were *not* at home.

We are watching TV. → We are *not* watching TV.

(2) 含有助動詞的句型，在助動詞後面加 not。

$$\boxed{\textbf{Subj AV V} \cdots} \quad \Rightarrow \quad \boxed{\textbf{Subj AV not V} \cdots}$$

I will do it. → I will *not* do it.

You must smoke. → You must *not* smoke.

He should go. → He should *not* go.

We have seen him before. → We have *not* seen him before.

如果同一個句子裡有兩個以上的助動詞，就在第一個助動詞後面加 not。

I will be studying at nine o'clock tomorrow.

　　　→ I will not be studying at nine o'clock tomorrow.

He may have seen you. → He may not have seen you.

(3) 不含有 Be 動詞或助動詞的句型，在動詞前面加 Do 動詞（do, does, did），然後在 Do 動詞後面加 not。

$$\boxed{\textbf{Subj V} \cdots} \quad \Rightarrow \quad \boxed{\textbf{Subj Do not V} \cdots}$$

They go to school. → They *do not* go to school.

He goes to school. → He *does not* go to school.

She went to school. → She *did not* go to school.

Do 與 does 用於現在式（does 只用在第三身單數主語後面），did 用在過去式。

在口語英語裡，常見下面的簡寫式：

is not = *isn't*	are not = *aren't*	do not = *don't* 〔dont〕
did not = *didn't*	has not = *hasn't*	will not = *won't* 〔wont〕
can not, cannot = *can't* 〔kænt, kɑ:nt〕		could not = *couldn't*
must not = *mustn't* 〔ˊmʌsnt〕		
shall not = *shan't* 〔ʃænt, ʃɑ:nt〕		should not = *shouldn't*
may not = *mayn't*	need not = *needn't*	was not = *wasn't*
were not = *weren't*	does not = *doesn't*	have not = *haven't*
had not = *hadn't*	would not = *wouldn't*	might not = *mightn't*
dare not = *daren't*		

習　題　2

　　把下面的句子變成否定句。

1. She could understand everything.

2. They had time to tell her.

3. We're coming tomorrow morning.

4. He comes here every morning.

5. There were many people at the concert.

6. Our teacher wants the homework now.

7. You must look out of the window.

8. We could see as far as the mountains.

9. She came with him.

10. He'll come if he can.

參考：在美式英語裡，一般動詞的 have（表示「有」的 have，非助動詞的 have）常用 do 來否定；但也有人（尤其是英國人）不用 do，而把 not 直接放在 have 後面，例如：

　　　　I have not (*haven't*) an English book.

　　　　They *have not* (*haven't*) many friends here.

　　　　Mary *has not* (*hasn't*) a bicycle.

1-3. 問　句

　　英語有兩種主要的問句：yes / no 問句與 wh- 問句。「**yes / no 問句**」（yes / no question）又叫做「是非問句」或「一般問句」，是可以用 yes 或 no 來回答的問句。例如有人問我們："Is he a student?"，我們就可以回答說 "Yes" 或 "No"。「**wh- 問句**」（wh-question），又叫做「特定問句」，是含有「**wh- 詞**」（wh-word）或「疑問詞」（question word）（如 who, whom, whose, which, what, when, where, why, how）的問句，不能用 yes 或 no 來回答。例如 "Who is he?" 就是一個 wh- 問句。

1-4. yes / no 問句

英語的 yes / no 問句是改變敘述句的詞序而成的。

(1) 含有 Be 動詞的句型，把 Be 動詞調到句首。

$$\boxed{\textbf{Subj Be}\cdots} \quad\Rightarrow\quad \boxed{\textbf{Be Subj}\cdots?}$$

He is busy. → *Is he* busy?

They were at home. → *Were they* at home?

You are studying. → *Are you* studying?

The house was burnt. → *Was the house* burnt?

(2) 含有助動詞的句型，把助動詞**調**到句首。

$$\boxed{\textbf{Subj AV V}\cdots} \quad\Rightarrow\quad \boxed{\textbf{AV Subj V}\cdots?}$$

You must smoke. → *Must you* smoke?

He should go. → *Should he* go?

We have seen him before. → *Have we seen* him before?

如果同一個句子裡有兩個以上的助動詞，就把第一個助動詞**調**到句首。

He will be studying at nine o'clock tomorrow.

　　　→ *Will he* be studying at nine o'clock tomorrow?

He could have seen you. → *Could he* have seen you?

(3) 不含有 Be 動詞或助動詞的句型，在句首加 Do 動詞（do, does, did）。這個時候原來的動詞都要變成動詞原形。

$$\boxed{\textbf{Subj V}\cdots} \quad\Rightarrow\quad \boxed{\textbf{Do Subj V}\cdots?}$$

They go to school. → *Do they* go to school?

He goes to school. → *Does he* go to school?

She went to school. → *Did she* go to school?

習 題 3

把下面的句子改成問句。

1. Winter is colder than summer.

2. He's opened the window on your right.

3. Peter was born and brought up in China.

4. You've studied English for two years.

5. Shoes are made in pairs.

6. Many old customs have died out in China.

7. It took you a month to get rid of the cold.

8. His mother asked you to send for a doctor.

9. They have to finish their work by tomorrow.

10. I should have prepared my lesson last night.

參考一：在口語英語裡，主語與動詞常用下面的簡寫式連起來。

I am = *I'm*	you are = *you're*	she will = *she'll*
I have = *I've*	you have = *you've*	they are = *they're*
I will = *I'll*	you will = *you'll*	they have = *they've*
we are = *we're*	he is, he has = *he's*	they will = *they'll*
we have = *we've*	he will = *he'll*	I, etc. had = *I'd*, etc.
we will = *we'll*	she is, she has = *she's*	I, etc. would = *I'd*, etc.

參考二：在美式英語裡，一般動詞的 have（表示「有」的 have）常用 Do 動詞來做問句。但也有人（特別是在英式英語裡）把 have 調到句首來做問句：

Have you an English book?　　*Has* he any relatives here?

1-5 長答句與短答句

回答英語的問句，可以用**長句**（完整的句子）來回答，也可以用**短句**（只用主語與助動詞）來回答。短答句在口語英語裡特別常見。

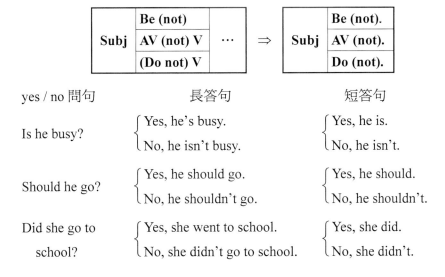

yes / no 問句　　　　　　　　長答句　　　　　　　短答句

Is he busy?

$\left\{\begin{array}{l}\text{Yes, he's busy.}\\ \text{No, he isn't busy.}\end{array}\right.$
$\left\{\begin{array}{l}\text{Yes, he is.}\\ \text{No, he isn't.}\end{array}\right.$

Should he go?

$\left\{\begin{array}{l}\text{Yes, he should go.}\\ \text{No, he shouldn't go.}\end{array}\right.$
$\left\{\begin{array}{l}\text{Yes, he should.}\\ \text{No, he shouldn't.}\end{array}\right.$

Did she go to school?

$\left\{\begin{array}{l}\text{Yes, she went to school.}\\ \text{No, she didn't go to school.}\end{array}\right.$
$\left\{\begin{array}{l}\text{Yes, she did.}\\ \text{No, she didn't.}\end{array}\right.$

習　題　4

用長答句與短答句回答下列問句。

1. Can you speak English?

2. Are you enjoying yourself?

3. Have you met my sister Alice?

4. Would you like another cup of tea?

5. Must I be there in time?

6. Did you meet him yesterday?

7. Does he play chess?

8. May I go out?

9. Were you at the theater last night?

10. Should we do our assignments now?

習 題 5

把適當的 Be 動詞，Do 動詞或其他助動詞填入下面的句子裡。

Examples: I'm from China. *Are* you?

He comes from China. I *do*, too.

1. My sister is getting married soon. _____ yours?

2. Jack is looking for another job. I _____, too.

3. I like to make speeches. My roommate _____, too.

4. I can speak French very well. _____ you?

5. Your English is improving. _____ mine?

6. Bob gets two tickets to the graduation. _____ I get any?

7. You should go with him. _____ I?

8. I want to insure my house. Mr. King _____, too.

9. This calendar is out of date. _____ that one, too?

10. I polish my shoes every night. _____ you?

參考：Be 動詞、助動詞、Do 動詞常可以用來代替主語以外的整個述語。例如：

I am tired. *Are* you?

I always got there on time. Everyone *did*.

Bob should take an examination tomorrow. I *should*, too.

1-6. 否定問句

英語的否定問句是把 not 加於肯定問句而成的。

Be		…?		Ben't		…?
AV	Subj	V…?	⇒	AVn't	Subj	V…?
Do		V…?		Don't		V…?

Is he busy? → *Isn't* he busy?

Will he do it? → *Won't* he do it?

Does he go to school? → *Doesn't* he go to school?

在比較正式的英語裡，not 可以加在主語後面。

Be		…?		Be		…?
AV	Subj	V…?	⇒	AV	Subj not	V…?
Do		V…?		Do		V…?

Is he *not* busy?

Will he *not* do it?

Does he *not* go to school?

否定問句並不一定表示否定，而常預期對方表示同意，尤其是用升調說出來的時候。

A: Didn't Mary pass the examination? (= I think she did.)

B: Yes, she did.

A: I knew I was right.

習　題　6

把下面的問句改成否定問句再回答。

1. Did you tell her to leave right away?

2. Is the elevator out of order?

3. Are there three windows in the room?

4. Has Mr. Smith put off his trip until next week?

5. Does the class begin at 8:30 sharp?

6. Must you write your exercises in pencil?

7. Will Mary be in class tomorrow?

8. Are they going to the movies tonight?

9. Is he going to have the radio repaired?

10. Did he tell you not to come here any more?

參考：否定問句的答句可能是肯定式，也可能是否定式。例如：

Isn't she pretty?

Yes, she is.

You may think so, but I don't.

Haven't you cleaned your room yet?

Of course, I have; I cleaned it yesterday.

No, I've been too busy studying.

1-7. 追問句

我們說完一句話以後，常在後頭加上一個簡短的問句，去問對方是不是同意我們的意思。這種問句就叫做「**追問句**」（tag question）。

He is an American, isn't he?

She can't speak English, can she?

(1) 如果前面的句子是肯定式，後面的追問句要用否定式。追問句裡的名詞都要改成代名詞（PN）。

Subj	Be / AV V / V	⋯		⇒	Subj	Be / AV V / V	⋯,	Ben't / AVn't / Don't	PN?

He is in your class. → He is in your class, *isn't he?*

Jane will do it. → Jane will do it, *won't she?*

Bob left for New York.

　　→ Bob left for New York, *didn't he?*

(2) 如果前面的句子是否定式，後面的追問句要用肯定式。追問句裡的名詞還是要改成代名詞。

Subj	Ben't / AVn't V / Don't V	⋯		⇒	Subj	Ben't / AVn't V / Don't V	⋯,	Be / AN / Do	PN?

He isn't in your class. → He isn't in your class, *is he?*

Jane won't do it. → Jane won't do it, *will she?*

Bob didn't leave for New York.

　　→ Bob didn't leave for New York, *did he?*

追問句可以兩種不同的音調說出來。

He's an American, isn't he?（表示對於所說的話相當有把握。）

He's an American, Isn't he?（表示對於所說的話沒有多大把握。）

習 題 7

在下面的句子後面加一個追問句。

1. Mr. Brown is an American.
2. They are late.
3. We weren't hungry.
4. Bob can explain.
5. You have your lunch at one o'clock.
6. You don't have to go just yet.
7. This winter hasn't been cold.
8. You shouldn't smoke.
9. Jane speaks English well.
10. I didn't hurt you.

參考一：I am 的追問句在比較正式的英語裡用 am I not，但在口語裡也常用 aren't I。

I'm going to the store now, *aren't I* (*am I not*) ?

參考二：命令句後面如果加上含有 will 或 shall 的追問句，就可以變成比較客氣的請求。

Stop that noise, *will you?*

Don't go away, *will you?*

Let's go for a walk, *shall we?*

Let's not argue again, *shall we?*

1-8. 強意肯定句

當我們想強調某一句話的真確性的時候，常把句子裡的 Be 動詞或助動詞說得重些，例如：

He is busy.

I will do it.

在這兩句裡 is 與 will 的音說得最重。如果句子裡沒有 Be 動詞或助動詞，那麼就要加上 Do 動詞（do, does, did），然後再把這個 Do 動詞說得重些。例如：

I dó know him.

You díd see her yesterday.

這種把 Be 動詞、助動詞、Do 動詞唸重的句子就叫做**強意肯定句**（emphatic statement）。

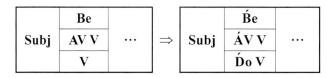

He is busy. → He *ís* busy.

(Why do you think he isn't busy?)

I will do it. → I *wíll* do it.

(Why do you think I won't do it?)

I know him. → I *dó* know him.

(Why do you think I don't know him?)

習　題　8

把下面斜體部分的動詞改成強意肯定式。

1. I *mailed* the letter. I swear it.

2. She *lives* in Taipei. I'm sure of it.

3. Dick *took* the book. He told me so.

4. He *wrote* that letter. I am positive of it.

5. You're mistaken. I *want* to learn English.

6. John didn't visit me but he *called* me on the phone.

7. I didn't do it today but I *did* it yesterday.

8. Maps were then very poor but they *showed* that the earth was round.

9. Jim doesn't study hard but he *attends* class regularly.

10. I didn't go away on my vacation but I *had* a good rest.

1-9. 連　句

　　當相連兩個句子的句型一樣的時候，我們常把這兩個句子用 and 或 but 連起來，並且把第二個句子重複的語詞省掉。這種句子就叫做**連句**（connected statement），例如：

> I want to go to the game.
>
> They want to go to the game (too). $\Bigr\}\rightarrow$

　　　I want to go to the game, and they do too.

> I don't want to go to the game.
>
> They don't want to go to the game (either). $\Bigr\}\rightarrow$

　　　I don't want to go to the game, and they don't either.

> I want to go to the game.
>
> They don't want to go to the game. $\Bigr\}\rightarrow$

　　　I want to go to the game, but they don't.

> I don't want to go to the game.
>
> They want to go to the game. $\Bigr\}\rightarrow$

　　　I don't want to go to the game, but they do.

　　第一個連句是由兩個肯定句相連而成，第二個連句是由兩個否定句相連而成；最後兩個連句是由一個肯定句和一個否定句相連而成。

1-10. 肯定句的連句

　　肯定句的連句有兩種：

(1) 兩個肯定句用 and … too 連起來。

	Be			Be	
Subj 1	**AV V**	**…, and Subj 2**		**AV**	**too.**
	V			**Do**	

　　Mary is a student, and Jane is too.

　　Susan has been to Japan, and I have too.

　　Jack can play tennis, and you can too.

They left early, and we did too.

(2) 兩個肯定句用 and so … 連起來。

Subj 1	Be	…, and so	Be	Subj 2.
	AV V		AV	
	V		Do	

Mary is a student, and so is Jane.

Susan has been to Japan, and so have I.

Jack can play tennis, and so can you.

They left early, and so did we.

注意：第二個圖式與例句裡的 Be 動詞、助動詞、Do 動詞要調到主語前面去。

習　題　9

把下面每一對句子用 and … too 和 and so … 連起來。

Example:

John is good. ⎱ → ⎰ *John is good, and Bob is too.*
Bob is good. ⎰　　 ⎱ *John is good, and so is Bob.*

1. He can run fast.
   His brother can run fast. ⎰ →

2. He has gone home.
   She has gone home. ⎰ →

3. Mr. Smith is a doctor.
   Mr. Rand is a doctor. ⎰ →

4. The boy seems happy.
   The girl seems happy. ⎰ →

5. Tom voted Bill chairman.
   Robert voted Bill chairman. ⎰ →

6. He has been lazy lately.
   His friend has been lazy lately. ⎰ →

7. The teacher has read the book.
   His students has read the book. ⎰ →

8. He speaks English well.　⎫
   I speak English well.　　⎬ →

9. We would go with him.　⎫
   They would go with him.⎬ →

10. I should have finished the assignment.　⎫
    You should have finished the assignment.⎬ →

1-11. 否定句的連句

否定句的連句也有兩種：

(1) 兩個否定句用 and … either 連起來。

Subj 1	Be AV Do	n't …, and Subj 2	Be AV Do	n't either.

I am not a teacher, and you aren't either.

He can't play tennis, and I can't either.

Mary doesn't like coffee, and you don't either.

(2) 兩個否定句用 and neither … 連起來。

Subj 1	Be AV Do	n't …, and neither	Be AV Do	Subj 2.

I am not a teacher, and neither are you.

He can't play tennis, and neither can I.

Mary doesn't like coffee, and neither do you.

再注意第二個圖式與例句裡的 Be 動詞、助動詞、Do 動詞要調到主語前面來。

習　題　10

把下面每一對句子用 and … either 和 and neither … 連起來。

Example:

The necklace wasn't expensive.　　⎫
The bracelet wasn't expensive either.⎬ →

{
The necklace wasn't expensive, and the bracelet wasn't either.

The necklace wasn't expensive, and neither was the bracelet.
}

1. The train wasn't late.
   The bus wasn't late either. →

2. The steak wasn't very good.
   The salad wasn't very good either. →

3. Paul didn't buy a new tie.
   Bob didn't buy a new tie either. →

4. Dick doesn't have class on Friday.
   Jack doesn't have class on Friday either. →

5. This place won't cash checks.
   That one won't cash checks either. →

6. Ralph hasn't been to Japan.
   Sam hasn't been to Japan either. →

7. Peter isn't studying architecture.
   John isn't studying architecture either. →

8. He wasn't going to leave.
   They weren't going to leave either. →

9. Jane can't drive a car.
   Betty can't drive a car either. →

10. The Smiths won't be at the reception.
    The Bakers won't be at the reception either. →

1-12. 肯定句與否定句的連句

肯定句與否定句的連句要用 but 連起來：

(1) 第一個句子是肯定句，第二個句子是否定句。

Subj 1	**Be**		···, but Subj 2	**Be**	**n't.**
	AV V			**AV**	
	V			**Do**	

I am a teacher, but you aren't.

He can play tennis, but I can't.

Mary likes coffee, but you don't.

(2) 第一個句子是否定句，第二個句子是肯定句。

Subj 1	**Be**		n't ···, but Subj 2	**Be.**
	AV			**AV.**
	Do			**Do.**

I am not a teacher, but you are.

He can't play tennis, but I can.

Mary doesn't like coffee, but you do.

習　題　11

把下面每一對句子連起來。

Examples:

This problem is difficult. ⎫
That problem isn't difficult. ⎬ →

This problem is difficult, but that problem isn't.

I haven't seen that movie. ⎫
Ruth has seen that movie. ⎬ → *I haven't seen that movie, but Ruth has.*

1. This milk tastes sour. ⎫
   That milk doesn't taste sour. ⎬ →

2. Mr. Smith didn't call today. ⎫
   Mr. Brown called today. ⎬ →

3. This pen is broken. ⎫
   That pen isn't broken. ⎬ →

4. I have never met Mrs. March. ⎫
   Ben and Dick have met Mrs. March. ⎬ →

5. These sweaters aren't clean.
   Those sweaters are clean. $\Big\} \rightarrow$

6. Ann smokes.
   Margaret doesn't smoke. $\Big\} \rightarrow$

7. Ben can sing well.
   Nancy can't sing well. $\Big\} \rightarrow$

8. Ingrid passed the examination.
   Roy didn't pass the examination. $\Big\} \rightarrow$

9. Today's cloudy.
   Yesterday wasn't cloudy. $\Big\} \rightarrow$

10. On Thursday there won't be class.
    On Friday there'll be class. $\Big\} \rightarrow$

習 題 12

依照例句改寫下面的句子，把斜體部分的語詞放在句子前面。

Examples:

There is such delicious fruit *nowhere else in the world.*

Nowhere else in the world is there such delicious fruit.

I have *never* seen more beautiful flowers.

Never have I seen more beautiful flowers.

One *seldom* finds such a sincere interest in the arts.

Seldom does one find such a sincere interest in the arts.

1. I have *never* appreciated my friends and family so much.

2. We have *rarely* had such a great honor.

3. This town has *seldom* entertained such a famous guest.

4. Students *rarely* study as hard as they should.

5. The weather is very hot here *only in August.*

6. Such a thing could happen *only in a big city like New York.*

7. We *rarely* see such beautiful dancing in our small town.

8. People are interested in this problem *in no other part of the world.*

9. We had *no sooner* arrived than all the lights went out.

10. Miss Helen *not only* dances well; she also sings beautifully.

參考：在比較正式的英語裡，常常把含有否定意味的語詞（如 not, never, seldom, rarely, little, not only, only 等）放在句首。這個時候，句子的主語與動詞的位置必須調換：

I was never so surprised. → Never *was I* so surprised.

I have never been there. → Never *have I* been there.

I never saw him before. → Never *did I* see him before.

注意：這種倒序與問句的倒序完全一樣。

第2章
十個基本句型

2-1. 主語與述語

所有英語的句子在結構上都可以分為兩部分。一個是講「誰？」或「什麼？」的部分；另外一個是講「是什麼？」、「做什麼？」、「怎麼樣？」的部分。前一個部分叫做「**主語**」（subject），後一個部分叫做「**述語**」（predicate）。寫英語的時候，每一個句子的開頭第一個字母都要大寫，最後一個字還要加標點：句號（•）、問號（？）、或驚嘆號（！）。

主　語	述　語
Jack	is ill.
They	are my friends.
The little boy	likes to collect stamps.
A tall lady in a blue dress	gave me this book yesterday.
His brother who lives in Taipei	has written to his family that he is coming home next week.

習　題　13

把下列句子的主語與述語分開。

Examples:

    |This| is my pen.

    Where did |the little boy| put his book?

1. This is a book.　　　　　　2. Isn't that dress beautiful?

3. The three men walked for five miles.

4. How beautiful the moon is tonight!

5. We all breathe, eat and drink.

6. Bob, Jack and Dick went downtown with me yesterday.

7. That John eats cabbage means that he likes cabbage.

8. It is important for us to practice English every day.

9. Who do you think won the election?

10. Never have I seen this man before.

2-2. 主語的形式

英語的詞類中可以當主語用的有「名詞」、「代名詞」、the +「形容詞」、由「動詞」變出來的「動名詞」和「不定詞」等。其他的片語或子句也可以當主語用。

(1) NOUNS: *Fortune* began to smile on her. （名詞）

(2) PRONOUNS: *We* enjoyed talking to her. （代名詞）

(3) ADJECTIVES: *The rich* are not always happy. （the + 形容詞）

(4) VERBS: *Swimming* is a good exercise. （動名詞）

To see is to believe. （不定詞）

(5) PHRASES: *Over the fence* is out of bounds. （介詞片語）

How to get there puzzled all of us. （不定詞片語）

(6) CLAUSES: *Whatever I do* is always wrong. （子句）

習　題　14

把 A 欄的主語與 B 欄的述語連成一個句子。

A	B
_5_ 0. The story of the Sphinx	(0) is to stay in bed.
___ 1. I	(1) need to be fed.
___ 2. Dinner	(2) is better than in the woods.
___ 3. Modern China	(3) is not decided yet.
___ 4. Shooting	(4) keeps up with modern science and ideas.
___ 5. The hungry	(5) came from Egypt.
___ 6. On the beach	(6) can get up by Wednesday, can't I?
___ 7. The main trouble	(7) is almost ready.

___ 8. To be a great scientist   (8) is that they don't follow the traffic regulations.

___ 9. Whether he is coming   (9) is my ambition.

___10. The best way to get rid   (10) is against the law.
         of cold

2-3. 述語的形式

述語的結構比較複雜，而且有好幾種不同的結構。但是每一種結構都是由一定詞類的詞按照一定的詞序排下來。這種詞序，我們就叫做「**句型**」（sentence patterns）：

John is a fool.   John is foolish.

John is here.   John became my friend (friendly).

John seems friendly.   John smiled.

John speaks English.   John gave me a book.

2-4. 第一個基本句型

主語	述語	
NP	**Be**	**NP**

John is a fool.   They are my good friends.

The dinner was a feast.   The girl in a red dress is Mary.

前三個本句型的述語都含有 Be 動詞。Be 動詞在英語裡是一個很特殊的動詞。它的現在式有三種——am, are, is，過去式有兩種——was, were。Be 動詞本身不能單獨使用，必須另外有名詞、形容詞，或表示場所的副詞做「補語」。這種補語在文法上就叫做「**主語補語**」（subject complement）。

NP（名詞組）代表名詞或其他具有與名詞相同功能的詞。NP 可能是名詞（John, Mary），可能是代名詞（they），也可能是帶有修飾語的名詞（the dinner, my good friends, the girl in a red dress）。Be 動詞後面帶著名詞組的時候，可以翻譯成國語「是」。

習　題　15

填入適當的語詞使下面的句子成為屬於第一個基本句型的句子。

1. I am a _____.
2. They were his _____.
3. A dog is a _____.
4. The student in the next room is my _____.
5. John is an _____.
6. You are _____, aren't you?
7. Jane is a very _____.
8. John and Jane are _____ from England.
9. They used to _____ good friends.
10. The _____ will be a great success.

2-5. 第二個基本句型

主語	述語	
NP	Be	Adj

John is strong.　　　　　　　They are very kind.

The flowers have been beautiful.

第二個基本句型的述語含有 Be 動詞和「**形容詞**」（Adj, adjective）。形容詞是像 strong, kind, beautiful, diligent 這類的詞。這些詞一般都可以加 -er, -est 或 more, most 來變化成比較級和最高級：stronger, strongest; kinder, kindest; more beautiful, most beautiful; more diligent, most diligent。後面帶著形容詞的時候，Be 動詞可以翻譯成國語「很」，也可以不翻。

習　題　16

填入適當的語詞，使下面的句子成為屬於第二個基本句型的句子。

1. I am very _____.
2. They were _____ than you.
3. It is quite _____ today.
4. The dinner was _____.
5. This book is more _____ than that one.

6. He used to be very _____ .

7. I have been _____ for the past three days.

8. Jane is too _____ to walk.

9. The party last night _____ very successful.

10. You should _____ more careful from now on.

2-6. 第三個基本句型

主語	述語	
NP	Be	Adv-p

John is here.　　　　　　　　They are upstairs.

The garage is three miles away.

The chair was behind the desk.

　　第三個基本句型的述語，含有 Be 動詞和「**表示場所的副詞**」（Adv-p, adverbial of place）。表示場所的副詞可能是單獨的副詞（如 here, there, inside, outside, upstairs, downstairs, up, down, in, out），也可能是「副詞片語」（如 over there, three miles away, in the house, at the door, behind the desk, by the river）。後面帶著場所副詞的時候，Be 動詞可以翻譯成國語的「在」。

　　如果這個句型的主語是無定的名詞的話，就要變成由 there 帶頭的句子：

My book is on the desk.（有定主語：「我的書在桌子上。」）

There is *a* book on the desk.（無定主語：「桌子上有一本書。」）

A book is here. → There is a book here.

Three boys are outside. → There are three boys outside.

Some money has been in the purse.

　　　→ There has been some money in the purse.

習　題　17

填入適當的語詞，使下面的句子成為屬於第三個基本句型的句子。

1. The books are _____.
2. Your friends are _____.
3. His house is across _____.
4. She is at _____.
5. He is out of _____.
6. Spain is _____.
7. Bob is over _____.
8. The bathroom is _____.
9. The bedrooms are _____.
10. The nearest town is _____ away from here.

習　題　18

把下面的句子改為由 there 帶頭的句子。

Example: Two dogs are in the garden.

　　　　→ *There are two dogs in the garden.*

1. A car is outside.
2. Only a footpath was here last year.
3. A sign is over the door.
4. A gasstation is three miles away.
5. Some letters for you are on the table.
6. No one was in the room.
7. A lot of people were in the park yesterday.
8. An old friend of yours was at the concert last night.
9. A check will be in the mail next month.
10. Several students might have been in the library.

習　題　19

按照例句把下面的語詞擴充為句子。

Examples:

　　　an accident → Thĕre's an ác|cident.

　　　the accident → Thére's the accident.

1. a letter for you
2. the letter for you

3. a good movie   4. the good movie

5. a new teacher   6. the new teacher

7. some questions   8. the questions

9. the dictionary   10. your friends

參考：與有定主語一起出現的 there 或 here 是副詞，要念重音。含有這樣的 there 或 here 的句子不能變成否定句或問句。

比較：Thére's / Hére's the accident.   Thĕre's an áccident.

There / Here isn't the accident.（×）   There isn't an accident.（○）

Is there / here the accident?（×）   Is there an accident?（○）

2-7. 第四個基本句型

主語	述語	
NP	**V-b**	$\left\{\begin{array}{c}\textbf{NP}\\\textbf{Adj}\end{array}\right\}$

John became president.   John became famous.

My uncle remains a bachelor.   My uncle remains single.

第四個基本句型的述語含有「**become 類的動詞**」（V-b, Verbs of the become-type），後面再跟著名詞組或形容詞。屬於 become 類的動詞，美式英語中只有四個：become, remain, stay, continue。英式英語則除了這四個動詞以外，seem, appear, look turn，等也可以用名詞或形容詞做主語補語。下面是英式英語的一些例句：

The captain *seemed a nice fellow*.

The captain *seemed very nice*.

They *appeared friends* to all of us.

They *appeared very much surprised*.

He *looks an honest man*.

He *looks honest*.

習 題 20

用括號裡的字來代替原來句子裡的 Be 動詞。

Example:

John was a soldier. (become) → *John became a soldier.*

1. The weather was still cold. (continue)

2. She is faithful to him for the rest of her life. (stay)

3. Mr. Green is the richest man in town. (become)

4. Mr. Higgins is a very nice man. (seem)

5. They have been good friends for years. (stay)

6. He was silent and said nothing. (remain)

7. Dick is my best friend, despite our differences. (continue)

8. She was a widow until death. (remain)

9. He was afraid and said nothing. (become)

10. She will be a fine woman when she grows up. (become)

2-8. 第五個基本句型

主語	述語	
NP	V-s	Adj

John seems friendly.　　　　They grew sleepy.

My uncle looks very happy.　　The milk tasted sour.

The flowers smell sweet.　　The story sounds interesting.

　　第五個基本句型的述語含有「**seem 類的動詞**」（V-s, Verbs of the seem-type）
和形容詞。屬於 seem 類的動詞有 seem, look, appear, grow, get, keep, smell, taste,
sound, ring, feel 等，這些動詞只能用形容詞來做主語補語。

習 題 21

從下面的動詞裡選出一個字，並改為適當的形式以後再填入空白裡：*look,*

turn, get, keep, smell, taste, sound, feel。

Example: His face *turned* pale at the news.

1. A rose _____ sweet.

2. Good medicine _____ bitter to the mouth.

3. How sweet the music _____ !

4. Doesn't the milk _____ sour to you?

5. Ice _____ cold.　　　　6. His statement _____ true.

7. He _____ disappointed when I told him the news.

8. I wish those children would _____ quiet.

9. The days are _____ warmer and warmer.

10. The leaves are beginning to _____ red.

習 題 22

依照例句改寫下面的句子。

Examples:

　　Is the child happy? (sad) → *No, he isn't. He's sad.*

　　Did the lesson seem easy? (hard) → *No, it didn't. It seemed hard.*

1. Is the soup hot? (cold)　　　　2. Did Mrs. King get fat? (thin)

3. Was the room dark? (light)　　　4. Does the floor look clean? (dirty)

5. Did the students become quiet? (noisy)

6. Was the typewriter heavy? (light)

7. Did you feel well? (sick)　　　　8. Were the streets wet? (dry)

9. Does your friend seem worried? (confident)

10. Do these flowers smell good? (awful)

2-9. 第六個基本句型

主語	述語
NP	VI (Adv- m)

John is smiling (happily).

They walked (slowly).

The baby is sleeping (soundly).

第六個基本句型的述語只含有「**不及物動詞**」（VI, intransitive verb）。不及物動詞後面常常用「**表示狀態的副詞**」（Adv-m, adverbial of manner）如 happily, slowly, soundly 等來修飾。表示狀態的副詞大多數都是由形容詞加 "ly" 而成的。比較：

$\begin{cases} \text{The boy is } \textit{careful}. & \text{（這個孩子很細心。）} \\ \text{The boy studies } \textit{carefully}. & \text{（這個孩子很細心地讀書。）} \end{cases}$

$\begin{cases} \text{They were very } \textit{happy}. & \text{（他們很快樂。）} \\ \text{They lived very } \textit{happily}. & \text{（他們很快樂地生活。）} \end{cases}$

有些不及物動詞後面可以跟著另外一類副詞，如 up, down, on, off, in, out, over, by, away 等。例如：

They didn't show *up*.　　　　The dog ran *off*.

John walked *away* quickly.

這一類的副詞叫做「**助詞**」（particles），也叫做「**介副詞**」（preposition adverbs），因為其中有很多都可以當介詞用。

習　題　23

把 Be 動詞用括號裡的動詞來代替，並且把形容詞改成副詞。

Example:

The soldier is brave. (fight) → *The soldier fights bravely.*

1. The students were careful. (listen)　　2. Mary is gentle. (speak)

3. Bob is honest. (work)　　4. Jack was slow. (walk)

5. They were patient. (wait)　　6. She was nervous. (talk)

7. He was quick. (answer)　　8. You are diligent. (study)

9. Miss Taylor is beautiful. (dress)　　10. They are loud. (speak)

習 題 24

把括號裡的助詞放在句子裡適當的位置。

Example:

Why don't we start the next day? (out)

→ Why don't we start *out* the next day?

1. Please sit, gentlemen. (down)
2. They can't move now. (in)
3. Did John come yesterday? (over)
4. Can we start right now? (off)
5. What time did you wake this morning? (up)
6. Everybody please stand. (up)
7. Will you stop later on? (in)
8. He didn't show yesterday. (up)
9. Don't go before I tell you to. (away)
10. I can't hold any longer. (on)

2-10. 第七個基本句型

主語	述語	
NP	VT	NP (Adv-m)

John can speak English (fluently).

They finished the game (quickly).

The boy has prepared his lesson (carefully).

第七個基未句型由「**及物動詞**」（VT, transitive verb）加上名詞組而成。這個名詞組在語法上叫做及物動詞的**賓語**（object）。賓語後面可以用狀態副詞來修飾。

有些及物動詞後面還可以跟著助詞。這個時候助詞可以出現在賓語的前面，也可以出現在賓語的後面。

$\begin{cases} \text{John } \textit{turned on} \text{ the radio.} \\ \text{John } \textit{turned} \text{ the radio } \textit{on.} \end{cases}$

$\begin{cases} \text{The student is } \textit{looking over} \text{ his exercise.} \\ \text{The student is } \textit{looking} \text{ his exercise } \textit{over.} \end{cases}$

　　但是如果賓語是「人稱代名詞」（如 me, you, him, her, it, them 等）或「不定代名詞」（如 someone, something, anyone, anything, everyone, everything 等），那麼賓語一定要放在助詞前面。

$$\begin{cases} \text{John turned } \textit{it} \text{ on.（○）} \\ \text{John turned on } \textit{it}. \text{（×）} \end{cases}$$

$$\begin{cases} \text{I must look } \textit{them} \text{ up in the dictionary.（○）} \\ \text{I must look up } \textit{them} \text{ in the dictionary.（×）} \end{cases}$$

　　因為及物動詞與助詞可以由賓語隔開，所以有人管這些動詞叫做「**可分動詞**」（separable verbs）。

　　還有一些動詞可以跟後面的介詞一起當及物動詞用：

John *looked at* his friends.

The dog is *waiting for* his master.

　　因為這些動詞是由動詞與介詞構成的，所以有人稱它為「**介詞動詞**」（prepositional verbs）。介詞動詞與可分動詞不同，賓語一定要放在介詞的後面，不能放在介詞的前面。比較：

$$\begin{cases} \text{John looked over his exercise.} \\ \quad \rightarrow \text{John looked his exercise over.（○）} \\ \text{John looked at his exercise.} \end{cases}$$

$$\rightarrow \text{John looked his exercise at.（×）}$$

習　題　25

　　在含有「主語補語」的句子後面注 "SC"，在含有賓語的句子後面注 "DO"。

Examples:

He became a soldier. (SC)　　　　I know the soldier. (DO)

1. He remained a soldier all his life.

2. Mr. Wilson won the election.　　3. I love dogs.

4. The students enjoyed the picnic.　5. We stayed good friends.

6. She had long hair.　　　　　　7. The kitten became a cat.

8. The cat chased a mouse.　　　　9. He is our schoolmaster.

10. They became parents.

習 題 26

把括號裡的副詞放在動詞（或賓語）後面。

Examples:

> The children came into the room. (noisily)
>
> → The children came *noisily* into the room.
>
> She closed the door. (quietly)
>
> → She closed the door *quietly*.

1. He always answers my letter. (promptly)
2. The monkey climbed the tree. (easily)
3. They arrived after a long journey. (safely)
4. She waited for three hours. (patiently)
5. The children spent their money. (foolishly)
6. She makes decisions. (fast)
7. He walked into the room. (boldly)
8. The firemen climbed up the ladders. (rapidly)
9. The wind blew all afternoon. (violently)
10. They thought about the matter. (carefully)

參考：有些及物動詞，如 have, resemble, cost, weigh 等，不能用狀態副詞修飾，也不能改成被動式：

> John *has* a lot of friends.
>
> The children *resemble* their father.
>
> The book *cost* twenty dollars.

習 題 27

把賓語改放在動詞與助詞的中間，然後再改成人稱代名詞。

Example:

She has turned on the light. → *She has turned the light on.*

She has turned it on.

1. They drove out the cat.
2. The soldiers blew up the bridge.
3. We have given up our plans.
4. She sent away her maid.
5. I will look over the reports.
6. Did the firemen put out the fire?
7. I'd like to try on that yellow wool coat.
8. Why are you holding off your decision?
9. The carpenter put away his tools and left the building.
10. He reached down and picked up the newspaper.

習　題　28

把適當的介詞填進空白裡。如果不需要介詞，就寫一個 "×" 的記號。

Examples:

We looked *at* the boy.　　We watched × the boy.

1. He thought _____ the idea.
2. We laughed _____ the question.
3. They arrived _____ the airport.
4. How did you get _____ the station?
5. They waited _____ a signal.
6. We decided _____ the plan.
7. She listened _____ the story carefully.
8. He is looking _____ his lost pen.
9. He found _____ his lost watch.
10. We called _____ the Johnsons last Wednesdey.

習　題　29

用人稱代名詞的受格（it, him, her, them）回答下列問句。

Examples:

Has he looked over the plan?

    → *Yes, he has looked it over.*

Did the class go over the words?

    → *No, the class did not go over them.*

1. Does Jane take after her mother? Yes, _____ .

2. Did he pick up the newspaper? Yes, _____ .

3. Should I take off my coat? Yes, _____ .

4. Can you turn off the machine? No, _____ .

5. Did he think over the matter? No, _____ .

6. Will you look into the problem? Yes, _____ .

7. Oughtn't he to try out that radio before he buys it? Yes, _____ .

8. Don't you care for this kind of candy? No, _____ .

9. Have they decided to put off their meeting? Yes, _____ .

10. Aren't you going to see about the reservation for the concert? No, _____ .

2-11. 第八個基本句型

主語	述語		
		indirect object	direct object
NP	VT-d	NP$_1$	NP$_2$

John gave me a book.

They are going to buy their daughter a nice present.

The student has asked the teacher a few questions.

第八個基本句型的述語由「**雙賓動詞**」（double-object verbs）和兩個賓語合成。第一個賓語叫做「**間接賓語**」（indirect object），第二個賓語叫做「**直接賓語**」（direct object）。

間接賓語通常可以省去。例如：

John gave a book.

They are going to buy a nice present.

The student has asked a few questions.

但是直接賓語通常都不能省去。例如：

John gave me.（×）

They are going to buy their daughter.（×）

間接賓語也可以調到直接賓語的後面去。這個時候間接賓語前面要加 to, for 等介詞。

NP	VT-d	NP₁	NP₂	⇒	NP	VT-d	NP₂	Prep + NP₁

John gave my younger brother a book.

　　→ John gave a book *to* my younger brother.

They are going to buy their daughter a nice present.

　　→ They are going to buy a nice present *for* their daughter.

The student has asked the teacher a few questions.

　　→ The student has asked a few questions *of* the teacher.

They are going to play you a basketball game.

　　→ They are going to play a basketball game *with* you.

如果直接賓語是代名詞的話，間接賓語一定要放在直接賓語的後面。比較：

⎰ Bring John the book.（○）
⎱ Bring the book to John.（○）

⎰ Bring John it.（×）
⎱ Bring it to John.（○）

雙賓動詞可以根據間接賓語前面可以加那一種介詞（to, for, of 等）而分成下面幾類：

(a) **To**（間接賓語表示「接受者」）：*give, take, send, lend, rent, owe, pay, sell, tell, teach, bring, show, pass, throw, hand, offer, serve, read, write, sing, feed, drop, grant, deliver, do* (good), etc.

(b) **For**（間接賓語表示「受惠者」）：*buy, make, cook, order, save, choose, get, paint, play, build, find, leave, call, pour, win, earn, catch, write, do* (a favor), etc.

(c) **Of**（間接賓語表示「來源」）：*ask, expect, beg, demand, require,* etc.

(d) **With**（間接賓語表示「對手」）：*play, run,* etc.

還有一些動詞祇能出現在「動詞＋直接賓語＋介詞＋間接賓語」這個句型裡：

$$\begin{cases} \textit{Say} \text{ "hello" to him.（○）} \\ \textit{Say} \text{ him "hello".（×）} \end{cases}$$

$$\begin{cases} \text{John } \textit{introduced} \text{ Mary to his friend.（○）} \\ \text{John } \textit{introduced} \text{ his friend Mary.（×）} \end{cases}$$

(a) **To:** *say, speak, talk, explain, report, describe, mention, remember, announce, propose, introduce, repeat, suggest,* etc.

(b) **For:** *open, close, change, correct, keep, sign, answer, repeat, prepare, pronounce, translate, fix,* etc.

習 題 30

把代名詞放進下面的句子裡做間接賓語用。

Examples:

Give a dollar. (him) → Give *him* a dollar.

Give a dollar to *him*.

Ask a question. (us) → Ask *us* a question.

Say "hello". (me) → Say "hello" *to me*.

1. Speak English. (me)　　　　2. Write a letter. (him)

3. Take the money. (her)　　　4. Tell your story. (me)

5. Repeat the answer. (them)　6. Explain the problem. (her)

7. Send a check. (us)　　　　8. Give your order. (them)

9. Lend your car. (me)　　　10. Report the accident. (them)

習 題 31

把代名詞放進下面的句子裡做間接賓語用。

Examples:

Read the book. (me) → Read *me* the book.

Read the book *to me / for me*.

Buy the book. (me) → Buy *me* the book.

Buy the book *for me*.

Open the door (me) → Open the door *for me*.

Repeat the answer. (me) → Repeat the answer to *me / for* me.

1. Show the pictures. (us)
2. Close the window. (him)
3. Get a table. (her)
4. Keep these papers. (them)
5. Find a place. (him)
6. Introduce your friend. (me)
7. Correct this sentence. (us)
8. Cook some dinner. (me)
9. Throw the ball. (them)
10. Call a taxi. (me)

習　題　32

刪去可以省略的直接賓語。

Examples:

Did he pay you the money? → *Did he pay you?*

Did he read a story to Jane? → *Did he read to Jane?*

1. Did he teach her English?
2. Did he sing songs to the children?
3. Did he feed the birds crumbs?
4. Did he give money to the Red Cross?
5. Did he tell the police his story?
6. Did he write a letter to his family?
7. Did he serve his guests lunch?
8. Did he rent his house to a family of seven?
9. Did he pay the employees last week's salary?
10. Did he contribute all his money to charities?

參考：在「動詞＋間接賓語＋直接賓語」這個句型裡，出現在動詞 teach, tell, write, pay, feed, serve, supply 後面的直接賓語可以省去：

He *taught* us (English) in high school.

She *wrote* us (a letter) every week.

在「動詞＋直接賓語＋to 間接賓語」這個句型裡，出現在動詞 give, lend, sing, write, play, rent, deliver, contribute 後面的直接賓語可以省去：

They *gave* (the book) to him yesterday.

She *wrote* (a letter) to her family last week.

習 題 33

把直接賓語改成代名詞，然後把間接賓語改成由 to 或 for 引導的介詞片語。

Examples:

The teacher gave the students some books.

→ *The teacher gave them to the students.*

They bought me that present.

→ *They bought it for me.*

1. Please give that lady the apples.
2. Mrs. Harris brought her children the toys.
3. Let's offer Bob the job.
4. Mother read us the story.
5. I showed my friends the pictures.
6. The merchant promised the boy the reward.
7. Hand him the books.
8. We sold the Taylors our house.
9. I told the officer the truth.
10. The reporter sent his paper the story.

2-12. 第九個基本句型

主語	述語		
NP	VT-e	object	object complement
		NP₁	NP₂

The city elected Mr. Wood mayor.

John named his new boat 'Hurricane'.

They voted Jane the most popular girl.

　　第九個基本句型的述語由「**elect 類的及物動詞**」（VT-e, transitive verbs of elect-type：如 elect, choose, vote, appoint, name, nominate）與兩個名詞組合成。這兩個名詞組的功用與第八個句型中雙賓動詞後面的兩個名詞組的功用不同。第八個基本句型的兩個名詞組是間接賓語與直接賓語，指兩個不同的人或物；第九個基本句型的兩個名詞組是賓語與「**賓語補語**」（object complement），指同一個人或物。比較：

They elected John their captain.

（第九個基本句型：John 和 captain 指同一個人。）

They gave John their captain (as a partner).

（第八個基本句型：John 和 captain 不是同一人。）

習　題　34

　　用括號裡的語詞回答下列問句。

Examples:

Did you elect John? (captain)

　→ *Yes, we elected John captain.*

What did they name the ship? ('Queen Mary')

　→ *They named the ship 'Queen Mary'.*

1. Did the committee appoint him? (chairman)
2. What did they name the baby? (Jane)
3. Did the students choose him? (president)
4. What did they nominate him? (treasurer)
5. Did they appoint him? (manager)
6. What did they vote her? (the most popular girl in the class)
7. Did you choose Tom? (spokesman for the family)
8. What are they going to elect him? (president)
9. Did the company appoint him? (superintendent)

10. What did you name the dog? ('Snow White')

2-13. 第十個基本句型

主語	述語		
		object	object complement
NP	**VT-c**	**NP₁**	$\begin{Bmatrix} \textbf{NP}_2 \\ \textbf{Adj} \end{Bmatrix}$

John considered me a fool.

John considered me foolish.

They thought it a wonderful idea.

They thought the idea wonderful.

第十個基本句型的述語是由「**consider 類的及物動詞**」(VT-c, transitive verbs of consider-type： 如 consider, think, prove, judge, imagine, believe, keep, make, find, leave, call, label）與名詞組或形容詞合成。這個句型和第九個基本句型很相似，所不同的是除了名詞以外形容詞也可以當賓語補語用。

注意：同一個動詞常常可以出現在不同的句型裡。例如：

$\begin{cases} \text{John } appeared \text{ surprised.} & （第五個基本句型） \\ \text{John } appeared \text{ suddenly.} & （第六個基本句型） \end{cases}$

$\begin{cases} \text{John } called \text{ me a taxi.} & （第八個基本句型） \\ \text{John } called \text{ me a fool.} & （第十個基本句型） \end{cases}$

參考：在 get, feel, set, wear, like, prefer, want, paint 等動詞後面只有形容詞可以當賓語補語用。例如：

She *wears* her hair *long*.　　　　　I *like* my tea *hot*.

We *set* him *free*.

習　題　35

用括號裡的語詞回答下列問句。

Example:

How do you like your tea? (iced) → *I like it iced.*

1. How does Jane wear her hair? (short)
2. How did you find the hotel? (delightful)
3. What color did you paint the walls? (white)
4. How do you want your coffee? (strong)
5. How does Bob play his radio? (loud)
6. How do you find English, simple or complicated? (simple)
7. How do you like your steak, rare, medium or well-done? (well-done)
8. How do you prefer your vegetables, cooked or raw? (cooked)
9. How do they serve fruit in China, peeled or unpeeled? (unpeeled)
10. What do historians call George Washington? (the father of his country)

習　題　36

照例句改寫下面的句子。

Examples:

We found him a sick man. → *He was a sick man.*

We found him a job. → *He got a job.*

1. We made him a member.
2. We made him an offer.
3. We called him a taxi.
4. We called him a pest.
5. We left him a happy person.
6. We left him a tip.
7. We made him a promise.
8. We made him a success.
9. We found him an audience.
10. We found him an unhappy person.

習　題　37

照例句完成下面的句子。

Examples:

find / empty → *(Did you) find (the box) empty?*

hold / responsible → *(I'll) hold (you) responsible.*

1. push / open
2. set / free
3. keep / warm
4. make / angry
5. cut / short
6. believe / innocent
7. judge / insane
8. consider / good English
9. find / a hard worker
10. leave / a mess

第3章
十二種動詞時變式

3-1. 英語的助動詞

　　在前面的一章裡我們討論了英語基本句型的結構，在這一章與後面的幾章裡我們要研究「**動詞組**」（verb phrase）的結構。英語的動詞組由兩個部分合成：「**助動詞**」（auxiliary or helping verb）與「**主動詞**」（main verb）。主動詞可以說是動詞組裡最主要的動詞；助動詞加在主動詞之前，用來表示各種「**時變式**」（tenses and aspects）或「**語氣**」（modes）。

Be

He *is* in England.（現在單純式）

He *was* in England.（過去單純式）

He *has been* in England.（現在完成式）

He *had been* in England.（過去完成式）

He *may be* in England.（may + 單純式）

He *might be* in England.（might + 單純式）

He *may have been* in England.（may + 完成式）

He *might have been* in England.（might + 完成式）

Study

She *studies* English.（現在單純式）

She *studied* English.（過去單純式）

She *is studying* English.（現在進行式）

She *was studying* English.（過去進行式）

She *has studied* English.（現在完成式）

She *had studied* English.（過去完成式）

She *has been studying* English.（現在完成進行式）

She *had been studying* English.（過去完成進行式）

She *should study* English.（should＋單純式）

She *should be studying* English.（should＋進行式）

She *should have studied* English.（should＋完成式）

She *should have been studying* English.（should＋完成進行式）

習 題 38

按照例句把助動詞與主動詞分開。

Examples:

He <u>might</u> <u>have</u> (be)en in England.   Has she <u>been</u> (study) ing English?

1. I am smelling a flower.

2. I have just heated up the coffee.

3. Did you ever talk to him?

4. You should read this more carefully.

5. You should have finished it long time ago.

6. He must have been tired.

7. Will you please help me on this?

8. I must be going now.

9. I have been hearing a good deal about you.

10. She may not be able to see you.

3-2. 時式與時間

英語的動詞只有兩種「**時式**」（tense）：**現在式**（present）與**過去式**（past）：

She *is* not here.（現在式）

She *was* not here.（過去式）

I *work* here.（現在式）

I *worked* here.（過去式）

They *have* been to Europe.（現在式）

They *had* been to Europe.（過去式）

He *will* go with you.（現在式）

He *would* go with you.（過去式）

You *may* have seen him.（現在式）

You *might* have seen him.（過去式）

　　為了要了解英語動詞的時式，我們必須區別時式與時間（time）這兩個不同的
概念。時間指過去、現在、未來所有的時間；時式卻指動詞的形式。我們用各種不
同的時式來表示各種不同的時間，但是現在式不一定表示現在時間，過去式也不一
定代表過去時間。例如，我們可以用現在式的動詞來描述發生在現在、過去或未來
的事情：

　　　Mr. Smith *doesn't understand* the question.（現在時間）

　　　Mr. Smith *sells* books and magazines.（包括現在、過去、未來三個時間）

　　　Mr. Smith *leaves* for New York tomorrow.（未來時間）

　　　So Mr. Smith *goes* up to the police. "There's a burglar in my house!" he *says*.
　　　　（過去時間—「歷史的現在」（historic present））

同樣的，我們也可以用過去式的動詞來描述發生在現在、過去或未來的事情：

　　　If Mr. Smith *had* money now, he *would* buy the car.（現在時間）

　　　Mr. Smith *bought* the car yesterday.（過去時間）

　　　Mr. Smith *might buy* the car tomorrow.（未來時間）

因此我們可以用不同的時式來表示同樣的時間：

　　　┌ Mr. Smith *leaves* for Japan tomorrow.
　　　│ Mr. Smith is *leaving* for Japan tomorrow.
　　　│ Mr. Smith *will leave* for Japan tomorrow.
　　　└ Mr. Smith *is going to leave* for Japan tomorrow.

　　　┌ John *talks* all the time.
　　　└ John *is* always *talking*.

　　　┌ How *do* you *feel* now?
　　　└ How *are* you *feeling* now?

習　題　39

把動詞的時式與所描述的時間指出來。

Examples:

　　　John is talking now.（現在式；現在時間）

　　　John is always talking.（現在式；現在、過去與未來時間）

John leaves for Japan tomorrow evening.（現在式；未來時間）

He didn't know the answer.（過去式；過去時間）

He might go tomorrow.（過去式；未來時間）

1. I smell something.

2. He may come next week.

3. I would like some tea, please.

4. She will go tomorrow.

5. Did you have your breakfast?

6. How brightly the sun is shining!

7. What brought you back tonight?

8. I have been in America and Europe.

9. She said she had been there.

10. He had made A on all three tests.

3-3. 現在式：V, V-s

英語動詞的「**現 在 式**」（present tense）有兩種：「**簡 單 式**」（V, simple form）與「**第三身單數式**」（V-s, third-person-singular form）。第一身（I, we）、第二身（you）、第三身複數（they, the boys, John and Mary）用簡單式，第三身單數（he, she, it, the boy, Mary）用第三身單數式，也就是在簡單式後面加 -s 或 -es。

	單數（singular）	**複數**（plural）
第一身	I work.	We work.
第二身	You work.	You work.
第三身	He works.	
	She works.	They work.
	It works.	
	John works.	John and Mary work.

唯一的例外是 Be 動詞。它有三種不同的形式：am, are, is。

I am.	We are.
You are.	You are.
He is.	
She is.	They are.
It is.	
John is.	John and Mary are.

參考一：拼字的規則：

(a) 如果動詞的字尾是子音加 y（-Cy, Consonant＋y），把 y 改成 i 後加 es。

-Cy → -Cies

cry　　cr*ies*　　　　try　　tr*ies*　　　　fly　　fl*ies*

（比較：buy buy*s*）

(b) 如果動詞的字尾是 s, z, x, sh, ch, o，加 es。

pass	pass*es*	waltz	waltz*es*
tax	tax*es*	rush	rush*es*
touch	touch*es*	go	go*es*

參考二：發音的規則：

(a) 在齒擦音〔s, z, ʃ, ʒ, tʃ, dʒ〕後面的 es，唸〔ɪz〕。

pass*es*, ris*es*, rush*es*, roug*es*, touch*es*, judg*es*.

(b) 在不帶聲的子音（清音）〔p, t, k, f〕後面的（e）s，唸〔s〕。

hope*s*, pat*s*, ask*s*, laugh*s*.

(c) 其他（e）s（濁音與母音後面的 s 或 es）唸〔z〕。

brib*es*, beg*s*, read*s*, cri*es*, go*es*.

(d) 不規則的讀音：does〔dʌz〕，says〔sɛz; sez〕。

習　題　40

把括號裡的動詞的現在式填進空白中，並且用音標注出 -（e）s 的發音。

Examples:

— 91 —

(work)　　He *works* every weekday.〔s〕

(return)　She *returns* every August.〔z〕

(play)　　We *play* tennis every spring.

1. (come) He ＿＿＿＿ to dinner every Sunday.

2. (listen) She ＿＿＿＿ to the radio in the evening.

3. (study) John ＿＿＿＿ every afternoon from four to six.

4. (paint) We ＿＿＿＿ every nice afternoon.

5. (meet) He and I ＿＿＿＿ every weekend.

6. (write) He ＿＿＿＿ his mother every week.

7. (strike) It ＿＿＿＿ every quarter-hour.

8. (read) She ＿＿＿＿ a story every evening.

9. (play) Bob ＿＿＿＿ baseball with his friends after school.

10. (complain) Mary ＿＿＿＿ all the time.

3-4. 過去式：V-ed

　　英語動詞的「**過去式**」（V-ed, past tense）有規則式與不規則式的區別。規則動詞的過去式由簡單式加 ed 而成，並不因為主語的身與數而有分別。

I worked.　　　　　　　We worked.

You worked.　　　　　　You worked.

He worked.　⎫

She worked.　⎬　　　　 They worked.

It worked.　 ⎭

John worked.　　　　　　John and Mary worked.

　　不規則動詞的過去式則有特別的變化, 必須一一記住。我們把所有不規則動詞的變化都列在 3-8 裡。

參考一：拼字的規則：

　　(a) 如果動詞是單音節而且字尾是短母音加子音字母，把子音字母重複後加 ed。

-VC　→　-VCCed

beg	beg*ged*	wed	wed*ded*
fit	fit*ted*	stop	stop*ped*

(b) 雙音節動詞如果重音在最後的音節，而且字尾是短母音加子音字母，把子音字母重複後加 ed。

-V́C　→　-V́CCed

Permít	permít*ted*		admít	admít*ted*
omít	omít*ted*	（比較：	límit	límit*ed*）
refér	refér*red*		prefér	prefér*red*
defér	defér*red*	（比較：	óffer	óffer*ed*）
occúr	occúr*red*		concúr	concúr*red*
		（比較：	cónquer	cónquer*ed*）

(c) 如果動詞的字尾是子音字加 y，把 y 改成 i 後加 ed。

-Cy　→　-Cied

cry	cr*ied*		try	tr*ied*
ply	pl*ied*	（比較：	play	play*ed*）

(d) 例外：

picnic	picnic*ked*	mimic	mimic*ked*
frolic	frolic*ked*		
trável	trável*led* (Br.)	trável*ed* (Am.)	
kídnap	kídnap*ped* (Br.)	kídnap*ed* (Am.)	
wórship	wórship*ped* (Br.)	wórship*ed* (Am.)	

參考二：發音的規則：

(a) 在〔t〕與〔d〕後面，唸〔ɪd〕。

　　start*ed*, tast*ed*, skat*ed*, need*ed*, attend*ed*, trad*ed*.

(b) 在不帶聲的子音（清音）後面，唸〔t〕。

　　tapp*ed*, pick*ed*, laugh*ed*, pass*ed*, rush*ed*, touch*ed*.

(c) 其他地方（在濁音與母音後面），唸〔d〕。

　　handl*ed*, nam*ed*, brib*ed*, begg*ed*, answer*ed*, play*ed*, cri*ed*, mov*ed*.

習 題 41

把括號裡的動詞的過去式填進空白中，並且用音標注出 -ed 的發音。

Examples:

(cook) She *cooked* the food this morning. 〔t〕

(snow) It *snowed* last winter. 〔d〕

1. (try) They _____ to get in after the show had begun.

2. (stay) He _____ after the other guests had left.

3. (watch) They _____ TV last nisht.

4. (help) The review course _____ me pass my exams.

5. (close) The store _____ early last Sunday.

6. (wash) The janitor _____ windows all day yesterday.

7. (use) We _____ a lot of coal during the last cold spell.

8. (start) The train _____ late last night.

9. (promise) He _____ to deliver the goods promptly.

10. (arrive) The package _____ last Saturday.

3-5. 未來時間

我們在前面已經提過，英語的動詞只有現在式與過去式而沒有未來式。但是英語仍有許多方式來表示未來時間：

(1) **Will 或 Shall + V**：

I *will let* you know as soon as the work is finished.

Shall we *go* to the play tomorrow night?

關於 will 與 shall 的用法請看 4-9。

(2) **Be going + to V**：

I *am going to visit* my uncle tomorrow.

Is Mr. Smith *going to have* his house painted?

(3) **Be + to V**：

I *am to give* a talk for her club next week.

éçà

Are we *to finish* this work by ourselves?

(4) **Be about + to V**：

I *am about to leave.*

Are you *about, to finish* your letter?

　因為以前文法書都把英語的時式分為現在、過去與未來，大家也習慣這種時式的三分法，所以為了教學方便我們也要把 will 或 shall＋V 看做「未來式」。但是我們必須把時間與時式這兩種概念分清楚，這樣才能把英語的時變式學得好。

參考：比較下列句子含義的不同。

　　　I'll go to visit my aunt.（單純未來）

　　　I *will* go to visit my aunt.（表示答應或決心）

　　　I *am going to* visit my aunt.（在未定的將來，可能就是下星期。）

　　　I *am to* visit my aunt.（媽媽要我這樣做，姑媽希望我這樣做，我計劃這樣做。）

　　　I *am about to* leave.（就要走開了。）

習　題　42

　把括號裡的動詞用適當的形式表示未來時間。每一個題目都可能有好幾個答案。

Examples: He (start) next month.

　　　　　He will start next month.

　　　　　He is going to start next month.

　　　　　He is to start next month.

1. She (arrive) tomorrow.
2. I (be) back at noon.
3. We (take) a walk in the park.
4. You (buy) a dictionary.
5. He (go) home by subway.
6. I (eat) by myself.
7. Nobody (tell) him what to do.
8. Alice (wear) her best suit.
9. They (put) the mail on my desk.
10. It (cost) ten dollars.

3-6. 變式：單純式、完成式、進行式、完成進行式

英語的動詞除了表示動作時間的時式以外，還有表示動作狀態的「**變式**」（aspect）：**單純式**（simple aspect），**完成式**（perfect aspect），**進行式**（progressive aspect），**完成進行式**（perfect progressive aspect）。因此從三個時式與四個變式，我們可以獲得十二種英語動詞的「**時變式**」（tense-aspect forms）。

時式 ＼ 變式	單純式	完成式	進行式	完成進行式
現在	*Simple Present*	*Present Perfect*	*Present Progressive*	*Present Perfect Progressive*
過去	*Simple Past*	*Past Perfect*	*Past Progressive*	*Past Perfect Progressive*
（未來）	*Simple Future*	*Future Perfect*	*Future Progressive*	*Future Perfect Progressive*

習　題　43

按照例句說出（或寫出）答句。用括號裡的語詞做答句的主語。

Examples:

He lives in Chicago now. (she) → *She lives in Chicago now, too.*

I worked in the bookshop last year. (Henry)

　　→ *Henry worked in the bookshop last year, too.*

They will go to Europe next month. (we)

　　→ *We will / shall go to Europe next month, too.*

1. I travel a lot. (you)

2. We played handball last week. (they)

3. They will travel by plane. (I)

4. Mary studies all the time. (Alice)

5. I enjoy going to concerts. (my brother)

6. Lawers and actors talk a lot in their work. (businessmen)

7. I like studying in the library. (Bob)

8. Jack asked a lot of questions. (Joe)

9. They will have a meeting tomorrow. (we)

10. Dick will get a raise this week. (you)

3-7. 進行式：Be + V-ing

動詞的「**進 行 式**」（progressive form）係 由 Be 與「**現 在 分 詞**」（present participle）合成。現在分詞由動詞原式加字尾 -ing 而成，因此又叫做「**ING（式）動詞**」（V-ing form）。

時式＼變式	進行式
現在	$\left. \begin{array}{l} am \\ are \\ is \end{array} \right\}$ + V-ing
過去	$\left. \begin{array}{l} was \\ were \end{array} \right\}$ + V-ing
未來	$\left. \begin{array}{l} will \\ shall \end{array} \right\}$ + be + V-ing

例如：

I am eating.

You (we, they) are eating.

He (she, it) is eating.

I (he, she, it) was eating.

You (we,they) were eating.

I (you, he, she, it, we, they) will be eating.

動詞的進行式表示一件事情在現在、過去或未來的某一點時間正在進行之中。

參考：拼字的規則：

(a) 如果動詞的字尾是不讀音的 e，把 e 去掉後加 ing。

-Ce → **Cing**

bite	bit*ing*	give	giv*ing*
write	writ*ing*	（例外：dye	dye*ing*）

(b) 如果動詞是單音節而且字尾是短母音加子音字母，把子音字母重複後加 ing。

-VC — **-VCCing**

put	put*ting*	run	run*ning*
stop	stop*ping*	quiz	quiz*zing*

（比較：rain　rain*ing*）

(c) 雙音節的動詞如果重音在最後的音節而且字尾是短母音加子音字母，把子音字母重複後加 ing。

-V́C → **-V́CCing**

omít	omit*ting*	（比較：límit	limit*ing*）
prefér	prefer*ring*	（比較：óffer	offer*ing*）

(d) 如果動詞的字尾是 ie，把 ie 改成 y 後加 ing。

- Cie — **Cying**

lie	*lying*	die	dy*ing*
tie	ty*ing*		

習 題 44

按照例句用括號裡的名詞和動詞說出（或寫出）問句。

Excamples:

Is John working today? (Bob, study) → *Is Bob studying today?*

Was he smiling? (you, talk) → *Were you talking?*

Will you be studying? (she, read) → *Will she be reading?*

1. Was he studying? (Ken, write on the blackboard)

2. Are they coming today? (he, leave)

3. Were you talking? (the man, lie in the next room)

4. Are you eating now? (your mother, bake a cake)

5. Was it raining? (the stars, shine brightly)

6. Will they be swimming? (you, take a piano lesson)

7. Is the typist improving? (you, improve your English pronunciation)

8. Is the patient in Room 103 getting better today? (the little boys, behave well)

9. Was she standing at the gate? (the car, go at a full speed)

10. Are the little boys learning to swim? (Miriam, get dressed up for the party)

3-8. 完成式：Have + V-en

動詞的「**完成式**」（perfect form）是由助動詞 Have 與「**過去分詞**」（past participle）合成。

時式 ＼ 變式	完成式
現在	$\left\{ \begin{array}{l} \text{have} \\ \text{has} \end{array} \right\}$ + V-en
過去	had　　+ V-en
未來	will (shall) + have + V-en

例如：

I (you, we, they) have eaten.

He (she, it) has eaten.

I (you, he, she, it, we, they) had eaten.

I (you, he, she, it, we, they) will have eaten.

動詞的完成式表示一件事情在現在、過去或未來的某一點時間之前已經完成。

過去分詞又叫做「**EN（式）動詞**」（V-en form）。一般動詞的過去分詞與過去式完全相同。

V (-s) Form	V-ed Form	V-en Form
work (s)	worked	(have) worked
learn (s)	learned	(have) learned

但是少數的常用動詞有特定的過去式與過去分詞。我們把這一些動詞按照它們的語音變化整理在下面。希望大家能把這一些變化牢牢記住。

動詞的不規則變化

I. A─A─A 型

現在式、過去式與過去分詞的基本式都一樣。

a. A─A─A

beat	「連擊」	beat	beat (beaten)
*bet	「打賭」	bet	bet
bid	「吩咐，開價」	bid (bade)	bid (bidden)
burst	「爆炸」	burst	burst
cast	「投」	cast	cast
cost	「值」	cost	cost
cut	「切」	cut	cut
*fit	「適合」	fit	fit
hit	「擊中」	hit	hit
hurt	「傷害」	hurt	hurt
*knit	「編結」	knit	knit
let	「讓」	let	let
put	「放置」	put	put
quit	「停止，放棄」	quit	quit
*rid	「驅除」	rid	rid
set	「安置」	set	set
shed	「流出」	shed	shed
shut	「關閉」	shut	shut
slit	「割裂」	slit	slit
*spit	「吐出」	spit (spat)	spit (spat)
spread	「散佈」	spread	spread

*sweat	「流汗」	sweat	sweat
thrust	「衝刺」	thrust	thrust
*wed	「嫁，娶」	wed	wed
*wet	「弄溼」	wet	wet

b. A—At—At

*burn	「燃燒」	burnt	burnt
dwell	「居住」	dwelt	dwelt
*learn	「學習」	learnt	learnt
*smell	「聞，嗅」	smelt	smelt
*spell	「拼字」	spelt	spelt
*spill	「溢出」	spilt	spilt
*spoil	「損壞」	spoilt	spoilt

c. A—Ad—An

*hew	「砍，劈」	hewed	hewn
*prove	「證明」	proved	proven
*saw	「鋸（木）」	sawed	sawn
*sew	「縫（衣）」	sewed	sewn
*show	「指出」	showed	shown
*sow	「播種」	sowed	sown
*strew	「散播」	strewed	strewn

d. Ad—At—At

bend	「彎曲」	bent	bent
build	「建築」	built	built
lend	「借（出）」	lent	lent
rend	「撕裂」	rent	rent
send	「送，寄」	sent	sent
spend	「花費」	spent	spent

II. A—B—B 型

過去式與過去分詞的基本式一樣。

a. A—B—B

1. 〔ɪ〕→〔ʌ〕

cling	「抓緊」	clung	clung
dig	「挖（洞）」	dug	dug
fling	「投，擲」	flung	flung
shrink	「退縮」	shrunk (shrank)	shrunk (shrunken)
sling	「投擲」	slung	slung
slink	「溜走」	slunk	slunk
spin	「紡織」	spun	spun
spring	「跳躍」	sprung (sprang)	sprung
stick	「插入」	stuck	stuck
sting	「刺，螫」	stung	stung
stink	「發臭」	stunk (stank)	stunk
*string	「捆紮」	strung	strung
win	「贏，獲」	won	won
wring	「絞扭」	wrung	wrung

〔æ〕→〔ʌ〕

*hang	{ hung	hung	「吊、掛」
	hanged	hanged	「吊死」

〔aɪ〕→〔ʌ〕

strike	「打擊」	struck	struck

2. 〔i〕→〔ɛ〕

bleed	「流血」	bled	bled
breed	「養育」	bred	bred
feed	「餵（養）」	fed	fed
lead	「引導」	led	led

meet	「遇見」	met	met
*plead	「抗辯」	pled	pled
read	「閱讀」	read	read
*speed	「加速」	sped	sped

〔o〕→〔ɛ〕

| hold | 「抓住」 | held | held |

3. 〔aɪ〕→〔ɪ〕

bite	「咬」	bit	bit
chide	「責罵」	chid	chid (chidden)
hide	「躲藏」	hid	hid (hidden)
*light	「點亮」	lit	lit
slide	「滑行」	slid	slid

4. 〔aɪ〕→〔aʊ〕

bind	「綑綁」	bound	bound
find	「發現」	found	found
grind	「碾，磨」	ground	ground
wind	「捲，上發條」	wound	wound

5. 〔aɪ〕→〔o〕

*bide	「等待」	bode	bode
*shine	「照亮」	shone	shone
strive	「努力」	strove	strove (striven)

〔i〕→〔o〕

| heave | 「挺舉」 | hove | hove |

〔e〕→〔o〕

| *wake | 「（喚）醒」 | woke | woke (woken) |

6. Others

get	「得到」	got	got (gotten)
tread	「踐踏」	trod	trod (trodden)
shoot	「射擊」	shot	shot
fight	「戰鬥」	fought	fought
sit	「坐」	sat	sat

b. A—Bt—Bt

1. 〔i〕→〔ε〕

creep	「爬行」	crept	crept
deal	「分發，經管」	dealt	dealt
*dream	「做夢」	dreamt	dreamt
feel	「覺得」	felt	felt
keep	「保持」	kept	kept
*kneel	「跪下」	knelt	knelt
*lean	「斜靠」	leant	leant
*leap	「跳躍」	leapt	leapt
mean	「表示」	meant	meant
sleep	「睡覺」	slept	slept
sweep	「掃除」	swept	swept
weep	「哭泣」	wept	wept

2. 〔i〕→〔ɔ〕

*beseech	「懇求」	besought	besought
seek	「尋找」	sought	sought
teach	「教（授）」	taught	taught

〔ɪ〕→〔ɔ〕

| bring | 「帶來」 | brought | brought |
| think | 「想」 | thought | thought |

〔æ〕 → 〔ɔ〕

catch	「捕捉」	caught	caught

〔aɪ〕 → 〔ɔ〕

buy	「買」	bought	bought

3. 〔iv〕 → 〔ɛf〕

*bereave	「奪去」	bereft	bereft
*cleave	「劈開」	cleft (clove)	cleft (cloven)
leave	「離開」	left	left

4. 〔uz〕 → 〔ɔs〕

lose	「遺失」	lost	lost

c. A－Bd－Bd

1. 〔ɛ〕 → 〔o〕

sell	「賣」	sold	sold
tell	「告訴」	told	told

2. Others

flee	「逃走」	fled	fled
hear	「聽到」	heard	heard
make	「製造」	made	made
say	「說」	said	said
*shoe	「穿鞋」	shod	shod
stand	「站（立）」	stood	stood

d. A－B－Bn

1. 〔ɛr〕 → 〔ɔr〕

bear		bore	born 「出生」（borne）「搬運、忍受」
*shear 〔ɪr〕「修剪」		shore	shorn
swear	「發誓」	swore	sworn
tear	「撕裂」	tore	torn

wear 「穿著」	wore	worn

2. 〔i〕→〔o〕

freeze 「冷凍」	froze	frozen
speak 「講」	spoke	spoken
steal 「偷」	stole	stolen
weave 「織（布）」	wove	woven

〔e〕→〔o〕

break 「打破」	broke	broken

〔u〕→〔o〕

choose 「選擇」	chose	chosen

〔ε〕→〔o〕

*swell 「膨脹」	swoll	swollen

3. Others

lie 「躺下」	lay	lain

III. A—B—A 型

現在式與過去分詞的基本式一樣。

a. A—B—A

come 「來」	came	come
become	became	become 「變為，適於」
overcome	overcame	overcome「得勝，壓倒」
run 「跑」	ran	run

b. A—B—An

1. 〔e〕→〔ʊ〕

forsake 「遺棄」	forsook	forsaken
shake 「搖動」	shook	shaken
take 「拿去」	took	taken

2. 〔o〕→〔ʊ〕

blow	「吹」	blew	blown
grow	「生長」	grew	grown
know	「知道」	knew	known
throw	「投，丟」	threw	thrown

〔ɔ〕→〔u〕

draw	「拖拉」	drew	drawn

〔e〕→〔u〕

slay	「殺害」	slew	slain

3. Others

eat	「吃」	ate	eaten
see	「看到」	saw	seen
give	「給」	gave	given
fall	「落下」	fell	fallen

IV. A─B─C 型

現在式、過去式與過去分詞的基本式都不一樣。

a. A─B─C

〔ɪ〕→〔æ〕→〔ʌ〕

begin	「開始」	began	begun
drink	「喝」	drank	drunk (drunken)
ring	「鳴響」	rang	rung
sing	「唱歌」	sang	sung
sink	「下沉」	sank	sunk
swim	「游泳」	swam	swum

b. A─B─Cn

1. 〔aɪ〕→〔o〕→〔ɪ〕

drive	「駕駛」	drove	driven
ride	「騎坐」	rode	ridden
rise	「升（起）」	rose	risen

*shrive	「聽懺悔」	shrove	shriven
smite	「重擊」	smote	smitten
stride	「大步行走」	strode	stridden
strive	「努力，抗爭」	strove	striven
*thrive	「興盛」	throve	thriven
write	「寫」	wrote	written

2. Others

do	「做（事）」	did	done
fly	「飛」	flew	flown
go	「去」	went	gone

　　星號「*」表示這些動詞也可以用規則變化；附括號（　）者表示這個動詞有幾種不同的不規則變化。

3-9. 完成進行式：Have + been + V-ing

　　完成進行式由 Have, been 與現在分詞（V-ing）三者合成。

時式＼變式	完成式
現在	$\left\{\begin{array}{l} \text{have} \\ \text{has} \end{array}\right\}$ + been + V-ing
過去	had + been + V-ing
未來	will (shall) + have + been + V-ing

例如：

　　I (you, we, they) have been eating.

　　He (she, it) has been eating.

　　I (you, he, she, it, we, they) had been eating.

　　I (you, he, she, it, we, they) will have been eating.

　　完成進行式描寫一個動作一直繼續到某一個時間，而且可能還要繼續下去。

習　題　45

把動詞的完成式改為完成進行式。

Example:

I have studied. → *I have been studying.*

1. He has written a letter.
2. They have listened.
3. We have heard about that.
4. She has thought about that.
5. I have ridden this train.
6. They have built a new building.
7. We have paid taxes.
8. She has worried about her job.
9. It has rained for an hour.
10. The government has talked about it for years.

第4章
各種時變式的用途

在這一章裡我們要從兩個不同的觀點來討論各種時變式的用途。首先我們要把每種時變式的用途逐一加以討論，然後在 5-3 的複習裡以摘要的方式來敘述我們心裡有關時間的概念，究竟可以用那幾種時變式來表達。

4-1. 現在單純式的用途：V, V-s

我們用現在單純式的動詞來表示種種永恒性、習慣性或頻繁性的行為。這一種行為，過去是如此，未來也是如此，可以說是超時間的。因為英語裡沒有超時間的時式，就用現在單純式來表示。

(1) 普遍的真理與現在的事實

The sun *rises* in the east.

The earth *moves* around the sun.

Two and two *are* four.

Children *need* love and care.

Experience *teaches* us many things.

Alaska *is* the largest state in the United States.

It *snows* a great deal in some parts of Alaska.

Water *contains* hydrogen and oxygen.

This milk tastes sour.

(2) 習慣與頻繁性的行為（如習慣、職業、興趣、嗜好、才能等）

V	every day, every morning.
V-s	always, often, usually, seldom, etc.

I *go* to church every Sunday.

Mr. Brown *broadcasts* every morning.

The hiking club *goes* on a picnic every weekend.

The Chinese people *eat* a great deal of rice.

John *plays* the violin well.

Professor White *teaches* philosophy.

Mrs. White usually *pays* her bills on time.

We seldom *go* to the movies.

I often *hear* my neighbors arguing.

現在單純式

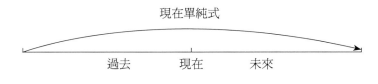

過去　　　　現在　　　未來

習　題　46

按照例句完成下面的句子。

Example: He _____ Chinese, but he _____ English. (speak)

　　　　He *speaks* Chinese, but he *doesn't speak* English.

1. Miss Harris _____ English, but she _____ geography. (teach)

2. Bob _____ German, but he _____ French. (know)

3. My father _____ tea, but he _____ coffee. (like)

4. That author _____ novels, but he _____ poems. (write)

5. Jack's wife _____ blue, but she _____ green. (wear)

6. The baker _____ bread, but he _____ cake. (make)

7. We _____ rice, but we _____ potatoes. (eat)

8. This class _____ music, but it _____ painting. (study)

9. The cafeteria _____ lunch, but it _____ breakfast. (serve)

10. The students here _____ baseball, but they _____ football. (play)

4-2. 現在進行式的用途：am, are, is + V-ing

我們用現在進行式的動詞來表示一件事情在說話的時候正在進行之中。

$$\left.\begin{array}{l} \textbf{am} \\ \textbf{are} \\ \textbf{is} \end{array}\right\} \text{V-ing} \left\{\begin{array}{l} \text{now, right now, just now, at} \\ \text{present, at this moment, etc.} \end{array}\right\}$$

I *am learning* English now.

John *is doing* his assignment right now.

They *are watching* television.

We *are trying* to fix a flat tire.

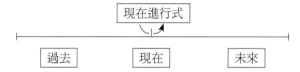

現在單純式表示一件事情過去是如此，現在是如此，未來也是如此，因此又叫「**超時間的現在**」（timeless present）；現在進行式則表示一件事情在說話的時候正在進行，因此又叫做「**真實的現在**」（real present）。

我們也用現在進行式的動詞，和表示未來時間的副詞，來表示未來的打算。

$$\left.\begin{array}{l} \textbf{am} \\ \textbf{are} \\ \textbf{is} \end{array}\right\} \text{V-ing} \left\{\begin{array}{l} \text{tomorrow, next week, next month,} \\ \text{in an hour, in ten minutes, etc.} \end{array}\right\}$$

He *is leaving* tomorrow on the six o'clock plane.

I *am picking* you up in an hour.

參考一：「**外動詞**」與「**內動詞**」

有些動詞 am, have, know, love 是無所謂「正在是」、「正在有」、「正在知道」、「正在愛」的，因此雖然表示現在的事實，但也只能用現在單純式，而不能用現在進行式：

$$\begin{cases} \text{I } \textit{am} \text{ a student.（○）} \\ \text{I } \textit{am being} \text{ a student.（×）} \end{cases}$$

$$\begin{cases} \text{He } \textit{has} \text{ a lot of money.（○）} \\ \text{He } \textit{is having} \text{ a lot of money.（×）} \end{cases}$$

$$\begin{cases} \text{We all } \textit{know} \text{ the answer.（○）} \\ \text{We } \textit{are knowing} \text{ the answer.（×）} \end{cases}$$

這些動詞主要的是表示「存在」、「所有」與「知覺、情感」的動詞。這些動詞在語意上有一個共同的特點，那就是它們所表示的行為是無法由外表判斷出來的。我們就把這些動詞叫做**內動詞**（private verbs），以便與可以由外表判斷行為的**外動詞**（public verbs）區別。比較：

$$\begin{cases} \text{I } \textit{see} \text{ him now.（「看見、看到」：內動詞）} \\ \text{I } \textit{am looking at} \text{ him now.（「看」：外動詞）} \end{cases}$$

$$\begin{cases} \text{I } \textit{hear} \text{ the music now.（「聽見、聽到」：內動詞）} \\ \text{I } \textit{am listening to} \text{ the music now.（「聽」：外動詞）} \end{cases}$$

$$\begin{cases} \text{I } \textit{am finding} \text{ my watch.（×）（「找到」：內動詞）} \\ \text{I } \textit{am looking for} \text{ my watch.（○）（「找」：外動詞）} \end{cases}$$

下面是一些不能用在進行式的內動詞：

see, hear, smell, notice; remember, forget, know, understand, recall, recollect, believe, trust (= believe); feel (that), think (that); suppose, mean, gather (= understand); need, want, wish, desire; refuse, forgive; care, love, hate, like, prefer, adore; seem, signify, appear (= seem); belong to, contain (= hold); matter, possess, own, consist of; have, be.

注意，下面動詞的用法是外動詞不是內動詞：

I'm *seeing* him tomorrow.（訪問，見（人））

The judge is *hearing* the case.（審理）

How are you *liking* it?（享受）

They are *having* dinner.（吃）

I am *having* a good time.（過）

Are you *forgetting* your manners?（你的禮貌到那裡去了？）

I was just *thinking* it might be a good idea ……（我正在考慮……）

有些形容詞也可以出現在進行式裡：

Now you're *being* naughty again.（你又在淘氣了。）

I am only *being* cautious.（我只不過是小心點罷了。）

Stop that. You are *being* ridiculous.（你又在招人家笑話了。）

參考二：現在進行式也可以跟 always, constantly, continually, for ever 等副詞用在一起來強調一件事情經常發生。例如：

He's *always thinking* (and *thinking*).

George *is continually arguing* with people.

習 題 47

　　把現在單純式改成現在進行式。注意除了動詞以外，時間副詞也要做適當的調整。

Example: 　　John studies in the library every day.

　　　　　　　→ *John is studying in the library now.*

1. John always finishes his lessons early.

2. The wind always blows hard at this season of the year.

3. Both children dress very quickly every morning.

4. He often brings flowers to her.

5. Mr. Connor always begins his lectures with a joke.

6. She speaks with an accent.

7. He generally writes detective stories.

8. We usually put the mail in this box.

9. A car stops in front of the house.

10. They save money for their vacation.

習 題 48

　　把現在進行式改成現在單純式。注意：除了改變動詞的形式以外，利用時間副

詞如 always, often, generally, every day 等做適當的調整。

Example: He is talking loudly now. → *He always talks loudly.*

1. Robert is trying hard.   2. They are coming here now.

3. He is making furniture as a hobby.

4. Walter is driving much too fast.

5. Mary is doing her shopping with her mother.

6. John is walking to school with me.

7. We are waiting for you in the street.

8. She is helping me with my lesson.

9. He is lying on the bed at this moment.

10. We are studying in the same class now.

習　題　49

把括號裡面的動詞改成現在進行式。

1. He (prepare) his homework now.

2. The leaves (begin) to fall from the trees.

3. Helen (write) a letter to her friend.

4. Look! That is Stephen who (get) on the bus.

5. The telephone (ring) in the next room.

6. The paper (lie) on my desk.

7. Several people (sit) in the lobby.

8. The students (argue) with the professor.

9. The plant (die) from lack of water.

10. I (work) my way through college.

習　題　50

按照句子的意思填入動詞的現在單純式或現在進行式。

1. Henry and Helen (walk) to school with us every morning.

2. We (learn) our lesson well.

3. Ralph often (use) my book during the lesson.

4. He (count) all the books in the library now.

5. It generally (snow) very hard at this time of the year.

6. The alarm clock (ring) at six in the morning every day.

7. Listen! The telephone (ring) in the next room.

8. The teacher (praise) Jane. She (want) the girl to try harder.

9. Now that the flowers (bloom), the garden (smell) good.

10. Today Jane (wear) her sister's dress. She certainly (resemble) her, doesnt' she?

習 題 51

按照例句把下面每一對句子連起來。

Examples:

Is he outside?
Is he waiting?
$\rightarrow$ *Is he outside waiting?*

Is she busy?
Is she writing letters?
$\rightarrow$ *Is she busy writing letters?*

1. Are they in the kitchen?
   Are they eating? $\rightarrow$

2. Is he standing?
   Is he talking? $\rightarrow$

3. Is she back home?
   Is she watching TV? $\rightarrow$

4. Is he in his room?
   Is he sleeping? $\rightarrow$

5. Are they in the other room?
   Are they arguing? $\rightarrow$

6. Are you sitting?
   Are you waiting? $\rightarrow$

7. Are they at the bank?
   Are they cashing a check? $\rightarrow$

8. Are you busy?
   Are you doing your assignment? $\rightarrow$

9. Are they downtown?
   Are they having dinner? $\rightarrow$

10. Is he with his students? ⎫
    Is he answering questions? ⎬ →

4-3. 現在完成式的用途：have, has + V-en

　　我們用現在完成式的動詞來表示：

(1) 一件事情到現在為止已經完成。這個時候可以用表未定時間的副詞（just, already, not … yet）或包括現在時間在內的副詞（如 today, this morning, this week, recently 等）。

$$
\begin{Bmatrix} \textbf{have} \\ \textbf{has} \end{Bmatrix} \textbf{V-en}
\begin{Bmatrix} \text{just, already, not … yet, today,} \\ \text{this morning, this week, this} \\ \text{month, this winter, this year,} \\ \text{recently, lately, etc.} \end{Bmatrix}
$$

I *have* just *finished* my assignment.

She *has* already *eaten* her supper.

John *hasn't fixed* his car yet.

I *have had* three colds this winter.

We *haven't heard* from him recently.

現在完成式

過去　　現在　　未來

(2) 到現在為止有過的經驗。這個時候可以與表示到現在為止的時間副詞（如 so far, till now, up to the present）或表次數的副詞（如 once, twice, three times, never 等）用在一起。

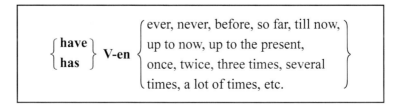

$$
\begin{Bmatrix} \textbf{have} \\ \textbf{has} \end{Bmatrix} \textbf{V-en}
\begin{Bmatrix} \text{ever, never, before, so far, till now,} \\ \text{up to now, up to the present,} \\ \text{once, twice, three times, several} \\ \text{times, a lot of times, etc.} \end{Bmatrix}
$$

So far I *haven't made* any mistake.

We *have* never *discussed* the subject.

Have you ever *seen* a camel?

This is one of the best books that I *have* ever *read*.

I *have met* this man before.

They *have seen* the same movie twice.

Mr. White *has written* three books of poems.

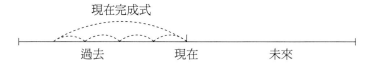

現在完成式

過去　　　　現在　　　　未來

(3) 一件事情從過去的某一點繼續到現在。這個時候可以有表時間長短的副詞（for an hour, for two weeks, for three months, for some time 等），或從什麼時候起的副詞（如 since yesterday, since two weeks ago, since 1965 等）。

$$\begin{Bmatrix} \text{have} \\ \text{has} \end{Bmatrix} \text{V-en} \begin{Bmatrix} \text{for an hour, for two weeks, for} \\ \text{three months, since yesterday,} \\ \text{since two weeks ago, since I was} \\ \text{sixteen, etc.} \end{Bmatrix}$$

I *have practiced* English for an hour.

We *haven't seen* each other for a year.

Bob *hasn't eaten* anything since yesterday.

I *have lived* here since I was sixteen.

We *have known* the whole family for a long time.

I *have* always *admired* his courage.

現在完成式

過去　　　　現在　　　　未來

顧名思義，現在完成式是一個和現在時間有關的時變式。說得更清楚一點，它是由現在回顧過去的一種時變式。所提到的一件事情儘管發生在過去，可是所注意

的不足那件事情的本身或發生的時間，而是是否曾經有過這麼一回事，對於現在有什麼影響。比較：

> I *have seen* a camel.（我現在知道駱駝長什麼樣子。）
> When *did* you *see* it? I *saw* it last year at a zoo.

> Edison *has made* many useful inventions.（我們現在仍受益不淺。）
> He *invented* the electric light in 1879.

因此，現在完成式不能與表確定過去時間的副詞用在一起。比較：

> He has *just / already* finished writing the letter.
> He has written three letters *this week / this month*.
> He wrote a letter *last night / just now*. (= a few moments ago)

現在完成式也不能用在 "When …?" 或 " How long ago …?" 開頭的問句裡，因為這種問句非用確定過去時間的副詞回答不可。比較：

> *Have* you *finished* your assignment?

> When / How long ago *did* you *finish* your assignment?

習　題　52

把括號裡面的動詞改成現在完成式。

1. I (already read) the book.
2. He (go) to the United States.
3. She (be) to Japan several times.
4. The man (never speak) to me.
5. George (bring) my book at last.
6. I (not hear) from him since last year.
7. She (not buy) a new hat for six months.
8. I (often walk) to school with her.
9. Up to the present, I (never meet) him.
10. The boy said, "I (make) a mistake."

參考：比較下面的句子。

> He has *gone to* the park.「他到了公園去了（他現在還在公園）。」
> He has *been to* the park.「他已經去過公園了。」

習 題 53

按照例句完成下面的句子。

Example: I haven't seen him ⋯⋯ (a) Christmas; (b) two months.

      I haven't seen him since Christmas.

      I haven't seen him for two months.

1. They have lived in this street ⋯⋯ (a) 1920; (b)the last three years; (c) a long time; (d) over a year.

2. It hasn't rained here ⋯⋯ (a) more than a month; (b) April; (e) two months; (d) many weeks.

3. I haven't bought any new dress ⋯⋯ (a) a week; (b) ages; (c) then; (d)longer than I can remember.

4. Bob hasn't eaten any meat (a) his childhood; (b) over a year; (c) he was a boy; (d) at least a month.

5. You have asked the same question every day ⋯⋯ (a) last Sunday; (b) fifteen days; (c) the beginning of the year; (d)your birthday.

參考：Since 表示「從過去的某一點時間（到現在）」，常與現在完成式用在一起。
For 表示「到現在為止的一段時間裡」，也常與現在完成式用在一起。比較：

      John *has worked* there *since* ten years ago.

      John *has worked* there *for* ten years.

For 又表示「一段時間」，因此可以用在現在、過去或未來。比較：

      John *has stayed* here for three years.

      John *stayed* here for three years.

      John *will stay* here for three years.

習 題 54

用 since 或 for 完成下面的句子。

1. Where have you been _____ last week?

2. You haven't been here _____ a week.

3. He has practiced English _____ three hours.

4. He has practiced French _____ three o'clock this afternoon.

5. We haven't done any work _____ a month.

6. Nothing has been done _____ January.

7. They have been talking _____ an hour and a half.

8. I have been very busy _____ last week.

9. My wife has been very happy _____ the last week.

10. Alice has been reading that book _____ the last two hours.

4-4. 現在完成進行式的用途：have, has + been + V-ing

　　現在完成進行式的用途與現在完成式的第三種用途「表示一件事情從過去某一點繼續到現在」相似；但是現在完成進行式特別強調一直不斷的繼續到現在。這一件事情可能還在進行之中。

He *has been lying* there for three hours.（他仍然躺在那裡。）

It *has been raining* all the morning.（雨還在下。）

也可能已經中止：

I'm cold because *I've been swimming* for an hour.

　　　　（我不再游泳了。）

He is very tired; he's *been running* around all day.

　　　　（他已經休息，不再跑來跑去了。）

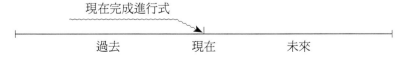

　　現在完成進行式的動詞常與表時間長短的副詞（如 for three hours, since yesterday, all the morning, all day 等）用在一起。但是現在完成進行式與現在完成

式不同，沒有這些期間副詞仍能表示一件事情從過去某一點一直繼續到現在。比較：

> He has been reading the book (for an hour).（他一直在看書。）
>
> He has read the book for an hour.（他看書看了一個鐘頭。）
>
> He has read the book.（他把書看完了；他看過書了。）

表示繼續性行為的動詞，如 stay, wait, sit, stand, lie, study, learn, read, live, rest, sleep 等，用在現在完成進行式的機會比用在現在完成式的機會多，因為這些動詞所表示的行為多半都會繼續到現在。比較：

> The books *have lain* on the desk.（很少這樣用）
>
> The books *have been lying* on the desk.（比較常用）

習 題 55

把括號裡面的動詞改成現在完成進行式。

1. I (live) here since 1956.   2. (You wait) long for me?

3. He (work) here for many years.

4. The man (stand) at the gate since noon.

5. They (play) tennis all the afternoon.

6. He (speak) English all his life.

7. My mother (feel) much better recently.

8. Look! That light (burn) all night.

9. I know you (talk) about grammar for the last half an hour, but I'm afraid I (not listen).

10. What (you do) while I have been out? We (sit) here writing our homework.

習 題 56

按照句子的意思，填入動詞的現在完成式或完成進行式。

1. I (not see) you for a long time.

2. He (not be) here since Christmas. I wonder where he (live) since then.

3. That book (lie) on the table for weeks. (You not read) it yet?

4. He (not have) a holiday for nine years because he (be) too busy.

5. I (try) to learn English for years, but I (not succeed) yet.

6. I (wait) here for her since seven o'clock and she (not come) yet.

7. (You be) asleep all the morning? I (ring) the bell for the last twenty minutes.

8. He (work) so hard this week that he (not have) time to go to the barber's.

9. We (live) here for the last six months, and (just decide) to move.

10. I (not find) a wife, though I (look) for one ever since I was twenty-five.

習　題　57

按照例句把下面每一對句子連起來。

Examples:　　She is studying in the other room. ⎫
　　　　　　　She started about an hour ago. ⎭ →

　　　　She has been studying in the other room since an hour ago.

　　　　He is always worrying about his job. ⎫
　　　　It all began in April. ⎭ →

　　　　He has been worrying about his job since April.

1. I began to look for an apartment three months ago. ⎫
   I am still looking. ⎭ →

2. Yesterday afternoon the temperature started rising. ⎫
   It is still rising. ⎭ →

3. She always rides the train. ⎫
   It started five years ago. ⎭ →

4. He began to think about getting a job last year. ⎫
   He is still thinking. ⎭ →

5. We started studying English three years ago. ⎫
   We are still studying. ⎭ →

4-5. 過去單純式的用途：V-ed

過去單純式表示一件事情在過去某一個確定時間發生。

$$\mathbf{V\text{-}ed}\begin{cases}\text{just now, a few minutes ago,}\\ \text{yesterday, last week, three}\\ \text{years ago, in 1961, etc.}\end{cases}$$

John *left* an hour ago.

Mr. Smith *went* to Japan two months ago.

We *did not enjoy* the party last night.

I *recognized* his face, but I *didn't remember* his name.

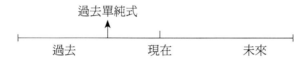

參考：與 just, already, ever, never, before 等時間副詞用在一起的現在完成式，常用過去單純式來代替。例如：

$$\text{I}\begin{cases}\textit{have} \text{ just } \textit{talked}\\ \text{just } \textit{talked}\end{cases}\text{to him.}$$

$$\begin{cases}\textit{Have} \text{ you ever } \textit{read}\\ \textit{Did} \text{ you ever } \textit{read}\end{cases}\text{this book?}$$

$$\text{This is the most interesting picture I}\begin{cases}\textit{have} \text{ ever } \textit{seen.}\\ \text{ever } \textit{saw.}\end{cases}$$

習 題 58

把現在單純式改為過去單純式，並把 yesterday, last week, an hour ago, 1970 等表示過去時間的副詞用在句子裡面。

1. We go to a shop.
2. He hides the key.
3. He loses his bag.
4. They drink tea every day.
5. You lie to me.
6. She tells us a story.
7. The hen lays five eggs.
8. Tom falls and hurts his arm.
9. The picture hangs on the wall.
10. They build a house.

習　題　59

按照句子的意思，填入動詞的現在完成（進行）式或過去單純式。

1. My sister (not write) to me lately.

2. I (write) a letter to them yesterday.

3. She (not buy) a new dress since last year.

4. I (buy) one last week.

5. They (visit) Japan a few years ago.

6. I (never visit) Japan up to the present.

7. I (not have) a good sleep last night.

8. I (not have) a good sleep since last week.

9. She (not have) a holiday for four years.

10. We (finish) our supper half an hour ago.

11. I (not finish) these sums yet.

12. We (not pay) our rent for over three weeks.

13. I (pay) this bill last Wednesday.

14. He (study) English for two years.

15. She (study) music since she (be) a child.

16. He (certainly arrive) by this time.

17. Since when (you know) him?

18. When (you meet) him?

19. How long ago (you arrive) here?

20. Although he (study) at the university for four years, he (not get) his degree yet.

習　題　60

按照例句用 since 或 ago 完成下面的句子。

Examples:

　　　　I know it (last week). → *I have known it since last week.*

　　　　I know it (a week). → *I knew it a week ago.*

1. She is away (this morning).

2. I see her (three months).

3. A lot happens (my arrival here).

4. She does not eat (the day before yesterday).

5. It all begins (a few years).

6. I have a physical checkup (quite a long time).

7. The property is in her name (their marriage).

8. He reads three books (breakfast).

9. She makes the beds (then).

10. They do not see each other (last summer).

參考：Ago 表示「離現在到過去的一段時間」，常與過去單純式用在一起。Since 表示「從過去到現在一段時間的起點」，常與現在完成式用在一起。例如：

> I *met* him three years *ago*.

> I *have known* him *since* then.

習 題 61

按照句子的意思，填入動詞的現在單純式、現在進行式、現在完成式，或過去單純式。

1. He (go) downtown every weekend.   2. He (go) abroad last week.

3. I (be) sick since last week.   4. She (read) a newspaper now.

5. My last car was a Ford. I (have) it for two years.

6. My present car is a Ford. I (have) it for one year.

7. He (not look) so strong as he (do) last semester.

8. I (hear) the news last night, but I (not hear) it today.

9. At present he (write) a letter; it is the tenth letter he (write) this week.

10. When we (exercise) in the sun, we (feel) very hot.

11. I (feel) much better since I (come) here.

12. I (feel) much better since I (be) here.

4-6. 過去進行式的用途：was, were + V-ing

　　過去進行式除了比較特殊的情形以外很少單獨使用。大多數是和過去單純式連絡起來用。進行式用來描寫一種事態，一種情境；單純式用來敘述在這個事態或情境中所發生的事故：

$$\cdots \left\{ \begin{array}{l} \textbf{was} \\ \textbf{were} \end{array} \right\} \textbf{V-ing} \cdots \text{ when} \cdots \textbf{V-ed} \cdots \qquad , \qquad \text{When} \cdots \textbf{V-ed} \cdots, \left\{ \begin{array}{l} \textbf{was} \\ \textbf{were} \end{array} \right\} \textbf{V-ing} \cdots$$

$$\cdots \textbf{V-ed} \cdots \text{ while} \cdots \left\{ \begin{array}{l} \textbf{was} \\ \textbf{were} \end{array} \right\} \textbf{V-ing} \cdots \qquad , \qquad \text{While} \left\{ \begin{array}{l} \textbf{was} \\ \textbf{were} \end{array} \right\} \textbf{V-ing} \cdots, \cdots \textbf{V-ed} \cdots$$

　　I *was studying* when the earthquake occurred.

　　(When the earthquake occurred, I *was studying*.)

　　The earthquake occurred while I *was studying*.

　　(While I *was studying*, the earthquake occurred.)

　　He *was having* a good time when I saw him at the party.

　　We had a flat tire while we *were crossing* the bridge.

　　從上面的例句，我們可以知道過去進行式總是表示比較長的動作（was studying, was having, were crossing），過去單純式總是表示比較短的動作（occurred, saw, had）。

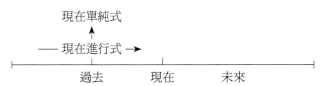

　　如果我們要強調有兩件事情在過去同時進行，那麼就可以用兩個過去進行式來表示這兩件事情。

　　I *was reading* newspapers while she *was playing* the piano.

　　While the child *was struggling* in the water, the mother *was screaming* on the
　　　　bank.

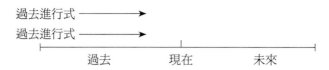

過去進行式如果有表雙重過去時間的副詞（如 at seven o'clock this morning, at ten o'clock last night），或表整段過去時間的副詞（如 all this morning, all afternoon），也可以單獨使用。

It *was raining* at seven o'clock this morning.

I *was studying* English at ten o'clock last night.

She *was washing* clothes all this morning.

What *were* you *doing* all afternoon?

參考一：「**持續性動詞**」（verbs of duration）與「**瞬間性動詞**」（verbs of point-action）：

根據能否有表示時間長短的副詞，英語的動詞可以分為兩種。「**持續性動詞**」（如 live, stay, wait, sit, stand, sleep, lie, work, study, read, write, listen 等）可以有由 for, till, until 引導的期間副詞。例如：

They *waited* for a long while.

He *slept* till / until nine o'clock.

「**瞬間性動詞**」（如 come, go, leave, start, arrive, die, appear, disappear 等）不可以有由 for, till, until 引導的期間副詞。

They *came* for a long while.（×）

He *left* till / until nine o'clock.（×）

持續性的動詞不管是單純式與進行式都能夠出現在由 while 引導的副詞子句中。

The band was playing while I $\left\{ \begin{array}{l} \text{was waiting.} \\ \text{waited.} \end{array} \right\}$

She was reading while he $\left\{ \begin{array}{l} \text{was writing.} \\ \text{wrote} \end{array} \right\}$

瞬間性的動詞只有進行式才能出現在由 while 引導的副詞子句中。

The band was playing while I $\begin{cases} \text{was leaving. (○)} \\ \text{left. (×)} \end{cases}$

注意，出現在由 when 引導的副詞子句裡面的動詞，多半都是瞬間性的動詞。比較：

The band was playing when I $\begin{cases} \text{waited. (×)} \\ \text{left. (○)} \end{cases}$

持續性的動詞本身已經含有動作持續的意思，如果用進行式，則更能強調這種持續性。如果我們用虛線（……）來表示動作的持續，用實線（——）來加強動作的連續，那麼下面的四個句子可以這樣的分析：

The band played while I waited. (…… , ……)

The band played while I was waiting. (…… , ——)

The band was playing while I waited. (—— , ……)

The band was playing while I was waiting. (—— , ——)

參考二：過去進行式也可以跟 always, constantly, continually 等副詞用在一起來強調一件事情在過去經常發生。

She *was always complaining* about something.

習　題　62

把括號裡面的動詞改成過去進行式。

1. We (study) when the teacher arrived.

2. I (read) a book when he came in.

3. They (eat) in a restaurant when I saw them.

4. The sun (shine) when we went out.

5. When you telephoned, I (still have) my dinner.

6. He came in while you (write).

7. He (work) all day yesterday.

8. It (rain) at six o'clock this morning.

9. I took another cake when you (not look).

10. While you (play) the piano I (write) a letter.

習 題 63

把過去單純式改成過去進行式，並按照例句加上適當的副詞或子句，使句子的意思變得完整些。

Example:

They traveled in France.

→ $\left\{ \begin{array}{l} \text{\textit{They were traveling in France at that time.}} \\ \text{\textit{They were traveling in France when the war began.}} \end{array} \right.$

1. He sat in the garden.
2. They walked home.
3. She ate her dinner.
4. The man left his home.
5. Mrs. Brown drank a cup of coffee.
6. Mr. Wood listened to the radio.
7. The teacher explained the grammar.
8. Mary spoke English.
9. We had supper.
10. They went to the movie.

習 題 64

按照句子的意思，填入動詞的過去單純式或過去進行式。

1. The sun (shine) at two o'clock.
2. The fire (still burn) at five o'clock this morning.
3. He (rest) all the afternoon.
4. I (go) to the movies last night.
5. I (go) to the movies when you telephoned.
6. The First World War (begin) in 1914 and (end) in 1918.
7. He (sit) in the room when I (see) him.
8. We (become) friends when we (be) students in the university.
9. The boy (fall) down while he (run).
10. When I (be) at school, I (learn) English.
11. He (walk) across the bridge when his hat (blow) off.
12. We (drink) coffee every day when we (be) in the United States.

13. The boy (jump) off the train while it (move).

14. The house (burn) fast, so we (break) a window to get out.

15. When I (see) him, he (sing) and (smoke) a cigar at the same time.

16. While he (get) off the street car, he (fall) and (cut) his face.

17. I (speak) to her several times, but she (always read) and (not hear) me.

18. He (think) of something else all the time you (talk) to him.

19. I (open) the door just as he (ring) the bell.

20. While she (write) a letter, the telephone (ring); as she (go) to answer it, she (hear) a knock at the door; the telephone (still ring) while she (walk) to the door, but just as she (open) it, it (stop).

4-7. 過去完成式的用途：had + V-en

　　我們用過去完成式來表示一件事情在過去確定時間以前，或另外一件事情發生以前發生。

$$\text{had V-en} \begin{cases} \text{by nine o'clock last night,} \\ \text{by six o'clock this morning,} \\ \text{before yesterday, before last night, etc.} \end{cases}$$

He *had gone* to bed by nine o'clock last night.

I *had* never *seen* him before yesterday.

> ⋯ **had V-en** ⋯ before ⋯ **V-ed** ⋯

> ⋯ **V-ed** ⋯ after ⋯ **had　V-en** ⋯

> ⋯ **had V-en** ⋯ when ⋯ **V-ed** ⋯
> ⋯ **V-ed** ⋯ when ⋯ **had V-ed** ⋯

$$\cdots \begin{Bmatrix} said \\ discovered \\ knew, \text{etc.} \end{Bmatrix} \text{(that)} \cdots \textbf{had V-en} \cdots$$

John (*had*) *shot* before the deer started to run.

The stenographer typed two letters after the manager (*had*) fired her.

We *had finished* our dinner when the guests arrived.

He said he *had seen* the movie.

　　過去完成式，與過去進行式一樣，很少單獨使用。大多數是和過去單純式連絡起來用：在過去先後有兩件事情發生，先發生的用過去完成式來敘述，後發生的用過去單純式來敘述。

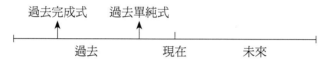

　　如果過去有兩件事情幾乎同時發生，沒有長短或先後之分別，那麼這兩件事情都用過去單純式來敘述。比較：

When I *saw* her, she *was crying*.

(She was crying before I saw her.)

When I *saw* her, she *started* to cry.

(She was not crying before I saw her.)

參考一：當兩件事情用連詞 before, after, by the time 等連起來的時候，因為事情的先後已經由這些連詞的含義交待清楚，故可以用過去單純式來代替過去完成式；換句話說，兩件事情都可以用過去單純式來敘述。例如：

We got to the hall after the concert (*had*) *started*.

The concert (*had*) *started* before we got to the hall.

　　如果兩件事情用連詞 when, as soon as, once 等連起來的話，事情的先後必須

靠過去完成式與過去單純式來表達。換句話說，先發生的必須用過去完成式，後發生的用過去單純式。

> When we got to the hall, the concert *had* already *started*.

參考二：hope, expect, think, intend, mean (= intend), suppose, want 等動詞的過去完成式常表示過去的希望、期望、企圖或渴望未能實現：

> We *had hoped* that you would be able to cotne.（結果你沒能來。）
>
> We *had intended* to go to Japan this summer.（結果我們沒有去。）

習　題　65

把括號裡面的動詞改為過去完成式。

1. He (go) away when we arrived.

2. They (have) dinner when I got there.

3. She (do) nothing before she saw me.

4. After you (go), I went to sleep.

5. When we got there, the dinner (already begin).

6. I was sorry that I (hurt) him.

7. As soon as she (leave), I wanted to see her again.

8. She thanked me for what I (do).

9. He told me that he (take) the medicine.

10. He discovered that the servant (steal) his watch.

習　題　66

按照例句，把過去單純式改為過去完成式。用 He（she, you, etc.）said（told me, knew）等來做你答句的開頭。

Examples:

> He saw her. → *He said that he had seen her.*
>
> She turned in the assignment yesterday. →
>
> > *She told me that she had turned in the assignment yesterday.*

1. He waited one hour for the bus.　　　　2. She saw him before.

3. You read the book.

4. He was ill for a long time.

5. He went to the movies with you.

6. She enjoyed her food.

7. You went to the seaside for a holiday.

8. A fire broke out in the neighborhood.

9. Her mother helped her with her homework.

10. He liked this picture very much.

習　題　67

按照句子的意思，填入動詞的過去單純式或過去完成式。

1. When we (arrive), they (already leave).

2. He (say) that he (have) his lunch.

3. I (tell) him that I (see) the movie previously.

4. We (get) there just ten minutes after he (leave).

5. He (wonder) why I (not visit) him before.

6. She (just go) out when I (call) at her house.

7. We (ask) him what countries he (visit).

8. After I (hear) the news, I (hurry) to see him.

9. When we (arrive), the dinner (already begin).

10. Before we (go) very far, we (find) that we (take) the wrong road.

習　題　68

按照句子的意思，填入動詞的過去單純式，過去進行式或過去完成式。

1. I (sleep) when you (telephone).

2. I (write) several letters last night.

3. My mother (prepare) dinner when I (get) home.

4. He (tell) me that he (visit) France several times.

5. She (fall) while she (get) off the bus.

6. He (live) there two years when the war (begin).

7. I (be) sure that I (never see) him before.

8. It (rain) hard last night.

9. It (rain) hard when I (leave) home.

10. It (rain) three hours when we (start).

11. The sun (shine) brightly when I (get) up this morning.

12. By the time we (reach) here, all the other guests (leave).

13. The teacher (write) on the blackboard when we (enter) the room.

14. They (drive) to Taipei when the accident (happen).

15. The fire (spread) to the next building before the firemen (arrive).

16. His mother (worry) a lot about him before she (hear) that he (be) safe.

17. The house (be) much bigger than he (think) at first.

18. After he (see) *The Longest Day*, he (tell) his friends that he (never see) a better war film.

19. After he (go), I (feel) sorry that I (hurt) him.

20. While I (walk) through the park with my sister last night, a man (snatch) her bag from her and (run) away.

4-8. 過去完成進行式：had been + V-ing

　　過去完成式表示過去有一件事情比另外一件事情（過去單純式）先發生，過去完成進行式強調這件先發生的事情一直繼續到另一件事情發生。

$$
\cdots \textbf{had been V-ing} \cdots \left\{ \begin{array}{l} \text{for two hours when} \\ \text{for three weeks when} \\ \text{for four years} \left\{ \begin{array}{l} \text{before} \\ \text{by the time} \end{array} \right. \end{array} \right\} \cdots \textbf{V-ed} \cdots
$$

He *had been studying* for two hours when they arrived.

He *had been living* there two years when the war began.

We *had been corresponding* regularly for many years before his death.

Mr. White *had been living* in Austin before he moved to New York.

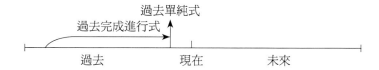

比較：

He *phoned* you when I got there.

（我到達那裡以後他才給你打電話。）

He *had* (already) *phoned* you when I got there.

（我到達那裡的時候他已經打了電話給你。）

He *had been phoning* you when I got there.

（我到達那裡以前他一直在打電話給你。）

習　題　69

把括號裡面的動詞改為過去完成進行式。

1. He (study) for two hours when we arrived.

2. She (wait) for an hour when he got to the station.

3. I (live) there two years when the war began.

4. Paul (study) French for many years when he went to France.

5. She (read) the letter when we visited her.

6. Mrs. Brown (sleep) a long time when the servant woke her up.

7. He (work) too hard and that is why he got sick.

8. She (study) every night until one o'clock.

9. It (rain) two hours when we started.

10. Mother (prepare) our breakfast when I got up.

習　題　70

把過去完成式改為過去完成進行式，並說明把動詞改成過去完成進行式以後在語意上有怎麼樣的變化。

1. He told me that he had worked there.

2. It was said that he had lost much money in his business.

3. It had rained two hours when we started.

4. She had had a music lesson when I telephoned.

5. They had had their dinner when we visited them.

6. Jane had played the piano when George came to see her.

7. Paul had written the letter when we arrived.

8. They had talked about it when I met them.

9. He said he had studied French.

10. Mother had prepared our dinner when I got up.

4-9. 未來單純式的用途：will (shall) + V

　　過去的文法書對於 will 與 shall 的用法常舉出一些複雜而不實用的規則。但是在現代口語裡 will 與 shall 的用法卻十分簡單：除了第一身打聽對方意思的問句用 shall 以外統統用 will。

I will leave tomorrow.	**We will** leave tomorrow.
You will leave tomorrow.	**You will** leave tomorrow.
He (she) will leave tomorrow.	**They will** leave tomorrow.
Will you leave tomorrow?	**Will you** leave tomorrow?
Will he (she) leave tomorrow?	**Will they** leave tomorrow?
Shall I leave tomorrow?	**Shall we** leave tomorrow?

　　最後兩個用 shall 的問句是請對方對於我（們）可否這樣做表示意見，即「我（們）可以不可以明天離開？」或「你是否要我（們）明天離開？」，但是如果不是問對方的意思，而只是問將來是否有這樣的事情發生，那麼就要用 Will I …? 或 Will we …?

　　Will we leave tomorrow?（我們是否明天要離開？）

　　Will I get a chance to talk to her?（我會不會有機會跟她談話？）

比較：

　　Shall we go?（請你告訴我們：我們該不該去？）

　　Will we go?（請你告訴我們：我們會不會去？）

除了 will 與 shall 以外，我們還常常用 Be going to 來表示未來：

I *am going to study* tomorrow.

Are you *going to travel* by plane?

It *is going to* rain.

They *are going to go* next week.

Was / were going to V 表示一件事本來想做，但是後來沒有做成：

We *were going to play* tennis yesterday, but it rained.

I *was going to phone* you, but I could not find your number.

參考一：我們用 Be about to + V 與 Be on the point of + V-ing 來表示事情在極近的將
來發生。

We *are about to finish* our job.

He *is on the point of going* out.

She *was about to cry* out when her mother came to her help.

參考二：未來的 " 安排、計畫 " 或 " 義務、責任 " 常用 Be + to V 來表示。

We *are* (= have arranged or agreed) *to meet* at the station at six o'clock.

比較：We *were* (= agreed or arranged) to be married in May (but we didn't get
married).

Am I *to* (= Must I) *stand* here for ever?

Nobody *is to* (= must) know the secret.

比較：You *were to* (= should) have finished your assignment yesterday (but you
didn't).

參考三：我們也可以用動詞的現在式來表示未來：

(a) 現在單純式與表示未來時間的副詞連用：

Mr. Brown *leaves* for New York next week.

Bob *goes* to town tomorrow.

What time *do* you *start*?

(b) 現在進行式與表示未來時間的副詞連用：

He *is coming* here tonight.

When *are* you *going* to Japan?

常用現在式來表示未來的動詞，主要的是 go, come, start, depart, return, arrive, sail, fly 等表示「出發、到達、往來」的動詞。

參考四：在較正式的書面英語裡，常在直述句中用 I shall … 或 we shall …。

習　題　71

按照例句用 Be going to 做問句以接下面的句子。如果原來的句子含有名詞做主語或賓語，就把名詞改成代名詞。

Examples:

The store is staying open late today.

→ *Is it going to stay open late* (*tomorrow*), *too?*

He's studying French this semester.

→ *Is he going to study it* (*next semester*), *too?*

1. We are all working late today.
2. The boys are playing football this afternoon.
3. She is working nights this week.
4. They are visiting some classes this morning.
5. We are really working hard this semester.
6. The family are feeling very hungry today.
7. He is playing baseball again this season.
8. They are eating at the restaurant today.
9. The students are having a parade today.
10. They are helping us tonight with our work.

習　題　72

用各種不同的方式表示未來時間（複習）。

1. She (arrive) tomorrow.
2. I (be) back at noon.
3. We (take) a walk in the park.
4. You (buy) a dictionary.
5. He (go) home by subway.
6. I (eat) by myself.
7. Nobody (tell) him what to do.
8. Alice (wear) her best suit.

9. They (put) the mail on my desk. 10. It (cost) ten dollars.

11. The boat (sail) for Europe next month.

12. The plane (take off) in a few minutes.

13. He (leave) some money for his sons.

14. She (leave) for the United States tomorrow morning.

15. I (go) downtown and (visit) my uncle this week

4-10. 未來進行式的用法 will (shall) be + V-ing

　　正如我們用過去進行式來表示一件事情在過去的某一個確定時間，或當另外一件事情發生的時候正在進行，我們用未來進行式來表示一件事在未來的某一個確定時間，或當另外一件事情發生的時候正在進行。

> **will (shall) be V-ing** $\left\{\begin{array}{l}\text{at this time tomorrow,} \\ \text{at this time next year, etc.}\end{array}\right\}$

I wonder what he *will be doing* at this time tomorrow.

We *will be traveling* together at this time next year.

> **⋯ will (shall) be V-ing ⋯ when ⋯ V(-s) ⋯**

> **When ⋯ V(-s) ⋯, ⋯ will (shall) be V-ing ⋯**

I *will be studying* when you come.

When we get there, they *will be eating*.

　　從上面的例句，我們也可以知道未來進行式與過去進行式一樣很少單獨使用，大多數都是與另外一個表示未來的現在單純式，或表示未來確定時間的副詞連絡起來用。

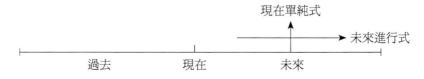

從上面的圖解，我們可以明白未來進行式的用法與過去進行式的用法極相似，只是時間由過去移到未來而已。

參考一：我們也用未來進行式來表示：

  (a) 一件事情在未來繼續一段時間。

     I *will be playing* tennis all afternoon.

     We *will be studying* for a long while.

     He *will be doing* his military service next year.

  (b) 一件事情在最近的未來就要發生。

     Let's get ready. Guests *will be coming*.

     Run away home. Your mother *will be inquiring* after you.

  比較：I *must be going* now, or I'll be late for the party.

參考二：在表示時間或條件的副詞子句裡面，常用現在單純式來代替未來單純式。
        用現在完成式來代替未來完成式。

     I will pay you when / if I *have* the money tomorrow.

     He will come as soon as he *has finished* writing his letter.

習　題　73

把括號裡面的動詞改成未來進行式。

1. I (study) when you come.　　2. They (eat) when we get there.

3. When you telephone, he (take) a nap.

4. At six o'clock tomorrow morning, I (take) a walk in the park.

5. She (probably sleep) in her room at that hour.

6. If you come in the afternoon, he (work) in his garden.

7. When we are ready to leave, it (probably rain).

8. At this time next year, I (travel) in Europe.

9. How long (you stay) here?

10. When you come back at midnight, he (probably still work) on this same problem.

習　題　74

把過去進行式改為未來進行式，並做其他適當的調整。

Example:

He was sleeping when I arrived.

→ *He will be sleeping when I arrive.*

1. He was eating his lunch when I got there.

2. They were having a party at nine o'clock last night.

3. The sun was shining when I got to the station.

4. He was working hard as usual when I met him.

5. She was watching television when he returned.

6. He was working in his garden when we called.

7. I wonder what he was doing at this time yesterday.

8. I was getting ready to go to the movie at seven o'clock.

9. He was having his music lesson when she telephoned.

10. We were traveling together at this time last year.

4-11. 未來完成式的用法：will (shall) have + V-en

我們用未來完成式來表示一件事情在未來某一個確定時間以前，或者另外一件事情發生以前完成：

… **will (shall) have V-en** … $\begin{cases} \text{When} \cdots \textbf{V(-s)} \cdots \\ \text{by six o'clock this evening, etc.} \end{cases}$

John *will have finished* his work when you come again this evening.

John *will have finished* his work by six o'clock (this evening).

未來完成式在表示時間或條件的副詞子句中常用現在完成式來代替：

He will come when he *has finished* his work.

注意：未來完成式的用法與過去完成式的用法，在基本上是一樣的，只不過是時間由過去移到未來罷了。

參考：假如有一個人是 1950 年結婚的，在 1970 年說話，就可以說：

I *have been* married twenty years.（現在完成式）

In 1960, *had been* married ten years.（過去完成式）

In 1980 (if I am still alive), I *will have been* married thirty years.（未來完成式）

習　題　75

把括號裡的動詞改成未來完成式。

1. By July, we (study) English for three years.

2. By the end of next month, all the leaves (fall) from the trees.

3. By the time we get there, he (finish) the lesson.

4. When you arrive, all the others (leave).

5. On next Sunday, John (be) in Taiwan six months.

6. By the time he leaves Taiwan, he (see) many interesting things.

7. He (visit) most of the important places in Taiwan.

8. If we don't drive faster, they (leave) when we get there.

9. On January 20, I (be) here ten months.

10. I (finish) my letter by six o'clock.

習　題　76

把括號裡的動詞，從過去完成式改為未來完成式，並做其他適當的調整。

Example:

They had left when we arrived.

They will have left when we arrive.

1. The party had begun when we got there.

2. He had finished the work when we saw him.

3. She had gone away when he arrived.

4. When we got there, the guests had already left.

5. The leaves had fallen from the trees when we visited the park.

6. He had spent all his money before he began his vacation.

7. He had forgotten all about it when you spoke with him.

8. She had told her mother before I saw her.

9. He had already written the letter when she telephoned him.

10. He had come and had left when she arrived.

4-12. 未來完成進行式：will (shall) have been + V-ing

我們用未來完成進行式來表示當一件事情在未發生的時候，另外一件事情早已發生而且仍在進行：

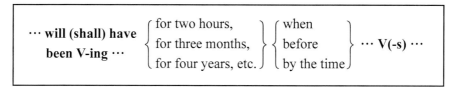

We'*ll have been practicing* for two hours when the teacher comes.

John *will have been studying* for three months by the time he takes his
examination.

未來完成進行式的用法也與過去完成進行式的用法很相似。但是我們平時很少使用未來完成進行式，而常用未來進行式或未來完成式來表示。

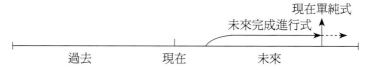

參考：假如有一個大學生，在學校裡已經唸了三年書，再過一年就可以得到他的學
位，那麼我們就可以說：

By this time next year, he *will have got* his degree.（未來完成式）

When he gets his degree, he *will have been studying* at the university for four
years.（未來完成進行式）

習　題　77

把括號裡的動詞從未來完成式改為未來完成進行式。

Example:

By July, we will have studied English for three years.

By July we will have been studying English for three years.

1. By the end of this month, the carpenter will have worked on the new house three
months.
2. By next year, you will have stayed here two years.
3. By the time you get to the town, you will have driven for five hours.
4. The teacher will have corrected our papers two hours before he goes home.
5. The wind will have blown for ten hours by midnight.
6. On next Friday, the Johnsons will have lived in Taiwan six months.
7. We'll have waited for two hours when the guest arrives.
8. On June 30, Mr. Hayworth will have taught at high school for twenty years.
9. When you see them, they will have discussed the subject more than an hour.
10. The house will have burned more than an hour by the time the fire engine gets there.

4-13. 時式的一致

英語的時式有一個規定，如果主要子句的動詞是過去式，那麼從屬子句裡的動
詞都一律要用過去式。比較：

> He says that his name is John.
> He *said* that his name *was* John.

> She says that she has met you.
> She *said* that she *had* met you.

同樣的，如果助動詞 will, shall, can, may 等出現在從屬子句裡面也要改成
would, should, could, might 等。這種時式，有人叫做「過去裡的未來式」：

$$\left\{ \begin{array}{l} \text{I think I can do it.} \\ \text{I } \textit{thought} \text{ I } \textit{could} \text{ do it.} \end{array} \right. \qquad \left\{ \begin{array}{l} \text{He says he will come.} \\ \text{He } \textit{said} \text{ he } \textit{would} \text{ come.} \end{array} \right.$$

有關時式一致的規定，只有一個例外：如果從屬子句裡面的動詞是表示真理或習慣的話，那麼仍然用現在單純式而不改用過去式。

He teacher taught us that Paris *is* the capital of France.

The teacher taught us that Paris *is* the capital of France.

We knew that the earth *is* round.

He said you always *enjoy* a merry company.

習　題　78

把下面的句子改為過去式。

Example:

I hear that he may be drafted.

I heard that he might be drafted.

1. He says they can learn a lot in a few weeks.

2. We expect that you'll have enough to keep you busy.

3. He knows that he will be happy there.

4. She imagines she may have to take examinations again.

5. They hope he can spend a little more time with them.

6. Do you feel you'll know it well enough to perform?

7. He thinks they may not want to help him any more.

8. We see that we can go ahead with our plans.

9. They tell me you'll soon be having a new job to do.

10. I notice that they won't be allowed to smoke in this room.

4-14. 間接直述句

我們把別人說的話照原來的句子一字不改地引用時，叫做**直接引句**（direct speech）；把別人說的話，不照原來的句子而間接的加以引述的時候，就叫做**間接引句**（reported speech, indirect speech）。

比較：

He said, "I am busy today." (直接說法)
He said that he was busy today. (間接說法)

He said to me, "I saw them come by car." (直接說法)
He told me that he had seen them come by car. (間接說法)

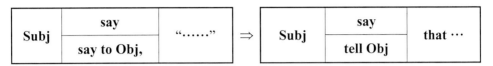

注意：上面的句子從直接引句改為間接引句的時候，有以下的變化：

(1) 引號（" "）與引號前面的逗號（，）要去掉。

(2) 連詞 that 要放在間接引句的前面。連詞 that 也可以省略。

(3) 如果動詞 say 後面帶有表示人的間接賓語，平常都用**傳達動詞**（reporting verb）、tell 來代替。

(4) 如果傳達動詞是過去式的話，那麼按照時式一致的原則，間接引句裡面的動詞也要改為過去式。

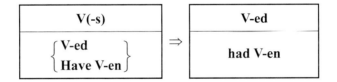

I said, "I am tired." → I said that I *was* tired.

He said, "I have studied English for three years."

　　→ He said that he *had studied* English for three years.

She said, "I went to Taipei last week."

　　→ She said that she *had gone* to Taipei last week.

He said, "I will come at noon."

　　→ He said that he *would* come at noon.

　（如果在引述的時候他還沒有來，就可以用 will：

　　He said that he *will* come tomorrow at noon.）

　　但是如果間接引句的內容是表示普遍的真理、常習的動作或歷史的事實的話，那麼就不一定要改成過去式或過去完成式：

He said that honesty *is* the best policy.

She said that she *takes* a walk in the park every morning.

The teacher told us that Columbus *discovered* (not *had discovered*) America in 1492.

參考：注意，從直接引句改為間接引句的時候，常常牽涉到代名詞與副詞的改變：

He said to me, "I will see you here tomorrow." →

He told me that *he* would see *me there the next day*.

但是如果在同一天，或同一個地方，引述別人的話的時候，時間副詞與場所副詞就不必改變：

He told me that he would / will see me *here tomorrow*.

---

here → there, now → then, ago → before, today → that day, yesterday → the day before (the previous day), last night (week, month, etc.)

→ the $\begin{cases} \text{night (week, month, etc.) before} \\ \text{previous night (week, month, etc.),} \end{cases}$

tomorrow, tomorrow night, next week (month, etc.) →

the $\begin{cases} \text{next} \\ \text{following} \end{cases}$ day, night, week, (month, etc.)

習 題 79

學生 A 把句子唸出來。學生 B 轉向學生 C 問："What did he say?" 最後學生 C 用 "He said that …" 起頭的句子引述學生 A 的話。

Example:

Student A: I'm listening to the teacher.

Student B: *What did he say?*

Student C: *He said that he was listening to the teacher.*

1. I am going to town with my sister.

2. I'm reading the newspaper.

3. My name is Bob.   4. I will answer the phone.

5. I have finished my work.

6. I have been to the museum many times.

7. I have been studying too much.   8. I want to speak to you.

9. We are very late.   10. He is ready to come with us.

習　題　80

用 He told me that … 起頭的句子，把下面的句子改為間接引句。

Example: I met you last year.

$$\rightarrow \textit{He told me that he had met me} \begin{cases} \textit{last year.} \\ \textit{the year before.} \\ \textit{the previous year.} \end{cases}$$

1. She didn't prepare her lessons.   2. They will be here soon.

3. He is going to London tomorrow.

4. I have just been to the barber's.

5. I can come next week.   6. They went away yesterday.

7. I was very ill yesterday.

8. I lost my temper yesterday morning.

9. I have never been here before.

10. You have done your homework well.

4-15. 間接問句（yes / no 問句）

把直接問句改為間接問句的時候，原來的問句就變成直述句。因此主語與動詞倒裝的詞序就要回復到原來主語前、動詞後的詞序：

{ He said, "Are you busy today?"（直接說法）
He asked whether I was busy today.（間接說法）

{ She said to me, "Didn't you finish your homework?"（直接說法）
She asked me whether or not I had finished my homework.（間接說法）

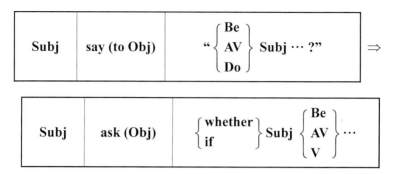

注意：連接詞 whether（or not）或 if 要放在間接問句的前面，動詞 say 用傳達動詞 ask 來代替。

習 題 81

按照例句把下面的問句用 if, whether, whether or not 改為間接問句。

Examples:

"Are you a student?" he asked me.

He asked me if I was a student.

He asked me whether I was a student.

He asked me whether or not I was a student.

"Were you at the game yesterday, John?" Bob asked.

Bob asked John if he had been at the game the day before.

Bob asked John whether he had been at the game the day before.

Bob asked John whether or not he had been at the game the day before.

1. "Is there any work, Miss Hopkins?" the students asked.

2. "Is there another road to the museum?" asked the tourist.

3. "Is Bob good at music?" Dick asked his friend.

4. "Do you enjoy swimming?" he asked me.

5. "Do you know how to dance?" she asked the boy.

6. "Was your picture in the newspaper?" I asked my friend.

7. "Did you hear about the accident?" he asked me.

8. "Have you studied your lesson carefully?" Mrs. Smith asked her daughter.

9. "Will you be staying at the Grand Hotel?" Mrs. Taylor asked her husband.

10. "May we stay up late?" the children asked their mother.

習　題　82

把下面的問句改為用 He asked me whether 起頭的間接問句。

Example:

   Are you enjoying yourself?

    He asked me whether I was enjoying myself.

1. Was the train very full?   2. Is it time to go?

3. Are my shoes cleaned yet?   4. Can you hear a noise?

5. May I use your telephone?   6. Do you sleep in the afternoons?

7. Do I look all right?   8. Is it raining very heavily?

9. Do you think it greedy to eat more than two at a time?

10. Do you know why Dick ran away when he saw a policeman?

4-16. 時間與時式（複習）

前面我們已經把每一種英語時變式的用法詳細討論過，下面我們要用摘要的方式說明，各種不同的時間觀念如何用各種不同的時變式來加以表達。

(1) **確實現在**：事情在講話的時候正在進行。

過去　　　　　現在　　　　　未來

(a) 現在進行式：

 I *am writing* a letter now.

(b) 現在單純式：

 （內動詞）：I *hear* a strange noise.

 （用 here 與 there 起首的有感歎意味的句子）：

 Here he *comes!*　There she *goes!*

(2) **超時間的現在**：事情發生在包括過去、現在、未來所有的時間。

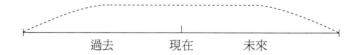

(a) 一般的真理：現在單純式。

The sun *shines* during the day.

She *speaks* English well.

(b) 習慣性或頻繁性的行為：

(i) 現在單純式（常與表示次數多寡的副詞合用）

She never *arrives* at school late.

(ii) 現在進行式（常與 always, ever, constantly 等副詞合用）

He *is* always *thinking* and *thinking*.

She *is* ever *complaining*.

(3) **兼包過去在內的現在**：

(a) 現在完成式：

一種事態從過去某一點延續到現在。

I *have practiced* English for an hour.

We *have lived* here since we got married.

過去的事態對於現在的效果。

He *has bought* a motorcycle.

She *has spent* many years in Japan.

(b) 現在完成進行式：

強調一種事態一直不斷的繼續到現在。

He's tired; he's *been running* around all day.

表示這種事態現在還在繼續。

It *has been raining* all morning.

(4) **過去時間：**

過去　　　　現在　　　　未來

(a) 過去單純式：表示事情在過去某一點發生。

The First World War *broke* out in 1914.

(b) 過去進行式：強調事情在過去進行一段時間。

He was watching television all evening.

(c) 過去完成式：表示事情在過去某一個確定的時間以前發生。

He *had gone* to bed by nine o'clock last night.

(d) 過去進行式（V_1）與過去單純式（V_2）：第一件事情（V_1）正在進行的時候，第二件事情（V_2）又發生。

I *was studying* when he *came*.

(e) 過去完成式（V_1）與過去單純式（V_2）：第一件事情（V_1）發生以後，第二件事情（V_2）才發生。

I *had finished* my letter when he *came*.

(f) 過去完成進行式（V_1）與過去單純式（V_2）：第一件事情（V_1）早已發生而且仍在進行的時候，第二件事情（V_2）發生。

I *had been sudying* for two hours when he *came*.

(g) 過去單純式（V_1）與過去單純式（V_2）：兩件事情（V_1, V_2）幾乎同時發生。

The students *kept* quiet as soon as the teacher *came* in.

(h) 過去進行式（V_1）與過去進行式（V_2）：兩件事情（V_1, V_2）同時進行。

I *was studying* while he *was talking* with his friends.

(i) was (were) to V, was (were) going to V：本來打算做一件事情，後來因故沒有實現。

We *were going to play* tennis yesterday but it rained.

I *was to go out* when the telephone started ringing,

(j) 過去常發生的事情。

(i)　used to V：事情經常發生。

He *used to play* football before his marriage.

　(ii) would V：事情偶爾發生。

　　　He *would* often *come* home tired out.

　(iii) 過去進行式：與 always, ever, constantly 等副詞合用。

　　　He *was* always *grumbling*.

(k)「剛剛」或「剛才」發生的事情：

　現在完成式，與 just 合用。He *has* just *finished* his letter.

　過去單純式，與 just（now）合用。

　He *finished* his letter just now.

(5) **未來時間：**

過去　　　　現在　　　　未來

(a) will (shall) + V, 'll + V：「單純未來」僅表示事情將在未來發生，並沒有別的含義。

　Tomorrow *will be* Sunday.

　I'm sure he'*ll come* tomorrow.

(b) will + V：「意願未來」（表示願意或決心。）

　I *will do* it whether you like it or not.

(c) is（am, are）to + V：表示計劃或義務。

　We *are to finish* the work tomorrow.

(d) is (am, are) going to + V：

　〔單純未來〕

　I am seventy now, and I'*m going to live* to be ninety.

　〔意願未來〕

　I'*m going to work* harder next week.

　〔不久的將來〕

　It'*s going to rain* (soon).

(c) is (am, are) + $\left\{\begin{array}{l}\text{about to V} \\ \text{on the point of V-ing}\end{array}\right\}$ ：「最近的將來」

They *are about to start.*

She *is on the point of crying.*

(f) 未來進行式：強調一種事態會在未來繼續一段時間。

I'*ll be playing* tennis all this afternoon.

(g) 未來進行式（V_1）與現在單純式（V_2）：第一件事情（V_1）在未來正在進行的時候，第二件事情（V_2）發生。

I'*ll be studying* when you *come.*

(h) 未來完成式（V_1）與現在單純式（V_2）：第一件事情（V_1）在未來發生以後，第二件事情（V_2）才發生。

I'*ll have finished* the report by the time you *come.*

(i) 未來完成進行式（V_1）與現在單純式（V_2）：第一件事情（V_1）在未來發生，並且還在繼續進行的時候，第二件事情（V_2）發生。

We'*ll have been practicing* for two hours when the teacher *comes.*

(j) 現在單純式：

與表示未來時間的副詞合用。

He *leaves* for New York tomorrow.

用在表示時間或條件的副詞子句裡面，以代替未來單純式。

I'll tell him when he *comes.*

He'll go if you *ask* him.

(k) 現在進行式：

與表示未來時間的副詞合用。

He *is leaving* for New York tomorrow.

用在表示時間或條件的副詞子句裡面，以代替未來進行式。

I'll cook supper while you *are resting.*

I'll do it if you *are coming* with me.

(l) 現在完成式：用在表示時間或條件的副詞子句裡面，以代替未來完成式。

I'll go with you after I *have* asked my mother.

They'll tell us if they have agreed on the price.

(m) 未來常發生的事情：will + V

Sometimes he *will work* for six or seven hours without stopping.

(n)「過去裡的未來」：should, would, might, could + V

He said he *would come* the next day.

She told me that she *might have* to take the exam again.

習 題 83

把括號裡面的動詞改成適當的時式。

1. I (lose) my keys; I cannot remember where I last (see) them.

2. I (never forget) what you (just tell) me.

3. They (meet) only yesterday and (already decide) to get married.

4. Whenever he (go) to town nowadays, he (spend) a lot of money.

5. They (just decide) that they (take) the job.

6. She (play) the piano when our guests (arrive) last night.

7. She (just come) in and (see) you in five minutes.

8. He (walk) very quickly when I (meet) him yesterday.

9. We (meet) you tomorrow after you (finish) your work.

10. I am sorry that I (not know) you (leave) your pipe when you (come) to see me last Thursday.

11. He (be) so good to me when I was a boy, that to this day I (not forget) his kindness, and I hope that I (never forget).

12. He (sleep) and (not understand) what you (say) to him. He (wake) if you (speak) louder.

13. Some animals (not eat) during the winter and only (come) out in spring; we (call) them hibernating animals.

14. I (go) there when I (be) told, not before!

15. I expect he (go) to England as soon as he (get) a visa.

16. He (visit) his friend yesterday and (find) that he (be) out.

17. They (sell) all the dresses before we (get) there.

18. After she (work) at the hospital for two years, she (decide) to give up the job.

19. By the time you get back I (finish) all my correspondence, and then I (can) help you with yours.

20. He will come at once because I (tell) him by phone that you (need) him urgently. I'm sure he (find) his way easily, although he (never visit) this house before.

21. In a few minutes' time, when the clock (strike) six, I (wait) here three hours.

22. I hope it (not rain) when the bride (leave) the church.

23. They (intend) to go there next week, but now they (find) they (not have) enough money.

24. What (you do) just now while I (wash) the dishes?

25. I (read) in yesterday's paper that a boy (steal) a watch and (sell) it, and that the police (look) for him everywhere but (not find) him.

26. When he grew old he often (think) of all the things he (do) when he (be) young.

27. I (never read) a story that (interest) me so much as the one I (read) last night.

28. When we (go) to see them last night, they (play) cards; they (say) they (play) since six o'clock.

29. By the end of last year he (read) four Shakespeare plays, and by next year he (read) two more. I (not see) him since last Monday, but I (believe) he (write) an essay on Hamlet at present.

30. This is the second time you (break) a cup; you (break) one yesterday. My last servant (never break) anything, and you (break) nearly half the things in the house.

31. Mother (just go) to the market; John (see) her just now in the main road as he (come) home from school.

32. I (always tell) you to comb your hair, but you never (do) what I (say).

33. When the bell (ring), we (finish) our work. The bell (ring) after we (finish) our work.

34. When I (meet) George, he (not yet hear) the news. I (meet) George before he (hear) the news.

35. If you (not write), everybody (wonder) what (happen) to you.

36. You (forever misunderstand) what I (explain) to you! Why you (not listen) while I (speak) to you?

第5章
表示情態的助動詞

5-1. 表示情態的助動詞

在英語裡，我們常把表示情態的**助動詞**（modal verbs）放在**主動詞**（main verbs）的前面來表示未來、能力、許可、可能、需要、情願等意思。例如在 "I can speak English." 這個句子裡，助動詞 can 表示能力。同樣地，在 "You may go now." 這個句子裡，助動詞 may 表示許可。

助動詞與主動詞不同，不因為主語的身與數而變化。因此助動詞只有現在式（can, may, will, shall, must）與過去式（could, might, would, should, must），沒有第三身單數現在式（V-s），也沒有現在分詞式（V-ing）或過去分詞式（V-en）：

$$\begin{cases} \text{He } \textit{will} \text{ come tomorrow.（○）} \\ \text{He } \textit{wills} \text{ come tomorrow.（×）} \end{cases}$$

英語裡主要的助動詞除了 will, would, shall, should, can, could, may, might, must 以外還有 ought to, need, dare 等。

習　題　84

在表示情態的助動詞上面加圈，在其他助動詞下面加線。

Example:

  I (shall) be waiting for you.

1. Bob should have been working.

2. You ought to have done better.

3. Could you hold these books for me?

4. The secretary may have made a mistake.

5. Those words must be justified.

6. They could have come by plane.

7. You might have seen him before.

8. They should be studying now.

9. Would you please sit down?

10. Can she do a good job?

5-2. Will 的用法

(1) 表示未來時間：「要，將」（這個時候 will 不重讀)。

    I *will* (= am going to) prepare my lesson tonight.

    You *will* (= are going to) like him when you see him.

    He *will* (= is going to) go with you.

    Will we (= Are we going to) have many examinations in this course?

    Will the meeting (= Is the meeting going to) take place tomorrow?

(2) 表示願意、答應或決心：「要、願意、決心」（這個時候 will 常重讀）。

    I *will* (= am willing to) lend you the book if you need it.

    Will you (= Are you willing to) sing at the concert tomorrow evening? Yes, I will.

    I *will* (= promise to) be there to help you.

    I *will* (= am determined to) do as I like.

    否定式 will not 用來表示拒絕「不要、不願意」：

    I *won't* (= refuse to) listen to you talk nonsense.

    She *won't* (= refuses to) come unless he comes too.

(3) 表示請求：與第二身主語用在問句中「請你…好嗎？」。

    Will you please come with me? (= Please come with me.)

    Will you kindly mail this letter for me? (= Be so kind as to mail the letter for me.)

    Won't you be quiet, please? (= Be quiet, please.)

    Will 還用在命令句後面的追問句：「…好不好？」

    Shut the window, *will* you?

    Be here by seven o'clock, *will* you?

參考：

(1) 表示常常發生的事情：

He *will* often sit up reading all night.

Sometimes he *will* go out for the whole day, and sometimes he *will* sit alone in the room.

(2) 表示無可避免的事情：「總」。

Boys *will* be boys.

Accidents *will* happen.

習　題　85

按照例句完成下面的問句與答句。用代名詞代替名詞。

Example:

Mr. Lyons will correct the homework. *Will he* correct the examinations, too?

Yes, *he will*.

1. The boys will bring paper. _____ bring pencils, too? Yes, _____.

2. Jane will sing for us. _____ play the piano, too? Yes, _____.

3. Jack will try to get that book for me. _____ try to get this one, too? Yes, _____.

4. The company will employ another clerk. _____ employ a stenographer, too? Yes, _____.

5. The professor will get a year to study abroad. _____ receive a financial grant, too? Yes, _____.

習　題　86

照例句把 will 的用法（願意、拒絕、請求、單純未來）注明。

Examples:

Will you open the door, please?（請求）

I will try again if you wish.（願意）

I will never see you again.（拒絕）

Tomorrow will be Sunday.（單純未來）

1. Will you mail this letter for me?

2. I won't do it no matter how much you pay me.

3. My grandmother will be ninety-three in November.

4. I will lend you the book if you need it.

5. They won't accept your offer.　　6. The holidays will soon be here.

7. Pass the butter, will you?　　8. Won't you stay a little longer?

9. It's very late. Won't the shops be closed now?

10. Why won't she do what you ask her to do?

5-3. Shall 的用法

(1) 表示提供服務或提出建議：與第一身主語用在問句中「要不要我…？」，「我們要不要…？」。

> *Shall* I (= Do you want me to) close the window?

> *Shall* we (= Do you allow us to) go to the play tomorrow night?

> *Shall* 還用在 Let me / Let's … 後面的追問句中「…要不要？」、「…好不好？」。

> Let me carry your bags, *shall* I?

> Let's catch that bus, *shall* we?

(2) 表示未來時間：只限與第一身主語合用，在現代口語中常用 will 來代替。

> We *shall* (= will = are going to) know the answer to this problem tomorrow.

參考：

　　表示說話者的諾言、恐嚇、決心：與第二身與第三身主語合用「我就答應你…」，「你非…不可」（這個時候常重讀）。

> If you pass the examination, you *shall* have (= I promise you) a new bicycle.

> You *shall* marry him! (= I insist on your marrying him.)

> 否定式 shall not 用來表示禁止：「我不准…」。

> You *shall not* (= I forbid you to) enter the house.

> The children *shall not* (= I forbid the children to) play in the yard.

習　題　87

按照句意填入 shall 或 will。

1. _____ you, please, stop talking?

2. Let me show you how to do it, _____ I?

3. Just come here a moment, _____ you?

4. Let's go for a walk, _____ we?

5. Let me try again, _____ you?

6. Let us stay here a little longer, _____ you?

7. Be so kind as to close the window, _____ you?

8. _____ I tell him to come again later?

9. _____ you explain that point to me again, please?

10. For heaven's sake don't let him touch that, _____ you?

5-4. Would 的用法

(1) Will 的過去式：用在間接引句表示過去裡的未來「要」。

　　　　He says he *will* go.（現在）

　　　　He said he *would* go.（過去）

(2) 表示願意：「要」、「願意」。

　　　　I *would* (= am willing to) lend you the book if you need it.

　　　　Would you (Are you willing to) sing at the concert tomorrow evening?

　　　　Would like 表示需要或渴望「要」、「很想」：

　　　　I *would like* (= want) a cup of tea.

　　　　I *would like* (= wish) to speak to you.

　　　　也有人用 I / We should like 來代替 I / We would like。

　　　　I *should like* (= would like) to go with you.

(3) 表示過去的習慣：「過去常…」。

　　　　When I was a child, I *would* often (= used to) walk in the country.

(4) 表示客氣的請求：用 would 表示請求比 will 還要客氣：「請你好……嗎？」

Would you kindly show me the way? (= Please show me the way.)

Would you mind opening the door for me? (= Please open the door for me.)

參考：

在假設句裡表示願意或渴望：

I *would* do it if I knew how. (But as I don't know, I can't do it.)

He *would* have bought the car, if he had had money.

   (But as he didn't have money, he didn't buy the car.)

5-5. **Would rather, would sooner, would just as soon 的用法**

Would rather（sooner, just as soon）用來表示選擇「寧願」、「較愛」。

I *would rather* (= prefer to) stay at home (than go for a walk).

I *would rather* have chicken than steak. (= I would prefer chicken to steak.)

Wouldn't you *rather* walk (than ride)? It's a nice day.

Would rather（sooner, just as soon）not 表示「寧願不」：

I *would rather not* (= prefer not to) talk about that any more.

I'*d rather not* be put in charge of the program.

習 題 88

照例句把 would 的用法（願意、過去的習慣、客氣的請求）注明。

Examples:

I would like to leave early.（願意）

Would you rather walk or ride?（選擇）

He would arrive late every morning.（過去的習慣）

Would you mind opening the window, please?（客氣的請求）

1. Would you rather have coffee or tea?

2. Would you please sit down?

3. Would you mind waiting until later?

4. I would like to sit down for a minute.

5. Sometimes the boys would play a trick on their teacher.

6. Would you pass the salt, please?

7. He would prefer to have coffee.

8. Would you mind not smoking in the dining room, please?

9. Would you be so kind as to come here a moment?

10. I would just as soon sit down.

5-6. Should 的用法

(1) 表示義務或責任：「應該」。

> We *should* (= ought to) be courteous to our parents.

> You *shouldn't* (= oughtn't to) laugh at his mistakes.

　　過去應該做而沒有做的事情，用 should have V-en「本應該…（而實際上沒有這樣做）」；過去不應該做而做的事情，用 should not have V-en「本不應該…（而實際上這樣做了）」：

> I *should have* given you my telephone number. (But I didn't.)

> You *shouldn't have* lied to me. (But you did.)

　　Should 還可以用來表示一件事情該這樣做比較妥當：

> You *should* (= had better) start at once (if you want to catch your train).

> *Should* I (= Had I better) leave tomorrow morning?

> It is proper (fitting / natural / important / necessary / essential, etc.) that you
> > *should* go.

(2) 表示驚訝或惋惜：用在表示驚訝或惋惜的「that- 子句」或「wh- 問句」裡，「竟然」。

> It is strange that you *should* say so.

> Why *should* you say so?

> How *should* I know? (= I don't know.)

> I am sorry that I *should* have spoken so rudely.

> It is a pity (a shame) that he *should* fail.

(3) 表示可能性或期望：「（照理）應該」

> I *should* get a letter from my insurance company today.

> > (= There is a strong possibility of my getting a letter.)

They *should* be there by now, I think. (= I expect that they are there. = They are probably there.)

參考：

表示不確定的事情：在敘述句裡表示「倒是」，在條件句裡表示「萬一」。

I *should* think so. (But I am not sure.)

I *should* expect George to be chosen.

If you *should* see him by any chance, please tell him.

習 題 89

按照句意填入 should 或 would。

1. He _____ rather drink French coffee than American coffee.

2. I _____ prefer not to give any explanation.

3. It is surprising that he _____ be so foolish.

4. I _____ go now, but I don' t want to.

5. You _____ n't speak so loud in here.

6. _____ you do me a favor and take this letter to the post?

7. According to the timetable, they _____ arrive any moment now.

8. Do you think he _____ mind helping us for a few minutes?

9. He decided that he _____ have to work harder.

10. The teacher told the students that they _____ work harder.

習 題 90

按照例句改寫下面的句子。

Example:

He went to the movies last night, but he shouldn't have.

He shouldn't have gone to the movies last night.

1. John didn' t practice English, but he should have.

2. Jane told you about the accident, but she shouldn't have.

3. I didn't speak English in class, but I should have.

4. Mr. Brown smoked in the theater, but he shouldn't have.

5. Bob went to the movies last night, but he shouldn't have.

6. They borrowed the money yesterday, but they shouldn't have.

7. We didn't write that exercise last week, but we should have.

8. You wrote your composition in pencil, but you shouldn't have.

9. James didn't deliver newspapers yesterday, but he should have.

10. Miss Brown didn't visit her aunt last week, but she should have.

5-7. Can 的用法

(1) 表示能力：「能」、「能夠」。

> I *can* (= am able to) speak three languages.（現在）
>
> I *can* (= will be able to) help you next week.（未來）

(2) 表示許可：「可以」。

> You *can* (= may) hang your coat here.
>
> *Can* (= May) I borrow your book?

(3) 表示可能性：用在問句中，後面常跟著 be（指現在）或 have V-en（指過去），「可能…嗎？」。

> *Can* the news be true? (= Is it possible that the news is true?)
>
> *Can* he have told a lie? (= Is it possible that he (has) told a lie?)

否定式 cannot 表示「不可能」：

> The news *can't* be true. (= It is impossible that the news is true.)
>
> He *can't* have told a lie. (= It is impossible that he (has) told a lie.)

5-8. Could 的用法

(1) Can 的過去式：用在間接引句裡「能」，「能夠」。

> He says he *can* (= is able to) fix your radio.（現在式）
>
> He said he *could* (= was able to) fix your radio.（過去式）

(2) 表示能力：有表示過去時間的副詞的時候，指過去的事情；沒有表示過去時間

的副詞的時候，可能指現在或未來的事情。這時候的 could 比 can 更多保留，較沒有把握。

> When I was six years old I *could* (= was able to) speak only one language; now I can speak three.（過去時間）

> I *could* never get all these clothes into that suitcase.（現在或未來）

(3) 表示客氣的請求：用 could 比用 can 還要客氣些，正如用 would 比用 will 來得客氣，「請你⋯好嗎？」，「我⋯可以嗎？」：

> *Could* you tell me how I can get to the station?

> *Could* I turn in my paper tomorrow?

(4) 表示可能性：「可能」，用法與 can 相似，但是不限於問句與否定句，在肯定句裡也可以用。

> *Could* the news be true, she wondered. (= Was it possible that the news was true, she wondered.)

> I hear someone coming down the hall. It *could* be John. (= Perhaps it is John.)

參考：

　　用在假設句裡表示能力或可能性，對於現在的用 could + V，對於過去的事情用 could have V-en「本來能 / 可以⋯（但是實際上沒有這樣做）」：

> I *could buy* a new car if I had the money. (= But I don't have the money, so I cannot buy a new car.)

> I *could have* asked him if I had seen him. (= But I did not see him, so I could not ask him.)

　　注意：Could 後面用完成式表示過去有一件事情本來可以做但是實際上沒有做：

> He *could* easily *have done* it. (But he didn't do it.)

習 題 91

　　把下面的句子改成過去式。如果括號裡的副詞表示「能力」的話，can 就改為 was able to；如果表示「許可」的話，can 就改為 could。

Examples:

Mary can cook well. (when she took the trouble)

Mary was able to cook well when she took the trouble.

John can visit his friends. (whenever Mary let him)

John could visit his friends whenever Mary let him.

1. She says I can go. (if my father agreed)

2. He can play football. (before he broke his leg)

3. His son can do arithmetic. (when he was only four)

4. He can borrow the money. (if he promised to repay)

5. He agrees that they can drive the car. (if they were seventeen)

6. I'm sure they can't understand. (because it was too difficult)

7. We can play in the garden. (Mother said)

8. They can't talk to each other. (because her father had forbidden it)

9. They can't talk to each other. (because the telephone was out of order)

10. My father says we can buy some sweets. (because we have been good)

習　題　92

Can 表示有無能力或可能性，should 表示是否妥當。用 can（can't）或 should（shouldn't）完成下面的句子。

1. It's cold today. You _____ wear plenty of clothes.

2. The teacher talks too fast. The students _____ understand him.

3. My car is working well. I _____ reach the city in half an hour.

4. John is a good mechanic. He _____ fix my car.

5. We have to finish the job. We _____ waste time.

6. That doesn't belong to him. He _____ take it.

7. Jim was at the meeting. He _____ tell you what was said.

8. We must be in by midnight. Perhaps we _____ go home now.

9. Cigarettes are unhealthy. Young people _____ smoke.

10. The light is good. The students _____ be able to read comfortably.

5-9. may 的用法

(1) 表示許可：「可以」，指現在或未來的時間。

> You *may* (= are allowed to) leave now.（現在）
>
> You *may* (= have permission to) go out and play when you have finished your homework.（未來）
>
> *May* I talk to you for a minute? (= Is it all right for me to talk to you for a minute?)

May not 表示「不可以」：

> *May* I borrow your toothbrush? No, you *may not*.

(2) 表示猜測：「可能」，對於現在或未來的事情用 may V，對於過去的事情用 may have V-en：

> It *may rain* tomorrow. (It is possible that it will rain tomorrow.)
>
> It *may have rained* while we were gone. (It is possible that it rained while we were gone.)

(3) 表示讓步：「無論…」，常與含有 -ever 的「wh- 詞」連用：

> Wherever he *may* be, he must be found.

5-10. Might 的用法

(1) May 的過去式：用在間接引句裡表示「可以」、「可能」。

> He says that I *may* go with him.（現在式）
>
> He said that I *might* go with him.（過去式）

(2) 表示猜測：「可能」，用法與 may (2) 一樣，只是 might 比 may 更多保留，更沒有把握。

> It *might* rain tomorrow. (The speaker is not very sure.)
>
> It *might* have rained while we were gone.
>
> I *might* buy a new car if I had the money. (But since I don't have the money, I don't know whether I will buy it or not.)
>
> I *might* have bought a new car if I had had the money. (But since I didn't have

the money, I didn't buy a new car.)

參考一：表示猜測的 may 與 might 通常不用在問句中。比較：

$$
\begin{cases}
\text{He } \textit{may} \text{ be there.} \\
\textit{Can} \text{ he be there?} \\
\textit{Is} \text{ he } \textit{likely to be} \text{ there?}
\end{cases}
$$

參考二：May not 用來表示「拒絕許可」；must not 用來表示「禁止」。

May I borrow your toothbrush? No, you *may not*.

You *must not* use other people's toothbrush.

Cannot 在口語中也常用來表示「禁止」：

You *cannot* (=must not, are not allowed to) go now.

習　題　93

在空白裡填入適當的助動詞，使等號兩邊的句子表示同樣的意思。

1. I am willing to try again if you wish. = I _____ try again if you wish.

2. Do you wish me to help you? = _____ I help you?

3. I know how to swim. = I _____ swim.

4. I was able to swim well when I was young. = I _____ swim well when I was young.

5. We can go as soon as we like. = We _____ go as soon as we like.

6. We were allowed to go out whenever we wanted. = We _____ go out whenever we wanted.

7. There is a possibility that he will come tomorrow. = He _____ come tomorrow.

8. You have permission to go home after school. = You _____ go home after school.

9. Is it all right for me to use the telephone? = _____ I use the telephone?

10. It is possible that he knows something about it. = He _____ know something about it.

5-11. Must 的用法

(1) 表示必須：一般指現在或未來的事情。

We *must* (= have to) eat in order to live.

I *must* go now.

在間接引句裡，must 可以指過去的事情：

He said I *must* (= had to) do as I was told.

除了間接引句以外，must 的過去式都一概由 had to 代替：

I *had to* do as I was told.

(2) 表示禁止：must not 表示禁止，「不可以」、「不准」。

You *must not* (= are not allowed to) bring the books out of the reading room.

(3) 表示可能性：「一定」、「準是⋯無疑」。

must V 用來指現在的事情：

Your grandmother *must be* over eighty now.

It *must rain* a lot at this time of the year.

must be V-ing 指現在或未來事情：

You look happy. You *must be having* a good time.

According to the telegram, he *must be arriving* tonight.

must have V-en 指過去的事情：

John looks very pleased. He *must have won* the prize.

You're on time. You *must have got* up early today.

習 題 94

用 must, mustn't, can, can't, could 或 couldn't 完成下面的句子。

1. The theater was crowded. We _____ get in.

2. This pot needs to be fixed. I _____ use it with a hole in it.

3. It is important to be prompt. Students _____ get to class on time.

4. The car is almost out of gas. We _____ stop at a filling station.

5. She's a marvelous singer. You _____ try to hear her.

6. Now we have finished our work. We _____ take a good holiday.

7. You must try harder. You _____ do it if you would try.

8. I don't have tickets. Dick bought them; they _____ be in his pocket.

9. The weather is perfect. It ＿＿＿ be better.

10. Bob practices faithfully every day. He ＿＿＿＿ really like music.

習　題　95

照例句把斜體部分的字用 must V,　must be V-ing,　must have V-en 或 must have been V-ing 代替。

Examples:

  Surely John is older than Mary. → *John must be older than Mary.*

  I suppose he was thirty when I first met him.

   → *He must have been thirty when I first met him.*

1. *I think* you are mistaken.　　　　2. *I think* it is going to rain.

3. John was working late at the office, *I suppose.*

4. Mr. Smith is a rich man nowadays, *I suppose.*

5. *Surely* those children over there are playing football.

6. *Surely* he was very busy if he couldn't come to the party.

7. *Surely* that is Mrs. Smith I can see over there.

8. *I suppose* I was dreaming when I saw her walk in.

9. *I think* you are mad to do that.

10. *I should think* the chickens were stolen by a fox.

5-12. Ought to 的用法

(1) Ought to 的用法與 should 的用法極相似：表示責任、義務、或事情的妥當性。可以指現在或未來，在間接引句裡也可以指過去：

  You *ought to* (= should) start at once.（現在時間）

  You *ought to* (= should) leave early tomorrow morning.（未來時間）

  I told him that he *ought to* (= should) do it.（過去時間）

(2) 過去應該做而沒有做的事情用 ought to have V-en，過去不應該做而已做了的事情用 ought not to have V-en：

  You *ought to have* (= should have) helped him. (but you didn't)

— 173 —

He *ought to have* (= should have) been more careful. (He was not careful enough.)

You *oughtn't to have* (= shouldn't have) laughed at his mistakes

(3) 表示可能性或期望：「（照理）應該」

He *ought* to know how to get there.

習 題 96

以 must 或 ought to (should) 完成下列問答。

1. Mary: Your shoes are wet. It _____ be raining outside.

2. Jane: Yes, it is. It _____ have started when I was shopping at the store, because, when I came out it was pouring. However, it was only a small cloud so the rain _____ have finished by lunchtime.

3. Mary: I hope so. John _____ be here very soon to take me out to lunch.

4. Jane: Yes, it _____ be half past twelve now.

5. Mary: Half past twelve? Then John's late. He _____ have been delayed by something at his office.

6. Jane: Yes, but he _____ be on his way here now.

7. Mary: I'll phone his office. (*She dials.*) No answer. They _____ have all gone to lunch.

8. Jane: Well, then John _____ arrive at any moment.

9. Mary: Yes, here he is! We thought you _____ have been delayed at the office, John!

10. John: No. I _____ have been here ten minutes ago, but I got into a traffic jam. There _____ have been a mile of cars in front of mine.

11. Mary: It _____ have been raining all the time too.

12. John: Yes, it was. Well, you _____ be hungry. Let's walk. We _____ get there quicker that way.

13. Mary: You _____ have decided where to take me, then.

John: Yes, Lin's.

14. Mary: We _____ be able to get Chinese food there.

15. John: Yes, we can. We _____ get a good meal there. Dicye recommended it, so it _____ be good.

16. Mary: Yes, they _____ have given him really good Chinese food for him to recommend it.

習　題　97

把括號裡的動詞改成適當的時式。

Examples:

They should *go* to the library tomorrow night. (go)

They should *have gone* to the library last night. (go)

1. We should _____ our lessons every night. (study)

2. You should _____ the question now. (answer)

3. Tom should _____ his lessons long ago. (practice)

4. Dick should _____ the book next week. (finish)

5. We ought to_____ that exercise yesterday. (write)

6. One should _____ carefully always. (drive)

7. They should _____ the money last month. (return)

8. We ought to _____ our parents. (love).

9. I should _____ you everything that week. (tell)

10. Mary ought to _____ in bed last night. (stay)

5-13. Had better (had best), had sooner 的用法

Had better / sooner 表示勸告或建議，「最好」、「…比較好」：

You *had better* (= it will be better for you to) take care of your cold.

We'*d sooner* start early.

Had (n't) we *better* go at once?

Had better / sooner not 表示「最好不要」：

You *had better not* go out without a coat.

He'*d sooner not* be late again.

5-14. **Have to 的用法**

Have to / has to〔hǽftə, hǽstə〕與 must 一樣表示必需：「必須」、「非⋯不可」：

I *have to* (= must) leave now.

Do I *have to* (= Must I) pay my fees today?

對於過去的事情用 had to：

I *had to* (= it was necessary for me to) leave then.

Did I have to (= Was it necessary for me to) pay my fees yesterday?

否定式 do / did not have to 表示「不必」：

I *don't have to* leave now.

I *didn't have* to pay my fees yesterday.

在口語英語常用 have / has / had got to 來代替 have / has / had to：

I'*ve got to* leave now.

Had I *got to* pay my fees yesterday?

He *hasn't got to* answer all the questions.

參考：not have to 表示不「必」，must not 表示不「可以」。比較：

You *do not have to* drive so fast. We have plenty of time to get there.

(It is not necessary you drive so fast.)

You *must not* drive so fast. We might have an accident.

(It is necessary you not drive so fast.)

習 題 98

填入適當的字，使左右兩邊的句子表示同樣的意思。

1. I am determined never to speak to that man again. = I _____ never speak to that man again.

2. I prefer not to say anything. = I _____ rather say nothing.

3. I refuse to listen to you unless you talk sense. = I _____ listen to you unless you talk sense. (Use a contracted negative form.)

4. Surely John is older than Mary. = John ＿＿＿ be older than Mary.

5. I suppose the servant took the money. = It ＿＿＿＿ be that the servant took the money.

6. We are obliged to help our neighbors. = We ＿＿＿＿ help our neighbors.

7. Must he work so late? = ＿＿＿＿ he ＿＿＿＿ to work so late?

8. I was obliged to tell him everything. = I ＿＿＿＿ to tell him everything.

9. Was it necessary for you to drive so fast? = ＿＿＿＿ you ＿＿＿＿ to drive so fast?

10. It will be better for you to start early. = You ＿＿＿＿ better start early.

11. It is better for us to stay, isn't it? = We ＿＿＿＿ better stay, ＿＿＿＿ we?

12. You prefer to go, don't you? = You ＿＿＿＿ rather go, ＿＿＿＿ you?

13. I must leave now. = I have ＿＿＿＿ to leave now.

14. Would it be right for me to take this job? = ＿＿＿＿ I better take this job?

15. It was not necessary for you to come in person. = You ＿＿＿＿ have ＿＿＿＿ come in person.

5-15. Be able to 的用法

　　Be able to「能、能夠」與 can（could）一樣表示能力，但是用法比較廣。指現在（或未來）的事情可以用 am（is, are）able to，指過去的事情可以用 was（were）able to，指未來的事情可以用 will be able to 或 am（is, are）going to be able to：

　　　　I *am able to* drive in traffic now.

　　　　They *were able to* go after all.

　　　　You'*ll be able to* speak French in six months.

　　　　So far we *haven't been able to* get in touch with him.

　　Be not able to, be unable to, be powerless to 表示「不能」：

　　　　I *am not able* (*unable, powerless*) to help you.

5-16. Used to 的用法

　　Used to「過去（經）常」表示一件事情過去經常發生，但是現在已不再發生：

　　　　He *used to* smoke. (He smoked for some time in the past but now he does not smoke.)

I *used to* buy my clothes at Dixon's. (Now I buy them at other stores.)

Used 的否定式與問句式，美式英語多用 did not use to 與 did … use to：

He *didn't use to* talk much.

Did he *use* to play tennis?

You *used to* smoke a pipe, *didn't* you?

參考：Used to 表示過去經常發生的事情；would 表示過去偶爾發生的事情。

比較：

$$\left\{\begin{array}{l} \text{He } \textit{used to} \text{ live in London.} \\ \text{He } \textit{would} \text{ often go to London for a visit.} \end{array}\right.$$

習 題 99

填入適當的字，使左右兩邊的句子表示同樣的意思。

1. I wish you would do as I tell you. = I _____ like you to do as I tell you.

2. I think you are mad to do that. = You _____ be mad to do that.

3. He prefers tea to coffee. = She _____ rather have tea than coffee.

4. She was unable to come yesterday. = She _____ come yesterday.

5. He had the habit of getting up early when he was young. = He _____ to get up early when he was young.

6. She was quite different from what she was before. = She was no longer what she __ _____ to be.

7. I couldn't come because of the rain. = I wasn't _____ to come because of the rain.

8. Can you finish your job by next week? = _____ you _____ able to finish your job by next week?

9. He drank a lot for some time in the past but now he does not drink. = He _____ drink a lot.

10. I tried to see him several times but so far I couldn't see him. = I _____ unable to see him.

5-17. Need 的用法

Need「需要，須要」可以當助動詞用，也可以當主動詞用。

(1) 當主動詞用：

He *needs* to work so late.

Does he *need* to work so late?

He doesn't *need* to work so late, does he?

(2) 當助動詞用：只限於否定句與帶有否定意味的問句裡。

Need he work so late? No, nobody *need* work so late.

He *needn't* work so late, *need* he?

參考：用 need 做問句的時候，說話的人預期對方的回答是否定的；用 must 做問句的時候，說話的人卻沒有這種心理。比較：

{ Need he come tomorrow?（他明天要來嗎？不必要吧。）
{ Must he come tomorrow?（他明天要不要來？）

習　題　100

用 mustn't 或 needn't 完成下面的句子。

1. He _____ eat so much; it makes him fat.

2. You _____ drive slowly; it's quite safe.

3. You _____ drive fast along this narrow road.

4. You _____ hurry; there's plenty of time.

5. The doctor said I _____ smoke so much.

6. The doctor said I _____ take those drugs any more.

7. You _____ walk in the middle of the road; it's dangerous.

8. I _____ tell you how foolish it would be to do that.

9. I _____ tell you the answer because I promised not to.

10. They _____ be late at the office, or the manager will get angry.

習 題 101

用肯定式與否定式的簡易答句回答下列問題。

Example:

>Must I go now?
>
>*Yes, you must.*
>
>*No, you needn't.*

1. May I go now?
2. Can you play tennis?
3. Will we have any trouble getting there?
4. Can the news be true?
5. Must I come again?
6. Need he come tomorrow?
7. Must you talk so loud?
8. Need it be finished by tomorrow?
9. Shall I open the window for you?
10. Could I use your phone?

習 題 102

按照句意把 it was not necessary 改成 needn't have 或 didn't need。

Examples:

>It wasn't necessary for me to tell him but I did tell him.
>
>*I needn't have told him.*
>
>It wasn't necessary for me to tell him and I didn't tell him.
>
>*I didn't need to tell him.*

1. It was not necessary for me to put on a coat as it wasn't raining.

2. It was not necessary for you to bring a coat as I could have lent you one.

3. It was not necessary for him to telephone Mary; he could have saved himself the trouble.

4. It was not necessary for us to visit our aunt as, when we got there, she was out.

5. It was not necessary for him to turn on the light as the sun was shining brightly.

6. It was not necessary for the children to go to bed early, as they had rested all afternoon.

7. It was not necessary for me to wear my glasses as I could see perfectly well without them.

8. It was not necessary for him to speak to her as he had already explained everything to her.

參考：Need 沒有過去式，但是可以用 need have V-en 來表示過去的事情。

　　比較：

　　　　He needn't have worked late.（他本來不必要工作，但是實際上他工作了。）

　　　　He didn't need to work late.（他不必要工作，不管他實際上有沒有工作。）

5-18. Dare 的用法

　　Dare「敢」也跟 need 一樣，可以當助動詞用，也可以當主動詞用。

(1) 當主動詞用：

　　　　Does he *dare* to tell you the truth?

　　　　He doesn't *dare* to tell me the truth.

(2) 當助動詞用；只限於否定句，帶有否定意味的問句，或在 how 後面（「竟敢」）。

　　　　Dare he tell you the truth?

　　　　He *daren't* tell me the truth.

　　　　How dare you speak to me like that?

參考：Daren't 可以用來指現在、過去或未來的事情：

　　　　John met me yesterday, but he *daren't* tell me the truth.

　　　　Will you tell Bob that I have lost his fountain pen? I *daren't* tell him.

習　題　103

　　照例句把句子裡面的 need 與 dare 從主動詞改為助動詞用。

Examples:

　　　　They don't need to send the letter after all.

　　　　　　They needn't send the letter after all.

　　　　We don't dare to light a fire among the trees.

　　　　　　We daren't light a fire among the trees.

1. He doesn't dare to touch the wire with his finger.

2. I don't need to tell you how sorry I am.

3. Do you really need to be so rude to her?

4. Does he dare to show himself in front of them?

5. Why don't you dare to keep a big dog?

6. Do I need to bring my raincoat with me?

7. How do you dare to say such things!

8. Tell the children that they don't need to do their homework.

9. I bet you don't dare to pull his beard.

10. We don't need to explain it all again, do we?

11. You don't dare to challenge me, do you?

12. She doesn't need to finish the work today, does she?

參考：need 與 dare 可以當主動詞與助動詞用，因此有兩種不同的追問句。

比較：

$\left\{ \begin{array}{l} \text{You don't need to drive so fast, } \textit{do you?} \\ \text{You needn't drive so fast, } \textit{need you?} \end{array} \right.$

$\left\{ \begin{array}{l} \text{He doesn't dare to ask him, } \textit{does he?} \\ \text{He daren't ask her, } \textit{dare he?} \end{array} \right.$

習 題 104

照例句用助動詞與完成式來敘述過去的事情。

Example:

John should come with us. He *should have come* with us yesterday.

1. Dick shouldn't stay in bed so late. He _____ up so late last night.

2. Mary must eat a lot. She _____ a lot when she was little, too.

3. Bob would help you, if you asked him. He _____ you yesterday, too.

4. They wouldn't like this food. They _____ the food we had last night, either.

5. There might be a different teacher there today. There _____ a different teacher

there yesterday.

6. You ought to take more exercise. You _____ more exercise when you were a boy.

7. I should ask my friends to stay. I _____ my friends to stay last week.

8. Jane must not hear the bell. She _____ it yesterday.

9. Ted need not buy the book. He _____ the book last week.

10. Bill cannot be very bright. He _____ very bright when he was young.

習 題 105

把下面的句子改為由助動詞與進行式合成的句子。

Example:

John is sleeping. (must) → Dick *must be sleeping*, too.

1. Bob is working in the garden. (will)

   He _____ in the garden tomorrow, too.

2. Jane is studying now. (could) Alice _____ now, too.

3. Tom isn't coming. (may) His brother _____, either.

4. I am saving money toward college. (should) You _____ money, too.

5. You are losing weight. (must) I _____ weight, too.

6. They are getting ready for school. (ought to)

   We _____ ready for school, too.

7. The Millers are not playing tennis today. (will)

   They _____ tennis tomorrow, either.

8. The Whites are looking for a house. (may)

   The Blakes _____ for a house, too.

9. Mary is not wearing her new hat today. (must)

   She _____ her old hat.

10. They are not playing tennis now. (could) They _____ playing golf.

習 題 106

把下面的句子改為由助動詞與完成進行式合成的句子。

Example:

John must be studying now.

He *must have been studying* last night, too.

1. You should be paying attention to your teacher. You _____ attention yesterday, too.

2. Mr. Hill will be working here next year. By then, he _____ here ten years.

3. Bob should be wearing warm clothing. He _____ warm clothing when he went skiing.

4. Jane might be helping her mother today. She _____ her mother all the week.

5. The visitor may be waiting in the next room. He _____ for a long time.

6. Dick can't be listening. He _____ when I explained the problem to him.

7. John could be studying. He _____ all day long.

8. Henry must be sleeping now. He _____ when I tried to telephone him.

習 題 107

在空白裡填入適當形式的助動詞。否定句用簡寫式。

1. _____ you please show me the way? (two possibilities)

2. Will the weather clear up this afternoon? No, I'm afraid it _____.

3. Do you think he would come if I asked him? No, I don't think he _____.

4. They _____ have arrived by now, but they didn't. (two possibilities)

5. Must I finish all this work in an hour? No, you _____.

6. You _____ to respect your teachers.

7. It is strange that he _____ do such a thing.

8. It is a pity that she _____ have died so young.

9. _____ it be true? (= Is it possible that it is true?)

10. He _____ have told a lie. (= It is impossible that he has told a lie.)

11. You _____ go out, but must come back before dark. (two possibilities)

12. May I open the window? No, you _____. (two possibilities)

13. He _____ drop in and have a chat with me whenever he passed by my house.

14. Paul is ill and hasn't come to school this week. Probably he _____ be able to come next week, either.

15. _____ you mind if I didn't come?

16. My sister _____ to oppose me, but my brother occasionally did.

17. I am surprised that he _____ have failed.

18. However hard you _____ work, you _____ not finish the job in a few days.

19. What has he done that you _____ be so angry?

20. He is working hard so that he _____ pass the exam.

21. You _____ not to neglect your duty.

22. How _____ you talk to me like this!

23. There _____ to be a big oak tree around here when I was a child.

24. _____ he rest in peace!

25. Need you bring your brother with you? Yes, I am afraid I _____.

26. Must you always wear that old coat? No, I suppose I _____.

27. Oughtn't you to be more careful? Yes, we _____.

28. Dare you pull your uncle's beard? No, I _____.

29. Do you really think he used to live here? (a) Yes, I _____; (b) I am sure he _____.

30. There _____ to be some trees in this field, _____ there?

31. He _____ have been hurt; we do not yet know.

32. He was not hurt, but he _____ have been hurt.

33. She isn't back yet. I'm afraid she _____ have had an accident.

34. You _____ not to have driven that car with the brakes out of order. You _____ have had an accident.

第6章
被動句

6-1. 主動語態與被動語態

英語的動詞有兩種語態（voice）：**主動語態**（active voice）與**被動語態**（passive voice）。前面兩章我們所討論的都是主動語態。在主動語態的句子裡，主語多半都是指做動作的人；在被動語態的句子裡，主語卻指接受動作的人或物。從下面的例句裡，我們可以明白被動句是由主動句變出來的。主動句的賓語變成被動句的主語；主動句的主語雖然可以用介詞 by 保留在被動裡句，但是多半都加以省略；

Active				Passive		
Subj	**V**	**Obj**		**Subj**	**Be V-en**	**by Obj**
主動者	動作	受動者	$\Rightarrow$	受動者	動作	主動者

John welcomed May. → Mary *was welcomed* by John.

Farmers raise rice in China. → Rice *is raised* in China (by farmers).

我們用被動語態，主要的是為了一件事情往往說不出誰是主動者，或是雖然說得出但是不值得指明：

His father *was killed* in the war.

English *is spoken* in many countries.

This book *was published* in China.

或者是說話的重點在受動者而不在主動者：

The man *was hit* by a speeding car.

This book *was given* to me by my uncle.

習 題 108

英語的動詞只有及物動詞才能變成被動語態。下面這些句子裡，凡是你認為可以變成被動語態的，都在句子後面打一個 √ 的記號。

1. She is singing.   2. They sing that song often.

3. They went fishing.

4. They caught six fish.

5. He had a big house.

6. He sold the house last year.

7. The students laughed a great deal.

8. They laughed at him.

9. She taught Chinese at college.

10. She married a Chinese professor.

6-2. 動詞的被動式

　　英語動詞的被動式都是由 Be 動詞和 V-en（過去分詞）合成。每一個主動的時變式都有一個相平行的被動式。只有完成進行式與未來進行式的被動式平常很少使用。

主動：V	被動：Be + V-en
（現在單純）He finishes the work.	The work is finished.
（過去單純）He finished the work.	The work was finished.
（未來單純）He will finish the work.	The work will be finished.
（現在完成）He has finished the work.	The work has been finished.
（過去完成）He had finished the work.	The work had been finished.
（未來完成）He will have finished the work.	The work will have been finished.
（現在進行）He is finishing the work.	The work is being finished.
（過去進行）He was finishing the work.	The work was being finished.

習　題　109

　　依照例句把下面的句子改成主動語態。

Examples:

　　　　It was done by me. → *I did it.*

　　　　It was done by telephone. → *They did it by telephone.*

1. It was done by radio.

2. It was done by a radio announcer.

3. It was done by machine.

4. It was done by workers.

5. It was done by a mailman.

6. It was done by mail.

7. It was done by a kind old woman.

8. It was done by special delivery.

6-3. 單純式的被動語態：B + V-en

單純式的被動語態由 Be 動詞（am, are, is, was, were）與 V-en（過去分詞）合成。

Subj	V	Obj
NP_1	$\begin{Bmatrix} V \\ V\text{-}s \\ V\text{-}ed \end{Bmatrix}$	NP_2

$\Rightarrow$

Subj	Be + V-en	Obj
NP_2	$\begin{Bmatrix} am \\ are \\ is \\ was \\ were \end{Bmatrix}$ V-en	(by NP_1)

The mailman brings the mail.

The mail *is brought* by the mailman.

The secretary typed the letters.

The letters *were typed* by the secretary.

They signed the treaty in Paris.

The treaty *was signed* in Paris.

習 題 110

把下面的句子改成被動語態。在這些句子裡誰是主動者都不重要，所以在被動句裡可以省去，不必用 by 保留。

1. They made this gun in England.

2. Somebody left the dog in the garden.

3. He wrote the book beautifully.　　　　4. People always admire this picture.

5. People speak English all over the world.

6. He hurt his leg in an accident.

7. They punished me for something I didn't do.

8. One uses milk for making butter and cheese.

9. Did anyone tell you how to get in touch with him?

10. Didn't they tell you to be here by six o'clock?

參考：在被動句裡「表示狀態的副詞」常放在 V-en 的前面：

He wrote the book beautifully. → The book was *beautifully written*.

The secretary typed the letter neatly. → The letter was *neatly typed*.

6-4. 含有助動詞的單純式的被動語態

如果動詞的單純式含有表示情態的動詞（will, shall, can, must, may, should, would, could, might, ought to, have to 等），那麼在助動詞後面加 be 後再加 V-en（過去分詞）。

Subj	AV V	Obj		Subj	AV be V-en	Obj
NP₁	will can may must etc.	NP₂	⇒	NP₂	will can may must etc. be V-en	(be NP₁)

He will finish the work tomorrow. →

The work *will be finished* tomorrow.

We must do this today. → This *must be done* today.

Yon can bring it tomorrow. → It *can be brought* tomorrow.

You have to do it now. → It *has to be done* now.

習　題　111

把下面的句子改為被動語態。

1. He must do this right away.
2. They ought to do it right away.
3. She can do it right away.
4. You should send the letter today.
5. They used to do that work.
6. You have to do this today.
7. They are going to build a bridge next year.
8. He cannot write the letter unless he has all the information,
9. I can assure you I will arrange everything in time. (Two passives.)

10. People will forget it in a few years' time, won't they?

11. He was supposed to do it yesterday.

12. What ought we to do about this?

6-5. 完成式的被動語態：Have + been + V-en

完成式的被動語態，在 have 動詞（have, has, had）後面加 been 後再加 V-en（過去分詞）而成。

Subj	Have V-en	Obj
NP₁	have / has / had / AV have } V-en	NP₂

⇒

Subj	Have been V-en	Obj
NP₂	have / has / had / AV have } been V-en	(by NP₁)

The secretary has typed the letters.

　　The letters *have been typed* by the secretary.

They had discussed the plan before I was consulted.

　　The plan *had been discussed* before I was consulted.

A servant must have stolen the money.

　　The money *must have been stolen* by a servant.

You should have mailed the letter yesterday.

　　The letter *should have been mailed* yesterday.

習　題　112

把下面的句子改成被動語態。

1. Someone has spilt some ink on the carpet.

2. Somebody has already shut the door.

3. Somebody must have stolen the money.

4. They have built the house of stone and cemept.

5. You should have mailed this letter yesterday.

6. Nobody has answered my question properly.

7. By the time you come back, I will have finished my letter.

8. Has anybody answered your questions?

9. Has somebody done all the work?

10. What have people done about this?

6-6. 進行式的被動語態：Be + being + V-n

進行式的被動語態，在 Be 動詞（am, are, is, was, were）後面加 being 後再加 V-en（過去分詞）而成。

Subj	Be V-ing		Obj
NP$_1$	am are is was were } V-ing		NP$_2$

$\Rightarrow$

Subj	Be being V-en		Obj
NP$_2$	am are is was were } being V-en		(by NP$_1$)

He is writing the letter now.

　　The letter *is being written* now.

The secretaries are typing the contracts.

　　The contracts *are being typed* by the secretaries.

She was cooking the food when I was there.

　　The food was *being* cooked when I was there.

They were preparing breakfast at six this morning.

　　Breakfast *was being prepared* at six this morning.

習　題　113

把下面的句子改成被動語態。

1. They were testing him at the time.

2. They are putting the horse in a stable.

3. We are arguing about that case now.

4. They are building a new subway in that town.

5. He was writing the letter when I was there.

6. They are tearing up the road in front of our house.

7. They are writing the letter now, aren't they?

8. He is preparing those reports today, isn't he?

9. Why are they tearing up the street?

10. They are going to deliver it tomorrow, aren't they?

習　題　114

把下面的句子改成以人做主語的被動句。

1. They gave her a new watch.

2. They will ask you several questions.

3. Somebody has shown her the new buildings.

4. The officials denied him his right.

5. They asked us to be there at eight o'clock.

6. Someone is showing her how to do it.

7. They have made him a captain.

8. They recommended me another doctor last week.

9. Somebody will tell you what time the train leaves.

10. Someone taught him French and gave him a dictionary

參考：如果主動句有兩個賓語，那麼就可以變成兩種不同的被動句：

Someone gave me the book.

　　→ *I* was given the book.

　　　The book was given to me.

Father bought my brother a new bicycle.

　　→ *My brother* was bought a new bicycle.

　　　A new bicycle was bought for my brother.

注意：用直接賓語做被動句的主語的時候，間接賓語前面通常都要加介詞 to 或 for 等。

習　題　115

把下面的句子改成被動語態。

1. We must look into the matter.　　　　2. People speak well of him.

3. They will look after you well.

4. Someone reads to the old lady every morning.

5. People often ask for that book.

6. Nobody has slept in that room for years.

7. A car ran over our dog.

8. People will simply laugh at you for your trouble.

9. People are talking about her.

10. The principal will speak to the children who are failing.

參考：「可分動詞」的助詞與「介詞動詞」的介詞，在被動句裡要跟動詞放在一起：

> They will *look after* you well. → You will be well *looked after*.
>
> They has *set up* the monument. → The monument has been *set up*.

習　題　116

依照例句把下面的句子改成以 it is V-en（that）…開頭的句子。

Examples:

> They expect that he will go. → *It is expected that he will go.*
>
> Someone explained that the project would need more than ten thousand dollars.
>
> > → *It was explained that the project would need more than ten thousand dollars.*

1. They hope that everything will be all right.

2. Someone suggests that we take a break before going on.

3. They announced that there won't be any class tomorrow.

4. We agree that no action will be taken until next week.

5. Someone found that they didn't give their right address.

6. They assumed that there was no chance to succeed.

7. You cannot deny that his handwriting has improved.

8. They have decided that a new branch will be opened next year.

9. You must never say that he was selfish.

10. You must understand clearly that this is your last chance.

參考：It is V-en（that）…的句型多半都用在比較正式的英文裡。這種句型不以人做主語，可以避免予人主觀獨斷的印象。

習　題　117

　　按照例句把下面的句子改成用 get 的被動句。

Example:

　　A bandit killed him last year. → *He got killed by a bandit last year.*

1. Peter defeated Dick in the contest.

2. Somone shot the man in the arm.

3. The teacher punished Mary for not being punctual.

4. The master hit the poor boy every day.

5. The police found the missing boy.

6. Bill has disappointed me before.

7. They are building a new hotel now.

8. The man has been whipping the dog for more than an hour.

9. His friends blamed him for the mistake he made.

10. Somebody used to beat that poor animal every day.

參考：在口語英語裡，我們常用 get + V-en 來表示被動。用 get 的被動句常表示「行動」而用 Be 動詞的被動句常表示因動作而引起的「狀態」。比較：

　　The man *was killed* when they found him.

　　　　（被殺死的狀態「已經死了」。）

　　The man *got killed* when he was alone in the house.

　　　　（被殺死的行為「被殺了」。）

習　題　118

把下面的句子改成被動語態。

1. He grabbed it from his hand.

2. They will put the horse in a stable.

3. He has already written the letter.

4. They are going to deliver it tomorrow.

5. Someone asked him a very difficult question.

6. People ought not to speak about such things in public.

7. Somebody has locked the box and I can't open it.

8. Her beauty struck me deeply.

9. You needn't think you took me in by your joke.

10. They told you to be here by six o'clock, didn't they?

11. Did the noise frighten you?

12. The doctor had to operate on him to find out what was wrong.

13. Did nobody ever teach you how to swim?

14. They did nothing until he came.

15. A sudden increase in water pressure would break the dam.

16. Men can shell cities from a distance of several miles.

17. Who can finish that?

18. I hate people looking at me.

19. It is time for her to put the children to bed.

20. People shan't speak to me as if I were a child.

21. Don't let the others see you.

22. The police are sure to ask you that question.

23. I should love someone to take me out to dinner.

24. I can assure you I will arrange everything in time. (Two passives.)

25. One cannot eat an orange if nobody has peeled it. (Two passives.)

26. They tell me somebody has shot your uncle. (Two passives.)

27. Naturally one expects you to interest yourself in the job they have offered you. (Three passives.)

28. It must have disappointed him terribly that people told him they didn't want him. (Three passives.)

29. We haven't moved anything since they sent you away to cure you. (Three passives.)

30. Nobody would have stared at him if they had told him beforehand what clothes one had to wear in such a place. (Three passives.)

31. They would have to look into the question of how to release themselves without people bringing them to trial. (Three passives.)

32. People no longer say that anyone inhabits the moon any more than Mars. (Three passives.)

參考一：注意以 Who 帶頭的 wh- 問句的被動式，例如：

Who can finish that?

    → *By whom* can that be finished?

參考二：注意動名詞，不定詞或原式動詞片語中所含有的被動式，例如：

I hate *people looking at me*.

    → I hate *being looked at* (*by people*).

It's time *for her to put the children to bed*.

    → It's time *for the children to be put to bed by her*.

Don't let *the others see you*.

    → Don't let *yourself be seen by the others*.

第7章
假設、願望與提議

7-1. 表示假設語氣的動詞

在這一章裡，我們要特別討論下面幾種結構裡面動詞的用法：

(1) 表示與事實相反的假設的子句：

If I *knew* how to swim, I *would go* to the beach every day.

If I *had known* how to swim last summer, I *would have gone* to the beach every day.

(2) 由 wish (that), as if, it is time (that), would rather (that) 等所引導的子句：

I wish I *knew* English well.

He looks as if he *were* very sick.

It is time you *went* to bed.

I would rather you *stayed* at home.

(3) 由 suggest that, it is important that 等所引導的子句：

The doctor suggested that the patient *stop* smoking.

It is important that he *follow* directions.

在這些句子裡，動詞的用法與前面幾章裡所討論的用法不同。在 (1) 與 (2) 表示假設與希望的例句裡面，所用的動詞雖然是過去式，但是所講的卻常常是指現在或是未來的事情。在 (3) 表示提議的例句裡面，動詞的用法不但違背了時式一致的原則（在過去式動詞後面的子句裡面應該用過去式），而且第三身單數的動詞也沒有加 -（e）s。這種動詞的用法，有些文法書上叫做**假設語氣**（subjunctive mood），以與叙述事實的**直說語氣**（indicative mood）區別。

就動詞的形式來說，英語動詞的假設語氣與直說語氣沒有什麼分別。譬如，「假設法過去式」（Subjunctive Past）與直說法過去式一樣，唯一的例外是在假設語氣裡常常用 were 而不用 was。

假設法過去式：

If I (you, he, she, we, they, etc.) *worked* harder, ……

If I (you, he, she, we, they, etc.) *were* rich, ……

假設法過去進行式：

If I (you, he, she, we, they, etc.) *were living* in Africa, ……

假設法過去完成式：

If I (you, he, she, we, they, etc.) *had worked* hader, ……

If I (you, he, she, we, they, etc.) *had been* rich, ……

假設法過去完成行式：

If I (you, he, she, we, they, etc.) *had been living* in Africa, ……

同樣地，「假設法現在式」（Subjunctive Present）也與直說法現在式一樣，唯一的例外是 Be 動詞（am, is, are）統統用 be，第三身單數的動詞不加 -（e）s。

假設法現在式：

It is important that I (you, he, she, we, they, etc.) *work* harder.

It is important that I (you, he, she, we, they, etc.) *be* there by nine o'clock.

7-2. 表示假設的句子

表示假設的句子通常都由兩個子句合成。一個是由 if（或其他連詞如 unless, even if, suppose, supposing, provided, in case 等）帶頭而表示假設的從屬子句，另外一個是表示結論的主要子句。我們把第一個子句叫做「**如果子句**」（if-clause），把第二個子句叫做「**結果子句**」（answer-clause）。

If-Clause	Answer-Clause

If he comes, I will tell him.

If I knew him, I would ask him to come.

表示假設的句子，從用法上可以分成四種：(1) 可能的假設（Future-possible），(2) 可疑的假設（Future-unlikely），(3) 與現在的事實相反的假設（Present-unreal），(4) 與過去的事實相反的假設（Past-unreal）。

習　題　119

讀一讀下面的句子，然後用 in 和 unless 把兩個表示假設的句子連起來。

Examples:

The weather is nice. I'll go to town.

> *If the weather is nice, I'll go to town.*

> *Unless the weather is nice, I won't go to town.*

You don't have an appointment. You can't see the doctor.

> *If you don't have an appointment, you can't see the doctor.*

> *Unless you have an appointment, you can't see the doctor.*

1. You study hard. You will get a scholarship.

2. You don't keep your promises. You'll lose your friends.

3. You tell me what you want. I can get it for you.

4. He doesn't know the way. He might get lost.

5. It's very cold. We'll probably have snow.

6. I'm not mistaken. That is Mr. Jones.

7. The weather was warm. I swam.

8. He had a good book to read. He didn't go to bed early.

9. She didn't know the answer. She wouldn't give the information.

10. Mr. Miller didn't have a newspaper to read. He didn't enjoy his breakfast.

7-3. 可能的假設

第一類的假設是**可能的假設**（future-possible）。這是對於未來的事情的假設，並且假設它是可能（或很可能）實現的。這個時候，「如果子句」用現在式，「結果子句」用未來式：

If-Clause	Answer-Clause	
V(-s)	will shall may can must be going to, etc.	V

If I *see* him, I *will tell* him.

If he *comes*, I *may go* with him.

If you *try*, you *can do* it.

If you *buy* that car, *drive* carefully.

同樣地，在由 until, when, as soon as, before, after, while, by the time, the moment 等所引導的副詞子句裡面，我們也用現在式來指未來時間：

If I *see* him, I will tell him.

When I *see* him, I will tell him.

As soon as I *see* him, I will tell him.

I will wait here until he *comes*.

He will come after he *has finished* the work.

Mother will have prepared your lunch before you *come* back.

You may read the magazine while you *are waiting*.

參考一： 在非常正式的書面英語裡（例如有關法律的文件中），「如果子句」有時候用動詞的基本式（即第三身單數主語動詞不加 -（e）s）。

If any person *be* found guilty, he shall have the right of appeal.

參考二： 對於過去的事情，我們也可以敘述可能的假設。這個時候，「如果子句」與「結果子句」都用過去式，例如：

If you *came* to the meeting yesterday, I *didn't* see you.

    (= I don't know whether you came to the meeting yesterday. But if you did, I didn't see you.)

習　題　120

把括號裡面的動詞改為適當的形式。

1. If dinner is not ready, I (go) without it.

2. I won't go unless he (invite) me.

3. If it (be) fine tomorrow, I'm going to play tennis.

4. I plan to wait here until the mail (arrive).

5. Keep an eye on my bag while I (get) my ticket.

6. Please give him this report as soon as you (see) him.

7. If you (not arrive) on time, you will not get a seat.

8. If he wants to play the violin, I (play) the piano for him.

9. We (not find) our seats until the concert has begun.

10. Sit down and when you (rest) I'll show you the garden.

7-4. 可疑的假設

　　第二類的假設是**可疑的假設**（future-unlikely）。這種假設含有「萬一」的意思，實現的可能性較第一類為少。這個時候，「如果子句」用 should（不用 would）與動詞的基本式，「結果子句」用 would, should, could, might 與動詞的基本式，偶爾也可以用未來單純式或祈使句。

If-Clause	Answer-Clause	
should V	would, should, could, might will, can, may, must, etc.	V

　　If I *should see* him, I *would tell* him.

　　If he *should come*, I *might go* with him.

　　If I *should have* the money on Monday, I *will pay* you.

　　If you *should see* him, *tell* him to wait.

　　如果要強調某種假設將來決無實現的可能（也就是「不可能的假設」），那麼就用 were to 來代替 should。這個時候「結果子句」就一定要用 would, should,

— 201 —

could 或 might 與動詞的基本式。這種句式出現於較為正式的書面英語裡。

If-Clause	Answer-Clause
were to V	$\left\{\begin{array}{l} \textbf{would} \\ \textbf{should} \\ \textbf{could} \\ \textbf{might} \end{array}\right\}$ V

If you *were to* buy a car, it *would cost* you a lot of money.

If I *were to* see him, I *might know* him.

習 題 121

依照例句寫出表示可能的假設與可疑的假設的句子。

Example:　　have the time / go swimming

　　　　　　If I have the time, I will go swimming.

　　　　　　If I should have the time. I would (/ will) go swimming.

1. have enough money / go boating
2. find a bicycle / go riding
3. buy a pole / go fishing
4. have the time / go hiking
5. stay near a lake / go swimming
6. stay near a lake / go boating
7. buy a bicycle / go riding
8. see a high mountain / go hiking
9. see a river / go fishing
10. get a boat / go boating

7-5. 不可能的假設：與現在的事實相反的假設

第三類的假設是「不可能的假設」，也就是與事實不符的假設。這種假設又可以分兩種：一種是與現在的事實相反的假設（present-unreal），一種是與過去的事實相反的假設（past-unreal）。與現在的事實相反的假設，「如果子句」用動詞的過去式（Be 動詞通通用 were），「結果子句」用 would, should, could, might 與動詞的基本式。

If-Clause	Answer-Clause
$\left\{\begin{array}{l}\text{V-ed}\\\text{were}\end{array}\right\}$	$\left\{\begin{array}{l}\text{would}\\\text{should}\\\text{could}\\\text{might}\end{array}\right\}$ V

If he *had* money now, he *might* buy the car.

If I *saw* him, I *would tell* him.

If I *were*n't so busy, I *should go* with you.

If today *were* a holiday, you *could go* to the beach.

　　在這些句子裡面所表示的假設都與現在的事實不符。例如「他現在沒有錢，但是如果他有錢就可能買那部車子」，又如「我現在很忙，但是如果我不忙就會跟你一道去」。

參考：在口語英語中常用 I was, he was 等來代替 I were, he were. 例如：

If John *were*〔*was*〕here, we would learn the truth.

If it *were*〔*was*〕to rain, we should get wet.

習　題　**122**

依照例句寫出表示可能的假設與不可能的假設的句子。

Example: have time / will write some letters

　　If he has time, he will write some letters.

　　If he had time, he would write some letters.

1. make an appointment / can see the doctor

2. slip on the ice / may break his leg

3. don't get sick / won't need a doctor

4. haven't enough money / can't buy a new car

5. study hard / will get good marks

習　題　123

按照句子的意思把括號裡面的動詞改為適當的形式。

1. I (show) you how to do it if I knew myself.

2. They would do it if they (can).

3. The Green Lake (be) ideal for a holiday, if there were not so many people there.

4. I would buy that hat if it (be) not so expensive.

5. I would knit another sweater if I (have) more wool.

6. My uncle would be able to help us if he (be) here.

7. If you (want) me to help you, why didn't you say so?

8. If she were older, she (have) more sense.

9. If you (read) that paper carefully, you would understand it.

10. I should be very grateful if you (will) do that for me.

參考：在徵求別人同意的時候，要用比較客氣的說法，就是在「如果子句」裡 if 的後面加上 will 或 would。

> If you *will* wait a moment, I'll cook you a supper.
>
> I would *tell* you everything, if you *would* just believe me.

7-6. 不可能的假設：與過去的事實相反的假設

第二種不可能的假設是與過去的事實相反的假設（past-unreal）；「如果子句」用動詞的過去完成式，「結果子句」用 would, should, could, might 與動詞的完成式。

If-Clause	Answer-Clause
had + V-en	would / should / could / might $\rbrace$ + have + V-en

> If he *had had* money last week, he *might have bought* the car.
>
> If I *had seen* him, I *would have told* him.

If I *hadn't been* so busy, I *should have gone* with you.

If yesterday *had been* a holiday, you *could have gone* to the beach.

在這些句子裡面所表示的假設，都是與過去的事實不符的假設。例如，「我事實上沒有看到他，但是要是看到的話我就會告訴他的」。又如，「昨天不是假日，但是要是假日的話你就可以到海邊去了」。

習　題　124

依照例句改為與現在及過去的事實相反的假設。

Example: If I have a car, I will go to the beach.

         If I had a car, I would go to the beach.

         If I had had a car, I would have gone to the beach.

1. If you study hard, you will pass.

2. If he has enough money, he will buy a new suit.

3. If he doesn't have enough money, he can't buy a new car.

4. I want to go if Joe does.

5. I won't get lost if I take the map.

6. If the news spreads, everyone will come to see the boy.

7. My wife doesn't mind if I bring a friend home to dinner.

8. If we get there in time, we can see the circus pass by.

9. If the troops advance, they may soon meet the enemy.

10. I'll pay for supper tomorrow if you'll pay tonight.

習　題　125

按照句子的意思把括號裡面的動詞改為適當的形式。

1. I (go) if I had known.

2. If the dog had not woke us, we (never hear) the burglar.

3. The dog (bite) you if it had not been tied up.

4. The child (be killed) if the train hadn't stopped quickly.

5. I should have come yesterday if I (have) nothing to do.

6. We should not have dispatched the goods if they (not be) in good condition.

7. I would have come sooner if I (know) you were here.

8. If she (not answer) the telephone, she would never have heard the good news.

9. It (be) better if they hadn't come.

10. If he had fallen into the river, he (be drowned).

習 題 126

依照例句用假設句表達下面的話。

Examples:

I don't have a pole, so I can't go fishing.

If I had a pole, I could go fishing.

The climate wasn't cool, and we didn't grow apples.

If the climate had been cool, we would have grown apples.

1. I don't have a bicycle, so I can't go riding.

2. I have a bicycle, so I can go riding.

3. I didn't have heavy shoes, so I couldn't go hiking.

4. I had heavy shoes, so I could go hiking.

5. We don't have enough rain, and we can't grow rice.

6. We didn't grow grapes, and we couldn't make wine.

7. I didn't know you were there, so I didn't telephone.

8. Betty got up on time, and she caught the bus.

9. She speaks English perfectly, so she won't have to be in this class.

10. He didn't start earlier, so he didn't catch the train.

習 題 127

依照例句用 if 和 not 改寫下面的句子。

Example:

Mr. Bell's car hit a taxi last night because he was driving too fast.

Mr. Bell's car would not have hit a taxi last night if he had not been driving

too fast.

1. He was driving too fast because he needed to get home quickly.

2. He needed to get home quickly because his family was in danger.

3. His family was in danger because his house was on fire.

4. His house was on fire because there were many cans of paint in his basement.

5. There were many cans of paint in his basement because he was planning to paint his kitchen.

6. He was planning to paint his kitchen himself because he didn't have enough money to pay someone else high wages for painting it.

7. The fire started because the cans of paint were too near the furnace.

8. His car hit that taxi because he wasn't driving carefully.

9. He wasn't driving carefully because he was worrying about the fire.

10. He will have to go to court next Wednesday because his car hit that taxi last night.

習　題　128

依照例句改寫下面的句子，使 had、should、were 出現在句首。

Examples:

> If I had known, I would never have gone.
>
> *Had I known, I would never have gone.*
>
> If you should decide to buy a car, please tell me.
>
> *Should you decide to buy a car, please tell me.*
>
> If I were a bird, I could fly to you.
>
> *Were I a bird, I could fly to you.*

1. If it should stop raining, I would go for a walk.

2. If they were stronger, they could lift the table.

3. If they had been stronger, they could have lifted the table.

4. If he were to listen more carefully, he wouldn't make so many mistakes.

5. I would go to the university if I were accepted.

6. I would have taken music lessons last year if I had had time.

7. If I had known the answer, I would have told it.

8. You would be as surprised as I if I should become a great artist.

9. If Shakespeare were alive, he would have been very surprised at our actors.

10. If the policeman hadn't shown me the way, I would have got lost.

參考：在比較正式的書面英語裡，常把 had, should, were, could 提前到句首，去取代連詞 if, suppose 等：

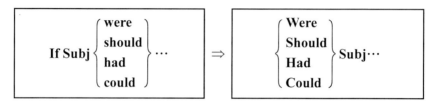

> *Were* it (= if it were) not for his idleness, he would be a good student.
>
> *Should* anybody (= if anybody should) call, say I will not be home till evening.
>
> *Had* it not (= if it had not) been for your help, I would have been ruined.

7-7. 表示願望的句子：wish (that) + 子句

我們常用動詞 wish 來表示無法實現或不容易實現的願望。因此，wish 後面的子句常用假設法語氣，也就是動詞要用過去式。

(1) 對於現在或未來的願望用過去單純式，過去進行式（Be 動詞統統用 were），或 would, should, could, might 與動詞的基本式：

wish		
	V-ed, were	now
	were V-ing	today
	would should could might } V	tomorrow this week this month this year

> I am not a scientist, but I wish I *were*.
>
> He has freckles, but he wishes he *didn't*.

I *wish* there *were* no class today.

We *wish* that you *were coming* with us.

　　(= We are sorry you are not coming with us.)

He wishes that he *could fly* like a bird.

　　(= He wishes to fly like a bird.)

They wish that you *would change* the subject.

　　(= They want you to change the subject.)

　(2) 對於過去未能實現的願望用動詞的過去完成式，過去完成進行式，或 would, should, might 與動詞的完成式：

wish	had V-en	yesterday two days ago last night
	would should could might } have V-en	last week last month last year three years ago
	had been V-ing	all day all morning all afternoon

I wish that I *had taken* your advice.

　　(= I am sorry I didn't take your advice.)

She wishes that she *hadn't bought* a new car.

　　(= She is sorry she bought a new car.)

They wish they *could have been* here for the class reunion.

　　(= They are sorry they could not be here.)

I wish you *hadn't been playing* all day.

　　(= I am sorry you have been playing all day.)

參考：有一些慣用的成語用「假設法現在式」（也就是動詞的本式）來表示願望。

(God) *bless* you! God *save* the Queen! Long *live* the king!

Grammar *be hanged!*（帶有玩笑的口氣）

在比較正式的英語裡用 may 與動詞的基本式來表示願望。這個時候，may 要提前放在句首：

May God *bless* you!

May you *have* a long and happy life!

May we never *forget* each other!

在一般口語裡就用祈使句來表示願望：

Have a good time! (= May you have a good time!)

Enjoy yourselves! (= May you enjoy yourselves!)

習 題 129

在空白裡面填進適當形式的動詞或助動詞。否定式用簡寫式 n't。

Examples:

My parents aren't here now, but I wish they *were*.

I often make foolish mistakes; I wish I *didn't*.

1. My exercises aren't always right; I wish they _____.

2. There are often mistakes on my compositions; I wish there _____.

3. I can't speak English very well; I wish I _____.

4. Today isn't a holiday; I wish it _____.

5. I don't like to study; I wish I _____.

6. They live in a small town; they wish they _____ in New York.

7. Tom has lost his pen; he wishes he _____.

8. I didn't get a good mark on our last test; I wish I _____.

9. Bob has been playing all the morning; he wishes he _____.

10. I have just bought a very expensive watch; I wish I _____.

習 題 130

依照例句用 I wish 改寫下面的句子。

Examples:

　　I'm late to class almost every day. →

　　　I wish I weren't late to class almost every day.

　　He wasn't home when I called. →

　　　I wish he had been home when I called.

1. It's time to leave now.
2. I didn't take any money with me.
3. I have to study now.
4. I failed the examination.
5. I am living in a big city.
6. He doesn't know how to speak French.
7. It has been raining all weekend.
8. We must go home early.
9. I couldn't help you with your problem.
10. My friend will be working all day tomorrow.

習　題　131

　　依照例句用括號裡面的語詞改寫下面的句子。

Examples:

　　They can't come. (If only)

　　　If only they could come!

　　Money does not grow on trees. (O that)

　　　O that money grew on trees!

1. They aren't here. (I wish)
2. I didn't go to the movies with you last night. (If only)
3. I can't speak English as well as you. (If only)
4. She doesn't have a handsome husband. (She wishes)
5. Today is not a holiday. (O that)
6. He was not invited to the party. (He wishes)
7. I didn't know it yesterday. (If only)
8. My parents are not here with me. (O that)

9. He won't tell me the whole story. (If only)

10. We are not living in a dreamland. (Don't you wish)

參考：除了 wish 以外，我們也可以用 if only, O that, would that, would to God 等較文言的說法來表示願望：

> *If only* the rain would stop! (= I wish the rain would stop.)
>
> *If only* I had known! (= I wish I had known.)
>
> *O that my father were* still alive! (= I wish my father were still alive.)
>
> *Would to God* he would return safely! (= I wish he would return safely.)

7-8. as if (as though) + 子句

用連詞 as if、as though「彷彿，好像」所引導的子句通常表示與事實不符的情況，因此裡面的動詞也常用假設語氣；對於現在的事情用過去單純式或過去進行式，對於過去的事情用過去完成式或過去完成進行式：

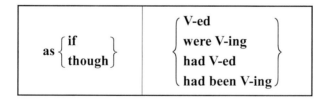

He looks as if he *were* very sick.

She looks as if she *were preparing* her lessons.

He looked as though he *had lost* his last friend.

They looked as though they *had been fighting*.

習 題 132

按照句子的意思，把括號裡面的動詞改成適當的形式。

1. He looks as if he (be) very tired.

2. He looked as if he (spend) all night studying.

3. He acts as if he (be) a Frenchman.

4. He talks as though he (live) in the United States many years.

5. He acted as if he (never see) us.

6. He talks as if he (be) a millionaire.

7. He laughed as if it (be) a big joke.

8. He treated her as if she (be) an old friend.

9. I feel as if my head (be) on fire.

10. It was as if the earth (stop) moving.

7-9. it is time (that) + 子句；would rather (that) + 子句

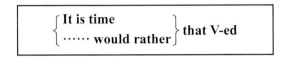

　　It is time「該是……的時候了」，後面的子句通常都用過去單純式來表示現在或未來該做的事情：

　　　　It's time we *started*. (= It is time for us to start.)

　　　　It's about time you *settled* down. (= It is about time for you to settle down.)

同樣地，在 would rather「寧願」後面的子句，也用過去單純式來表示現在或未來的事情：

　　　　I would rather you *stayed* at home.

　　　　　(= I would prefer you to stay at home.)

　　　　He would rather people *didn't* talk about his family.

　　　　　(= He would prefer people not to talk about his family.)

習　題　133

　　把括號裡面的動詞改成適當的形式。

1. It's time you (go) to bed.　　　　2. I'd rather you (pay) me now.

3. Jane wishes she (not go) last night.

4. If only he (try) again tomorrow!

5. It's about time you (get) the dinner ready.

6. I wish I (know) how to swim.

7. I would rather you (come) tomorrow than today.

8. He looks as though he (be) drunk.

9. It's high time you (write) a letter to your family.

10. I would rather your sister (stay) with me tonight.

7-10. 表示「提議」、「請求」、「命令」的句子

suggest, recommend, advise, propose, move, ask, require, request, pray, plead, demand, insist, urge, maintain, order, command, instruct, direct, intend, arrange, prefer, desire, authorize, etc.	(that)	(should) V

在表示「提議」、「請求」或「命令」的動詞（如 suggest, request, order 等）後面的子句，常用動詞的基本式（「假設法現在」）：

The doctor *suggested* that the patient *stop* smoking.

We *requested* that he *give* us another chance.

The judge *ordered* that the prisoner *be* set free.

She *demanded* that she *be given* a fair trial.

如果這個子句是否定句，那麼就把 not 放在基本式動詞的前面：

I suggest that we *not do* it now.

She insisted that you *not be* told.

在口語英語中也有人用 should 與動詞的基本式來代替假設法現在式：

The doctor suggested that the patient *should stop* smoking.

She insisted that you *should* not *be* told.

習　題　134

把括號裡面的動詞改成適當的動詞。

1. He insisted that she (go) with them at once.

2. The teacher demands that everyone (be) in his seat at nine o'clock.

3. The doctor recommended that Paul (take) the medicine regularly.

4. They suggested that we (wait) for them at the station.

5. The director asked that Betty (not stand) in the front row.

6. The rules required that they (be) in uniform.

7. The invitation requested that she (answer) promptly.

8. My suggestion is that he (have) another glass of punch.

9. The captain gave orders that they (not quarrel) with each other.

10. They propose that everyone (write) a composition as homework.

參考：除了動詞以外，在表示提議、請求、命令的名詞子句（例如 make a suggestion that ...,　his suggestion is that ...,　give an order that ...,　my proposal was that ...）裡面，也常用動詞的基本式：

The doctor *made a suggestion* that the patient *stop* smoking right away.

His suggestion is that each student *visit* the museum every week.

7-11. 表示「重要」、「需要」、「適當」的句子

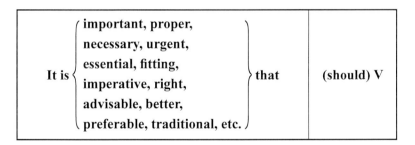

在表示「重要」、「需要」或「適當」的形容詞（如 important, necessary, proper 等）後面的子句，也常用動詞的基本式：

It is *important* that he *follow* the doctor's directions.

Is it *necessary* that he *be* there by noon?

It is *essential* that I *not be disturbed* before I finish my letter.

有些人也用 should 與動詞的基本式：

It is important that he *should follow* the doctor's instructions.

習 題 135

把括號裡面的動詞改為適當的形式。

1. It is important that she (meet) us all here at eight o'clock.

2. It is necessary that you (not discuss) the matter with anyone.

3. It's urgent that he (come) and (join) the rest of us.

4. It is essential that this (be) done immediately.

5. It is imperative that you (stop) smoking.

6. Is it necessary that Bob (take) an examination?

7. It is important that he (sign) the contract and (return) it at once.

8. Is it traditional that the table (be) decorated?

9. It is advisable that a lawyer (write) the contract.

10. They admitted the necessity that Mary (be) told ahead of time.

習 題 136

依照例句把下面的句子連起來。

Examples:

   This should be done immediately. That's essential.

   → *It's essential that this be done immediately.*

   She should wait for him. He recommended that.

   → *He recommended that she wait for him.*

1. He should return the book promptly. That's imperative.

2. I should come back a little later. He demanded that.

3. She should take the money. He suggested that.

4. You should not mention this to your brother. He insisted on that.

5. Everyone should practice English constantly. That's essential.

6. You should not make the same mistake again. That's important.

7. All people should be treated equal. The law requires that.

8. No smoking should be allowed. That's imperative.

9. Every student should work harder. The principal urged that.

10. I should not serve them Japanese food. They prefer that.

參考：在連詞 lest「以免」：後面的子句裡面，也常用動詞的基本式或 should 與動詞的基本式。比較：

　　　She walked softly *lest* she (*should*) *disturb* her husband.

　　　She walked softly *so that she would / might not* disturb her husband.

　　　She walked softly *for fear* she *might / should* disturb her husband.

習　題　137

按照句子的意思把括號裡面的動詞改成適當的形式。

1. You will be ill if you (eat) so much.

2. I (go) with you if I had known.

3. If my car (not break) down, I should have caught the train.

4. If you (read) that book carefully, you would understand it.

5. If the children (be) good, they can stay up late.

6. If they had waited, they (find) me.

7. We (enjoy) the play better if it had not been so long.

8. I shouldn't have thought it possible unless I (see) it.

9. I'm sure she will do well if she (go) to the university.

10. I'm sure my sister would go out with you if you (ask) her nicely.

11. If dinner is not ready, I (go) without it.

12. If you (go) away, please write to me.

13. If you (be) in, I should have given it to you.

14. If you (not turn) off that noisy radio, I will scream!

15. If men (be) only more reasonable, there would be no more war.

16. I wouldn't do that if I (be) you.

17. You would be taking a great risk if you (invest) your money in that company.

18. If it (be) convenient, let's meet at nine o'clock.

19. If I (have) the courage, I should have answered him back.

20. If the sentence that had "had had" had had "had", it (be) correct.

習　題　138

按照句子的意思把括號裡面的動詞改成適當的形式。

1. I wish I (know) his name.

2. It's time we all (go) home.

3. I'd rather you (go) now.

4. It's about time you (get) the tea ready.

5. Don't you wish you (come) earlier?

6. Would you mind if I (not go) with you?

7. He acts as if he (know) Russian perfectly.

8. If only he (not eat) so much garlic!

9. If only he (not drink) so much milk last night!

10. I'd rather you (pay) me now. Suppose he (ask) me for the money tomorrow!

11. Suppose I (get) there late!

12. What if he (not come) with us?

13. It's high time you (have) a haircut.

14. I feel as if my head (be) on fire.

15. A person who (refuse) to eat would be dead in a month.

16. He said he wished he (never see) me.

17. You look as if you (can) do with a drink.

18. Would to God you (be) a better husband to me!

19. Do you mind if I (open) a window?

20. (Will) you mind if I came a little late?

21. I'd rather you (give) me a new one instead of having it repaired as you did.

22. If only I (know) earlier, I'd have sent you a telegram.

23. I felt as if I (be pulled) through a hedge backwards.

24. I wish I (not break) it.

25. He came in, looking as if he (see) a ghost.

26. Isn't it about time you (set) to and (do) some work?

27. My wife says she wishes I (be) a thousand miles away; indeed I wish I (be).

28. He said it was essential that this (be done) at once.

29. He demanded that I (come) back a little later.

30. We all think it imperative that he (go) with us.

31. He recommended that she (get) in touch with him as soon as possible.

32. They made a suggestion that you (take) the money.

33. He copied the letter very carefully lest he (make) any mistakes.

34. Do you think it necessary she (be informed) of the accident?

35. He ran away lest he (be) seen.

36. Lest the plan (be discovered), we should take some precautions.

37. His instruction was that we (not borrow) any money from the bank.

38. Did he receive the order that he (start) out right away?

39. I'd rather we (have) a five-day week like they have in the United States.

40. We're going to propose that every worker (have) two weeks' vacation.

參考：表示條件或假設的句子，有時可以用關係子句的形式表達，例如：

> Students who *have finished* their assignments *may go* home.

比較：If they have finished their assignments they may go home.

> Students who *hadn't reviewed* their lessons *wouldn't have passed* the exam.

比較：If they *hadn't reviewed* their lessons, they *wouldn't have passed* the exam.

第8章
動詞的修飾語

8-1. 動詞的修飾語

英語的動詞可以用幾種不同的方法來加以修飾，使它變成動詞片語。在第三章裡我們曾經學過動詞可以用助動詞來修飾。當我們在句子裡遇到助動詞的時候，我們就知道助動詞後頭總有一個動詞要出現：

助動詞	動詞
can	come
should	come
is	coming
has	come

動詞也可以用「介詞片語」（prepositional phrase）或「從屬子句」（subordinated sentence）來修飾。當一個動詞同時用介詞片語與從屬子句修飾的時候，通常的詞序是介詞片語在前、從屬子句在後：

動詞	介詞片語	從屬子句
comes	on his bicycle	when he has time
will speak	to the group	if he is asked

但是最常見的動詞修飾語還是副詞。

8-2. 副　詞

修飾動詞的副詞通常表示「時間」（time），「場所」（place），或「狀態」（manner）。

	場所	狀態	時間
He went	home	suddenly	yesterday.
He went	there	thus	then.

因此我們可以把副詞分為三大類：「場所副詞」、「狀態副詞」、「時間副

詞」。

8-3. 狀態副詞 thus 類

　　在這三類副詞中，最大的一類是**狀態副詞**（manner adverbs），如 suddenly, sadly, happily, quickly, slowly 等。差不多所有的狀態副詞都是由形容詞加字尾 -ly 而成的：sudden → sudden*ly*, sad → sad*ly*, happy → happ*ily*。

> He went home *suddenly*.
>
> Bob told his story *sadly*.
>
> Mary sang *happily* yesterday.
>
> They walked to the river *slowly*.

　　可是有一小群的狀態副詞，字形卻與形容詞一樣，不加字尾 -ly，如 fast, hard, well, fine, straight。

> The car moved *fast*.
>
> My brother works very *hard*.
>
> She did her job quite *well*.
>
> We are doing *fine*.

　　一般說來，狀態副詞通常都放在它所要修飾的動詞後面。可是如果動詞後面還有賓語的話，那就放在賓語後面：

Subj	VI	Adv-m
	VT　Obj	Adv-m

> She answered *quickly*.
>
> She answered the question *quickly*.
>
> I always drive *fast*.
>
> I always drive my car *fast*.

字尾帶有 -ly 的狀態副詞有時候還可以放在動詞的前面：

$$\boxed{\textbf{Subj Adv-m V} \cdots}$$

> She *quickly* answered (the question).

He *suddenly* went home.

They *slowly* walked to the river.

We *happily* sang the song that was composed for the occasion.

甚至也可以提前放在句首：

```
Adv-m Subj V …
```

Suddenly he went home.

Slowly they walked to the river.

習 題 139

依照例句改寫下面的句子。

Examples:

He is a slow talker. → *He talks slowly.*

She is a good teacher. → *She teaches well.*

1. I am a slow learner.　　　　　2. He is a bad painter.

3. She is a fine singer.　　　　　4. You are a clear thinker.

5. Bob is a fast driver.　　　　　6. Mr. Taylor is a straight shooter.

7. Mrs. Smith is a patient listener.　　8. My uncle is a steady worker.

9. Jane is a careful reader.　　　10. Jack is a wonderful speaker.

習 題 140

依照例句回答下面的問句。

Example:

What kind of teacher is she? (good)

She is a good teacher; she teaches well.

1. What kind of swimmer is he? (fine)

2. What kind of worker is he? (hard)

3. What kind of typist is she? (fast)

4. What kind of driver are you? (careful)

5. What kind of dancer are you? (bad)

6. What kind of cook is she? (nice)

7. What kind of students are they? (diligent)

8. What kind of English teacher is he? (excellent)

9. What kind of tennis player are you? (poor)

10. What kind of speaker is he? (fast and clear)

11. What kind of reader is she? (slow but careful)

12. What kind of storyteller is he? (nervous and not very good)

習　題　141

把括號裡面正確的字選出來。

1. This cake tastes too (sweet, sweetly) for me.

2. The cook tasted the cake (delightful, delightfully).

3. The man looks (cold, coldly) to us.

4. The man looked (cold, coldly) at us.

5. A stranger appeared (sudden, suddenly) at the door.

6. He appeared (uneasy, uneasily) before the strangers.

7. She feels (strong, strongly) again after her illness.

8. She feels (strong, strongly) about this question.

9. She felt (uneasy, uneasily) in her pockets for the money.

10. She felt (safe, safely) with her husband.

習　題　142

把括號裡面的狀態副詞放在動詞或賓語的後面。

Example:

The boy climbed the tree. (easily)

The boy climbed the tree easily.

1. The boy walked into the room. (boldly)

2. The wind blew all afternoon. (violently)

3. Please answer my letter. (promptly)

4. They arrived after their long journey. (safely)

5. The firemen climbed their ladders. (rapidly)

6. She agreed to our proposal. (willingly)

7. She put the dishes away. (carefully)

8. The children are playing in the park. (happily)

9. He eats breakfast early in the morning. (quickly)

10. The package was wrapped. (attractively)

8-4. 場所副詞：there 類

第二類的副詞是**場所副詞**（place adverbs）：如 there, here, home, outside, inside, outdoors, indoors, upstairs, downstairs 等是。

Please, don't come *here*.

He went *home*.

Mary stayed *inside*.

Farm workers spend most of their time *outdoors*.

有些場所副詞有 -wise, -ways, -ward（s）等字尾，如 -sideways, crosswise, lengthwise, forward, backward, southward。

The crab always walks *sideways*.

The car lays *crosswise* in the road.

The boy walked *backward*.

The ship is sailing *southward*.

場所副詞通常都緊放在動詞後面或賓語後面：

They are talking *outside*.

We met (each other) *at the station*.

We'll discuss the problem *upstairs*.

較長的場所副詞，有時候還可以提前放在句首。比較：

There is a gas station *three miles away*.

Three miles away there is a gas station.

習　題　143

把括號裡面的場所副詞放在句子中適當的位置。

Example:

> She is standing. (on the corner)
>
> *She is standing on the corner.*

1. The children are playing happily. (outside)

2. They are arguing violently. (upstairs)

3. I met him yesterday. (at the station)

4. He has lived for three years. (there)

5. They are discussing now. (in the other room)

6. We are staying for a few days. (here)

7. He took a walk in the morning. (in the park)

8. Is there a telephone? (here)

9. Is she waiting? (downstairs)

10. Shall we go or stay? (inside, outside)

8-5. 時間副詞：then 類

第三類的副詞是**時間副詞**（time adverbs）：如 then, now, already, soon, later, earlier, today, yesterday, tomorrow。這些副詞通常都出現在句尾：

> He is studying *now*.
>
> She went home *soon*.
>
> Bob walked away *later*.
>
> Mary cried sadly *yesterday*.

有些時間副詞，尤其是表示不確定時間的副詞，如 already, soon, later, lately, recently, immediately 等，還可以放在動詞的前面：

> Bob *later* walked away.
>
> He *already* finished his work.
>
> I will *soon* let you know.

She has *recently* published a new novel.

還有些時間副詞，通常都是表示確定時間的，還可以出現在句首：

Yesterday she went home.

Now you can come with me.

Last week Mr. Lee died of a heart attack.

習 題 144

把括號裡面的時間副詞放在句尾，並把動詞的形式適當的改變。

Examples:

I eat in the cafeteria. (everyday, yesterday, tomorrow)

I eat in the cafeteria every day.

I ate in the cafeteria yesterday.

I'll eat in the cafeteria tomorrow.

1. I read the newspaper. (every morning, yesterday, tomorrow)

2. Dick has lunch with me. (every day, yesterday, tomorrow)

3. My brother doesn't go swimming. (every summer, last summer, lately)

4. Do you see Jane? (last week, since she returned from Europe, next month)

5. I finish my coffee. (before he leaves the house, a little while ago, by the time you arrived)

習 題 145

時間副詞一般都放在場所副詞的後面。把括號裡面的副詞放在句子裡適當的位置上。

Examples:

I went to the bank. (this morning)

I went to the bank this morning.

She arrived at ten o'clock. (here)

She arrived here at ten o'clock.

1. Everyone went after class. (outside)

2. The manager will be here. (soon)

3. I saw Julie last night. (at the party)

4. I have been waiting for a long time. (in the hall)

5. She left here. (a long time ago)

6. The guests arrived from Taipei. (at six o'clock)

7. We listened to records at Bob's house. (in the evening)

8. The guard passes here. (every ten minutes)

9. People in big cities spend most of their time. (indoors)

10. The sun will go down in a little while. (behind the mountains)

習 題 146

把下面的中文時間副詞翻成英文。

1. 今天早上	2. 今天晚上	3. 明天
4. 明天晚上	5. 昨天	6. 昨天晚上
7. 這星期	8. 下星期	9. 上星期
10. 兩星期以前	11. 後天	12. 前天
13. 上上個月	14. 下下個月	15.（某一天的）第二天
16.（某一天的）前一天	17. 五月的一個早晨	18. 七月的一個下午
19. 不久以前	20. 幾個星期以前	21. 整天
22. 整夜	23. 整年	24. 每星期一次
25. 每個月三次	26.（每）隔一天	27. 三天一次
28. 五個月一次		

參考：表示時間的名詞（如 morning, week, January, spring 等）可以與 this, that, next, last 等合成許多表示時間的副詞。

　　(a) **this / that:** ～ morning (afternoon, evening); ～ week (month, term, semester, year); ～ January (February, etc.); ～ spring (summer, etc.).

　　(b) **next / last:** ～ Sunday (Monday, etc.); ～ week (month, term, semester, year); ～ January (February, etc.); ～ spring (summer, etc.).

　　(c) **(the) next / the following:** ～ day (morning, afternoon, evening, night); ～

week (month, year); ～ January (February,etc.); ～ spring (summer,etc.).

(d) **the previous / the ～ before:** ～ day (morning, afternoon, evening, night); ～ week (month, year).

(e) **tomorrow:** ～ morning; ～ afternoon; ～ evening; ～ night.

(f) **yesterday:** ～ morning; ～ afternoon; ～ evening. (cf. last night)

(g) **others:** (the) day after tomorrow; (the) day before yesterday; the week (month, year) after next; the week (month, year) before last; one morning (afternoon, evening, nignt); Sunday (Monday,etc.) morning (afternoon, evenimg, night); one day (morning,etc.) in January (February,etc.); one January (spring, etc.) morning (afternoon, etc.) ; all day long; all the night through; all the year round; all one's life through.

(h) **adverbials of frequency:** every hour (day, morning, etc.); every other day (week, month, year) ; every two (three, four, etc.) days (weeks, etc.); every second (third, fourth, etc.) day (week, etc.); once (twice, three times, etc.) a week (month, year, etc.); (every) now and then (now and again, so often); etc.

習 題 147

把括號裡面的時間副詞放在句子裡適當的位置上。

Example:

He arrived this morning. (at ten o'clock)

He arrived at ten o'clock this morning.

1. It all happened in May. (one morning)

2. School will be over in the afternoon. (by four)

3. They had a fight last week. (on Saturday afternoon)

4. They see each other at three. (Sunday afternoon)

5. The game will start at nine o'lock. (tomorrow morning)

6. We'll discuss the matter again this day. (week)

7. He worked yesterday. (all day long)

8. I saw Mrs. Wilson shortly after lunch. (yesterday)

參考：英語的時間副詞裡，比較精確的時間副詞放在前面，比較籠統的時間副詞放在後面；國語的時間副詞，則是比較籠統的時間副詞放在前面，比較精確的時間副詞放在後面。比較：

He was born at eight o'clock on Christmas morning in the year 1923.

他在一九二三年聖誕節的早上九點鐘出生。

8-6. 頻度副詞

除了上面三類副詞以外，還有一類副詞叫做**頻度副詞**（frequency adverbs）。這是表示動作或狀態在一定時間內發生次數多少的副詞，如 often, always, ever, never, seldom, sometimes, usually, generally, rarely, occasionally, every day, every week, once in a while 等。

單字的頻度副詞通常都放在 Be 動詞或助動詞的後面。如果沒有 Be 動詞或助動詞，就放在動詞的前面。換句話說，頻度副詞最常見的位置就是否定句裡 not 所出現的位置：

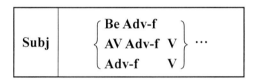

I *often* study in the library.

Jack *seldom* comes on time.

She was *never* late for class.

He has *always* wanted to be a doctor.

可是在短答句裡面，頻度副詞卻要放在 Be 動詞、助動詞、或 Do 動詞的前面：

Is he *ever* home? Yes, he *often* is.

Will he *always* drive home? Yes, he *always* will.

Do they *usually* stay home? No, they *seldom* do.

比較：

$$\left\{ \begin{array}{l} \text{He } \textit{always} \text{ comes in the morning. (He } \textit{always} \text{ does.)} \\ \text{He is } \textit{always} \text{ here in the morning. (He } \textit{always} \text{ is.)} \\ \text{He has } \textit{always} \text{ been here in the morning. (He } \textit{always} \text{ has.)} \\ \text{He must } \textit{always} \text{ work in the morning. (He } \textit{always} \text{ must.)} \end{array} \right.$$

有些頻度副詞（如 often, sometimes, usually, occasionally 等）還可以放在句首或句尾，但是最常見的位置還是句中：

$$\left\{ \begin{array}{l} \text{Tom } \textit{usually} \text{ studies at home.} \\ \text{Tom studies at home } \textit{usually.} \\ \textit{Usually} \text{ Tom studies at home.} \end{array} \right.$$

由兩個以上的字合成的頻度副詞，通常都放在句尾或句首：

$$\left\{ \begin{array}{l} \text{We go to school } \textit{every day.} \\ \textit{Every day} \text{ we go to school.} \end{array} \right.$$

$$\left\{ \begin{array}{l} \text{She comes here } \textit{once in a while.} \\ \textit{Once in a while} \text{ she comes here.} \end{array} \right.$$

習 題 148

把括號裡面的副詞放在句子裡適當的位置上。

Example:

> Jack has gone home. (already)
>
> *Jack has already gone home.*
>
> *Jack has gone home already.*

1. We go to the museum. (often)　　2. Have you been to the zoo? (ever)

3. She comes to the office on Saturdays. (occasionally)

4. I do. (always)　　5. Are you working there? (still)

6. He has been abroad. (never)　　7. They are. (often)

8. She is absent from school. (frequently)

9. I have seen him downtown. (seldom)

10. Do they live in England? (still)

11. They are found in high mountains. (sometimes)

12. Father has to work in the evening. (often)

13. He will come. (probably)

14. She was sick. (perhaps)

參考：表示推測的副詞（如 probably, perhaps, maybe, possibly）在句子中出現的
位置也跟表示頻度的副詞一樣。

習　題　149

把 already 或 yet 放在句子裡適當的位置上。

Examples:

The car has stopped.

The car has *already* stopped. / The car has stopped *already*.

The car hasn't stopped.

The car hasn't stopped *yet*. / The car *hasn't yet* stopped.

1. I have finished my homework.

2. The letter hasn't arrived. 　　　　3. He knew the answer.

4. She hasn't made progress in learning English.

5. Her sister has made great progress. 　　6. We can't get together.

7. Has he joined the army?

8. They were there when you came in.

9. We know why he is absent.

10. I don't know whether they have or not.

參考：Already 用在肯定直述句；yet 用在否定句或 yes / no 問句。

The car has *already* stopped.

The car hasn't stopped *yet*.

Has the car stopped *yet*?

用在 yes / no 問句的 *already*，表示驚訝。比較：

Is it five o'clock *yet*?「到了五點了嗎？」（單純的問句）

Is it five o'clock *already?*「（怎麼）已經到了五點了？（不會那麼快吧。）」

（表示驚訝或懷疑的問句）

習 題 150

把下面的句子改成否定句。注意肯定句與否定句裡可能要用不同的副詞。

Example:

I have already seen him. → *I haven't seen him yet.*

1. We already have the solution.   2. Bob speaks English too.

3. He is still teaching English. (two possibilities)

4. She can still sing. (two possibilities)

5. He always worked hard. (two possibilities)

6. They often go to church on Sunday. (two possibilities)

7. He sometimes gets here on time.

8. We usually have a meeting on Monday morning. (two possibilities)

9. They occasionally see each other on weekends.

10. We'll go on a picnic this weekend, too.

參考一：副詞 still 的用法與 always 很相似。比較：

$$He \begin{Bmatrix} still \\ always \end{Bmatrix} comes \ in \ the \ morning. \quad He \ is \begin{Bmatrix} still \\ always \end{Bmatrix} always \ here.$$

$$You \ can \begin{Bmatrix} still \\ always \end{Bmatrix} count \ on \ me. \quad You \begin{Bmatrix} still \\ always \end{Bmatrix} can.$$

注意，still … not 與 not … any more / longer 表示不同的含義：

John was a student, but he is *not* a student *any more / longer.*

「他再不是學生」。

Bob was not a student, and he still is *not*〔he's *still* not〕a student.

「他仍然不是學生。」

參考二：Seldom、rarely、never 是 often、usually、always 的相反詞，因為本身已經含有否定的意思，所以不能與 not 合用。Sometimes 與 occasionally 只能用在 not 的前面；often、usually、generally 可以用在 not 的前面，也可以用在 not 的後面，用在前與後所表達的意思不盡相同。比較：

$$\left\{\begin{array}{l}\text{He } \textit{seldom} \text{ comes to class on time.（○）}\\\text{He } \textit{seldom} \text{ doesn't come to class on time.（×）}\end{array}\right.$$

$$\left\{\begin{array}{l}\text{He } \textit{sometimes} \text{ doesn't come to class on time.（○）}\\\text{He doesn't } \textit{sometimes} \text{ come to class on time.（×）}\end{array}\right.$$

$$\left\{\begin{array}{l}\text{He } \textit{often} \text{ doesn't come to class on time.「他常常不準時來上課。」}\\\text{He doesn't } \textit{often} \text{ come to class on time.「他並不常常準時來上課。」}\end{array}\right.$$

習　題　151

依照例句用短答句回答下列問題。

Example:

　　　　Is he ever home? (Yes, … often) → *Yes, he often is.*

1. Do they usually stay home? (No, … seldom)

2. Does he ever study? (No, … never)

3. Is she generally there in the evening? (Yes, … usually)

4. Is she generally there in the morming? (No,… rarely)

5. Do you ever watch TV? (Yes, … often)

6. Do you often go to the movies? (Yes, … sometimes)

7. Do you always sleep late in the morning? (No, … rarely)

8. Do they still live in Japan? (Yes, … still)

9. Does he still work for your company? (No, … no longer)

10. Are you sometimes angry with your brothers? (No, … often)

習　題　152

依照例句改寫下面的句子，把斜體部分的語詞放在句首。

Examples:

　　　　He was *seldom* so angry. → *Seldom was he so angry.*

　　　　They have *never* been so late. → *Never have they been so late.*

　　　　She *rarely* visited her aunt. → *Rarely did she visit her aunt.*

1. She was *never* so angry before.

2. I *seldom* hear such beautiful music.

3. I have *never* seen so much rain.

4. We *rarely* see such beautiful scenery in our country.

5. The train has *never* been so late.

6. I *never* read such a dull book.

7. The weather is *seldom* hot here in August.

8. He was *rarely* seen with his wife.

9. Jane *never* seemed so beautiful.

10. I care *little* what he thinks of my plan.

11. You can succeed *only by hard work*.

12. You will find such nice people *in no other part of the world*.

13. Such a thing could happen *only in a hig city like New York*.

14. We saw *little* that we hadn't seen before.

15. There is such delicious fruits *nowhere else in the world*.

參考：在比較正式的英語，常常把含有否定意味的如 never、seldom、rarely（還有否定詞如 no、not、little、only 等）的頻度副詞放在句首。這個時候，句子的主語與動詞的位置必須調換：

I was never so angry. → Never *was I* so angry.

I have never been here. → Never *have I* been here.

I never came here. → Never *did I* come here.

注意：這種倒序與問句的倒序完全一樣。

8-7. 副詞的次序

(1) 當有兩類以上的副詞修飾動詞的時候，通常的次序是：「表起點的場所」（there）、「狀態」（thus）、「時間」（time）：

They	lived	here	happily	before.
He	went	home	suddenly	yesterday.
She	arrived	here	safely	this morning.
Mary	came	downstairs	angrily	just now.

(2) 當動詞的修飾語含有副詞、介詞片語，或從屬子句的時候，通常都把「單字副詞」放在最前面，「介詞片語」排在其次，「從屬子句」殿後；結果常形成 (1) 狀態、(2) 場所、(3) 時間的次序：

> She stayed comfortably at home throughout the summer.

> He went suddenly to the house at two o'clock.

> They walked angrily into the hotel when the clock struck two.

注意以 -ly 收尾的單字狀態副詞還可以放在動詞的前面：

> He *suddenly* went to the house at two o'clock.

> They *angrily* walked into the hotel when the clock struck two.

可見英語副詞的次序並不是一定不變的。

(3) 當屬於同類的兩個副詞修飾動詞的時候，要用連詞 and 或 or 把這兩個副詞連起來。

> He ate *quickly* and *greedily*.

> You can go *by train* or *by bus*.

習　題　153

把括號裡面的副詞放在句子裡適當的位置上。

1. He has prepared his lessons. (always)

2. I go for a walk on Sunday. (never)

3. Do you go for a walk on Sunday? (ever)

4. He prepares his lessons. (carefully)

5. I saw Mr. Lee in the cafeteria. (yesterday)

6. I have spoken to him about his lessons. (repeatedly)

7. He always does his work. (cheerfully)

8. We go to the theater in the summer. (rarely)

9. Nobody has a bad word to say about Jane. (ever)

10. I saw Mr. Jones on the twentieth floor. (shortly after breakfast)

習 題 154

把括號裡面的副詞放在句子裡適當的位置上。

1. Helen went. (to school, at eight o'clock)

2. I was born. (in the year 1931, at 6 a.m., on July 29th)

3. Your brother spoke to us. (in class, very rudely, this morning)

4. I drink coffee. (every morning, at home)

5. Father likes tea. (in the morning, very much)

6. Charles loved his wife. (all his life, passionately)

7. They stayed. (all day, quietly, there)

8. The letter was sent. (last week, to New York, by air mail)

9. She walked. (into the room, quietly, because her husband was sleeping)

10. Get up. (if you don't want to miss the train, tomorrow morning, early)

11. They are arguing. (in the next room, right now, in a loud voice)

12. We went. (last year, once a week, to a movie)

13. Dr. Hill graduated. (with high honors, in 1950, from our university)

14. We met the Taylors. (once in a while, unexpectedly, at the club)

15. They were discussing the project. (in the office, seriously, at that time)

16. I plan to go. (still, with my wife, to Japan, next year)

17. He comes home. (seldom, after 6 o'clock, from work, unless there is an emergency)

18. The president comes. (often, at 9 o'clock, with his secretary, in the morning)

19. They learned the news. (probably, through your friend, last night, before I told them)

20. You cannot do it. (possibly, by yourself, successfully, unless you follow the directions carefully)

第9章
感歎句與祈使句

9-1. 句子的種類

英語的句子可以根據句子的功能分成三類。這三類句子對於講話的對方發生不同的影響。第一類句子是表達命令或請求的**祈使句**（imperative sentences; requests）。祈使句要求對方做一些事情。例如：

Come here.（對方聽到這句話就要走過來。）

Please sit down.（對方聽到這句話就會坐下。）

Close the door, please.（對方聽到這句話就會關門。）

第二類的句子是提出問話的**疑問句**（interrogative sentences; questions）。疑問句要求對方回答問題。例如：

Is he a student?（對方回答 "Yes" 或 "No"。）

Are you going today or tomorrow?（對方回答 "Today" 或 "Tomorrow"。）

Where did he go?（對方回答 "Downtown"。）

第三類的句子是敘述事情的**直述句**（declarative sentences; statements)。直述句不要求對方說話或做事。例如：

He is a student.

You are closing the door.

I went downtown yesterday.

我們也可以把表達驚訝與感歎的**感歎句**（exclamatory sentences）放在這一類。例如：

What a beautiful day this is!

How beautifully she sings!

參考：除了祈使句、疑問句、敘述句以外，**招呼**（greetings）、**召喚**（calls）與**感歎**（interjections）也可以單獨成為一個句子。傳統的文法書管這些叫做**獨立成分**（independent elements）。

(1) **Greetings:**

(good) morning (day, afternoon, evening),

hi, howdy (= how are you, how do you do),

good-bye, good night, so long, see you later.

(2) **Calls:**

you there, the boy in the end seat.

(3) **Interjections:**

well, bravo, hurrah (*or* hurray), okay, oh, alas, my, dear me, ouch, oops,

phooey, tsk-tsk, whew, hush,

what the heck (*or* hell, dickens, devil),

for heavens (*or* goodness, gosh, gods) sake.

9-2. 感歎句

感歎句可以說是由直述句變來的。變的方法是：

(1) 在名詞組（NP）前面加 what，在形容詞（Adj）、副詞（Adv）前面加 how；

(2) 然後把 what 連同後面的名詞組，或 how 連同後面的形容詞、副詞移到句首來。

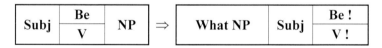

Subj	Be / V	NP	⇒	What NP	Subj	Be ! / V !

Peter is a smart student. → What a smart student Petter is!

     ∧
    what

He made a mistake. → What a mistake he made!

      ∧
     what

Subj	Be / V	Adj / Adv	⇒	How	Adj / Adv	Subj	Be! / V !

It is cold. → How cold it is!

   ∧
  how

She sings beautifully. → How beautifully she sings!
$\wedge$
how

　如果名詞組裡除了名詞以外還含有形容詞，那麼也可以變成由 how 開頭的感歎句。比較：

You have made a big mistake.
$\wedge$
what

→ *What a big mistake* you have made!

You have made a big mistake.
$\wedge$
how

→ *How big a mistake* you have made!

　注意：用 how＋名詞組開頭做感歎句的時候，名詞組一定要含有冠詞 a（n），同時形容詞要跟著 how 移到冠詞前面來。

習　題　155

　把下面的句子改成以 what 或 how 開頭的感歎句。

Examples:

This flower is very beautiful. → *How beautiful this flower is!*

This is a very beautiful flower. → $\begin{cases} \textit{What a beautiful flower this is!} \\ \textit{How beautiful a flower this is!} \end{cases}$

He runs very fast. → $\begin{cases} \textit{How fast he runs!} \\ \textit{What a fast runner he is!} \end{cases}$

1. That house is very big.
2. That is a very big house.
3. This story is very interesting.
4. Your brother is very intelligent.
5. These cameras are very expensive.
6. He has been very foolish.
7. She dances very gracefully.
8. She is singing very sweetly.
9. He teaches very well.
10. She is very fond of the dog.
11. He is very afraid of his father.
12. She made a very pretty doll.
13. He wrote a very long letter.

14. He wrote a letter very nicely.

15. Our life here on earth is very strange.

16. He behaved very strangely when he heard the news.

17. This world would be very lonely if you were away.

18. You will easily imagine I am very happy.

19. I wish to succeed.   20. He talked nonsense.

參考：有時候直述句雖然不含有形容詞或副詞，也照樣可以用 what 或 how 變成感

　　歎句：

　　　　What a noise! (The noise is very terrible.)

　　　　What a fool! (He〔she, etc.〕is a big fool.)

　　　　How I wished to succeed! (I wished to succeed very much.)

　　　　How he speaks! (He speaks very well.)

9-3. 祈使句：命令與請求

　　英語裡表示命令與請求的方式很多。有直接了當的命令，也有客氣而禮貌的請

求。

　　(1) 英語的祈使句可以看做是由 "You will …（你要…）" 的敘述句變來。把主

語 you 與助動詞 will 省掉就變成了命令句。

　　You will come here. → *Come here.*

　　You will close the door. → *Close the door.*

　　You will be careful. → *Be careful.*

　　You will be here by seven o'clock. → *Be here by seven o'clock.*

如果要指出下命令的對象，就可以把這個名詞或代名詞放在句首或句尾：

　　You sweep the floor, *John*, and *you girls* clean the kitchen.

　　Come on, *everybody!*

　　Call a doctor, *somebody!*

(2) 若要緩和命令的語氣，就在句首或句尾加 **please**，改為請求。

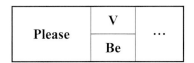 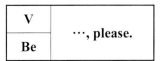

Please come here.

Close the door, *please*.

John, stand up, *please*.

Everybody *please* be here by seven o'clock.

(3) 也可以在命令前面或後面加上 **will you** 或 **won't you**，改為請求。

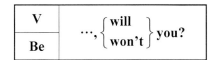 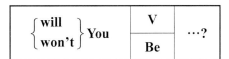

Be here by seven o'clock, *will you?*

Will you be here by seven o'clock?

Won't you 常含有邀請的語氣：

Have a cup of coffee, *won't you?*

Won't you come in?

(4) 如果要表示客氣的請求，就在命令句前面加 **will（won't）you please,**
would you please, do（would）you mind V-ing? 等：

Will you please be here by seven o'clock?

Won't you please be quiet?

Would you please come on time?

Would you sit over here *please?*

Do you mind closing the door?

Would you mind sitting here?

也可以用 **kindly** 或 **be so kind（good, nice）as to** 來代替 please：

Will you kindly be here by seven o'clock?

Would you be so kind as to close the door?

$$\left\{ \begin{array}{l} \textbf{Will} \\ \textbf{Won't} \\ \textbf{Would} \end{array} \right\} \textbf{you} \left\{ \begin{array}{l} \textbf{please} \\ \textbf{kindly} \\ \textbf{be so kind as to} \\ \textbf{be so good as to} \end{array} \right\} \left\{ \begin{array}{l} \textbf{V} \\ \textbf{Be} \end{array} \right\} \cdots?$$

$$\left\{ \begin{array}{l} \textbf{Do} \\ \textbf{Would} \end{array} \right\} \textbf{you mind V-ing} \cdots?$$

(5) 在非正式的談話裡（例如朋友間的交談），也可以用 **could**（**can**）**you** 或 **could**（**can**）**I** 來表示請求：

> *Could you* lend me five dollars until tomorrow?
>
> *Could you* tell me what time it is now?
>
> *Could I* have that newspaper, please?
>
> *Could I* see your railway time-table?

(6) **May**（**might**）**I, Do you mind if I V** ⋯, **Would you mind if I V-ed** ⋯，請求對方允許說話者做某些事情：

> *May I* have some coffee?
>
> *Might I* borrow your pen for a minute?
>
> *Do you mind* if I *turn* on the radio?
>
> *Would you mind if* I *didn't* come?

也可以用 **Let me**（**us, him, etc.**）**V** ⋯來請求允許：

> *Let* me go!
>
> *Let* him do the job.
>
> *Let* us know whether you can come, *will you?*

(7) **Let's V** ⋯表示包括說話者與對方在內的請求，也就是提議：

> *Let's* start early. (I suggest that we start early.)
>
> *Let's* help him, *shall we?* (I suggest that we help him.)
>
> Yes, let's (do). No, let's not.（也有人說 let's don't）

習 題 156

把下面的句子改為命令句。

1. You will come back later.
2. You will be careful.
3. You will wait for me on the corner.
4. You will be here by ten.
5. You will remove the stone from the road.
6. Girls! You will sit on these chairs.
7. Boys! You will study in the next room.
8. You will just let me try once.
9. You will pay attention to me while I am talking.
10. You will ask her to go to the movie with us this morning.

習 題 157

用各種不同的方式把下面的命令改為客氣的請求。

Examples:

        Stay a few minutes. →

$$\left\{ \begin{array}{l} \textit{Will} \\ \textit{Won't} \\ \textit{Would} \end{array} \right\} \left\{ \begin{array}{l} \textit{you stay a few minutes?} \\ \textit{you please stay a few minutes?} \\ \textit{you stay a few minutes, please?} \end{array} \right.$$

1. Come back a little later.
2. Wait for me after the lesson.
3. Get on this bus.
4. Call me by telephone tonight.
5. Ask her to go to the movie with us.
6. Tell him that we are waiting.
7. Help me to remove the stone from the road.
8. Give him your telephone number.
9. Step into the dining room.
10. Bring two or three friends.

習 題 158

把助詞移到賓語的後面，並且把整個命令句高聲念出來。

Example:

        Pùt dôwn the bóok. → *Pút the bôok dówn.*

1. Drink up your tea!   2. Cover up your legs!

3. Clear up this mess!   4. Do up your buttons!

5. Eat up your dinner!   6. Pick up that book!

7. Pull up all the weeds!   8. Wake up your brother!

9. Read out the message aloud!   10. Take out your friend to lunch!

11. Put out your tongue!   12. Pour out the tea!

13. Turn out the light!   14. Put on your coat!

15. Take off your shoes!   16. Take away these dishes!

17. Write down these sentences in pencil!

18. Put back the clock one hour!   19. Switch on the light!

20. Turn off the radio!

9-4. 否定祈使句與強意祈使句

(1) 表示禁止的命令或請求，在祈使句前面加 Do not 或 Don't。

    Come here. → *Don't* come here.

    Smoke in this room. → Please *don't* smoke in this room.

    Let him go. → *Don't* let him go.

注意 Be …的否定式是 Don't be …，而不是 Be not …。

    Don't be late for school. *Don't be* silly.

(2) Let's V …的否定式是 Let's not …。

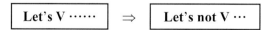

    Let's not start too early.

    Let's not talk about it any more.

Please *let's not* speak Japanese.

(3) 要加強命令或請求，在祈使句前面加 Dó。

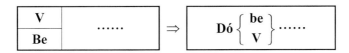

Come here right away. → *Dó* come here right away.

Please sit down. → Please *dó* sit down.

Be quiet, please. → *Dó* be quiet, please.

參考一：除了 Don't 以外也可以用 Never（＝ don't you ever）來表示禁止：

Never tell a lie again.

Never let him know the truth.

參考二：表示禁止的張貼常用動名詞，例如：

No smoking.（禁止抽煙。）

No parking.（禁止停車。）

習 題　159

把下面的命令或請求改成否定式。

1. Fold the paper.　　　　　　　2. Please leave the room.

3. Let's forget our homework.　　4. Listen to what he says.

5. Lay hands on the desk, please.　6. Let's play in class.

7. Be kind to me.　　　　　　　8. Put down your pens.

9. Let us wait.　　　　　　　　10. Read out the letter aloud, please.

習 題　160

依照例句回答下面的問句。

Examples:

　　Shall we go to the movies? → Yes, *let's. Let's go to the movies.*

　　Shall we go to the movies. → No, *let's not. Let's watch TV* instead.

1. Shall we open a window?

　　No, _____ . _____ open the door instead.

2. Shall we speak Chinese?

    No, _____. _____ English instead.

3. Shall we meet at noon?

    Yes, _____. _____.

4. Shall we go to the library? Yes, ⋯

5. Shall we ask George? No, ⋯ instead.

6. Shall we invite the Taylors? Yes, ⋯

7. Shall we ride Bob's car this time? No, ⋯ instead.

8. Shall we go to a Chinese restaurant this time?

    No, ⋯ instead.

習 題 161

依照 B 欄的句型或句義完成 A 欄的句子。

A	**B**
0. *Don't* wake him up now.	Don't try to be funny.
1. Let's go to a movie, _____?	Let me try, will you?
2. _____ _____ be lazy!	Don't go near the water!
3. _____ be nice to my daughter.	Do come and see us again.
4. Let's _____ argue any more.	Don't let him play in the street.
5. Let us go by bus, _____ _____?	Let's go by bus, shall we?
6. Let me show you, _____ I ?	Let me show you, will you?
7. _____ you _____ trust a stranger.	You will never trust a stranger.
8. _____ play with fire.	You will never play with fire.
9. _____ _____ beautiful garden it is!	= The garden is very beautiful.
10. _____ _____ a job we have!	= We have a very difficult job.
11. _____ take a taxi.	= I suggest that we take a taxi.
12. _____ _____ stay with you.	= Will you allow us to stay with you?

習　題　162

把 A 欄的祈使句與 B 欄的回答連在一起。

3	0. Open the door, please.	(0) I won't.
	1. Sit down, please.	(1) I'll never do it again.
	2. Don't forget the key.	(2) With pleasure.
	3. May I have some tea?	(3) Yes, sir.
	4. Let's go now.	(4) I'm sorry. I haven't finished it.
	5. Would you mind sitting here?	(5) No, I wouldn't mind.
	6. Quiet!	(6) Thank you.
	7. Do you mind if I sit here?	(7) Why?
	8. Would you please hand in your paper?	(8) That's fine with me.
	9. Come on; give me a hand.	(9) Help yourself.
	10. Don't you ever do it again.	(10) Of course not.

9-5. 間接祈使句

祈使句在間接引句中變成「**不定詞**」（infinitive）或「**To 動詞**」（to V …）。傳達動詞用 tell, order, command, ask, beg, request 等。

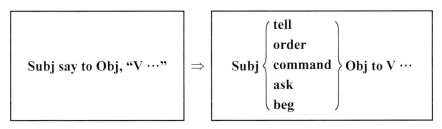

Subj say to Obj, "V …" ⇒ Subj {tell, order, command, ask, beg} Obj to V …

- He said to his friend, "Go right away."（直接說法）
- He told his friend to go right away.（間接說法）

- She said to me, "Bring me a cup of tea."（直接說法）
- She asked me to bring her a cup of tea.（間接說法）

否定式祈使句在間接引句中變成「否定式不定詞」（not to V …）。

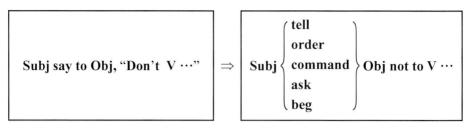

$$\left\{\begin{array}{l}\text{He said to his friend, “Don't go away.”（直接說法）}\\ \text{He told his friend not to go away.（間接說法）}\end{array}\right.$$

$$\left\{\begin{array}{l}\text{I said to him, “Don't make such big noise.”（直接說法）}\\ \text{I told him not to make such big noise.（間接說法）}\end{array}\right.$$

習 題 163

用括號裡面的主語與動詞把下面的句子改成間接祈使句。

Example:

Sit down! (We asked him) → *We asked him to sit down.*

1. Come here! (I asked her)
2. Pick it up! (He ordered me)
3. Do it again! (Tell him)
4. Wash your face! (She told me)
5. Give me another! (Ask them)
6. Don't put it on the desk! (She told me)
7. Get your hair cut! (Tell them)
8. Don't wait for me! (She told us)
9. Don't go away before I come back! (He begged them)
10. Never speak to a stranger! (She advised her)

習 題 164

把下面的句子改成間接祈使句。

1. I said to her, “Write quickly.”
2. He said to me, “Have another cup of tea.”
3. “Don't sit on my bed,” he said to me.
4. “Take a look at yourself in the mirror,” she said to him.

5. "Don't put your elbow on the table," Mother said to me.

6. "Never borrow money from your friends," Father said to us.

7. He said to her, "Don't speak until you are spoken to."

8. Mrs. Taylor said to her daughter, "Be a good girl and sit quietly."

9. He said to them, "Don't spend all your money and save some for the future."

10. "Go to bed and don't get up till you are called," he said to me.

習　題　165

依照例句把下面的句子改成間接感歎句。

Examples:

What a lovely house you have! (She cried out)

She cried out what a lovely house I had.

She cried out that I had a very lovely house.

How fine the weather is! (She said)

She said how fine the weather was.

She said that the weather was very fine.

What a terrible noise! (He exclaimed)

He exclaimed what a terrible noise it was.

He exclaimed that it was a very terrible noise.

1. What a fool I've been! (He cried out)

2. What a dirty face you have! (She said to me that)

3. How happy I am! (She exclaimed that)

4. What a charming daughter you have, Mrs. Smith! (She said to)

5. How cruel you have been! (She accused her husband that)

第10章
WH- 問句

10-1. wh- 問句

Wh- 問句（wh-question）是由「wh- 詞」或「疑問詞」（如 who, whom, whose, which, what, when, where, why, how）所引導的問句。這些問句不能僅用 yes 或 no 來回答。例如：

Who arrived late?	*John.*
When did he arrive?	*Last night.*
Where did he stay last night?	*At a hotel.*

Wh- 問句是由直述句變來的。變化的過程是：(1) 先把直述句變成 yes / no 問句，(2) 再用適當的 wh- 詞代替問句中的某些語詞，(3) 最後把 wh- 詞提前放在句首：

John arrived late. → Did *John* arrive late? → *Who* arrived late?

He arrived *last night.* → Did he arrive *last night?* → *When* did he arrive?

He stayed *at a hotel.* → Did he stay *at a hotel?* → *Where* did he stay?

注意：英語的疑問詞（與國語的疑問詞不同），一定要放在句首。比較：

$\begin{cases} \textit{When did you come?} \\ 你什麼時候來？ \end{cases}$

$\begin{cases} \textit{Where did he go last night?} \\ 他昨天晚上到什麼地方去了？ \end{cases}$

參考：Wh- 問句可以用兩種不同的音調說出來：

(1) （手裡拿著一本書問。）　　What's this?　　(It's a book.)

　　（指著某一個人問。）　　Who's he?　　(He's the principal.)

(2) 　This isn't a cap.　　　 What is it?　　(It's a hat.)
　　There's something
　　on the desk.

That's not Mr. Lee
Somebody's at the
door.
}　Who is he?　(He's Mr. Jones.)

10-2. 以 what, who, whom 開頭的 wh- 問句

Who（賓格 whom）用來代替表示人的名詞或代名詞；what 用來代替表示事物或動物的（代）名詞；which 用來代替特定的人、事物或動物。

(1) 如果 what, who, which 所代替的是句子的主語，那麼 wh- 問句的詞序與直述句一樣：

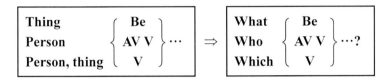

Somebody broke my pencil. → *Who* broke my pencil?

Something is on the desk. → *What* is on the desk?

Something has happened. → *What* has happened?

Something killed the rat. → *What* killed the rat?

Somebody is happy. → *Who* is happy?

Somebody will do it. → *Who* will do it?

Either Bob or Dick will do it. → *Which* will do it? (Bob or Dick)

Either this or that is correct. → *Which* is correct? (this or that)

(2) 如果 what, who, which 所代替的是句子的賓語或補語，那麼 wh- 問句的詞序與 yes / no 問句一樣：

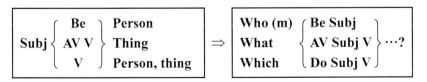

He is *somebody*. → Is he *somebody?* → *Who* is he?
who

Jack can help *somebody*.

→ Can Jack help *somebody?* → *Who* (*m*) can Jack help?

They saw *somebody* yesterday. → Did they see *somebody* yesterday?

→ *Who* (*m*) did they see yesterday?

It is *something*. → Is it *something?* → *What* is it?

He can play *something*.

→ Can he play *something?* → *What* can he play?

You will help *either Bob or Dick*. → Will you help

Bob or Dick? → *Which* will you help (Bob or Dick) ?

You prefer *either oranges or apples*. → Do you prefer

oranges or apples? → *Which* do you prefer

which --------------------- (oranges or apples) ?

在一般會話裡，who 可以用來做主語，也可以用來做賓語；在比較正式的英語裡，主語用 who，賓語用 whom。比較：

Who did you see?（非正式的英語）

Whom did you see?（較正式的英語）

「介詞動詞」（參看 2-10）的介詞可以放在句尾，也可以放在句首。放在句首的時候，後面的賓語一定要用 whom。比較：

Who did you speak *to?*（非正式的英語，介詞放在句尾。）

To whom did you speak?（較正式的英語，介詞放在句首。）

參考：我們也可以用 what 來問一個人的職業或身分。比較：

Who is he?

He is Mr. A. / He is Mr. B.'s son, and a friend of my brother's.

What is he? (= *What* does he do?)

He is a lawyer (a teacher, a student).

習　題　166

依照例句把下面的句子改為以 what 開頭的 wh- 問句，然後用括號裡面的話回答這個問句。

Examples:

It is something. (a dictionary)

What is it? It is a dictionary.

She bought something. (a new dress)

What did she buy? She bought a new dress.

1. This is something. (a gold watch)
2. They are something. (plans for the house)
3. Something caused the flood. (the rain)
4. The thief stole something. (a diamond ring)
5. The book is about something. (English grammar)
6. The artist is painting something. (a picture)
7. The driver ran over something. (a yellow dog)
8. The students are going to discuss something. (their plans for the summer)
9. The farmer has planted something. (a row of corn)
10. Jane's been copying something. (a letter)
11. There's something on the kitchen table. (a birthday cake)
12. There'll be something in the envelope for him. (some money)

習　題　167

依照例句把下面的句子改為以 who 或 whom 開頭的 wh- 問句，然後用括號裡面的話回答這個問句。

Examples:

Somebody told you that. (my brother)

Who told you that? My brother told me that.

You saw somebody. (John)

Who (m) did you see? I saw John.

Bob talked to somebody. (the principal)

Who did Bob talk to?
To whom did Bob talk? } *Bob talked to the principal.*

1. Somebody made the announcement. (the teacher)

2. Somebody broke the windows. (those boys)

3. Charles invited someone to the dance. (Susan)

4. You gave the money to someone. (his sister)

5. You spoke to somebody about the picnic. (Mrs. Taylor)

6. Someone is Mr. Jackson. (the tall man over there)

7. The girl with a book is somebody. (my sister)

8. Your sister is engaged to someone. (Bill Newman)

9. Somebody is going to type the book. (Miss Jones)

10. You are going to borrow the dress from someone. (Jane)

習　題　**168**

依照例句把下面的句子改為以 which 開頭的 wh- 問句。

Examples:

This answer is wrong. → *Which (answer) is wrong?*

I prefer those shoes. → *Which (shoes) do you prefer?*

1. This advice is useful.　　　　　　2. That magazine is cheap.

3. These books are expensive.　　　　4. You have read the blue book.

5. This phone is out of order.　　　　6. These eggs are fresh.

7. They are going to read those books.

8. You visited the art museum.

9. She borrowed the yellow dress from Jane.

10. He talked to the clerk at the counter.

習　題　169

　　針對下面的答句，用 what、which、who（m）做問句。斜體部分的語詞就是你所要問的話。

Examples:

　　　　Bob found Bill's book. → *Who found Bill's book?*

　　　　Bob found *this* book. → *Which (book) did Bob find?*

　　　　Bob found *Bill's book*. → *What did Bob find?*

　　　　Bob *found Bill's book*. → *What did Bob do?*

1. *Dick* talked to the teacher about it.　　　　2. The hunter shot *the lion*.

3. I met *two friends from the Army*. (informal)

4. I borrowed *these* books from the library.

5. Jane is going to *buy a ring*.

6. He gave the book to *the librarian*. (informal)

7. You should speak to *Mrs. Hill*. (formal)

8. *Mother* made a birthday cake for Johnny.

9. Mother made *a birthday cake* for Johnny.

10. Mother made a birthday cake for *Johnny*. (informal)

11. Mother *made a birthday cake for Johnny* today.

12. We visited *Uncle Joe* Sunday. (formal)

13. *We* visited Uncle Joe Sunday.　　　　14. We *visited Uncle Joe* Sunday.

15. *These* chairs are comfortable.　　　　16. *George* is a student.

17. *George* is the new student.　　　　18. George is *the new student*.

19. The trouble with the car is *that the clutch isn't working right*.

20. A truant is *a child who stays away from school without permission*.

21. The teacher announced *that school would close early*.

22. Betty borrowed *the green coat* from Alice.

23. Betty borrowed the green coat from *Alice*. (informal)

24. Betty borrowed *the green* coat from Alice.

25. *Betty* borrowed the green coat from Alice last week.

26. Betty *borrowed the green coat from Alice* last week.

習　題　170

依照例句把下面每對句子改成選擇問句。

Examples:

Are you a Chinese? Are you a Japanese?

Are you a Chinese or a Japanese?

Are you a Chinese? Aren't you a Chinese?

Are you or aren't you a Chinese?

1. Are you going today? Are you going tomorrow?

2. Do we pay you? Do we pay the cashier?

3. Is she playing? Is she studying?

4. Did he say "yes"? Didn't he say "yes"?

5. Do they usually eat here? Do they usually eat in a restaurant?

6. Is John buying a new car? Is his father buying a new car?

7. Do you eat with chopsticks? Do you eat with knife and fork?

8. Do you have a radio? Do you have a TV?

9. Will you drop me a line? Will you give me a ring?

10. Can you speak English? Can't you speak English?

11. Is your brother studying at a college? Is your brother studying at a university?

12. Can you write English? Can you speak English?

參考：**選擇問句**（alternative questions）要求對方在兩個答案之間選出一個來。這種問句不能用 yes 或 no 來回答。

Are you a Chinese or Japanese?

I am a Chinese (*or* I am a Japanese).

選擇問句，是把兩個 yes / no 問句用 or 連接以後，刪去第二個問句中與第一個

問句相同的部分而得來的：

> Are you going today?
> Are you going tomorrow? } →

> Are you going today or are you going tomorrow?

10-3. 以 whose、what、which 開頭的 wh- 問句

　　Whose 用來代替「所有格」（如 my, your, his, John's, the teachers' 等）；what 用來代替「無定」冠詞或限定詞（a, an, φ 等）；which 用來代替「有定」冠詞或限定詞（如 the, this, that, these, those 等）。（參 12-5）

(1) 如果 whose, what, which 所代替的是主語的一部分，那麼 wh- 問句的詞序與直述句一樣：

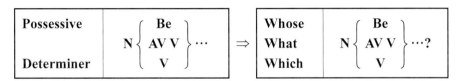

> *Somebody's* book is on the desk.
>
> 　　→ *Whose* book is on the desk?
>
> *Somebody's* mother will come tomorrow.
>
> 　　→ *Whose* mother will come tomorrow?
>
> *Some* person made this rule.
>
> 　　→ *What* person made this rule?
>
> *Either this person or that* person made this rule. →
>
> 　　*Which* person made this rule?

(2) 如果 whose, what, which 所代替的是賓語或補語的一部分，那麼 wh- 問句的詞序與 yes / no 問句一樣：

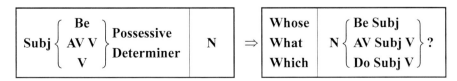

This is *somebody's* hat.

→ Is this *somebody's* hat? → *Whose* hat is this?

whose

He borrowed *somebody's* book.

→ Did he borrow *somebody's* book? → *Whose* book did he borrow?

whose

She suggested *some* plan?

→ Did she suggest *some* plan? → *What* plan did she suggest?

what

We are going to see either *this movie or that* movie.

→ Are we going to see *this movie or that* movie?

which

→ *Which* movie are we going to see?

注意：whose 可以跟後面的名詞一起出現，也可以單獨使用。

比較：

> *Whose* grade was the highest?
>
> *Whose* was the highest?

習　題　171

依照例句把下面的句子改為以 whose 開頭的 wh- 問句，然後用括號裡面的話回答這個問句。

Example:

Is this somebody's coat? (John's)

> *Whose coat is this? It's John's coat.*
>
> *Whose is this? It's John's.*

1. This is somebody's hat. (the teacher's)

2. That's someone's car. (Mr. Smith's)

3. These are somebody's gloves. (Jane's)

4. Those are someone's letters. (my sister's)

5. Alice found someone's book. (John's)

6. Betty is going to borrow somebody's dress. (Mary's)

7. Professor Jones will lecture on someone's plays tomorrow. (Shakespeare's)

8. They left somebody's name out of the list. (my brother's)

習　題　172

針對下面的答句，用 which 或 what（kind of）做問句。斜體部分的語詞就是你所要問的話。

Examples:

I like to read *history* books. → *What (kind of) books do you like to read?*

I took *the blue* book. → *Which book did you take?*

1. The thief stole *a diamond* ring.

2. I will carry *the heavy* luggage.

3. Bob won *a bronze* medal.

4. *This* chemical is dangerous.

5. I ate *the green* bananas.

6. He is drawing plans *for the house*.

7. They discussed *the* plans *for the summer*.

8. I borrowed *these* books from the library.

9. She lost *the* hat *that her mother bought for her last week*.

10. The driver ran over *a yellow* dog.

11. Mr. Jones used to smoke *cheap* cigarettes.

12. Jane lent *her best* sweater to Mary.

參考：Which 含有選擇的意思，因此指特定的人或事物；what（kind of）指一般的人或事物。比較：

Which books (among several) are expensive?

（問：「（這幾本書裡）那些書價錢很貴？」）

These books.（答：「這些書。」）

What (kind of) books (in general) are expensive?

（問：「（一般說來）什麼書價錢很貴？」）

Books with hard covers.（答：「硬精裝做封面的書。」）

習 題 173

在空白面填入 who, what 或 which。

1. _____ knows the answer? John does.

2. _____ is the answer to the question? I don't know.

3. _____ answer is yours? This one is.

4. _____ trees grow in China? Pine trees.

5. _____ color is it? Blue.

6. _____ is yours, the raincoat or the umbrella?

7. _____ is his fountain pen, the one on the desk or the one in the drawer?

8. _____ can answer this question? No one can.

9. _____ of you can answer this question?

10. _____ teaches you mathematics? Mr. Smith does.

11. _____ are you learning now? French.

12. _____ wants a piece of cake? Everyone does.

13. _____ piece of cake is mine?

14. _____ is the name of your teacher?

15. Here are the dictionaries! _____ is yours?

16. _____ wrote this letter? You did.

17. _____ are you waiting for? My brother.

18. _____ is the president of the United States?

19. _____ is the matter with you?

20. _____ color is the sky?

21. _____ time did you get up this morning?

22. _____ date is today?

23. _____ one do you prefer?

24. _____ ones do you drive?

25. _____ one earns 20,000 dollars a year? The rich one.

10-4. 以 when、where、how、why 開頭的 wh- 問句

(1) when 用來代替「時間副詞」，where 用來代替「場所副詞」，how 用來代替「狀態副詞」，why 用來代替表示理由或目的的副詞。

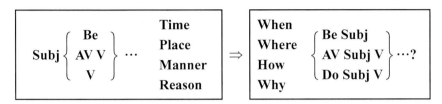

He went *home suddenly yesterday to see his mother*.

　　When did he go? (Yesterday.)

　　Where did he go? (Home.)

　　How did he go? (Suddenly.)

　　Why did he go? (To see his mother.)

所有這些 wh- 問句，也都是由含有各種副詞的 yes / no 問句變來的。

　　He went home *sometime*.

　　　→ Did he go home *sometime*? → *When* did he go home?

　　He went *somewhere* yesterday?

　　　→ Did he go *somewhere* yesterday? → *Where* did he go yesterday?

　　He went home *somehow*.

　　　→ Did he go home *somehow*? → *How* did he go home?

　　He went home *for some reason*.

　　　→ Did he go home *for some reason*? → *Why* did he go home?

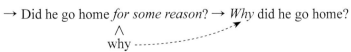

(2) How 除了單獨表示狀態（「怎麼，怎麼樣」）以外，還可以與 much、many、often、long、far、old、soon、deep、wide、high 等形容詞或副詞連用：

How much sugar do you want?	（分量）
How much does this dress cost?	（價錢）
How many times have you seen him?	（數量）
How often do you go to the movies?	（頻度）
How long will it take to finish this?	（期間）
How long is the road?	（長度）
How far is it from here to the station?	（距離）
How old is your brother?	（年齡）
How soon will the doctor come?	（時間）
How fast does the car run?	（速度）
How deep is the water?	（深度）
How wide is the street?	（寬度）
How high is the mountain?	（高度）

參考：口語英語中常出現不含助動詞的「wh- 問句」：

Why get so upset? Why not enjoy yourself?

What about the house? How about joining us? How goes it?

習 題 174

針對下面的答句，用 when 做問句。

Examples:

Supper is at six o'clock. → *When is supper?*

The train leaves at 8 a.m. → *When does the train leave?*

1. My birthday was last month.

2. Spring begins at the 21st of March.

3. Visiting hours are from 4 to 6 in the afternoon.

4. The airplane leaves every hour on the hour.

5. She's going shopping for a new suit this weekend.

6. The museum opens every day except Monday.

7. Jane is going to take French and German next year.

8. They arrived home late last night.

9. Mr. Jones will see you as soon as he can.

10. I took dancing lessons when I was a child.

習　題　175

針對下面的答句，用 where 做問句。

Examples:

> The book was on the desk. → *Where was the book?*
>
> I come from China. → *Where do you come from?*

1. We play tennis in the park.
2. They are going to the museum.
3. I saw the story in today's paper.
4. She put the watch on the table.
5. His house is on Roosevelt Road.
6. You can find a post office at the corner of the street.
7. I am studying English at the Language Center.
8. Miss Jones plans to go to England, France and Germany.
9. She found the book on the floor.
10. The truck ran over the little boy right in front of the house.

習　題　176

針對下面的答句，用 how 做問句。

Examples:

> He speaks fluently. → *How does he speak?*
>
> You get there by taking a taxi. → *How do I get there?*

1. The weather's fine.
2. You look very well.
3. The cake tastes delicious.
4. The team played poorly.
5. I always travel by train.
6. They got there by taking the train.
7. I can tell by his face.
8. He became a good speaker by practicing hard every day.
9. I'm enjoying my visit enormously.

10. She got interested in art by going to the museum.

習　題　177

針對下面的答句，用 how much, how many, how often, how long, how far, how old, how deep, how wide, how high, how fast, how tall, how thick 等做問句。

Examples:

I weigh 130 pounds. → *How much do you weigh?*

She repeated it six times. → *How many times did she repeat?*

She stayed there for a week. → *How long did she stay there?*

He is twenty. → *How old is he?*

I have my hair cut twice a month. → *How often do you have your hair cut?*

1. This dress costs twenty dollars.

2. I have fifty dollars.

3. I want three pounds of pork.

4. The movie lasts three hours.

5. He tried several times.

6. She needs two boxes of typewriter paper.

7. There are 50 students in my class.

8. We have six children.   9. The discussion lasted an hour.

10. New York is 225 miles from Washington.

11. The bus ran six times a day.   12. I am five feet tall.

13. The lake is 100 feet deep.   14. The school is 200 years old.

15. The windows are 4 feet wide.   16. The pool is 50 feet long.

17. She weighs 120 pounds.

18. The doctor will come soon.

19. The plane flies at 600 miles an hour.

20. The building is twenty stories high.

21. We go to the movies once a week.

22. The wind was blowing 20 miles an hour.

23. I have known him for years.

24. I can run 100 meters in 12 seconds.

25. The dictionary is 1000 pages thick.

26. The station is three blocks from here.

27. About 3000 people died in traffic accidents last year.

28. There were three hundred people at the meeting.

29. I need $1,000 to go shopping.

30. The new library cost $1,000,000 to build.

習　題　178

在空白裡面填入適當的疑問詞。

1. _____ would you like me to do?

2. _____ hat blew off? John's?

3. _____ left this book here?

4. _____ is your sister going to marry?

5. _____ of these cakes may I take?

6. _____ is your mother's name?

7. _____ is wrong with your camera?

8. _____ did you visit yesterday afternoon? The museum.

9. _____ dress was she wearing? The one you gave her.

10. _____ train shall we take, the 5:30 or the 7:10?

11. _____ is your family doctor?

12. _____ of these people have you met before?

13. _____ is this watch? Mine.

14. _____ kind of watch is this? A stop watch.

15. _____ are you talking about? Nothing.

16. _____ of them will come with us?

17. _____ is the shortest way to the station?

18. _____ do you like better, spring or fall?

19. _____ did you say just now?

20. _____ book did I borrow? Yours?

21. _____ did you meet her? I met her in the park.

22. _____ will he come back? He will come back in a short time.

23. _____ didn't you come? Because I was ill.

24. _____ is your mother? She is quite well, thank you.

25. _____ _____ is he? Eleven.

26. _____ _____ have you been waiting? More than two hours.

27. _____ _____ is it from here to the post office? About five minutes' walk.

28. _____ _____ brothers do you have? Three.

29. _____ _____ do you have? Half past ten.

30. _____ _____ is today? The fifth of July.

31. _____ is Mr. Jones? He's my uncle.

32. _____ is Mr. Jones? He's an engineer.

33. _____ does he do? He's a doctor.

34. _____ _____ will she come? Any minute.

35. _____ _____ ago did you see him? Last week.

習　題　179

依照例句用「短答句」回答下列問題。

Examples:

Who invented the electric light?

Edison did.

How many of your brothers can swim? (Every one of them)

Every one of them can.

1. Who teaches you English?

2. Who wrote *Hamlet*?

3. What makes people fat? (Eating)

4. How many of you play tennis? (Most of us)

5. How many of you can play chess? (None of us)

6. How many of you ought to know the answer? (All of us)

7. Which of you likes ice cream? (We all)

8. What fruit is good to eat? (All)

9. Which cost more, these or those?

10. Which of you finished your homework yesterday? (None)

11. Who dares to jump over the stream? (Nobody)

12. Who's the present queen of England?

13. Who's taken my books? (Your brother)

14. Who used to live in this old house? (My great - grandfather)

15. Which of you knows the shortest way to the station? (Jim)

習　題　180

把下面的 wh- 問句改為被動。

Example:

How do you spell it? → *How is it spelled?*

1. What do you use it for?	2. Where do you keep it?
3. When do they take it away?	4. How do you write it?
5. What do you eat it with?	6. How do they sell it?
7. How often do you tune it?	8. Who do you send it to?
9. How do you pronounce it?	10. Who broke the window?

10-5. 間接 wh- 問句

　　把直接 wh- 問句改為間接 wh- 問句的時候，原來的問句就要變成直述句。因此主語與動詞倒裝的詞序就要回復到原來主語在前、動詞在後的次序。但是 wh- 詞仍然要放在句首，「傳達動詞」可以用 ask, inquire, want to know 等。

　　　　He said to me, "Who are you?"（直接說法）
　　　　He asked who I was.（間接說法）

$\left\{\begin{array}{l}\text{She said to me, "Where does John work?" （直接說法）}\\\text{She asked me where John worked. （間接說法）}\end{array}\right.$

Subj	say (to Obj),	"Wh-X $\left\{\begin{array}{l}\textbf{Be}\\\textbf{AV V}\\\textbf{V}\end{array}\right\}$ subj ···?"

$\Rightarrow$

Subj	ask (Obj)	wh-X Subj $\left\{\begin{array}{l}\textbf{Be}\\\textbf{AV V}\\\textbf{V}\end{array}\right\}$ ···

習　題　181

依照例句把下面的 wh- 問句用 He asked me 改為間接問句。

Examples:

　　Why are you so worried? → *He asked me why I was so worried.*

1. How many languages can you speak?

2. What have you been studying?　　3. When did you eat lunch?

4. When will you return my book?

5. How well can you speak English?　　6. Where were you last night?

7. How long have you been waiting?

8. Who did you invite to the party?

9. Why didn't you come this morning?

10. What kind of work do you do?　　11. Whose plays have you read?

12. How much sugar do you use in your coffee?

13. Why have you not eaten anything?

14. How do you like this cake?

15. Which book have you been reading?　　16. What time is it?

17. What is the matter?　　18. What's wrong with you?

19. What's the English for " 花 "?　　20. Who called while I was out?

習　題　182

依照例句把下面的問句或直述句用 She asked me 或 She told me 改為間接引句。

Examples:

When did you call? → *She asked me when I called.*

Are you hungry? → *She asked me whether / if I was hungry.*

I'm a student. → *She told me (that) she was a student.*

1. I'm going to move to Taipei.
2. Why are you angry?
3. Have you heard from your brother?
4. Where are you going to spend your vacation?
5. Was the library open all day?
6. I'll graduate in June.
7. When will you graduate from high school?
8. Do you know the way to the station?
9. Can you tell me where I can find a rest room?
10. How far is it to the National Museum?
11. Who do you think is China's greatest scientist?
12. I hope you have a letter for me.

第11章
名　詞

11-1. 名　詞

在下面的句子裡用斜體表示的語詞都屬於**名詞**（nouns）。

John is ill.

They are all my *friends*.

Her *brother* lives in *Taipei*.

A tall *lady* in a blue *dress* gave me this *book* yesterday.

名詞可以分成兩類：專有名詞與普通名詞。

習　題　183

從下面一段文章裡把名詞找出來，並在下面劃線。

Bill and Sally White, their father and mother, and some of their friends were visiting Bill's Uncle George at the seashore. Uncle George was Bill's father's brother. He had a house and a sailboat. Bill and Sally had visited him many times. They liked the seashore very much.

It was late in August. The air was cool, but the water was warm enough for swimming. Uncle George had invited them all to go sailing with him. They were going to sail for two or three hours and then have a picnic on one of the islands in the bay.

11-2. 專有名詞

專指特定的人物或場所的名詞，如 John, Mary, Mr. Brown, China, Asia 等，叫做**專有名詞**（proper nouns）。英語專有名詞的開頭第一個字母必須大寫。

(1) 人　名：John Brown, Mrs. Wood, Captain Cory, President Chiang Ching-kuo.

(2) 地　名：Japan, South America, New York, Roosevelt Road（羅斯福路），National Taiwan University.

(3) 星球名：Venus（金星），Mars（火星），Jupiter（木星）。

(4) 日、月、節日：Sunday, Monday, January, Christmas, New Year's Day.

專有名詞一般都不能與「冠詞」（a、an、the）或其他「限定詞」（this, that, these, those 等）用在一起。因此我們不能說 a China, the China, this China 或 Chinas。

習　題　184

專有名詞通常都不能帶冠詞 the，但是有少數專有名詞卻必須帶冠詞 the。在需要帶冠詞的專有名詞前面的空白裡填 the，在不能帶冠詞的專有名詞前面的空白裡打（×）。

1. _____ Nancy is a charming girl.

2. _____ China is a great country.

3. _____ Chinese are a peace-loving people.

4. Is _____ Chinese a very difficult language to learn?

5. _____ Niagara Falls is the largest waterfall in _____ America.

6. _____ United States is a member of _____ United Nations.

7. _____ Netherlands is on the north of _____ Belgium.

8. _____ Amazon is the largest river in _____ South America.

9. In some places _____ Rocky Mountains are not far from _____ Pacific Ocean.

10. _____ Hudson River empties into _____ Atlantic Ocean.

11. We have visited _____ Congress but not _____ White House.

12. _____ Eskimos make houses of snow and ice.

13. Every Christian should read _____ Bible carefully.

14. _____ Canary Islands are group of Spanish islands in _____ Atlantic.

15. I heard that _____ Mr. Smith was going to France, _____ German and _____ Soviet Union.

參考：英語有些專有名詞本身含有 the，例如 the United States（美國），the Himalayas（喜馬拉雅山脈），the Sahara（撒哈拉沙漠），the Queen Elizabeth（伊利莎白女王號－船名）。這種 the 可以說是專有名詞不可分割

的一部分，我們必須一一記著。

(a) 河、運河：the Thames（泰晤士河），the Nile River（尼羅河），the Yangtze River（揚子江），the Suez Canal（蘇彝士運河）。

(b) 海洋：the Pacific Ocean（太平洋），the Atlantic Ocean（大西洋），the Red Sea（紅海），the Mediterranean（地中海）。

(c) 船舶：the Queen Mary（瑪利皇后號），the President Lincoln（林肯總統號）。

(d) 公共設施、建築物、紀念碑等：the Metropolitan Museum（紐約的大都會博物館），the Empire State Building（帝國大廈），the Sphinx（埃及的獅身女面像），the White House（白宮）。

(e) 書籍、報章、雜誌：the Four Books（四書），the Bible（聖經），the Arabian Nights（天方夜譚），the New York Times（紐約時報），the Newsweek（新聞週刊）。

(f) 帝國、朝代：the Ottoman Empire（鄂圖曼帝國），the Ming Dynasty（明朝）。

(g) 民族：the Chinese（中華民族），the English（英國人）。

(h) 山脈（多數）：the Himalayas（喜馬拉雅山脈），the Alps（阿爾卑斯山脈），the Rockies（落磯山脈）。

(i) 群島（多數)：the Philippines（菲律賓群島），the Pescadores（澎湖群島）。

(j) 聯邦、其他：the United States（美國），the Soviet Union（蘇聯），the United Kingdom（聯合王國—英國），the United Nations（聯合國），the Netherlands（尼德蘭—荷蘭），the North Pole（北極），the South Pole（南極），the Hague（海牙），the Bronx（布隆克斯—紐約市的一區）。

11-3. 普通名詞

不專指特定的人物或場所的名詞叫做**普通名詞**（common nouns）。普通名詞又可以分成兩個小類：可數名詞與不可數名詞。

11-4. 可數名詞

名詞如果可以有「單數形」（singular）與「複數形」（plural），就叫做**可數名詞**（count nouns）。例如，我們可以說 one student, two students, three students，因此 student 是可數名詞。

可數名詞的單數形，必須加上冠詞 a (n)，the 或其他「限定詞」（如 this, that 等）：

I saw *a boy* and *a girl* in *the room*.

可數名詞的複數形必須加 -(e)s，而且可以加上冠詞 the 或其他「限定詞」（如 these, those 等）：

I don't like *apples*, but *these apples* look delicious.

參考一：名詞複數形的拼法規則

(a) 大多數的名詞都在字尾加 -s：

books, pens, students, schools.

(b) 如果名詞的字尾是 s, ch, sh, x，或 z，加 -es：

bus (*s*) *es*, class*es*, match*es*, brush*es,* box*es* quizz*es*（測驗）.

注意：stomachs〔-ks〕（胃），monarchs〔-ks〕（君主）.

(c) 如果名詞的字尾是子音字加 o，加 -es：

hero*es*, potato*es*（馬鈴薯），torpedo*es*（魚雷），echo*es*（回聲）.

例外：zoo*s*, bamboo*s*（竹），radio*s*, curio*s*（古玩），piano*s*, solo*s*（獨唱，獨奏），soprano*s*（女高音），photo*s*（照片），auto*s*（汽車）.

注意：mosquito（*e*）*s*（蚊子），tobacco（*e*）*s*（菸草），buffalo（*e*）*s*（水牛），zero（*e*）*s*（零），cargo（*e*）*s*（貨物），volcano（*e*）*s*（火山），motto（*e*）*s*（格言）.

(d) 如果名詞的字尾是子音字加 y，把 y 改成 i 後加 -es：

bab*ies*, cit*ies*, countr*ies*, colloqu*ies*〔-kwiz〕（交談）.

注意：boy*s*, monkey*s*.

(e) 如果名詞的字尾是 f 或 fe，把 f（e）改成 v 後加 -es：

wol*ves*（狼），cal*ves*（小牛），hal*ves*（一半），shel*ves*（棚架），

leaves, knives.

例外：roofs, proofs（證明）, beliefs（信念）, griefs（傷心事）, chiefs
（首長）, handkerchiefs（手帕）, mischiefs（惡作劇的人）,
cliffs（懸崖）, cuffs（袖口）, safes（保險箱）.

(f) 有兩個名詞加 -en：

ox—oxen, child—children〔罕見 brother—brethren（同胞）〕.

(g) 有幾個名詞改變母音字：

foot—feet, tooth—teeth, goose—geese（鵝）, man—men, woman—women,
mouse—mice（老鼠）, louse—lice（蝨子）.

(h) 有幾個名詞的單數形跟複數形一樣：

sheep, deer（鹿）, swine（野猪）, fish（of the same kind）, trout（鱒
魚）, salmon（鮭）, quail（鵪）, dozen（一打）, score（二十）,
hundred, Chinese, Japanese, Swiss（瑞士人）, means（手段，方法）
series（系列）, species（種）.

(i) 由幾個詞形成的「複詞」（compound nouns）, 把其中最重要的詞變成
複數形：

mothers-in-law, editors-in-chief, aides-de-camp, courts-martial, men-of-
war, passers-by, by-standers, step-sons, mouse-traps, go-betweens, forget-
me-nots.

(j) 字母、數字或其他記號的複數形，加 -'s 或 -s。

A's, 3's, B.A.'s, 1970's（或 As, 3s, B.A.s, 1970s）；但是 e's, i's, a.m.'s.

參考二：名詞複數形的讀音規則：請注意這些讀音規則與第三身單數現在式動詞
（e）s 的讀音規則完全一樣。

(a) 在齒擦音〔s、z、ʃ、ʒ、tʃ、dʒ〕後面的 es，讀〔ɪz〕。

boxes, bus（s）es, quizzes, brushes, churches, ages.

(b) 在不帶聲的子音「清音」〔p、t、k、f、θ〕後面的（e）s，讀〔s〕。

cups, cats, books, roofs, months〔mʌnθs, mʌnts, mʌns〕.

(c) 其他（e）s（即「濁音」與母音後面的 s 或 es），讀〔z〕。

jobs, roads, dogs, knives, clothes, babies, radios, cows, names.

注意：house〔haʊs〕→ houses〔haʊzɪz〕，bath〔bɑɵ〕→ baths〔bɑðz〕，

path〔pɑɵ〕→ paths〔pɑðz〕，truth〔truɵ〕→ truths〔truɵs, -ðz〕，

youth〔juɵ〕→ youths〔juɵs, -ðz〕．

習　題　185

把下面的名詞改成複數形，並且用音標注出 -(e)s 的發音。

Examples:

day *days*〔z〕，desk *desks*〔s〕，speech *speeches*〔ɪz〕．

1. cook _____　　　2. part _____　　　3. egg _____

4. sound _____　　　5. sky _____　　　6. key _____

7. roof _____　　　8. loaf _____　　　9. race _____

10. moss _____　　　11. game _____　　　12. line _____

13. ball _____　　　14. door _____　　　15. month _____

16. bath _____　　　17. potato _____　　　18. radio _____

19. horse _____　　　20. house _____　　　21. match _____

22. stomach _____　　　23. knife _____　　　24. safe _____

25. page _____　　　26. garage _____　　　27. I _____

28. 8 _____　　　29. Ph. D. _____　　　30. 1970 _____

習　題　186

按照句意把括號裡面的名詞的單數形或複數形填在空白裡。

Examples:

chapter Read the next (chapter).

lessons Study these three (lesson).

1. _____ How many (bank) are there in this town?

2. _____ There are several (guest) waiting to see you.

3. _____ I had to have two (tooth) pulled the other day.

4. _____ Two of my uncles are (judge).

5. _____ You can always hear (echo) in these mountains.

6. _____ A group of (editor-in-chief) are holding a meeting now.

7. _____ The weather forecast is for blue (sky).

8. _____ I saw three (sheep) on the farm.

9. _____ Don't you think that (tax) are too high?

10. _____ She took two (spoonful) of medicine.

11. _____ Did you raise these (goose) yourself?

12. _____ We saw several (fish) in the pond.

13. _____ She is very proud of her (son-in-law) because they are all very rich.

14. _____ How many (passer-by) were killed in the accident?

15. _____ Men walk with two (foot) and animals with four (leg).

16. _____ (Ox-cart) are drawn by (ox) not by (horse).

17. _____ That millionaire has a dozen (servant) to wait on him.

18. _____ They invited two (Englishman) and three (German) to the party.

19. _____ (Mouse-trap) are set to catch (mouse).

20. _____ Get me two (dozen) of (egg) and three (loaf) of (bread).

習　題　187

把下面的名詞改為複數形。

1. crisis _____
2. basis _____
3. criterion _____
4. phenomenon _____
5. datum _____
6. curriculum _____ _____
7. stimulus _____ _____
8. focus _____ _____
9. index _____ _____
10. madame _____ _____
11. alumnus _____
12. alumna _____

參考：有些從外國傳來的名詞，保留原來的複數形：

　　(a) ～ is → ～ es：crisis—crises（危機），basis—bases（基礎），thesis—theses（論文），analysis—analyses（分析），parenthesis—parentheses（括弧），hypothesis—hypotheses（假設）

(b) ～ us → i：radi*us*—radi*i*（半徑），nucle*us*—nucle*i*（核心），alum*nus*—alum*ni*（校友）*cf.* alumn*a*—alumn*ae*（女校友）.

(c) ～ um → ～ a：dat*um*—dat*a*（資料），agend*um*—agend*a*（議程），bacter-i*um*—bacteri*a*（細菌），errat*um*—errat*a*（勘誤表）.

(d) ～ on → ～ a：criteri*on*—criteri*a*（標準），phenomen*on*—phenomen*a*（現象）。有些由外國傳來的名詞，除了原有的複數形以外，又加 -（e）s 的複數形。一般說來，加 -（es）的複數形比較常用：

formul*a*—formul*as* / formul*ae*（公式），curricul*um*—curricul*ums* / curricul*a*（課程），memorand*um*—memorand*ums* / memorand*a*（備忘錄），stimul*us*—stimul*uses* / stimul*i*（刺激），ind*ex*—ind*exes* / ind*ice*（索引），foc*us*—foc*uses* / foc*i*（焦點），madam*e*—madam*es* / m*es*dames（夫人）.

Mr. 的多數是 Messrs.〔ˈmɛsəz〕：

Mr. Brown（單數），Messrs. Brown and Taylor（不同姓複數），the Messrs. Brown（同姓複數，正式用語），the Mr. Browns（同姓複數，非正式用語）.

比較：Miss Brown（單數），Misses Brown and Taylor（不同姓複數），the Misses Brown（同姓複數，正式用語），the Miss Browns（同姓複數，非正式用語）。

習　題　188

在正確的答案下面劃線。

1. I saw two (deer, deers) running into the wood.

2. Professor Hill gave a (serie, series) of lectures on modern history.

3. Lend me a pair of (scissor, scissors), will you?

4. He always brushes his (trouser, trousers) clean.

5. She drew a circle with (a compass, compasses).

6. I am near-sighted, so I can't see without a pair of (glass, glasses).

7. It was (a spectacle, spectacles) worth watching.

8. She put on her (spectacle, spectacles) and started to read the letter.

9. I withdrew all my (saving, savings) from the bank yesterday.

10. Mr. Johnson used to take a walk as a (mean, means) of exercise.

11. Mathematics (is, are) my favorite subject.

12. (Many thanks, Much thank) for your help.

13. (Thank, Thanks) a lot for your wonderful present.

14. No news (is, are) good news.

15. Riches (have, has) wings.

16. The United States (is, are) composed of 51 states.

17. Statistics (is, are) not an exact science.

18. These statistics on population (is, are) very interesting.

19. (Is, Are) politics an interesting subject?

20. My politics (is, are) nobody's business but mine.

21. The Brown family (is, are) a very happy one.

22. The Brown family (is, are) in many parts of the world this winter: Mr. and Mrs. Brown are at home, George is in Asia, and Susan is in Europe.

23. The committee (is, are) not able to agree on the plan.

24. Middle-class people (spends, spend) a lot of money on clothes.

25. The peoples of the world (wants, want) peace and happiness.

參考：

(a) 有些名詞一定要用複數形，後面的動詞也常作複數。

  (i) 成雙一對的由兩個部分形成的工具、褲子等，前面常可以加（一雙），動詞常用複數：

scissors（剪刀），shears（大剪刀），pincers（鉗子），tongs（火鉗），pliers（老虎鉗），chopsticks（筷子），scales（天秤），compasses（圓規），spectacles（眼鏡），（eye）glasses（眼鏡），fetters（腳鍊），bellows（風箱），trousers（褲子），pants（褲子），pajamas / pyjamas（睡衣褲），slacks（寬褲），shorts（短褲），drawers（襯褲），pantaloons（長褲）.

Your scissors are rusty.

My trousers need washing.

She wore a pair of spectacles (slacks, pantaloons, etc.).

(ii) 其他：thanks（感謝），riches（財富），clothes（衣服），bowels（腸），intestines（腸），proceeds（收入），savings（積蓄），belongings（個人財富），victuals（食物），wages（工錢），arms（武器），whereabouts（下落），headquarters（司令部）.

Riches do not always bring happiness.

His present whereabouts are (*or* is) unknown.

(b) 有些名詞一定要用複數形，但是所表示的意義卻是單數。

news（新聞、消息），economics（經濟學），mathematics（數學），physics（物理學），measles（麻疹），mumps（腮腺炎），billiards（撞球）.

What's the latest news?

Is economics a difficult subject?

Measles is a childhood disease.

(c) 有些名詞一定要用複數形，但是所表示的意義可能是單數、也可能是複數，要看上下文而定。

ethics（倫理學、倫理觀），statistics（統計學、統計結果），politics（政治學、政見）。

Ethics（倫理學）*is* a challenging subject.

His personal ethics（倫理觀）*are* different from yours.

(d) 有些名詞一定要用單數形，但是所指的意義可能是單數（**集合名詞**（collective nouns）指整個集合），也可能是複數（**群眾名詞**（multitude nouns）指個別的元素或成員）。

tribe, family, team, committee, faculty, choir, crew, jury, crowd,

mob, gang, flock, bunch, collection, group.

The family was (*or* were) all present.

(e) 有些名詞有兩個複數形表示不同的意義。

brother	brothers（兄弟）	brethren（同胞）
cloth	cloths（布片、種類）	clothes（衣服）
die	dies（印模）	dice（骰子）
genius	geniuses（天才）	genii（精靈）

(f) 有些名詞，單數形與複數形表示不同的意義。

advice（勸告）	advices（通知）
air（空氣）	airs（架子）
beef（牛肉）	beeves（牛）
compass（範圍）	compasses（圓規）
content（滿足，容量，要旨）	contents（內容）
force（力量）	forces（軍隊）
good（善、益）	goods（動產）
ground（土地）	grounds（論據）
iron（鐵）	irons（腳鍊）
return（歸來）	returns（贏利，報告）
sand（沙）	sands（沙洲）
shot（砲彈）	shots（射擊）

(g) 有些名詞的複數形，除了單數形原有的含義外，多增加一種意義。

custom（習慣）	customs（習慣，關稅）
color（顏色）	colors（顏色，軍旗）
effect（結果）	effects（結果，動產）
letter（文字）	letters（文字，文學）
manner（方法）	manners（方法，禮貌）
number（數）	numbers（數，韻文）
pain（痛苦）	pains（痛苦，費力）
part（部分）	parts（部分，才能）
quarter（四分之一）	quarters（四分之一，軍營）

spectacle（奇觀）　　　　　　spectacles（奇觀，眼鏡）

scale（縮尺）　　　　　　　　scales（縮尺，天秤）

習　題　189

依照例句改寫下面的句子。

Examples:

　　The boy is five years old. → *He is a five-year-old boy.*

　　He gave me a bill worth ten dollars. → *It was a ten-dollar bill.*

　　She bought two dozen of eggs. → *She bought two dozen eggs.*

1. That baby is three months old.　　2. The rope is ten feet long.

3. This car has four doors.　　　　　4. The building is five stories high.

5. I bought a stamp for eight cents.

6. There were six men on the committee.

7. He bought a house that was twenty years old.

8. The vacation lasted two weeks.

9. We paid six dollars for the ticket.

10. They walked in the park for fifteen minutes.

參考：

(a) 當數目與名詞用做另外一個名詞的修飾語的時候，數目後面的名詞不能用複數形：

a five-dollar note（五元鈔票），a three-act play（三幕戲劇），a ten-year-old boy（十歲大的小孩），a twenty-story building（二十層樓的建築物）。

(b) 數目後面的 dozen（打）、score（二十）、hundred（百）、thousand（千）、million（百萬）常用單數：

two dozen（兩打），three score（六十），four hundred, five thousand.

注意：dozen*s* of eggs（成打的雞蛋），hundred*s* / thousand*s* / million*s* of people（成百、成千、成百萬的人）。

11-5. 不可數名詞

僅有單數形、不能有複數形的名詞叫做**不可數名詞**（noncount nouns）。例如，bread 與 courage 是不可數名詞，因此我們不能說 one bread、two breads 或 three courages、four courages；而只能說 some bread、some courage 或 a lot of bread、a lot of courage。

I want to eat some bread.

It takes a lot of courage to speak up in public.

不可數名詞不能加上 a（n），但是可以加上 some, the, this, that 等：

I wanted to drink *some milk*, but *the milk* in the jar didn't taste good.

不可數名詞主要地可以分為**物質名詞**（material nouns）與**抽象名詞**（abstract nouns）。

(1) 物質名詞：wood（木頭），metal（金屬），wool（羊毛），ivory（象牙），chalk（白堊、粉筆），paper（紙），gold（黃金），iron（鐵），oxygen（氧氣），fire（火），sugar（糖），salt（鹽），bread（麵包），rice（米），flour（麵粉），meat（肉），fish（魚），water（水），tea（茶），coffee（咖啡），wine（葡萄酒），oil（油），gas（瓦斯），air（空氣），smoke（煙）。

(2) 抽象名詞：love（愛），hatred（恨），time（時間），space（空間），friendship（友誼），democracy（民主），liberty（自由），slavery（奴役），philosophy（哲學），history（歷史），health（健康），wealth（財富），fun（樂趣），courage（勇氣），honesty（誠實），truth（真），goodness（善），beauty（美）。

(3) 其他：money（金錢），change（零錢、找頭），furniture（傢具），luggage（行李），baggage（行李—美語），information（消息、情報），mail（信件），advice（勸告），evidence（證據），work（工作），merchandise（商品），produce（農產品），laughter（笑 *cf.* laugh），company（同伴 *cf.* companion），scenery（風景 *cf.* scene），poetry（詩 *cf.* poem），the police（警察 *cf.* policeman）。

Chairs, tables and beds are kinds of *furniture*.

We bought several pieces of *furniture* for the new house.

Japan is famous for its beautiful *scenery*.

We enjoyed beautiful *scenes* all the way.

The *police* have not made any arrests.

The *policeman* finally caught the pickpocket.

習 題 190

在可數名詞前面加 a(n)，在不可數名詞前面加 some。

1. _____ pencil　　2. _____ ink　　3. _____ chalk

4. _____ pen　　5. _____ furniture　　6. _____ sofa

7. _____ friend　　8. _____ friendship　　9. _____ bag

10. _____ baggage　　11. _____ fruit　　12. _____ vegetable

13. _____ car　　14. _____ transportation　　15. _____ homework

16. _____ assignment　　17. _____ mail　　18. _____ letter

19. _____ money　　20. _____ dollar　　21. _____ lamp

22. _____ electricity　　23. _____ work　　24. _____ task

25. _____ flesh　　26. _____ bone　　27. _____ blood

28. _____ paint　　29. _____ wheat　　30. _____ fog

31. _____ pig　　32. _____ pork　　33. _____ cow

34. _____ beef　　35. _____ land　　36. _____ acre

37. _____ flower　　38. _____ grass

習 題 191

選出正確答案。

1. _____ The teacher brought us several (① ink, ② pen, ③ chalks, ④ erasers).

2. _____ Help yourself to some (① apple, ② orange, ③ fruit, ④ banana).

3. _____ Would you like a (① meal, ② food, ③ tea, ④ coffee)?

4. _____ I wrote a few (① mail, ② correspondence, ③ letters, ④ page) this morning.

5. _____ They need another (① milk, ② wine, ③ glass, ④ grass).

6 _____ We eat a lot of (① bean, ② potato, ③ rice, ④ vegetable).

7. _____ Is there any more (① egg, ② tomato, ③ butter, ④ biscuit) ?

8. _____ How many (① lesson, ② speech, ③ poetry, ④ poems) can you recite?

9. _____ A parade requires a great deal of (① plan, ② plans, ③ planning, ④ plannings).

10. _____ (① The furnitures, ② The furniture, ③ Furnitures, ④ A furniture) of this house has been removed.

習 題 192

在正確的答案下面劃線。

1. He gives a name to each (cow, cattle).

2. The rich farmer owns many (fields, lands).

3. Please lend me some (money, book).

4. We had a lot of (fun, funs) at the party last night.

5. He drank with (glass, a glass).

6. She cut the paper with (a piece of glass, a glass).

7. I know him by (sight, a sight) but I've never spoken to him.

8. The sunset is (beautiful sight, a beautiful sight).

9. A book is made of (paper, papers).

10. The newsboy delivers (paper, papers) every morning.

參考：有些不可數名詞偶爾也可以做可數名詞用。這個時候可以加上冠詞 a（n）或變成複數形。

(a) 物質名詞：

$\left\{\begin{array}{l}\text{These houses are built of } \textit{brick}. （「磚」物質名詞，不可數）\\ \text{He picked up } \textit{a brick}. （「磚塊」部分，可數）\\ \text{Don't throw } \textit{bricks}. （「磚塊」部分，可數）\end{array}\right.$

    I bought three yards of *cloth*.（「布」物質名詞，不可數）

    She covered the table with *a cloth*.（「桌布」成品，可數）

    This is *a* good *cloth* for summer wear.（「布料」種類，可數）

    These *clothes* are made in this country.（「衣服」成品，可數）

「種類」：a fish, fishes; a wine, wines; a tea, teas; a metal, metals.

「部分」：a stone, stones; a cloud, clouds; a light, lights; a fire, fires.

「成品」：a glass, glasses（玻璃杯）；a paper, papers（報紙、文件）；an iron, irons（熨斗）。

(b) 抽象名詞：

    Seek *truth* and do *good*.（「真、真實」抽象名詞，不可數）

    This is *a truth*.（「真事」具體的事實，可數）

    This book contains many *truths*.（「真理、真義」，可數）

    Everybody loves *beauty*.（「美」抽象名詞，不可數）

    She was once *a beauiy*.（「美人」，可數）

    She loves the *beauties* of art.（「美點、美術品」，可數）

其他：a virtue, virtues; an art, arts; a sight, sights; a kindness, kindnesses; a death, deaths.

第*12*章
限定詞

12-1. 限定詞

英語的名詞很少單獨出現，而多半都跟著 a(n), the, this, that 等**限定詞**（determiners）一起出現。我們見到了限定詞，就可以猜到後面總有一個名詞要出現。因此，限定詞可以說是表示英語名詞的信號。

英語主要的限定詞有下列幾種：

(1) **冠詞**（articles）：a, an, some, any, φ（零，不加冠詞）, the.

a	boy, girl, book, pen
an	aunt, uncle, apple, orange
some	ink, bread, courage, advice
φ	boys, aunts, ink, advice
the	boy(s), aunt (s), ink, advice

(2) **指示詞**（demonstratives）：this, that, these, those.

this	boy, apple, ink, advice
that	boy, apple, ink, advice
these	boys, apples
those	boys, apples

(3) **所有格**（possessives）：my, your, his, her, its, our, their, N's, N-s'

my / your, etc. boy, apple, ink, advice

John's / the student's, etc. pencil, book, ink

the students' etc. pencils, books, ink

NOUN	PHRASE	（名詞組）
Determiner（限定詞）	Noun	（名詞）

a   boy

some	eggs
this	book
my	family
John's	brother

注意，在同一個名詞之前只能用一種限定詞，不能同時用兩種限定詞：

my	*this*	book	（×）
the	*John's*	brother	（×）

習　題　193

依照例句在名詞下面畫線，在限定詞上面加圈。

Example:

When will (the) *party* take (φ) *place?*

1. The girl lives with her family in a big house.

2. That boy has spent all his money on these toys.

3. Get me tea instead of milk.

4. I live with my grandmother, my parents, my elder brother and a younger sister.

5. This house is famous for its garden.

6. People got off their train at the station.

7. Is he your father's brother, or your mother's?

8. Why did John's bicycle cost more than Mary's camera?

9. I want a pencil, an eraser and some paper.

10. Any stranger will get lost in London if he doesn't know the city well.

12-2. 無定冠詞「零」

冠詞（articles）可以分為兩種：**無定冠詞**（nondefinite articles）與**有定冠詞**（definite articles）。無定冠詞包括 φ（「零」，也就是不加冠詞）、some、any、a（n）。

如果我們用不可數名詞或複數可數名詞來指不特定的人或物，那麼這些名詞前面不用加冠詞：

Air and *water* are both necessary to us.（不可數名詞）

Friends and *books* are both very valuable.（複數可數名詞）

12-3. some 與 any

some 與 any 常用在不可數名詞或複數可數名詞前面來表示不特定的分量、數目或程度。

(1) 在肯定句裡，用 some。

Give me *some milk*.（物質名詞「分量」）

I still have *some faith* in him.（抽象名詞「程度」）

There are *some books* on the desk.（可數名詞「數目」）

(2) 在否定句、條件句裡，用 any。比較：

I want *some* pencils / *some* paper.

I don't want *any* pencils / *any* paper.

If you want *any* pencils / *any* paper, I can give you *some*.

(3) 在問句裡，some 與 any 表達不同的意思。比較：

Do you need *some* money?

= You need some money, don't you? I think you do.

Do you need *any* money?

= You don't need any money, do you? I don't think you do.

= I am asking you because I don't know whether you do.

習 題 194

在空白裡填進 some, any 或 a(n)。

1. I have _____ money.

2. You wrote _____ letters.

3. She is visiting _____ friend.

4. I didn't have _____ ink.

5. There wasn't _____ news.

6. They found _____ paint.

7. We're learning _____ new words.

8. She found _____ old watch.

9. They're showing _____ interesting movies.

10. We didn't eat _____ fruit.

11. The farmer is planting _____ corn.

12. Do you have _____ information on the subject?

習 題 195

把下面的句子改為否定句與問句。

Example:

> You bought some paper. → *You didn't buy any paper.*
>
> *Did you buy any paper?*

1. The engineers made some plans.

2. The factory hired some workers.

3. The boys are eating some candy.

4. The secretary was writing some letters.

5. She's got some money.　　　　　6. You'll need some help.

7. They received some good advice.

8. John has made some wonderful suggestions.

9. Betty had some strange ideas.　　　10. I can eat some ice-cream.

習 題 196

依照例句把下面的句子改為追問句與否定問句。

Examples:

> You have some money. → $\begin{cases} \textit{You have some money, don't you?} \\ \textit{Don't you hove some money?} \end{cases}$
>
> They won't get any help. → $\begin{cases} \textit{They won't get any help, will they?} \\ \textit{Won't they get any help?} \end{cases}$

1. He knows some English.　　　　2. He doesn't know any English.

3. She needed some money.　　　　4. She didn't need any money.

5. They can borrow some books.　　6. They can't borrow any books.

7. She is making some sandwiches for us.

8. She isn't making any sandwiches for us.

9. You have done some studying.   10. You haven't done any studying.

習　題　197

依照例句回答下列問句。

Examples:

    Do you want some bananas?

      Yes, *I want some bananas. I want some.*

    Did he ask you for any soap?

      No, *he didn't ask me for any soap. He didn't ask me for any.*

1. Did the factory hire any men? No, ⋯

2. Did she invite any friends? Yes, ⋯

3. Is there any mail for me? Yes, ⋯

4. Do you have any questions? No, ⋯

5. Are there any matches left? No, ⋯

6. Will you have any more tea? No, ⋯

7. Won't you have some more cake? Yes, ⋯

8. Can you eat any more potatoes? Yes, ⋯

9. Do you think there is any money in the purse? No, ⋯

10. Do you believe that he will lend you any books? Yes, ⋯

參考：

    some 與 any 後面的名詞，如果已經在前文提到，就可以省略。例如：

    Do you need any money?

      Yes, I need *some* (money).

      No, I don't need *any* (money).

    Are there any books on the desk?

      Yes, there are *some* (books on the desk).

      No, there aren't *any* (books on the desk).

習　題　198

在下面的空白裡填 some 或 any。

1. There isn't _____ sugar in this jar.

2. She asked me for _____ paper, but I can't find _____.

3. You can't have _____ more tomatoes because I want _____ for myself.

4. Please give me _____ more cake. I'm sorry but there isn't _____.

5. I can't eat _____ more ice-cream, but I would like _____ more pudding.

6. I asked him for _____ ink, and he gave me _____.

7. Don't make _____ noise. I want to get _____ sleep.

8. Have you had _____ tea? I can give you _____.

9. Go and ask him for _____ more paper. I don't have _____ in my desk.

10. If you need　more money, you must get _____ out of the bank; there is hardly _____ in the house.

11. We have _____ new shoes in today. Do you want to buy _____?

12. Would you like _____ coffee? (= Please have coffee.) Yes, I'd like _____.

13. Didn't I give you _____ money yesterday? (= I think I gave you _____.) No, you didn't give me _____.

14. I don't have _____ time to do _____ more now; you can do yourself.

15. Wouldn't you like _____ thing to drink? Have _____ lemonade?

12-4. 無定冠詞 a(n) 的用法

「無定冠詞」a(n) 的用法，有一點像數目的 one，只能用在單數可數名詞的前面。

> A stitch in time saves nine.「及時縫一針省却將來的九針（及時行事，事半功倍）。」

> I'll be here for an hour or two.「我會在這裡待一兩個鐘頭。」

a 用在以子音開頭的名詞（或形容詞）前面；an 用在以母音開頭的名詞（或形容詞）前面。

a book, *a* pen, *a* clever student, *a* delicious apple.

an apple, *an* egg, *an* old man, *an* American student.

注意：*a* hotel, *a* home, *a* hill 但是 *an* hour, *an* honor, *an* heir, *an* honest boy;

a university, *a* uniform, *a* useful thing 但是 *an* usher, *an* ugly duck;

a ewe, *a* European country 但是 *an* egg, *an* excellent book;

a one-story building, *a* one-way road 但是 *an* ox, *an* oven;

an e〔i〕, *an* h〔etʃ〕, *an* N〔ɛn〕, *an* S〔ɛs〕, *an* M.A.〔ɛm e〕（文學碩士）, *an* SOS〔ɛs o ɛs〕（海上求助信號）, *an* 8〔et〕-day vacation（八天的假期）。

無定冠詞 a(n) 的用法主要有下列三種：

(1) 「任指」：'one', 'any'：指「一個」或「隨便那一個」人或物。

I want to buy *a* fountain pen tomorrow.

Hand me *a* piece of chalk, please.

(2) 「殊指」'a certain', 'some particular'：指「某一個」或「有一個」人或物。

I bought *a* fountain pen yesterday.

A man is waiting for you outside.

There is *a* letter for you on the table.

(3) 「泛指」'that which is called…', 'every'：表示「凡是…」或「只要是…」。

A dog is a faithful animal.

A cat looks like a tiger.

參考：a(n) 除了上述「任指」、「殊指」、「泛指」以外，還有下列兩種比較特殊的用法：

(4) 「同一」（the same）：

No two men are of *a* mind.「沒有兩個人會有同一顆心（人心不同各如其面）。」

Two of *a* trade seldom agree.「兩個從事同一行業的人很少會同意（同行相忌）。」

Birds of *a* feather flock together.「同一色羽毛的鳥常聚在一起（物以類聚）。」

(5) 「每一」（per, every）：

I used to go to the movies once *a* week.

We eat three meals *a* day.

習　題　199

在下面的空白裡填入 φ, a 或 an。

1. _____ coffee is _____ drink.

2. _____ coat is made of _____ wool.

3. _____ iron is _____ metal.

4. _____ orange has _____ sweet taste.

5. _____ sugar is nice in _____ cup of _____ tea.

6. _____ cigarette is made of _____ tobacco and _____ paper.

7. _____ ring is made of _____ gold or _____ silver.

8. I like _____ jam on _____ piece of _____ bread.

9. I can write _____ letter in _____ ink or with _____ pencil.

10. _____ bread is made from _____ flour, and _____ flour is made from _____ wheat.

習　題　200

在下面的空白裡填入 φ, a, an，或 some。

1. _____ woman gave me _____ money yesterday.

2. _____ yard usually has _____ flowers in it.

3. Give me ink to write _____ letter.

4. _____ Austrian sheep give us _____ very good wool.

5. I want _____ glass of _____ lemonade with _____ sugar in it.

6. You must write in _____ ink; here is _____ pen.

7. _____ house made of _____ wood catches _____ fire very easily.

8. _____ book about politics is too difficult for _____ child.

9. There is _____ dirt on the floor and _____ dirty mark on _____ curtain.

10. There is _____ pencil and _____ writing paper.

習 題 201

在正確的答案下面劃線。

1. The machine is made of (metal, a metal).

2. (Iron, An iron) is (metal, a metal).

3. She pressed her dresses with (iron, an iron).

4. I prefer (tea, a tea) to coffee.

5. This is really (excellent tea, an excellent tea).

6. This is (tea, a tea) grown only in the mountains of Ceylon.

7. There is no smoke without (fire, a fire).

8. There was (fire, a fire) in the next street last night.

9. She always has (cold meat, a cold meat) on hand for the school lunch boxes.

10. She suggested (cold meat, a cold meat) for a summer luncheon.

11. This is (lace, a lace) seldom seen in New York.

12. She wore a dress of (old lace, an old lace).

13. He did it all out of (kindness, a kindness).

14. It would be (great kindness, a great kindness) to call and see him while he is so ill.

15. It was (excusable error, an excusable error).

16. (Error, An error) is unavoidable.

17. They sell books on (education, an education).

18. He wanted his son to have (education, an education).

19. She felt (pity, a pity) for the poor orphans.

20. What (pity, a pity) she couldn't go with you!

21. It's (mercy, a mercy) that he didn't take that train!

22. He never shows (mercy, a mercy) for the poor.

23. The old man is without (sight, a sight) and hearing.

24. She was (sight, a sight) pleasing to the eye.

25. I had (pain, a pain) in my leg yesterday.

26. (Death, A death) comes to all.

27. He felt (new happiness, a new happiness) growing within him.

28. Patience is (virtue, a virtue).

29. Eat more fruit; it will do you (good, a good).

30. He showed (amazing endurance, an amazing endurance).

參考：物質名詞與抽象名詞通常都不加冠詞a(n)；加冠詞的時候，常表示「種　類」

（a kind of）或「事例」（an instance of）。比較：

$\begin{cases} \text{I like } \textit{coffee.}（指一般的咖啡）\\ \text{I like } \textit{a coffee} \text{ from Brazil.}（特指一種來自巴西的咖啡）\end{cases}$

$\begin{cases} \text{She was filled with } \textit{pity} \text{ for the poor girl.}（同情心）\\ \text{It's } \textit{a pity} \text{ that you can't come.}（一件令人遺憾的事情）\end{cases}$

習　題　202

依照例句把下面的句子改為否定句。

Examples:

He gave me (some) books. → $\begin{cases} \textit{He gave me no books.}\\ \textit{He didn't give me any books.}\end{cases}$

There is no letter on the table. → $\begin{cases} \textit{There is a letter on the table.}\\ \textit{There isn't any letter on the table.}\end{cases}$

1. There is some sugar.
2. I can see a hat on the shelf.
3. He likes girls with red hair.
4. She has got some money to lend you.
5. I have some more money.
6. There are some apples on the tree.
7. The hen has laid eggs today.
8. Some ink spilled on the carpet.
9. Some people called last night.
10. He gave me some ink, so I could write some more.

參考：含有無定冠詞與名詞的句子可以變成兩種不同形式的否定句：

She has (some) money. →

$\begin{cases} \text{She has } \textit{no} \text{ money.}（用 no 代替 } \phi \text{ 或 some。）\\ \text{She does} \textit{n't} \text{ have } \textit{any} \text{ money.}（用 not … any 代替 } \phi \text{ 或 some）\end{cases}$

He gave me (some) books. →

{ He gave me *no* books.（用 no 代替 φ 或 some。）
  He did*n't* give me *any* books.（用 not ⋯ any 代替 φ 或 some）

There is a book on the table. →

{ There's *no* book on the table.（用 no 代替 a。）
  There is*n't* *any* book on the table.（用 not ⋯ any 代替 a）

12-5. 有定冠詞 the 的用法

除了無定冠詞 φ, some, any, a(n) 以外的限定詞都指出特定的人或物，因此可以叫做**有定限詞**（definite determiner）。英語的有定限詞包括「有定冠詞」the，「指示詞」this, that, these, those 與「所有格」。

有定冠詞 the 可以用在可數名詞之前，也可以用在不可數名詞之前，它主要的用法是表示說話者與聽話者之間，對於所講的事物有一個共同的認識或默契。換句話說，如果說話的人與聽話的人都明白彼此指的是什麼人或什麼東西，那麼就在這個名詞的前面加 the。這種情形又可以分為下列幾種：

(1)「後指」：指在前文裡已經出現過的名詞。注意，這些名詞前後用不同的冠詞。

I saw *a* cat in the tree this morning, but when I looked again this afternoon, *the* cat was gone.

A boy and *a girl* were walking down the street together, and *the* girl was shouting at *the* boy.

My uncle sent me *a* fountain pen and *some* books. I kept *the* fountain pen for myself but gave *the* books to my brother.

(2)「明指」：名詞的前後有修飾語，足以認定某一個特定的人或物。

Hand me *the* longer piece of chalk on the desk, please.

The principal of our school went to the United States last month.

This is *the* book I have been looking for.

(3)「暗指」：名詞的前後雖然沒有修飾語，但是從生活經驗或語言情況中仍可以判定所指的是一個特定的人或物。

The President will be on the air this evening.

The moon goes round *the* earth.

Please close *the* window. (i.e. the window that is open)

Did you wind *the* clock? (e.g. the clock in the drawing room)

He went to *the* post office to mail *the* letter. (e.g. the post office near by; the letter he has just written)

類例：*the* king, *the* Emperor, *the* Lord (= Christ), *the* world, *the* universe, *the* sun, *the* sea, *the* ocean, *the* weather, *the* sky, *the* wind 等。

(4) 「泛指」：用在單數可數名詞之前，以表示一類的所有分子。

The horse is a noble animal.

The early bird catches *the* worm.

參考：

(1) the 也可以與形容詞或「分詞」連用，表示一類的所有分子：

The rich (rich people) are not always happier than *the* poor (= poor people).

The dying and *the* wounded (those who were dying and wounded) were sent to the hospital.

類例：the old, the young, the dead, the living, the blind, the brave 等。

(2) the 也可以與名詞或形容詞連用，表示抽象的概念。

He felt *the patriot* (= his patriotic feeling) rise within his breast.

The pen (= the power of pen) is mightier than *the sword* (= the power of the sword).

We seek for *the true*, *the good* and *the beautiful* (= truth, goodness and beauty).

習　題　203

在下面的空白裡填 φ, a(n) 或 the。

1. I saw _____ woman the other day. _____ woman wore _____ big hat. _____ hat had _____ long feathers on it. _____ feathers were red, green and yellow.

2. Go and see who is at _____ door.

3. _____ bird can fly very high in _____ sky.

4. He came to see us twice _____ month.

5. China is _____ largest country in Asia.

6. _____ principal of our school was absent today.

7. _____ student of our school was run over by a bus.

8. John is _____ heir to a millionaire. (John is the only heir.)

9. John is _____ heir to a millionaire. (There are several other heirs besides John.)

10. _____ capital of Japan is Tokyo.

11. Tokyo is _____ city in Japan.

12. _____ man with a red necktie is Mr. Smith.

13. _____ man she loves must be very rich.

14. Who is _____ man teaching her English?

15. We need _____ woman who understands French.

16. _____ mailman has come, but there was no mail for us today.

17. _____ young can always learn something from _____ old.

18. I had _____ pain in my side yesterday, and I had _____ pain in my side again today.

19. _____ air is necessary to life, and so is _____ water.

20. _____ air in her room is heavy with _____ perfume of flowers.

21. I love _____ open air and outdoor life.

22. The children are having _____ exercise in _____ open air.

23. _____ wisdom is _____ gift of heaven.

24. _____ wisdom of Solomon is quite well-known among _____ students.

25. I cannot forget _____ kindness with which he treated me.

26. Would you have _____ kindness to pull up _____ window?

27. Have you had _____ kindness shown? Pass it on.

28. _____ money begets _____ money.

29. I wonder who took _____ money in _____ purse.

30. At last _____ warrior in him was thoroughly aroused.

習　題　204

在下面的空白裡填 φ, a(n) 或 the。

1. This is _____ most interesting story I ever heard.

2. Can you tell me which is _____ better of these two models?

3. We were married on _____ fifth of May, 1957.

4. You are _____ very man I wanted to see.

5. _____ very thought of going there frightened me.

6. This is _____ only example I can give you.

7. He is _____ only son.

8. They were both born on _____ same day and in the same town.

9. He was always _____ first guest to come and _____ last to leave.

10. Rice is sold either by _____ catty or by _____ pound.

11. Rice is sold here at _____ price of two dollars _____ catty.

12. It is cheaper to buy eggs by _____ dozen than apiece.

13. How much do eggs cost _____ dozen?

14. We rent our house by _____ month not by _____ week.

15. How often do you have your hair cut _____ month?

16. The garden lies to _____ south of the house.

17. He is _____ right man for _____ position.

18. I will not apologize because I am in _____ right.

19. He got onto _____ wrong train and got out at _____ wrong station.

20. His address is given at _____ left of _____ card.

21. You've come on _____ wrong day. Your music lesson is on _____ Friday.

22. Three loud knocks are heard on _____ door at _____ right.

23. She patted the boy on _____ back and comforted him.

24. The little boy pulled his sister by _____ sleeve and asked her to take him out.

25. Take what you want and throw _____ rest away.

參考：有定冠詞 the 常用在

(1) 最高級形容詞或比較級形容詞 + of the two 之前：

the best book, *the* highest mountain, *the* most important rule;

the taller of the two, *the* more useful of the two.

(2) 序數之前：

the third chapter (cf. chapter three), *the* fourth of July.

(3) first, next, last, same, very, only, right, wrong 等形容詞之前：

She came *the* (very) next day.

He used *the* (very) same words as you had.

This is *the* very thing I wanted to find out.

Which is *the* right side of the cloth?

(4) 由一些形容詞轉來的名詞，如 north, south, east, west, right, left, wrong 等之前：

Russia is in *the* north of Europe.

Please turn to *the* left.

You must be in *the* wrong.

(5) 習慣用法：

in *the* morning (afternoon, evening, day-time, etc.), in *the* dark (light, rain, etc.),

for *the* time being, in *the* meantime, etc.;

to rent or pay something by *the* day (week, month, year, etc.);

to buy or sell something by *the* pound (catty, yard, bushel, gallon, etc.);

to pull, seize or catch someone by *the* collar (sleeve, arm, ear, etc.);

to strike, hit or pat someone on *the* head (shoulder, back, etc.):

We rent our room by *the* week. (= We pay our rents every week.)

This cloth is sold by *the* yard.

He seized the thief by *the* collar and dragged him to the police station.

習　題　205

在下面的句子裡，除了 (14) 與 (15) 兩句以外，括號裡的名詞都指事物的總類。把不適當的說法劃掉。

1. (The milk, Milk) is very good for health, but some children don't like it.

2. (The foxes, Foxes) are cunning animals.

3. (An owl, Owl) cannot see in the day-time.

4. (The bees, Bees, Bee) make honey.

5. (The blood, Blood) is thicker than (the water, water).

6. (The man, Man) is in general stronger than (the woman, woman).

7. (A sentence, Sentence, Sentences) are made of (the words, words, word).

8. (The friend, A friend) in need is (a friend, the friend) indeed.

9. He is as poor as (the church mouse, a church mouse).

10. Do you know who invented (a telephone, the telephone) ?

11. (The cow, A cow) and (the horse, a horse) are domestic animals.

12. (The dinosaur, A dinosaur) no longer exists.

13. (The panda, A panda) is found only some part in China.

14. (The bee, A bee) is gathering honey from flowers these days.

15. (The dinosaur, A dinosaur) roamed here in prehistoric times.

參考：英語裡表示「泛指」的方法一共有四種：

(1) 單數名詞不加定冠詞：限於不可數名詞與 man「人類，男人」、woman「女人」

　　Smoke is lighter than *air*.

　　Woman is sometimes cleverer than *man*.

(2) 單數名詞加無定冠詞 a(n)：含有 any「任何」、every「每個」的意思。

　　A pig is a domestic animal.

　　An oak is harder than *a beech*.

　　注意：這種「泛指」只能用在現在單純式主動語態的句子。比較：

　　A bee gathers honey from flowers.（「泛指」，做「凡是蜜蜂」或「任何蜜蜂」
　　解。）

　　A bee gathered honey from flowers.（過去式）　　（非「泛指」，只
　　A bee is gathering honey from flowers.（進行式）　　能做「殊指，有一
　　Honey is gathered by a bee.（被動態）　　隻蜜蜂」解。）

(3) 單數名詞加有定冠詞 the：

The student should respect *the teacher*.（人）

The camel lives in a desert.（動物）

The rose is the sweetest of all flowers.（植物）

The diamond is a precious stone.（珠寶）

Alexander Graham Bell invented *the telephone*.（發明）

Can you play *the piano?*（樂器）

The small shop flourishes in this quarter.（店舖）

The book, *the play*, *the film* are strong influences on our social life.（文學、藝術）

We hired the motor-car by *the day*.（計算的單位）

注意：這種「泛指」雖然形式上屬於單數，但是在語義上卻表示複數。比較：

$\left\{\begin{array}{l}\text{A mosquito is increasing in numbers.（×）}\\ \text{The mosquito is increasing in numbers.（○）}\\ \text{Mosquitos are increasing in numbers.（○）}\end{array}\right.$

$\left\{\begin{array}{l}\text{A dinosaur is extinct.（×）}\\ \text{The dinosaur is extinct.（○）}\\ \text{Dinosaurs are extinct.（○）}\end{array}\right.$

(4) 複數名詞不加冠詞：限於可數名詞。

Rabbits have long ears and soft hair.

Potatoes originated in Peru.

(5) 複數專有名詞加定冠詞 the：*the* Johnsons, *the* Germans.

（注意：the Chinese）

習 題 206

在空白裡填 *φ*, a(n) 或 the。

1. _____ waiter, bring me _____ glass of _____ milk.

2. _____ young man, would you be interested in earning _____ couple of dollars?

3. _____ Professor Hill has already explained _____ problem to us.

4. Robert Louis Stevenson, _____ author of _____ *Treasure Island*, is also _____ great poet.

5. He became _____ Mayor of _____ Taipei _____ last year.

6. The knife is made of _____ special kind of _____ metal.

7. What _____ kind of _____ flower is this?

8. This is _____ very rare species of _____ fish which can be found only in _____ deep ocean.

9. _____ monkey resembles very much _____ man.

10. _____ Mother is doing dishes in _____ kitchen. She'll be here in _____ minute.

11. Do you take _____ walk before or after _____ dinner?

12. He is _____ Christian and goes to _____ church _____ every Sunday.

13. She left _____ school in _____ year 1956.

14. Do you go to _____ school on _____ foot or by _____ bus?

15. _____ day after _____ day, she worked hard from morning till _____ night.

16. This time I'm going to _____ United States by _____ sea, not by _____ air.

17. Some of the students are playing _____ basketball, while the others are playing _____ tennis.

18. When I am at _____ leisure, I like to play _____ chess with my friends.

19. They went away _____ arm in _____ arm.

20. They stood _____ side by _____ side, talking happily to each other.

21. _____ Washington was twice elected _____ president; he was elected _____ first president of _____ United States.

22. Stevenson is _____ English novelist and _____ poet.

23. _____ novelist and _____ poet are discussing literature and art on _____ air.

24. _____ watch and _____ chain belongs to my father.

25. I see _____ red and _____ white flower in the vase. (one flower)

26. There is _____ red and _____ white flower in the vase. (two flowers)

27. Both _____ red and _____ white flowers may be worn on this occasion.

28. _____ red and _____ white flower is _____ azalea.

29. _____ red and _____ white flowers look very lovely against the green leaves.
    (one kind of flowers)

30. _____ red and _____ white flowers in the vase are both my favorites. (two kinds of flowers)

參考 1：冠詞的省略

名詞在下列情形下通常不加冠詞。

(a) 招呼人家的時候（「呼格」）：

   Young man, tell me your name.

(b) 職位或階級當做同位語或補語用的時候：

   Mr. Young, *late Professor of English*.（同位語）

   His brother was *Duke of Lancaster*.（補語）

   We elected him *captain of our school team*.（補語）

(c) 表示自己家裡成員的名詞，如 father、mother、uncle、aunt、baby、nurse 等：

   Mother is going to cook us chicken this evening.

(d) 表示三餐（dinner、supper、lunch、breakfast）或運動、遊戲（baseball、basketball、tennis、golf、ping pong、chess、bridge）的名詞之前：

   Would you like to have *dinner* with us this evening?

   We eat bread and butter for *breakfast*.

   I like to play *bridge* in my leisure hours.

(e) a kind of、a sort of、a species of、a type of、a manner of 後面的名詞：

   The banyan is a kind of *fig tree*.

   What kind of *soap* is this?

(f) 兩個相同的名詞用介詞連起來的時候：

step by *step*、*day* after *day*, from *door* to *door*.

(g) 兩個相對或相關的名詞用連詞或介詞連起來的時候：

father and *mother*, *father* and *son*, *brother* and *sister*, *parent* and *child*, *husband* and *wife*, *teacher* and *student*, *doctor* and *patient*, *heart* and *soul*, *pen* and *ink*, *pen* and *paper*, *east* and *west*, *young* and *old*, *poor* and *rich*, from *morning* till *night*, from *hand* to *mouth*, etc.

(h) 含有 school、college、town、bed、church、prison 等名詞的慣用語：

school, college: at school, got to school, leave school, at college, …

town: in town, go to town, leave town, …

bed: go to bed, lie in bed, get out of bed, …

其他：go to *church* (*prison, market, mass, war, bank, court, sea*, …)

(i) 由下面的介詞所帶頭的慣用語：

By (car, bus, train, plane, steamer, ship, boat, land, water, river, sea, air, rail, foot, mail, telephone, radio, …)

On (foot, horseback, deck, shore, …)

At (dinner, table, desk, hand, …)

In (town, jail, prison, bed, …)

By (day, night, name, trade, profession, …)

At (night, noon, midnight, sunset, sunrise, daybreak, dawn, …)

In (trouble, debt, danger, fact, truth, …)

(j) 由下面的動詞所帶頭的慣用語：

Do (good, harm, justice, evil, wrong, …)

Make (haste, way, war〔upon〕, love〔to〕, …)

Take (place, care, breath, part〔in〕, heart, advantage〔of〕, …)

Give (way, attention, aid, battle, ear, …)

Catch (fire, cold, sight〔of〕, hold〔of〕, …)

參考 2：冠詞的重複與省略

如果兩個名詞同指一個人或物，那麼只要在第一個名詞前面加冠詞；如果兩個

名詞各指不同的人或物，那麼兩個名詞前面都要加冠詞。比較：

$$\left\{\begin{array}{l}\text{I have } a \text{ black and white dog.「一隻黑白雜色的狗」}\\ \text{I have } a \text{ black and } a \text{ white dog.「兩隻狗；一隻黑，一隻白」}\end{array}\right.$$

$$\left\{\begin{array}{l}The \text{ secretary and treasurer } is \text{ absent.「一人兼秘書與司庫的工作」}\\ The \text{ secretary and } the \text{ treasurer } are \text{ absent.「秘書與司庫兩個人」}\end{array}\right.$$

習 題 207

在空白裡填 ϕ, a(n) 或 the。

1. Is she _____ Miss Hopkins you asked me about?

2. You are not _____ John I used to know.

3. I can't believe I'm seeing _____ Margaret of my son's letters.

4. There is no _____ Anderson in this block, but we have two Addisons.

5. _____ Mr. Smith is waiting to see you outside.

6. Shanghai was once called _____ Paris of China.

7. Tagore is often called _____ Longfellow of India.

8. Bob wishes to become _____ Einstein (= a great physicist like Einstein).

9. He was _____ Napoleon (= the greatest general) of his age.

10. _____ China today is quite different from _____ China fifty years ago.

參考：專有名詞與冠詞：

(1) 在專有名詞之前加有定冠詞 the，表示特定的人、物或場所。比較：

$$\left\{\begin{array}{l}\text{I know } John\ Brown \text{ very well.}\\ \text{Is } the\ John\ Brown \text{ you spoke of an American?}\end{array}\right.$$

$$\left\{\begin{array}{l}Rembrandt \text{ is a great Dutch painter.}\\ \text{We compare } the\ Rembrandt \text{ (= the painting done by Rembrandt) in the}\\ \quad \text{Louvre with } the\ Rembrandt \text{ in Amsterdam.}\end{array}\right.$$

$$\left\{\begin{array}{l}New\ York \text{ is the biggest city in America.}\\ \text{Tokyo is } the\ New\ York \text{ of Japan.}\end{array}\right.$$

　　　注意：*the great Caesar, the immortal Shakespeare*。

(2) 在專有名詞之前加無定冠詞 a(n)，表示這個專有名詞變成普通名詞。比較：

$$\left\{\begin{array}{l} \textit{Edison} \text{ is a great inventor.} \\ \text{I hope there will be } \textit{an Edison} \text{ (= a great inventor like Edison) in my family.} \end{array}\right.$$

$$\left\{\begin{array}{l} \textit{Henry Ford} \text{ is a very well-known automobile manufacturer in the United} \\ \quad \text{States.} \\ \text{We bought } \textit{a Ford} \text{ (= an automobile produced by the Ford Company) last} \\ \quad \text{year.} \end{array}\right.$$

(3) a（n）加在人名之前，有時表示「一個名叫…的人」：

Do you know *a Mr. Brown* (= *one* Mr. Brown, *a certain* Mr. Brown)?

習　題　208

在空白裡填 φ, a(n)，some 或 the。

1. _____ page of _____ book is torn.
2. Can you play _____ violin?
3. _____ cat loves _____ milk.
4. He gave me _____ food and _____ glass of _____ wine.
5. There is _____ yard behind _____ house.
6. _____ mailman has just put _____ letter under _____ door.
7. She has bought _____ new dress with _____ long sleeves.
8. There are _____ beautiful flowers in _____ park.
9. _____ fruit and _____ vegetables are good for _____ health.
10. Put _____ butter on _____ bread.
11. I would like _____ house in _____ country.
12. It is enjoyable to watch _____ TV in _____ evening.
13. It is pleasant to play _____ game of _____ tennis on _____ summer afternoon.
14. _____ butcher opposite _____ library always sells _____ good meat.
15. Jane and Alice went down _____ hill to fetch _____ bucket of _____ water.
16. I want _____ can of _____ peaches, _____ sugar, and _____ pound of

_____ beef.

17. Father always smokes _____ cigarette with _____ cup of _____ tea.

18. _____ life without _____ wife is _____ life without _____ strife.

19. _____ book on that shelf is _____ interesting one about _____ history.

20. _____ student at _____ back of _____ class is readng _____ newspaper.

21. _____ man, who is _____ social animal, cannot live alone.

22. What _____ fun we had when we were at _____ seaside!

23. _____ book his uncle bought him last week is not _____ one he is reading now.

24. John majors in _____ history; he is _____ history major.

25. What do you usually eat for _____ lunch?

26. We ate _____ light lunch at the cafeteria.

27. _____ school is situated at _____ foot of the mountain.

28. _____ school begins at 8 a.m. and ends at 4 p.m.

29. My brother was killed during _____ Second World War.

30. _____ World War II brought _____ death to hundreds of thousands of people.

31. Mr. Tower is _____ most intelligent person I ever met.

32. _____ most children like to eat candies.

33. We enjoyed watching _____ football on _____ television.

34. Did you enjoy _____ football game last night?

35. Is _____ Chinese _____ difficult language to learn?

36. Miss Jones has _____ good command of _____ Chinese language.

37. "Hwa" is _____ Chinese for "flower".

38. The picture looks better at _____ distance. (= from a short distance)

39. I saw _____ small figure running away in _____ distance. (= far away)

40. Though he is _____ one-armed man, he is _____ best-experienced mechanic in our company.

41. _____ poor man as (= though) he was, he always tried to help those in _____ need.

42. Mr. Johnson became _____ president of _____ big electronic company.

43. Mr. Taylor is _____ poorly-paid clerk in _____ school library.

44. They came by _____ plane; they got here by taking _____ plane.

45. I met _____ Englishman on _____ train.

46. _____ late Mrs. Smith was _____ good wife and _____ mother.

47. Dr. Sun Yat-sen is _____ great scholar and _____ statesman.

48. My brother wishes he would be _____ Edison some day.

49. _____ John Smith that lives on _____ Main Street is _____ good friend of mine.

50. I don't mean _____ Cleopatra of _____ history but _____ Cleopatra of _____ *Bernad Shaw*.

12-6. 指示詞：this, that, these, those

(1) This 用來指較近的人或物；that 指較遠的人或物：

　　This camera is expensive.

　　That camera is expensive, too.

　　These 是 this 的複數形；those 是 that 的複數形。

　　　These books are not as interesting as *those* books.

(2) This, these, that, those 除了放在名詞前面做限定詞以外，也可以單獨做代名詞用。比較：

　　⎰ *This* camera is expensive.
　　⎱ *This* is an expensive camera.

　　⎰ I like *those flowers* in the vase.
　　⎱ I like *those* in the vase.

　　These books are not as interestig as *those* (books).

(3) 在文章裡，為了避免重複使用同一個名詞，常用 that 與 those 來代替這個名詞。這個時候，that 與 those 後面常有「介詞片語」等修飾語：

The tail of a fox is much longer than *that* (= the tail) of a rabbit.（代替單數名詞 the tail）

Our teachers are as well-trained as *those* (= the teachers) in the other coutries. （代替多數名詞 the teachers）

The people in cities live a much more complicated life than *those* (= the people) in the countryside.（代替多數名詞 the people）

(4) 我們也常連用 this 與 that 或 these 與 those 來表示「前者」、「後者」的意思。 This（these）指在前文中後提到的事物（「後者」）；that（those）指在前文中先提到的事物（「前者」）。

Work and *play* are both necessary to health; *this* (play = the latter) gives us rest, and *that* (= work = the former) energy.

Friends and *books* are valuable; *these* (= books = the latter), perhaps, more than *those* (= friends = the former).

參考：*This* 與 *that* 有時候還可以指前面的子句：

He is lazy, and you know *this* (= that he is lazy).

He has failed the examination, and *this* (= the fact that he has failed the exam) is the proof that he is lazy.

He is late for school, and *that* (= his being late for school) happens very often.

習 題 **209**

依照例句回答下列問句。

Examples:

Which book is new?	Which lessons are easy?
(STUDENT 1) *This one is.*	*These are.*
(STUDENT 2) *That one's old.*	*Those are hard.*

1. Which pencil is long?　　　　2. Which answers are right?

3. Which box is big?　　　　　　4. Which satchels are heavy?

5. Which watch is broken?　　　　6. Which eggs are fresh?

參考：我們可以說 this one 或 that one，但是不能說 these ones 或 those ones：

This book is much better than *that* (one).

These are much better than *those*.

習 題 210

在空白裡填入 this, that, these 或 those。

1. Come _____ way, please.

2. _____ is a good idea.

3. _____ are times that try men's souls.

4. Life was easier in _____ days.

5. What about _____ five dollars you borrowed from me last week?

6. Tom must have arrived home by _____ time.

7. He will have finished his assignment by _____ time.

8. _____ is Bob Smith speaking. May I speak to Mr. Johnson, please?

9. "Is _____ you, Mary?" "Yes, it's me."

10. Is _____ what you really think?

11. _____ much is certain: he will not come back today.

12. She left her home alone on Sunday morning, we know _____ much.

13. His behavior was not _____ of a gentleman.

14. The population of China is much bigger than _____ of Japan.

15. We compare Shakespeare's plays with _____ by Ibsen.

16. The book on the shelf is as interesting as _____ on the desk.

17. People from the country tend to spend less than _____ living in the city.

18. It is a different kind of car from _____ I am used to.

19. Will _____ who wish to go stand up?

20. All _____ that I saw were old.

21. _____ who are rich are not always happy. 「富者不常樂。」

22. _____ who respect others will be respected. 「敬人者，人恆敬之。」

參考：學習下面的慣用語：

　(a) *That's* right. 「對了。」 *That's* all right with me. 「我無所謂。」 *That'll* do.「那正好（正合適；行）。」*That* won't do.「那樣不行。」

That's certain.「一定的。」I am not sure of *that*.「這個，我就沒有把握了。」

That's right.「對了；好。」*That* can't be true.「那不可能是真的。」

That's it.「就是了；對了。」*That's* all.「這就是全部了（沒有了；完了）。」

So *that's that*.「這樣就完了；就這樣決定吧。」

(b) He ought to be ready *by this* (= by this time).「這個時候已經」

At this (or *that*) (= hearing this or that) he got angry.「聽到這個（或那個）；於是」

With this (or *that*) (= saying this or that) he went out.「這樣（或那樣）說著；於是」

The price of the tea is only five dollars, *and* a very good tea *at that* (= *besides*, it's a very good tea).「而且」

A fortnight tomorrow, *that is to say* (= in other words), May 10th.「那就是說；即」

He says he's not guilty, but I'm sure he's guilty *for all that* (= in spite of what has been said, done, etc.).「儘管那樣」

12-7. 代名詞所有格

所有格分為「代名詞的所有格」與「名詞的所有格」。**代名詞的所有格**（possessive pronouns）包括下列幾種：

單　數		複　數	
主　格	所有格	主　格	所有格
I	my	we	our
you	your	you	your
he	his	they	their
she	her		
it	its		

代名詞的所有格可以用在可數名詞之前，也可以用在不可數名詞之前：

Please take *your* time.

He wanted *his* money back.

She finally took *her* chance.

All the students should bring *their* books with them.

如果代名詞所有格後面的名詞要省略，那麼就要不同形式的代名詞來代替：

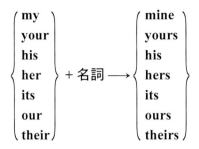

比較：

$\left\{ \begin{array}{l} \text{This is } \textit{your book} \text{ and that is } \textit{my book.} \\ \text{This is } \textit{your book} \text{ and that is } \textit{mine.} \\ \text{This is } \textit{yours} \text{ and that is } \textit{mine.} \end{array} \right.$

They lost all their money, so we gave them *ours* (= our money).

I prefer your company to *theirs* (= theircompany).

I thought my flowers are pretty, but *hers* (= her flowers) are prettier.

習 題 211

依照例句改寫下列句子。

Examples:

This is my book. → *This book is mine.*

That is her hat. → *That hat is hers.*

1. These are their magazines.　　2. Those are not his pencils.

3. I am sure these are our desks.　　4. Are those her new dresses?

5. Is this your fountain pen?

6. This is my pencil, but that is his knife.

7. This is my coat, but the other is your coat.

8. How many of these are your books?

習　題　212

依照例句改寫下列句子。

Examples:

> Our friend is staying with us tonight. (a)
>
> *A friend of ours is staying with us tonight.*
>
> You can borrow my book. (any)
>
> *You can borrow any book of mine.*

1. Your friend came to see you. (a)

2. May I borrow your book? (this)　　3. I don't know his sister. (any)

4. It is her fault. (no)

5. You should not repeat your mistakes. (these)

6. That is my business. (no)

7. The Smiths are paying a visit to their relative in town. (a)

8. They went to the park with their friends. (some)

9. I forgot where I left your magazines. (those)

10. Where did you put my new pen? (that)

11. We can show our sample. (another)

12. Which friend gave this to you? (your)

13. Which picture do you like best? (her)

14. I can't remember which book has interested you. (my)

15. I have my own reasons for not going there. (some)

參考：代名詞所有格不能與其他限定詞（a(n), some, any, no, this, that, those, another, which 等）一起放在名詞的前面，但是可以放在名詞的後面。這個時候，my, your, …等要改為 mine, yours, …同時前面要加介詞 of。比較：
我見過你這位朋友。

$$\begin{cases} \text{I have met } \textit{your this} \text{ friend. （×）} \\ \text{I have met } \textit{this} \text{ friend } \textit{of yours}. \text{（○）} \end{cases}$$

你看過我哪一本書呢？

$$\begin{cases} \textit{Which my} \text{ book have you read? （×）} \\ \textit{Which} \text{ book of } \textit{mine} \text{ have you read? （○）} \end{cases}$$

習 題 213

把 own 放在句子中適當的地方。

Examples:

> This is his book. → *This is his own book.*
>
> This book is mine. → *This book is my own.*

1. I have my trouble.
2. They have their plans.
3. I saw it with my eyes.
4. This house is mine.
5. I have a watch and my brother has his, too.
6. She makes all her clothes.
7. I cook my breakfast, but usually have my dinner in town.
8. She wrote her name, and I did mine, too.
9. I've lost my knife. Would you lend me yours?
10. Tell Jane not to forget her appointment; you mustn't forget yours, either.

參考：為了加強語氣，我們常把 own「自己的」加在代名詞所有格後面：

> It was her *own* idea, not mine.
>
> This book is your *own*.（注意，不能說 *your's own*）
>
> He has no house of his *own*.

習 題 214

在空白裡填入適當的代名詞所有格（my, mine 等）。

1. Tell him not to forget＿＿＿＿＿ ticket; she mustn't forget ＿＿＿＿＿, either.
2. I see that you have lost ＿＿＿＿＿ pen; perhaps I can lend you ＿＿＿＿＿.
3. Jane has come to see me; ＿＿＿＿＿ mother and ＿＿＿＿＿ were school friends.

4. This doesn't look like _____ book; it must be _____.

5. You can take _____ and give me _____.

6. I have finished _____ work; has she finished _____?

7. _____ is a very bad one; what's _____ like?

8. _____ lessons are all in, but _____ are not.

9. Let's collect some friends of _____ and some of _____ and have a big party.

10. "Tell me, isn't that _____ girl friend Mary over there?" "Oh no, she *was* _____ last week, but _____ dog doesn't like me!"

12-8. 名詞所有格

名詞的所有格（noun possessives）有兩種形式。一種是在單數名詞的字尾加上 's「一撇與 s」而成，如果名詞是複數而字尾已經加上了 s，就只加 '「一撇」。

比較：

the *boy's* toy「男孩子的玩具」

the *boys'* club「男孩子們的俱樂部」

a *girl's* picture「女孩子的相片」

a *girls'* school「女子學校」

the *lady's* glove「女人的手套」

the *ladies'* room「女人的化粧室」

John Smith's house「約翰，史密斯的房子」

the *Smiths'* house「史密斯家」

比較：

man's privilege「（男）人的特權」

men's clothes「男人的衣服」

a *child's* name「孩子的名字」

children's shoes「孩子的鞋子」

另外一種是在名詞的前面加介詞而成。比較：

名詞 + 's	of + 名詞
the *men's* clothes	the clothes *of men*

people's dreams   the dreams *of people*

Shakespeare's plays   the plays *of Shakespeare*

習　題　215

依照例句把斜體部分的名詞改為所有格，並把 's 的發音注出來。

Examples:

> the *girl* dog → *the girl's dog* 〔z〕
>
> a *horse* tail → *a horse's tail* 〔ɪz〕

1. a *rabbit* ears
2. a *teachers* room
3. a *women* college
4. a *bird* nest
5. the *students* lunch box
6. *James* report
7. *Confucius* sayings
8. for *Jesus* sake
9. the *PTA* decision
10. your *grandmother* visit
11. my *father-in-law* company
12. *men-servants* pay
13. *Queen Elizabeth* crown
14. his *sister Mary* school
15. *no one else* concern
16. the *King of France* palace
17. *Mr. Smith, the baker* house
18. *you know who* arrival
19. *Mary and Alice* school
20. *Mary and Alice* schools

參考一：所有格 's 的拼字規則

(a) 合成語、片語、子句的所有格 's，加在最後一個字後面：

my brother-in-law's child, *the editor in chief's* office

the President of the Board's daughter, *someone else's* shoes

Dixon, *the book-seller's store*（「同位語」（appositive））

the boy in the back of the room's remark

the runner who came in second's prize

(b) 如果兩個或兩個以上的名詞所代表的人共同所有（或參加）一件事物，那麼只把最後面的名詞變成所有格；如果這些名詞所代表的人分別所有（或參加）一件事物，那麼每一個名詞都要變成所有格。比較：

$$\begin{cases} \textit{Mary} \text{ and } \textit{Jane's} \text{ bicycle「Mary 與 Jane 共有一輛腳踏車。」} \\ \textit{Mary's} \text{ and } \textit{Jane's} \text{ bicycles「Mary 與 Jane 各有一輛腳踏車。」} \end{cases}$$

$$\begin{cases} \textit{Tom} \text{ and } \textit{John's} \text{ school「Tom 與 John 上同一個學校。」} \\ \textit{Tom's} \text{ and } \textit{John's} \text{ schools「Tom 與 John 上兩個不同的學校。」} \end{cases}$$

(c) 以 -sas, -ses, -sis, -sos, -sus 收尾的專有名詞，通常只加'：

　　Moses' laws, for *Jesus* sake, etc.

　　以〔s〕收尾的名詞如果出現在 sake 的前面，也只加'：

　　for *goodness'* sake, for *justice'* sake, for *appearance'* sake, for old
　　　acquaintance' sake, etc.

(d) 以 -s 收尾的專有名詞，可加'也可加's，視發音的難易而定：

　　Charles's / Charles' father, *James's / James'* record, *Confucius'* sayings.

參考二：所有格的讀音規則

　　所有格's 的讀音規則與第三身單數現在式動詞 -（e）s 或名詞複數形 -（e）s
讀音規則完全一樣：

(a) 在齒擦音〔s、z、ʃ、ʒ、tʃ、dʒ〕後面的's，讀〔ɪz;iz〕。

(b) 在不帶聲的子音「清音」〔p、t、k、f、θ〕後面的's，讀〔s〕。

(c) 其他's（即「濁音」與母音後面的's），讓〔z〕。

習　題　216

依照例句把下面的話用英語說出來。

Examples:

　　　　馬的尾巴（horse, tail）→ *a horse's tail, the tail of a horse*

　　　　中國沿海（China, coast）→ *the coast of China*

1. 貓的爪（cat, paws）　　　　　　　2. 樹枝（tree, leaves）

3. 鳥蛋（birds, eggs）　　　　　　　4. 屋頂（house, roof）

5. 月光（moon, light）　　　　　　　6. 山頂（mountain, top）

7. 總統的責任（president, duties）　　8. 旅行的費用（trip, cost）

9. 茶的味道（tea, taste）　　　　　　10. 司機的座位（driver, seat）

11. 博士學位（doctor, degree）　　　　12. 男廁所（men, room）

13. 他的生日（birth, date）　　　　14. 醫生的診所（doctor, office）

15. 肉價（meat, price）

16. 五元價值的茶葉（dollar, worth, tea）　　17. 一晚的休息（night, rest）

18. 十碼的距離（yard, distance）　　19. 汽車的銷售（car, sale）

20. 一個月的薪水（month, salary）

21. 人生的悲歡（life, joys and sorrows）

22. 約翰的老闆的女兒（John, boss, daughter）

23. 約翰跟迪克的父母（John, Dick, parents）

24. 你跟約翰的責任（you, John, duty）

25. 我父親的一位朋友（father, friend）

26. 你哥哥的那一位女朋友（brother, girl friend）

參考一：一般說來，「有生名詞」（表示人與動物的名詞）用 's 做所有格（但是
　　　　也可以用 of），「無生名詞」（表示事物或概念的名詞）用 of 做所有格。

　　　比較：$\begin{cases} \text{the dog's legs (the legs } of \text{ the dog)「狗的腿」} \\ \text{the legs } of \text{ the table「桌子的腿」} \end{cases}$

　　但是無生名詞在下列情形下也可以例外地用 's 做所有格。

(a) 擬人或人格化的名詞：

　　Fortune's smile「命運的微笑」，Nature's voice「大自然的聲音」history's
　　teaching「歷史的教訓」等。

(b) 表示時間、距離、價值、重量等的名詞：

　　today's paper「今天的報紙」，ten minutes' walk「十分鐘的步行」，one hundred
　　miles' journey「一百里的旅程」，a stone's throw「一擲之遠」，a dollar's worth
　　「一元的價值」，a pound's weight「一磅的重量」等。

(c) 表示尊貴事物的名詞：

　　the sun's rays「陽光」，the moon's rising「月出」，the earth's surface「地球的
　　表面」，a doctor's degree「博士學位」，a bachelor's degree「學士學位」等。

(d) 習慣用語：

　　for goodness'sake「看在老天爺的面上」，for justice'sake「為了公正起見」，

for convenience' sake「為了方便起見」，for mercy's sake「為了憐憫」，at one's wits' / wit's end「智窮才竭，不知所措」，to one's heart's content「盡情」，get to one's journey's end「到達旅途終點」，have something at one's finger's ends / tips「熟悉，精通」，to keep out of harm's way「避禍」等。

參考二：在同一個名詞組中連用兩個以上的 's 做所有格，常給人生硬不通順的感覺，因此常用 of 來代替其中的一個。

比較：　{ John's boss's daughter（欠通順）
　　　　{ the daughter of John's boss（較通順）

又名詞所有格 's 不能與其他限定詞（a(n), some, any, no, this / these, that / those, another, which 等）一起放在名詞的前面，但是可以與介詞 of 一起放在名詞的後面。

比較：　{ a John's picture （×）　　{ my father's this friend（×）
　　　　{ a picture of John's（○）　　{ this friend of my father's（○）

傳統的文法，把這種結構叫做「雙重所有格」（double Possessive）。

習　題　217

依照例句回答下列問句。

Example:

　　　Whose pencil is this? (John)

　　　(STUDENT 1) *It belongs to John.*

　　　(STUDENT 2) *It is John's.*

1. Whose book is this? (Alice)　　　　2. Whose watch is that? (my brother)

3. Whose money is this? (she)　　　　4. Whose coats are these? (her sisters)

5. Whose letters are those? (Bob's uncle)

6. Whose seat is this? (a friend of mine)

參考：名詞所有格後面的名詞在下列情形中可以省略。

(1) 如果這個名詞已經在前文中出現：

　　　These books are my brother's (*books*).

　　　We compare Lawrence's novels with Miller's (*novels*).

(2) 如果這個名詞是代表場所的名詞，如 house, home, store, shop, office 等：

　　We saw him at your uncle's (*house*).

　　She spent the whole day at the hairdresser's (*shop*).

習　題　218

　依照例句用完整的句子來解釋下面的片語。

Examples:

　　the boy's hat → *The hat belongs to the boy.*

　　John's return → *John returned (will return).*

　　the criminal's execution → *The criminal was (will be) executed.*

　　a five minutes' walk → *The walk takes (took) five minutes.*

　　the city of New York → *New York is a city.*

1. Mary's car
2. Edison's electric light
3. the driver's licence
4. Bob's death
5. the arrival of the bus
6. cow's milk
7. love of music
8. the hunting of lions
9. the peacock's beautiful feather
10. two months' vacation
11. ten dollars' worth of tea
12. men's love of God
13. Columbus's discovery of America
14. a picture of John
15. a picture of John's

參考：名詞的所有格有下列幾種含義：

(1) 表示「所有」或「所屬」：這個時候後面的名詞要念重。

　　John's hat, Mary's home, the dog's tail, the birds' nest, the city's principal museum.

(2) 表示「作者」、「發明者」或其他「來源」：

　　Shakespeare's plays「莎士比亞的的戲劇」，Picaso's paintings「畢卡索的繪畫」，Webster's dictionary「韋伯斯特的字典」，Watt's steam engine「瓦特的蒸汽機」，the baby's picture「嬰兒的相片」。

(3) 表示「種類」或「性質」：這個時候名詞所有格要念重。

a doctor's degree「博士學位」，a men's room「男厠所」，cow's milk「牛奶」，hen's eggs「雞蛋」。

(4) 表示時間、價值、距離、重量等「度量」：複數名詞後面的所有格記號「'」常可以省去。

an hour's wait「一個鐘頭的等候」，two weeks' / week rest「兩星期的休息」，five dollars' / dollar worth「五塊錢的價值」，ten pounds' / pound weight「十磅的重量」。

(5) 表示「主動者」，做動作的人：

John's return (= John returned.)

the judge's decision (= The judge decided (on the case).)

the comments of the press (= The press commented (on the matter).)

(6) 表示「受動者」，接受動作的人：

John's punishment (= John was punished; somebody punished John.)

the robber's execution (= The robber was executed.)

the selection of the committee (= The committee was selected.)

(7) 表示「同位」：

the city of Taipei (= Taipei is a city.)

第13章 數量詞

13-1. 數量詞

英語的名詞，除了限定詞以外還可以帶有表示數目（如 one, two, Three …）或分量（如 much, little, a great deal …）的**數量詞**（quantifiers）。

(1) 數量詞可以出現在限定詞的後面：

Determiner（限定詞）	Quantifier（數量詞）	Noun（名詞）
ϕ	one	boy
these	two	books
my	three	sons

(2) 數量詞也可以出現在限定詞的前面。這個時候，限定詞必須是有定限詞，而且數量詞後面必須帶著介詞 of：

Quantifier（數量詞）	of	Determiner（有定限詞）	Noun-s（複數名詞）
one	of	the	boys
two	of	these	books
three	of	my	sons

用在限定詞前面的數量詞表示「部分」，因此後面的名詞必須是複數可數名詞或單數不可數名詞。例如 one of the boys「孩子中的一個」，two of these books「這些書本中的兩本」，much of your money「你的錢裡有許多」，可以看做是由 one (boy) of the boys, two (books) of these books, much (money) of your money 把括弧中的名詞省略而得來。

比較： $\begin{cases} \text{my three sons} \ulcorner 總共有三個兒子 \lrcorner \\ \text{three of my sons} \ulcorner 兒子裡面的三個，至於一共有多少個兒子則不得而知 \lrcorner \end{cases}$

參考：

有時候，數量詞前後都有有定限詞。這個時候，名詞後面一定要帶著形容詞子句：

The two of *the* boys who had disagreed left.

The one of *the* books which are on the desk is very interesting to read.

習 題 219

依照例句改寫下面的名詞組。

Examples:

one boy of the boys → *one of the boys*

three friends of your friends →

　　three of your friends; *three friends of yours*

these five books of your books → *these five books of yours*

1. three girls of the girls	2. five pencils of these pencils
3. one-half cake of the cake	4. many students of those students
5. four mistakes of her mistakes	6. six answers of his ten answers
7. several teachers of my teachers	8. these three sons of your sons
9. three friends of my ten friends	
10. even some students of your students	

習 題 220

依照例句改寫下面的句子。

Examples:

My books are missing. (one)

　　One of my books is missing.

　　One of them is missing.

　　One is missing.

The students were here. (several)

> *Several of the students were here.*
>
> *Several of them were here.*
>
> *Several were here.*

1. The books are interesting. (two)

2. The girls could answer the questions. (three)

3. These boys want to go with you. (one)

4. The guests are in the garden. (some)

5. The suspects have disappeared. (one)

6. The money is in the purse. (half)

7. He bought my paintings. (two)

8. The pictures were left on the table. (one)

習　題　221

依照例句完成下面的句子。

Examples:

> three books ⋯ on the desk → *There are three books on the desk.*
>
> my books ⋯ on the desk → *My books are on the desk.*

1. the ten books ⋯ on the shelf

2. ten of the books ⋯ on the shelf

3. two pictures ⋯ on the wall

4. two of his pictures ⋯ on the wall

7. every student ⋯ in the classroom

8. all the guests ⋯ in the lobby

9. five other books ⋯ in the library

10. the other five books ⋯ in the library

參考：場所副詞做無定名詞的補語的時候，要改成由 there 帶頭的句子（請參考 2-6 的說明）。

比較：

> ⎧ *The three books* are on the desk.「三本書都在桌子上。」
>
> ⎨ *Three of the books* are on the desk.「書有三本在桌子上。」
>
> ⎩ There are *three books* on the desk.「桌子上有三本書。」

13-2. 數　詞

數量詞分為**數詞**（numbers）與**量詞**（classifiers）。數詞又可以分為**基數**（cardinals）與**序數**（ordinals）。基數是指 one, two, three, four, five …這一類的字，而序數是指 first, second, third, fourth, fifth …這一類的字。

基數可以放在名詞之前當修飾語用，也可以單獨做名詞用。

比較：

> *Ten* students went there, but only *three* students came back.
> *Ten* went there, but only *three* came back.

> I have *one* pen and *five* pencils.
> *One* and *five* are (is) six.

> I have seen him *four* times.
> *Four* times *three* makes (is) *twelve*.

> There are *two* boys in each row.
> The boys marched by *twos* (= two by two).

序數的前面常用有定冠詞 the。

比較：

> the *Second* World War　　the *Fifth* Lesson
> World War II (= two)　　Lesson 5 (= five)

參考一：一般說來，英語的序數放在基數的前面。

> I have finished reading the *first three* chapters.
> We'll study the *next two* lessons tomorrow.
> The *last three* sections were most difficult.

比較：

> first three prizes (= first-mentioned three prizes)「頭三個獎品」
> three first prizes (= first prizes which are three in number)「三個頭獎」

參考二：在序數前面用無定冠詞 a(n) 表示 another「另外一個」。

> This is my only chance; I will never get *a second* chance.
> *One* student said …, *another* said …, *a third* …, and *a fourth* said.

習　題　222

把下面的數目用英語說出來（或寫出來）。

Example:

　　1204 (*one thousand two hundred and four*)

1. 182　　　　　2. 407　　　　　3. 1,540　　　　　4. 3,026

5. 21,906　　　6. 564,719　　　7. 803,892　　　8. 5,372,694

9. 6,073,540　　10. 236,567,994

習　題　223

把下面的年代用英語說出來。

Example:

　　1965 (*nineteen sixty-five*)

1. 1968　　　　2. 1908　　　　3. 1874　　　　4. 1009

5. 842　　　　　6. 605　　　　　7. 1472　　　　8. 1056

9. 5 B.C.　　　10. 301 B.C.

習　題　224

把下面的時間用英語說出來。

Examples:

　　7:25 = *twenty-five* (*minutes*) *past* (or *after*) *seven*

　　10:45 = (*a quarter to* (or *before*) *eleven*

　　6:30 = *half past* (or *after*) *six*

　　12:19 = *nineteen minutes past* (or *after*) *twelve*

1. 1:05　　　　2. 4:45　　　　3. 10:35　　　4. 3:27　　　　5. 12:00

6. 2:50　　　　7. 8:15　　　　8. 7:30　　　9. 5:56　　　　10. 6:09

參考：五的倍數如（five, ten, fifteen, twenty, …）後面的 minutes 通常可以省略。

習 題 225

把下面的基數改為序數。

Example:

six (*sixth*); 6 (*6th*)

1. one; 1
2. two; 2
3. three; 3
4. four; 4
5. five; 5
6. eleven; 11
7. twelve; 12
8. thirteen; 13
9. nine; 9
10. twenty; 20
11. twenty-one; 21
12. twenty-two; 22
13. twenty-three; 23
14. ninety-nine; 99
15. one hundred; 100

習 題 226

念出下面的英語。

Examples:

Lesson 10 (*lesson ten; the tenth lesson*)

Chapter 3 and 4 (*chapter three and four, chapters three and four; the third and the fourth chapter, the third and fourth chapters*)

1. World War I
2. Page 3
3. Charles V
4. Henry VIII
5. Louis XVI
6. Room 204
7. No. 35
8. Lesson 9 and 10

習 題 227

把下面的日期用英語說出來。

Example:

Oct. 10 (*October the tenth*)

1. Jan. 1
2. Feb. 28
3. Mar. 29
4. Apr. 5
5. May 5
6. Jun. 24
7. Jul. 7
8. Aug. 17
9. Sep. 28
10. Oct. 25
11. Nov. 15
12. Dec. 31

習　題　**228**

把下面的分數用英語說出來。

Example:

　　　$^1/_6$ (*one sixth*)

1. $^1/_2$　　　　　2. $^1/_3$　　　　　3. $^2/_3$　　　　　4. $^1/_4$　　　　　5. $^3/_4$

5. $^1/_5$　　　　　7. $^2/_5$　　　　　8. $1^3/_5$　　　　　9. $3^4/_5$　　　　10. $^{11}/_{58}$

參考：分數的分母用序數，分子用基數：

　　$^1/_2$ one half　　　　　　　$^1/_4$ one fourth or a quarter

　　$^1/_3$ one third　　　　　　　$^3/_4$ three fourths or three quarters

　　$^2/_3$ two thirds　　　　　　　$1^4/_5$ one and four fifths

　　$^{13}/_{25}$ thirteen over twenty-five

　　One third of the *students have* dropped this course.

　　One third of the *money has* been contributed to organized charities.

習　題　**229**

把下面的次數（或倍數）念出來。

1. one; once　　　　　　　　2. two; twice; two times

3. three; thrice; three times　　4. four; four times

5. five; five times

習　題　**230**

用英語念出下面的算數式。

1. $5 + 3 = 8$　　　　　　2. $9 - 2 = 7$　　　　　　3. $7 \times 3 = 21$

4. $12 \div 4 = 3$　　　　　5. $\dfrac{2}{3} + \dfrac{3}{4} = 1\dfrac{5}{12}$

13-3. 量　詞

量詞主要的有下列兩種。

(1) 表示「不可數名詞」（物質名詞與抽象名詞）分量的量詞：

— 329 —

Would you like *a piece of* cake?

Give me *a glass of* water, please.

注意，這些量詞還可以用數詞或形容詞來修飾：

She ate *a small piece of* cake.

I drink *eight glasses of* water every day.

(2) 表示「群體」的量詞，可以用在「可數名詞」的前面：

We saw *a herd of* cattle grazing in the field.

A *swarm of* bees are gathering honey from the flowers.

參考一：表示「不可數名詞」分量的量詞主要的有——

(a) a *cup* of: tea, coffee, cocoa, hot chocolate, (warm) milk, etc.

(b) a *glass* of: water, ice-tea, milk, lemonade, orange juice, wine, etc.

(c) a *bottle* of: ink, milk, wine, whiskey, brandy, etc.

(d) a *can* of: oil, beer, orange juice, etc.

(e) a *tube* of: toothpaste, etc.

(f) a *piece* of: paper, chalk, wood, glass, land, luggage, furniture, work, news, information, advice, evidence, good luck, etc.

(g) an *article* of: news, furniture, clothing, etc.

(h) a *sheet* of: paper, tin, glass, metal, etc.

(i) a *loaf* of: bread, etc.

(j) a *slice* of: bread, ham, pork, beef, mutton, turkey, etc.

(k) a *bit* of: paper, news, fun, etc.

(1) a *lump* of: sugar, etc.

(m) a *cube* of: ice, etc.

(n) a *bar* of: soap, chocolate, metal, iron, etc.

(o) a *stick* of: chewing gum, chalk, dynamite, etc.

(p) a *grain* of: rice, corn, sugar, salt, sand, etc.

(q) a *drop* of : water, rain, blood, etc.

(r) a *mouthful / handful / spoonful / cupful* of: water, sugar, salt, etc.

(s) an *act* of: folly, kindness, cruelty, etc.

(t) a *gallon*（加侖）of gasoline / *pound*（磅）of meat / *yard*（碼）of cloth, etc.

(u) a *pair* of: shoes, boots, gloves, spectacles, scissors, horses, etc.

參考二：表示「群體」的量詞主要有：

(a) a *flock* of: sheep, goats, rabbits, geese, sparrows, birds, people, etc.

(b) a *drove* of: cows, oxen, sheep, deer (when moving or driven together), etc.

(c) a *herd* of: cattle, deer, elephants (when feeding or going about together), etc.

(d) a *pack* of: wolves, hounds, knaves, thieves, lies, etc.

(e) a *swarm* of: ants, bees, locusts, people, etc.

(f) a *brace* of: pheasants, hounds, ducks, etc.

(g) a *group* / *throng* / *crowd* / *multitude* of: people, students, etc.

(h) a *band* of: robbers, fugitives, rebels, etc.

(i) a *school* / *shoal* of: fish, etc.

(j) a *flight* of: stairs, birds (when on the wing), etc.

(k) a *couple* of: eggs, friends, days, weeks, months, years, etc.

習　題　231

依照例句填入適當的「量詞」。

Examples:

　　　　I drink a _c_ u p of coffee every morning.

　　　　She bought a new b _ott_ le yesterday.

1. Would you like a c_____p of tea? Yes, please.

2. May I have a g_____s of milk?

3. I'm going to buy a new p_____r of shoes.

4. Get me a l_____f of bread, please.

5. How many b_____rs of soap do you want?

6. There's a c_____ke of soap in the bath-room.

7. Let me give you a p_____ce of advice.

8. I ate three s_____ces of bread this morning.

9. We need several a_____les of furniture for our new house.

10. He wrote my name and address on a s_____t of paper.

11. She wrote the new words on the blackboard with a p_____ce of chalk.

12. Put two s_____ls of salt into the soup.

13. I put two l_____ps of sugar into my coffee.

14. Get me a t_____be of toothpaste, please.

15. How much does a g_____n of gasoline cost?

習 題 232

　　從下列的詞裡選出適當的「量詞」填入空白裡：piece, lump, head, ear, blade, drop, bar, flash, suit, mouthful, school, swarm, pair, flock。

1. I gave each of them a _____ of candy.

2. She went into the bathroom for a _____ of soap.

3. I need a _____ of sugar for my coffee.

4. She cut up a _____ of lettuce for the salad.

5. We saw a _____ of lightning in the sky.

6. He pulled a _____ of grass from the garden.

7. The bird had a _____ of bread in his mouth.

8. Her gift was an unusual _____ of jewelry.

9. There wasn't an _____ of corn left in the vegetable garden.

10. We haven't had a _____ of rain for at least a month.

11. He picked up a _____ of sand from the beach.

12. She drank a _____ of water from the pitcher.

13. He pulled out a _____ of change from his pocket.

14. I bought a _____ of clothes in Tokyo.

15. The black object was a _____ of coal.

16. Could you lend me a _____ of scissors?

17. A _____ of birds are hovering around the farm.

18. A _____ of people were crowding into the theater.

19. A _____ of bees were attacking the bear.

20. We saw a _____ of fish in the river.

13-4. 其他數量詞

　　數量詞，除了數詞與量詞以外，還包括一些表示不定數量或分量的語詞。這些數量詞主要的有：

(1) 「可數」與「不可數」名詞前面都可以通用的：如

　　　　all (*of*), *half* (*of*), *no* (*ne of*), *some*「某（些）」，*any*「任何」

　　　　a lot of, lots of, plenty of, enough, most, more, etc.

(2) 僅可以用在「可數」名詞前面的：如

　　　　every (*one of*), *each* (*one*), *either* (*one*), *neither* (*one*); *both* (*of*), *several, few,*

　　　　　a few, many, a good / *great many, a* (*large* / *small* / *great*) *number of*, etc.

(3) 僅可以用在「不可數」名詞前面的：如

　　　　little, a little, much, a good / *great deal of, a large* / *small* / *great quantity of,*

　　　　　a large / *small* / *great amount of*, etc.

　　注意，這些數量詞如果用在有定限詞的前面一定要帶介詞 of；又注意，這些數量詞都可以單獨（有時候，後面要加 one）當代名詞用。

Several of the men ⎫
Several men ⎬ are here.
Several ⎭

Some of the students ⎫
Some students ⎬ failed the exam.
Some ⎭

Any (*one*) *of* your friends ⎫
Any friend ⎬ can learn to speak English.
Any (*one*) ⎭

None of the students ⎫
No students ⎬ have passed the exam.
None ⎭

None of the money ⎫
No money ⎬ has been recovered.
None ⎭

I can answer ⎰ *a few of* your questions.
⎨ *a few* questions.
⎱ *a few*.

Much of John's energy ⎫
Much energy ⎬ has been wasted.
Much ⎭

Lots of the milk ⎫
Lots of milk ⎬ has been spoiled
Lots ⎭

She has spent ⎰ *a great deal of* the money.
⎨ *a great deal of* money.
⎱ *a great deal*.

He has read ⎰ *all (of)* the books.
⎨ *all of* them.
⎱ *all*.

I want ⎰ *half (of)* the money.
⎨ *half of* it.
⎱ *a half*.

Both (of) his sons ⎫
Both sons ⎬ are intelligent.
Both ⎭

Each (one) of her children ⎫
Each child ⎬ told a story.
Each (one) ⎭

$$
\left.\begin{array}{l}
\textit{Every one of}\text{ the boys} \\
\textit{Every}\text{ boy} \\
\textit{Every one}
\end{array}\right\}\text{ got a present.}
$$

$$
\left.\begin{array}{l}
\textit{(N) either (one) of}\text{ these two roads} \\
\textit{(N) either}\text{ road} \\
\textit{(N) either (one)}
\end{array}\right\}\text{ leads to the station.}
$$

注意，all、half、both 後面的 of 可以省略。

習 題 233

依照例句改寫下列句子。

Example:

These books are interesting. (every)

$$
\rightarrow \left\{\begin{array}{l}
\textit{Every one of these books is interesting.} \\
\textit{Every book is interesting.} \\
\textit{Every one of them is interesting.}
\end{array}\right.
$$

1. The names are unfamiliar. (some)　　2. Did the guests stay late? (any)

3. The news was incorrect. (half)

4. My books were missing. (a couple)

5. The questions were rather silly. (a few)

6. The talk was interesting. (not much)

7. These students have a dictionary. (each)

8. The members have attended the meeting. (enough)

9. The money is still in the bank. (most)

10. The rooms are empty. (none)

11. The girls need glasses. (both)　　12. The guests left early. (not all)

13. I need milk. (plenty)

14. The boys are good at mathematics. (either)

15. The girls know the answer. (neither)

16. The teachers were there. (not every)

參考：many 表示「（數目）很多」；a few 表示「（數目）不多，但是有一些」；

few 表示「（數目）很少，幾乎沒有」：

I have *many* friends in China but *few* in Japan.

比較：
$\begin{cases} \text{Are there } \textit{many} \text{ (books) ? No, there are } \textit{few}. 「否定」} \\ \text{Are there } \textit{any} \text{ (books) ? Yes, there are } \textit{a few}. 「肯定」} \end{cases}$

much 表示「（分量）很多」，而且多半用在否定句與問句；a little 表示「（分量）不多，但是有一些」；little 表示「（分量）很少，幾乎沒有」：

We have *much* rain in March, but little in June.

比較：

$\begin{cases} \text{Does he have } \textit{much} \text{ (money)? No, he has } \textit{little}. 「否定」} \\ \text{Does he have any (money)? Yes, he has } \textit{a little}. 「肯定」} \end{cases}$

quite a few 與 quite a little 表示「不少，很多」，very / but few 與 very / but little 表示「很少，幾乎沒有」，only a few 與 only a little 表示「只有一些」：

比較：

He has $\begin{cases} \textit{quite a few} \\ \textit{very few} \\ \textit{but few} \\ \textit{only a few} \end{cases}$ friends.（複數）

She has $\begin{cases} \textit{quite a little} \\ \textit{very little} \\ \textit{but little} \\ \textit{only a little} \end{cases}$ money.（單數）

many（and many）a 表示「很多」，後面跟著單數可數名詞：

We walked on *many* (*and many*) *a* mile.

習　題　324

在下面的空白裡填 many, few, a few, much, little 或 a little。

1. There are _____ books in the library, but _____ good ones.

2. There are no French schools, but _____ English schools.

3. This ore contains _____ silver, but _____ gold.

4. This ore contains silver, besides _____ gold.

5. He grows worse; there is _____ hope of his recovery.

6. He is not much better; but there is yet _____ hope.

7. It is not worth while to visit the country. It has _____ places of interest.

8. The town is worth visiting. It has _____ objects of interest.

9. Are there _____ navigable rivers in Japan? No, _____ are navigable.

10. I have only _____ money left.

11. These are all the books I have, but my brother has twice as _____.

12. We waited _____ and _____ a day.

13. They have as _____ as four thousand students.

14. We have but _____ furniture but plenty of room.

15. One who considers too _____ will accomplish _____.

<h1 style="text-align:center">習　題　235</h1>

　　依照例句用 many 或 much 做問句，並用 many, much, a lot of, a great deal of
回答這些問句。

Examples:

　　　　Do you see _____ movies?

　　　　Do you see many movies?

$$\text{Yes, I see} \begin{Bmatrix} \textit{many} \\ \textit{a lot of} \\ \textit{lots of} \end{Bmatrix} \textit{movies.}$$

　　　　No, I don't see many movies.

　　　　Does he have _____ time?

　　　　Does he have much time?

$$Yes, he\ has \begin{Bmatrix} a\ great\ deal\ of \\ lots\ of \\ a\ lot\ of \end{Bmatrix} time.$$

No, he doesn't have much time.

1. Do you have _____ time to study English?

2. Do you have _____ opportunities to speak English?

3. Don't you have _____ work to do now?

4. Does Betty have _____ social life?

5. Do Americans drink _____ coffee?

6. Doesn't she know _____ people here?

參考：在口語英語，much 多半用在問句與否定句。在敘述句裡則多用 a great deal of, a lot of, lots of 等來代替 much。

習　題　236

在下面的空白裡填入 a few, the few, a little 或 the little。

1. _____ knowledge is a dangerous thing.

2. _____ words spoken in earnest will convince him.

3. _____ tact would have saved the situation.

4. _____ Americans write Chinese correctly.

5. _____ information he has is not quite reliable.

6. _____ public libraries that we have are not well equipped.

7. _____ days' rest is all you need.

8. _____ trinkets she has are not worth much.

9. _____ precaution is necessary in handling that machine.

10. _____ knowledge of French he has will be very useful to him in France.

參考：the few 與 the little 用在「關係子句」的前面：

There were only few guests, and the few who attended the party were poor.

I gave him *the little* money that I had left.

習　題　237

在下面的空白裡填 every, each 或 any。

1. _____ of these boys has his own bicycle.

2. All the students present shouted for joy. _____ one looked happy.

3. Five boys were seated on _____ bench.

4. He has read _____ book in the library.

5. I do not know _____ one of them; I know only some of them.

6. Such things do not happen _____ day.

7. Leap year falls in _____ fourth year.

8. He came to see us _____ three days.

9. The four boys _____ make his own decisions.

10. Not _____ man can be a genius.

11. There is _____ reason to believe that he has enjoyed one of his holidays.

12. They were drowned, _____ one of them.

13. There was a baker's shop on _____ side.

14. _____ of them wanted to try.

15. He ate up bit of it. There was not _____ left.

參考：each「各」偏重個別的人或物；every「每」偏重全體的人或物。比較：

> Each student has his own desk.「各個學生都有他自己的書桌；即一人一
> 個。」
> Every student has a desk.「每個學生都有書桌；即人人都有一個。」

因此 every 雖然在形式上是單數，但是語義上卻是複數；等於 each and all「大家（無例外地）」，語氣比 each 或 all 都要重。

比較：
> Take *each* (*one*) of them (and examine them).「一個個拿起來（檢查）。」
> Take *every one* of them.「全部拿走（一個也不要留）。」

any「任何」，表示隨便哪一個或幾個：

> *Any* of these books *is* / *are* interesting.

比較：
$$\begin{cases} \text{Take } \textit{any one} \text{ of them.「隨便拿一個。」} \\ \text{Take } \textit{any} \text{ of them.「隨便拿幾個。」} \end{cases}$$

every, any, all 後面可以用任何數詞；each 卻不能這樣用。比較：

He writes to his mother *every ten* days.

You may take *any two* of them.

I know *all* (*the*) *five* students.

習 題 328

在下面的空白裡填入 both, one, either 或 neither。

1. _____ the brothers are here.

2. I do not know _____ ; I know only _____ of them.

3. You may choose _____ of the two languages.

4. _____ you or he may go.

5. Do you want a pen or a pencil? _____ will do.

6. Do you know _____ of the two brothers? I do not _____ know of them.

7. Do you know _____ of the two? No, _____ .

8. There is a restaurant at _____ side of the street.

9. I have studied _____ French nor German.

10. There is a door at _____ end of the room.

11. There are doors at _____ ends of the room.

12. "I don't like coffee." " _____ do I."

參考：both「兩個都」、either「兩個裡的任何一個」、neither「兩個都不」用在兩個人或物之間：

Both (of) the (two) boys (*Both* boys, *Both*) are here.

Either of the (two) boys (*Either* boy, *Either* one, *Either*) is here.

Neither of the (two) boys (*Neither boy, Neither one*、*Neither*) is here.

注意，both 要用複數；either, neither 要用單數。比較：

$$\begin{cases} \textit{Both have} \text{ brought } \textit{their} \text{ books with } \textit{them.} \\ (N) \textit{ either has} \text{ brought } \textit{his} \text{ books with } \textit{him.} \end{cases}$$

習 題 239

在下面的空白裡填入 all, any, some 或 none。

1. _____ the students are here.

2. I do not know _____ of them; I know only _____ of them.

3. You may choose _____ of these books.

4. _____ one of you may come with me.

5. What kind of paper do you want? _____ paper will do.

6. Do you know of these students? No, I know _____ of them.

7. Jack has three brothers but I have _____.

8. _____ the teachers are present. The teachers are _____ present.

9. Not _____ of the teachers were present; only _____ of them were present.

10. Not _____ of his poems are well-known. _____ of his poems are well-known.

參考：all「全部」、any「任何（一個或幾個）」、some「某一（些）」、none「沒
有一個」可以用在表示三個以上的人或物的可數名詞之前：

　　　All (the ten students) are here.

　　　Any (of the ten students) are here.

　　　Any one (of the ten students) is here.

　　　Some (of the ten students) are here.

　　　None (of the ten students) are here.

也可以用在物質名詞之前：

　　　All (the money) was wasted.

　　　Some (of the money) was wasted.

　　　None (of the money) was wasted.

　　　Not *any* (of the money) was wasted.

　　注意，all, any, some, none 在可數名詞之前用複數（但是 any one 用單數），
在不可數名詞之前用單數。

　　one「一個」、each「各個」可以用在兩個或三個以上的人：

　　　One of the two / three students knows the answer.

Each (one) of the two / three students has a new pen.

習 題 240

依照例句用 neither 或 none 回答下列問句。

Examples:　　Which of the two boys are clever enough to do the job?

　　　　　　Neither of them is clever enough to do the job.

　　　　　　Neither is clever enough to do the job.

　　　　How many lessons have you learned by heart?

　　　　　　I have learned none of them by heart.

　　　　　　I have learned none.

1. How many exercises have you done today?
2. Which of these two books have you read?
3. How many have I given you already?
4. How many of these are mine?
5. Which of the two do you want?
6. Which foot have you hurt?
7. How many glasses did you break at the party?
8. Which glove of this pair has a hole?
9. Which of the two girls is your sister?
10. How many of these cameras belong to you?

習 題 241

依照例句改寫下列句子。

Examples:　　Some of the students are here.

　　　　　　Some of the students are not here.

　　　　　　None of the students are here.

　　　　Either of us can speak English.

　　　　　　Neither of us can speak English.

　　　　　　Not either of us can speak English.

Any of the boys can answer the question.

None of the boys can answer the question.

Not any of the boys can answer the question.

1. Some of the questions are very easy.

2. Any of my friends will help me.

3. Either of the two sisters is very pretty.

4. All the students are present.

5. Every one of the members was interested in the program.

6. Each one of the brothers has a new watch.

7. Both of them went to the movies.

8. I know any of these girls.

9. Some of my friends speak French.

10. One of these tourists has been here.

11. I have seen one of those gentlemen.

12. Many of the books are John's.

參考：無定冠詞 some〔sə̀m〕與數量詞 some〔sʌ́m〕，不僅讀音不同而且意義、用法也不同。前者（「一些」）只能用在肯定句，後者（「某一（些）」）肯定句、否定句都可以用。比較：

> ⎰ I have *some* books.「我有（一些）書。」
> ⎱ I don't have *any* books.「我什麼書都沒有。」

> ⎰ I like *some* (of the) books.「有一些書，我喜歡。」
> ⎱ I don't like *some* (of the) books.「有一些書，我不喜歡。」

> ⎰ *Some* (of the) books are good.「有一些書很好。」
> ⎱ *Some* (of the) books are not good.「有一些書不好。」

同樣地，數量詞 any「任何」與無定冠詞 any「一些」的用法也不同。前者肯定句、否定句都可以用，後者只可以用在否定句或問句：

> ⎰ You may take *any* (of the) books.
> ⎱ Not *any* (of the) books are useful.

注意，用 none 與 not 做的否定句常有不同的含義：

$\left\{ \begin{array}{l} \textit{None of} \text{ the books are interesting.} 「沒有一本書是有趣的。」 \\ \textit{Not} \text{ all of the books are interesting.} 「並不是所有的書都是有趣的。」 \end{array} \right.$

Not one 用在可數名詞之前，語氣比 none 還要重些。比較：

One of the books is *not* interesting. 「（許多書裡頭）有一本沒有趣。」

$\left\{ \begin{array}{l} \textit{Not one} \text{ of the books} \\ \textit{Not one} \text{ book} \end{array} \right\}$ is interesting. 「有趣的書連一本都沒有。」

習 題 242

依照例句改寫下面的句子。

Examples:

> All of the students are waiting. → *The students are all waiting.*
>
> Both of the boys came. → *The boys both came.*
>
> Each of the girls sings a song. → *The girls each sing a song.*

1. Both of the children are playing in the yard.

2. Each of the guests brought a gift.

3. All of the money has disappeared.

4. Both of the students have failed the examination.

5. Each of the boys owns a bicycle.

6. She gave all of us a present.

7. Each of them should at least try.

8. We took all of them to the museum.

9. All of it came originally from China.

10. Each of the members receives a card.

11. Both the mayor and the governor have influence.

12. Does each of you get a haircut?

參考：all、both、each 除了做數量詞以外，還可以放在句中當副詞用。比較：

$$\begin{cases} \textit{Both} \text{ (of) the students are clever.} \\ \text{The students are } \textit{both} \text{ clever.} \end{cases}$$

$$\begin{cases} \textit{All} \text{ (of) the children must get a haircut.} \\ \text{The children must } \textit{all} \text{ get a haircut.} \end{cases}$$

$$\begin{cases} \textit{Each} \text{ of the boys won a prize.} \\ \text{The boys } \textit{each} \text{ won a prize.} \end{cases}$$

注意：這個時候 all、both、each 的位置與 not 在句子中的位置一樣（即 Be 動詞後面、助動詞與本動詞中間、其他動詞前面）。

習　題　243

依照例句完成下列「追問句」。

Example: One of the students is here, ⋯

　　　　One of the students is here, isn't he?

1. Some of them are taking music lessons, ⋯

2. All of us will be there, ⋯　　　　3. Each of them has a watch, ⋯

3. Three of them haven't arrived yet, ⋯

5. Each of us like our milk cold, ⋯　　　6. Each of us likes his milk cold, ⋯

7. Either of us can do it, ⋯

8. None of them are here right now, ⋯

9. No one of them watches TV any more, ⋯

10. Every one of you must have finished your assignment, ⋯

參考：含 有 each（one）、no one、every one、either（one）、neither（one）、any
　　（one）做主語的追問句可以有兩種不同的方式。比較：

$$\begin{cases} \text{Each (one) of us } \textit{know} \text{ the answer, } \textit{don't we}? \\ \text{Each (one) of us } \textit{knows} \text{ the answer, } \textit{doesn't he}? \end{cases}$$

$$\begin{cases} \text{Every one of them } \textit{likes} \text{ coffee, } \textit{don't they}? \\ \text{Every one of them } \textit{likes} \text{ coffee, } \textit{doesn't he}? \end{cases}$$

　　含有 none, few, some, several, many, most 做主語的追問句只能有一種方式：

　　　　All of us *know* the answer, *don't we*?

None of them *like* coffee, *do they?*

13-5. 限制詞

英語的名詞組除了限定詞、數量詞以外還可以含有 just, only, merely, even, especially, particularly 等限制詞（limiters）。這種限制詞通常都放在名詞組的最前面以限制整個名詞組：

NOUN			PHRASE		（名詞組）
Limiter （限制詞）	Quantifier （數量詞）	Determiner （限定詞）		Quantifier （數量詞）	Noun （名詞）

	Even	one	of	your	three	sons	came.
I like	especially	some	of	these	ten	pictures.	
	Only	a few	of	my		friends	were
							invited.

習 題 244

把括號裡的語詞填入句子適當的位置。

Example: Bob and Dick came. (just)

> *Just Bob and Dick came.*

1. I want no girls, boys. (just)

2. The cleverest student cannot solve the question. (even)

3. The judge can decide on the case. (only)

4. The witness knows what happened. (alone)

5. John is a nice fellow. (rather)

6. This is an expensive watch. (quite)

7. All the students attended the party. (almost)

8. He spent a little time on the project. (quite)

9. I wonder whether there is a thing. (such)

10. They don't think there is any thing. (such)

11. Ten students will make up a strong team. (such)

12. We need ten students. (more)

13. There are three students in the room. (other)

14. Where are the three students? (other)

15. A(n) disaster will ruin the country. (such, other)

16. Not a person was to be seen in the street. (single)

17. His remark had a meaning. (double)

18. Have you books? (any, other)

19. I don't go there every day, only day. (every, other)

20. Don't write on every line; write on lines. (every, two)

21. A friend of mine wants to buy the house. (certain)

22. Possibilities must be considered. (such, all)

23. I have met people. (such, many)

24. The manager is too busy to spare hour. (a(n), even, half)

25. Money in the world cannot buy happiness. (the, even, all)

26. What he needs is sympathy. (little, just, a)

27. This is example of your son's improvement. (another, just)

28. He is fool. (an, just, other)

29. I saw model. (first, his, only)

30. Many time did I warn him, but he paid attention. (a, no)

參考：

(1) Only 可以出現在名詞組的前面，也可以出現在名詞組的後面；just 只能出現在名詞組的前面，而 alone 只能出現在名詞組的後面。比較：

$$\left. \begin{array}{l} \textit{Only} \text{ your brother} \\ \textit{Just} \text{ your brother} \\ \text{Your brother } \textit{only} \\ \text{Your brother } \textit{alone} \end{array} \right\} \text{ can help me.}$$

Only 也可以出現在限定詞的後面、數詞的前面：

This is the *only* example I can give you.

You have *only* three months to go.

比較：
$\begin{cases} \text{His } only \text{ son came. (= He has no other son.)} 「他唯一的兒子來了。」 \\ Only \text{ his son came. (= No one else came.)} 「只有他的兒子來了。」 \end{cases}$

(2) Quite「相當、多少有一些」常出現在含有無定冠詞與形容詞的名詞組前面：

He is *quite a* good player / good singer / gentleman.

有時候，後面的形容詞可以不用：

He is *quite a* player / singer / man.

Rather「相當、多少有一些」也常與含有形容詞的名詞組一起出現；即放在無定冠詞的前面或後面、有定冠詞的後面。比較：

It was $\begin{cases} rather\ a \text{ surprising} \\ a\ rather \text{ surprising} \end{cases}$ result.

I know *the rather* tall boy in the corner.

(3) Such「這樣的」放在無定冠詞 a（n）的前面；但是放在 some, any, no, another, many, few, every, all 或其他數詞的後面：

I never said *such a* thing / *such* things.

I didn't say *any such* thing.

I said *no such* thing.

Some such plan was in his mind.

I hope never to have *another such* experience.

We need *ten such* players to make a team.

(4) Other「其他的、另外的」在有定名詞組放在數詞的前面，在無定名詞組放在數詞的後面。比較：

$\begin{cases} \text{There are } two\ other \text{ guests waiting to see you.} \\ \text{The } other\ two \text{ guests are in the lobby.} \end{cases}$

An other 經常都拼成一個字 another：

May I offer you *another* piece of cake?

I need *another* one (two / three, etc.) of these.

Every other（every two）, every three（every third）, every four（every fourth）等，

表示「每隔一」、「每隔二」、「每隔三」、「每隔四」等：

He doesn't come here every day, only $\left\{ \begin{array}{l} \textit{every other} \text{ day} \\ \textit{every two} \text{ days} \end{array} \right\}$.

Don't write on every line; write on $\left\{ \begin{array}{l} \textit{every three} \text{ lines} \\ \textit{every third} \text{ line} \end{array} \right\}$.

(5) single「唯一的、單一的」、double「雙…的」、triple「三部分合成的」…，通常放在冠詞後面：

He never made a *single* mistake.

This knife has a *double* edge.

The *triple* window has three parts.

但是如果這些語詞是表示倍數,就要放在冠詞前面：

I will pay you *double* (= twice) his price.

He earns *treble* (= three times) my salary.

(6) 數量詞 half(of)「一半」通常出現在限定詞的前面,同時 of 多半都加以省略：

He wasted *half* (*of*) his time.

Half (*of*) the people I met were strangers.

但是如果後面的名詞是表示單位的名詞(如 hour, day, year, mile, pound 等),那麼就可以說 half a(n) 也可以說 a half。比較：

We waited $\left\{ \begin{array}{l} \textit{half an} \text{ hour / one hour and } \textit{a half.} \\ \textit{a half} \text{ hour / one and } \textit{a half} \text{ hours.} \end{array} \right\}$

(7) Almost 與 nearly「差不多」可以出現在 all, every, no 與數詞前面：

Almost all the students were present.

I know *almost* every student.

He made *almost* no mistake.

It is *almost* three o'clock.

About「大約」可以用在數詞前面：

Give me *about* five.

It's *about* ten o'clock.

It happened on or *about* the fifth of May.

習 題 245

把括號裡的語詞依照英語正確的詞序排下來。

Example:

Don't be in (a, such, hurry).

Don't be in such a hurry.

1. Do you have (book, other, any) on this subject?

2. I'm busy now; ask me about it (time, other, some).

3. I'd like to buy (three, of, another, these).

4. Bob didn't come, but (other, boy, every) in the school came.

5. Mary didn't dance, but (girls, the, other, all) did dance.

6. Do you have (questions, more, any)?

7. I ate (a, half, eggs, dozen) this morning.

8. (his, every, almost, of, friend) was invited to his party.

9. I can never solve (question, difficult, a, such).

10. He told us (story, quite, interesting, an).

11. (members, of, some, the even) on the committee did not know the truth.

12. We invited (friends, few, just, of, a, ours).

13. This is (piece, news, of, astonishing, rather, an).

14. He was interested in (book, chapters, only, few, your, first, the, of).

15. (few, friends, my, only, a, of, best) know my secret.

16. My wife earns (my, double, almost, salary).

17. We enjoyed (two, first, his, the, of, acts, play, especially).

18. These are (only, examples, mistakes, a, his, few, many, stupid, of).

19. This book has (readers, only, few, a) because it has (few, merits,but) to recommend it.

20. That book has (a, stories, quite, interesting, few), but (people, few, very) ever read it.

第*14*章
代名詞

14-1. 人稱代名詞

人稱代名詞（personal pronouns）用來代替名詞或名詞組：

James studies at college; *he* is a college student.

This is *my new house*. I bought *it* only last month.

英語裡的人稱代名詞一共有七個：I「我」、we「我們」、you「你、你們」、he「他」、she「她」、it「它」、they「他（她，它）們」。I 與 we 指講話的人，叫做**第一身**（first person）；you 指講話的對方，叫做**第二身**（second person）；he, she, it, they 指第三者，叫做**第三身**（third person）。

You, *he* and *I* are going to visit Mr. Brown tomorrow.

We, *you* and *they* all had a good time last night.

參考：下面的表，表示那一種名詞可以用那一種代名詞來代替。

(1) 「陽性名詞」（he-nouns）

 a. 「屬人名詞」he（they）：

  boy, brother, father, uncle, husband, nephew, man, waiter, priest, monk, king, emperor, tenor.

 b. 「非屬人名詞」he / it（they）：

  bull, ram, rooster, buck, steer, tomcat.

(2) 「陰性名詞」（she-nouns）

 a. 「屬人名詞」she（they）：

  girl, sister, mother, aunt, wife, niece, woman, waitress, priestess, nun, queen, empress, soprano.

 b. 「非屬人名詞」she / it（they）：

  cow, ewe, hen, doe, heifer, bitch, ship.

(3) 「中性名詞」（it-nouns）it（they）：

book, pen, desk, house, tree, poem, friendship, kindness, complication, rock, sand, mountain.

(4) 「通性名詞」

　　a. 「屬人名詞」he / she（they）

　　　　child, parent, person, friend, teacher, student, singer, pianist, artist, doctor, invalid.

　　b. he / she / it（they）：

　　　　baby, dog, cat.

(5) 「集合名詞」（collective nouns）it / they（they）：

　group, team, bunch, gang, class, family, crowd, flock, mob, tribe, choir, jury, crew, committee, faculty, government, collection.

(6) 「不定代名詞」（indefinite pronouns）：

　　a. he / she（沒有複數）：somebody, someone, anybody, everybody.

　　b. he / she / it（they）：one, other.

(7) 「不可數名詞」（noncount nouns）it（沒有複數）：

　dirt, mathematics, news, information, furniture, baggage, poetry, music.

(8) （沒有單數）they：pants, scissors, pliers, clothes, people.

習　題　246

　　用適當的代名詞代替斜體部分的名詞組。

1. *Bob's grandmother* came from England.

2. Where have George and *George's* wife been?

3. Where had *George and George's wife* been?

4. *The child's clothes* were dirty.

5. How old is *Bill and Linda's baby?*

6. That's the cow I want; lead *the cow* over there, please.

7. That elephant lost *the elephant's* calf.

8. The baby had lost *the baby's* toy.

9. The police found the child and returned *the child to the child's* parents.

10. That's our *cow*; *the cow* gives a lot of milk.

11. Is that your baby girl? My, how *the baby girl* has grown!

12. The mother elephant bathes *the mother elephant's* baby in the river.

13. *The cattle* milled around uneasily in the pen.

14. *The rooster's* crowing woke us at dawn.

15. Is *Joe* a friend of *Jane's?*

16. The boat was *Harry* and *Bob's*.

17. *Dick* seemed to enjoy all *the group's* decisions.

18. This is *my vegetable garden*, and that's *my wife's flower garden*.

19. *The system in their office* seemed more efficient than *our system*.

20. *The jury* couldn't agree on *the case*.

習 題 247

從下面兩行名詞中把意義相對的陽性與陰性名詞配起來，並用代名詞 he 與 she 注出它的性別來。

Example: actor (*he*)　　　actress (*she*)

1. count	a. nephew	8. witch	h. horse
2. hen	c. madam	9. bride	i. cock
3. heir	c. hero	10. hostess	j. heiress
4. bachelor	d. maidservant	11. ewe	k. princess
5. mistress	e. ram	12. duchess	l. landlady
6. heroine	f. monk (*or* friar)	13. steward	m. host
7. sir	g. countess	14. nun	n. gentleman
15. mare	o. wizard	21. king	u. master
16. lady	p. stewardess	22. prince	v. son
17. bull	q. spinster	23. manservant	w. grandmother
18. grandfather	r. widower	24. daughter	x. queen
19. niece	s. bridegroom	25. widow	y. duke
20. landlord	t. cow		

14-2. 人稱代名詞的主格與受格

人稱代名詞，除了所有格以外，還有主格與受格兩種不同的形式。

單數		複數	
主格	受格	主格	受格
I	me	we	us
you	you	you	you
he	him		
she	her	they	them
it	it		

句子的主語，用主格；動詞與介詞的賓語，用受格：

> *He* told me a joke.（主語）

> They saw *him*.（動詞的賓語）

> We laughed at *him*.（介詞的賓語）

主語補語，正式的英語常用主格，但是口語英語常用受格：

> Who is it? It's *I*. (It's *me*.)

> It's *he* (*him*) that wants to see you, not *she* (*her*).

賓語補語，用受格：

> I thought it to be *him*.

> It was *him* that I wanted to see, not her.

習 題 248

依照例句改寫下列句子。

Examples: I know you. → *You know me.*

We look at her. → *She looks at us.*

1. I like him.   2. She needs them.

3. We take care of it.   4. You ran after her.

5. They understand us.   6. He is watching you carefully.

習 題 249

用適當的代名詞代替斜體部分的名詞或名詞組。

1. *John* brought *some sweets* for *his aunt*.

2. *The teacher* explained *the problem* to *the student*.

3. *My sister* and I told *my little brother* a story.

4. *Henry* and *his wife* came to see *Charles and Susan*.

5. *My friend and I* told *Mr. Smith* about *our trip* last month.

6. *Bob* will find *her coat* for *Jane*.

7. *Betty* gave a lot of *presents* to *Bob and Jane*.

8. *The boys* went into the garden, where *the boys* saw the *snake*.

9. Very soon *the Rabbit* noticed as *Alice* went hunting about, and called out to *Alice* in an angry tone.

10. *John* had taken *his watch* out of his pocket, and was looking at *the watch* uneasily, shaking *the watch* every now and then, and holding *the watch* to his ear.

習 題 250

選出正確的語詞。

1. (We, us) all went to the movies with (they, them).

2. What's the name of (he, him) who came first?

3. The best ones are always bought by (he, him) who can pay the most.

4. There's a friendly agreement between Mr. Smith and (I, me).

5. Let you and (I, me) try what we can do.

6. We scored as many goals as (they, them).

7. He loves you more than (I, me) 〔love you〕.

8. He loves you more than 〔he loves〕 (I, me).

9. You are a better golfer than (he, him).

10. Let (we, us) all go for a walk except (she, her), since (she, her) is so tired.

11. Do you think (he, him) is stronger than (I, me)?

12. It was (she, her) that went out just now, wasn't it?

13. It was (she, her) you meant, wasn't it?

14. I know you're bigger than (I, me), in fact you're bigger than (we, us) both, but it doesn't scare me.

15. John thought the visitor to be (I, me); he mistook (I, me) for the visitor.

16. I saw (she, her) fall down as (she, her) was walking across the street.

17. We thought (he, him) was the best player; we thought (he, him) the best player.

18. If you were (I, me), would you ever believe (he, him) to be honest?

19. They elected (you, he and I; me, you and him; you, him and me) to investigate the matter.

20. Well, let's pretend for a moment: I'll be (she, her) and you be (I, me). Now imagine there's a quarrel between (she, her) and (I, me). How would you settle it?

參考：(1) 在口語英語中，Be 動詞後面常用受格代名詞。例如：

That's *him*.

It's only *me*.

I wouldn't do that if I were *her*.

(2) than 與 as 是連詞，因此後面的代名詞用主格或受格應該有分別。例如：

I like you more than *him*. (= than I like him)

I like you more than *he* (does). (= than he likes you)

但是在口語英語中，特別是在 Be 動詞與不及物動詞後面，常用代名詞的受格而不用主格。

We're much stronger than *them* (they) at football.

You're as tall as *me* (I), so you can easily ride my bike.

I can run much faster than *him* (he).

You can sing as beautifully as *her* (she).

如果代名詞後面有 both 或 all，那麼就是書寫的英語也常用受格。例如：

He is cleverer than *us all*.

A stone is heavy and the sand weighty;

　　but a fool's wrath is heavier than *them both*. (*Bible*)

(3) such as 後面的代名詞通常都用主格：

    I don't know any man such as *he*.

但是如果 such as 前面有介詞，那麼也有用受格的。

    How can you talk to a woman such as *she / her?*

  比較：How can you talk to such a woman as *her?*

(4) except 與 but「⋯除外」是介詞，所以後面的代名詞原應該用受格。例如：

    There was no one except *me*.

但是現代英語，特別是書寫的英語，把這些介詞看做連詞，因此後面常用受格。

例如：   Nobody could answer except *I / me*.

    No one came home but *he / him*.

(5) 在口語秀語中，凡是說話者認為所指的人不是真正做這件事的人，都喜歡用受格不用主格。例如：

    "Who did that?" "Please, sir, *it wasn't me*.

    What! *Me* fight a big chap like him? No, *me*.

    Her marry George! Not *her*! She would rather die than marry him.

(6) 下面例句裡的代名詞，必須用受格，不能用主格。

    It was *him* I was talking about.（介詞 about 的賓語）

    Is it *us* they are referring to?（介詞 to 的賓語）

    It was *her* you meant, wasn't it?（動詞 meant 的賓語）

14-3. 反身代名詞

    帶有 -self（單數）或 -selves（複數）的代名詞叫做反身代名詞（reflexive pronouns）。

單數		複數	
I	myself	we	ourselves
you	yourself	you	yourselves
he	himself	they	themselves
she	herself		
it	itself		

反身代名詞主要有兩種用法。

(1) 放在（代）名詞的後面或句尾以表示「本人」或「親自」：

> I went *myself*.
> I *myself* went there.（較為正式，語氣也較重。）

> You did it *yourself*. / You *yourself* did it.

> I gave the money to John *himself*, not his sister.

> It was the Queen *herself* that I saw.

(2) 做為動詞或介詞的賓語以表示做動作與受動作的人是同一人：

比較：
> He shot him with a gun.「張三開槍殺了李四。」
> He shot himself with a gun.「他開槍自殺了。」

> She looked at *herself* in the mirror.

> One must take care of *oneself* (*himself*).

參考：

(1) 「反身動詞」（reflexive verbs）：下面的動詞常以反身代名詞為賓語。

pride oneself（up）on「以…自豪」，*absent* oneself from「缺席、不到」，*dress* oneself in「穿著」，*seat* oneself on「坐在」，*avail* oneself of「利用」，*apply* oneself to「集中精力做」，*associate* oneself with「與…為伍」，*possess* oneself of「擁有」，*prepare*（oneself）for「準備」，*engage*（oneself）in「從事」，*avenge* oneself on「向…報仇」，*interest* oneself in「對…感到興趣」，*accustom* oneself to「使自己習慣於」，*amuse* oneself with「以…自娛」，*submit* oneself to「服從」，*subject* oneself to「使自己遭受」，*devote* oneself to「獻身於」，*commit* oneself to「承諾、負責」，*break* oneself off「戒除（惡習）」，*guard* oneself against「防備」，*spend* oneself on「鞠躬盡瘁」，*help* oneself to「自己取用」，*present* oneself before「出席、參加」，*enjoy* oneself「享樂」，*behave* oneself like「舉止、行為」，*make* oneself at home「自在、不拘束」。

比較：
> He *prides* himself on his success.（動詞）
> He is *proud* of his success.（形容詞）

$$\begin{cases} \text{She } \textit{absented} \text{ herself from school.（動詞）} \\ \text{She was } \textit{absent} \text{ from school.（形容詞）} \end{cases}$$

$$\begin{cases} \text{He } \textit{dressed himself} \text{ in uniform.（主動式）} \\ \text{He } \textit{was dressed} \text{ in uniform.（被動式）} \end{cases}$$

$$\begin{cases} \text{She } \textit{seated herself} \text{ on the sofa.（主動式）} \\ \text{She } \textit{was seated} \text{ on the sofa.（被動式）} \end{cases}$$

$$\begin{cases} \text{He } \textit{accustomed himself} \text{ to getting up early.（主動式）} \\ \text{He } \textit{was accustomed} \text{ to getting up early.（被動式）} \end{cases}$$

$$\begin{cases} \text{She } \textit{devoted herself} \text{ to music.（主動式）} \\ \text{She } \textit{was devoted} \text{ to music.（被動式）} \end{cases}$$

(2) 介詞與反身代名詞：

He lives *by himself* (= alone).「單獨」

Studying has to be done *by oneself* (= without help).「靠自己」

Would you like to see *for yourself* (= in person)?「親自」

One should not live *for oneself* (= for one's own sake) alone.「為本身的利益」

The door closed *of itself* (= automatically).「自動」

She awoke *of herself* (= spontaneously).「自然、自己」

He is *beside himself* (= mad) with joy.「（欣喜）若狂」

I have the whole house *to myself*.「歸自己（住）」

A thing good *in itself* (= by its own nature) may become harmful by its use.「本身」

習　題　251

依照例句改寫下列句子。

Example: He bought a book.

　　　He bought a book himself; he himself bought a book.

　　　He bought himself a book; he bought a book for hirnself.

1. Jane is going to write a letter.　　　2. Jack has gone to buy a coat.

3. Miss Wood taught the lesson.　　　4. James made a big sandwich.

5. You told a lie.

6. The students asked a question.

7. I am going to find a job.

8. Mrs. White cut a slice of bread.

9. We are going to bake cake.

10. Charles and Susan will build a new house.

習 題 252

在下面的空白裡填入代名詞所有格（my, mine; your, yours; he, his; her, hers 等）或反身代名詞（myself, yourself, himself, herself 等）。

1. She makes all _____ own dresses _____ .

2. This book is _____ ; I wrote _____ name in it _____ .

3. That's not _____ , it's _____ ; he bought it _____ .

4. We enjoyed _____ very much at _____ party.

5. She has made _____ very unpopular among _____ friends.

6. It's _____ ; they bought it _____ .

7. George says that the hat is not _____ , although it looks like the one he bought _____ last month.

8. You must all look after _____ on _____ trip to Japan.

9. You have always to remind _____ that this book is _____ and not _____ ; otherwise you may take it away _____ with _____ own books by mistake.

10. One must remember to behave _____ in _____ own house just as well as in other people's.

習 題 253

依照例句回答下列各句。

Examples: I want you to do it.

    Why don't you do it yourself?

    She's a pretty good musician, isn't she?

    Yes, but you're a pretty good one yourself.

    Can't you go with me?

    No, you'll have to go by yourself.

1. He wants you to do it.

2. He's a pretty good player, isn't he?

3. Can't you go with them?

4. She expects you to get it for her.

5. You have a pretty good exam paper, don't you?

6. Can't you help them to finish?

7. They told you to write him a letter.

8. They know an awful lot of people, don't they?

9. Can't you walk downtown with her?

10. We're asking you to look for it.

11. He needs to spend some time in the lab, doesn't he?

12. Can't you practice English with them?

14-4. **It 的特殊用法**

人稱代名詞 it 除了代表第三人身單數動物或無生物「牠、它」以外，還有下列幾種特別的用法。

(1) a. 指天氣：

It is cold (warm, fine, wet, windy) today.

It rains heavily (snows a lot, blows hard) during January.

b. 指時間：

What time is *it* now?

It is two o'clock (five-thirty, striking eleven).

It is dark (light enough, dawning, still early, getting late) .

It is Wednesday (March, summer, Christmas).

It's a month to New Year.

It's time to go home.

c. 指距離：

How far is *it* from here to the station?

It is not far (ten minutes' walk, two miles) from here.

It's only a short way now.

d. 指不特定的人：

Who is *it? It*'s me.

I thought *it* was John.

(2) It is … that（who, when, where）：要強調句子中的某一些語詞的時候，可以把這些語詞放在 it is / was 的後面，其他的部分放在 that 的後面。

比較：Jack met Mary at the station yesterday.「傑克昨天在車站遇見瑪麗。」

It was *Jack* that / who met Mary at the station yesterday.

「昨天在車站遇見瑪麗的（人）是傑克。」

It was *Mary* that / who(m) Jack met at the station yesterday.

「昨天傑克在車站遇見的是瑪麗。」

It was *yesterday* that / when Jack met Mary at the station.

「傑克在車站遇見瑪麗的時間是昨天。」

It was *at the station* that / where Jack met Mary yesterday.

「傑克昨天遇見瑪麗的地方是車站。」

(3) 由「不定詞」（to V）、「動名詞」（V-ing）、「that- 子句」、「wh- 子句」開頭的句子都可以改為由 it 帶頭的句子；即先把不定詞、動名詞、that- 子句、wh- 子句移到句尾，然後把 it 放在句首。

$$\left.\begin{array}{l} \text{To V} \cdots \\ \text{V-ing} \cdots \\ \text{That} \cdots \\ \text{Wh} \cdots \end{array}\right\} \text{V} \cdots \quad \Rightarrow \quad \text{It V} \cdots \left\{\begin{array}{l} \text{to V} \cdots \\ \text{V-ing} \cdots \\ \text{that} \cdots \\ \text{wh} \cdots \end{array}\right.$$

比較：

$\left\{\begin{array}{l}\text{To learn to speak English is easy.（欠通順）}\\ \textit{It} \text{ is easy to learn to speak English.（較通順）}\end{array}\right.$

$\left\{\begin{array}{l}\text{Trying to do that is no use.（欠通順）}\\ \textit{It} \text{ is no use trying to do that.（較通順）}\end{array}\right.$

$\left\{\begin{array}{l}\text{That he hadn't come yesterday was strange.（欠通順）}\\ \textit{It} \text{ was strange that he hadn't come yesterday.（較通順）}\end{array}\right.$

$$\begin{cases} \text{When, he will come is uncertain.}（欠通順）\\ \textit{It} \text{ is uncertain when he will come.}（較通順）\end{cases}$$

$$\begin{cases} \text{Whether we start now or later doesn't matter.}（欠通順）\\ \textit{It} \text{ doesn't matter whether we start now or later.}（較通順）\end{cases}$$

參考：It 的習慣用法：

That's *it*. (= That's what I wanted to know.)「這就是（我要知道的）了。」

How is *it* with him? / How goes *it* with him? (= How is he?)「他好嗎？」

It is all over with us. (= There is no hope left for us.)「我們已經完（蛋）了。」

He had the best of *it*. (= He was successful.)「他很得意。」

We had a splendid / hard time of *it*.「那時候我們真快樂（辛苦）。」

It is always so with Jack.「傑克總是這樣的。」

There *it* is, do what you like.「好吧，你高興怎樣做就怎樣做。」

Now you have done *it*. (= You have done something wrong or foolish.)「這一下你可糟啦！」

Now you'll catch *it*. (= You'll be punished.)「這一下你可要挨罵了。」

It can't be helped.「沒有辦法啦！」

習　題　254

按照中文意思完成下列句子。

1. _____ is quite _____ _____.「今天天氣相當冷。」
2. _____ rains _____ _____ in spring.「春天裡雨下得很多。」
3. _____ a fine day _____ _____!「天氣多好啊！」
4. _____ dark _____ _____!「天好黑啊！」
5. _____ _____ a long _____ to the nearest station.「到最近的車站有不少路呢。」
6. _____ _____ five _____ walk.「走五分鐘就到了。」
7. _____ is _____ that I must see?「我要見的是誰？」
8. Go and see _____ _____ _____.「去看看是誰？」
9. _____ is right _____ do so.「這樣做是對的。」

10. _____ is _____ use _____.「試也沒有用。」

11. _____ is certain _____ he will succeed.「他一定會成功的。」

12. _____ is absurd _____ like that.「說那樣的話真荒唐。」

13. I found _____ easy _____ learn to speak English.「我覺得學說英語並不難。」

14. _____ is still undecided _____ he will go.「他去不去還沒有決定。」

15. Does _____ matter _____ you do next?「你下一步做什麼關係重大嗎？」

16. _____ _____ three years _____ I last met you.「自從上次見面以後已經三年了。」

17. _____ so happened _____ he was not there.「碰巧他不在那裡。」

18. _____ turn _____ _____ next?「下一個輪到誰啦？」

19. I think ____ a pity _____ you didn't try harder.「你沒有更加努力我覺得很可惜。」

20. _____ doesn't seem much use _____ on.「再繼續下去似乎沒有什麼用處。」

習 題 255

依照例句改寫下列的句子，以加重斜體字部分的意思。

Example: The Americans started it.

→ *It was the Americans that / who started it.*

1. *I* am fortunate.

2. He left *an hour ago*.

3. She wanted to go to *New York*.

4. They got married *in May*.

5. *The President* proposed the bill.

6. *His work during the weekend* exhausted him.

7. I want *the red book*, not the green one.

8. I gave the book to *John*, not Dick.

9. I saw him *on Sunday*, not on Saturday.

10. I am concerned about *the people*, not the dollars.

11. He doesn't have much *money*.

12. I'm not sure *whether I can go or not*.

13. We heard *him* playing the piano.

14. That young man doesn't have much *experience*.

15. They watched *her* walking across the street.

參考：注意下面幾個句子的變化：

> She wanted to go to New York.
>
>> It was New York *that* she wanted to *go to*.
>>
>> It was New York *where* she wanted to *go*.
>
> He doesn't have much money.
>
>> It is money that he doesn't have much *of*.
>
> I'm not sure whether I can go or not.
>
>> It is whether I can go or not that I'm not sure *of*.
>
> We heard him playing the piano.
>
>> It was *he* that we heard playing the piano.

習　題　256

依照例句改寫下列句子。

Example: He suggested that you report to the principal.

> → *It was his suggestion that you report to the principal.*

1. She requested that we help her.

2. They recommended that he not follow the order.

3. We proposed that they change the subject.

4. You advised that I not buy the car.

5. He ordered that his instructions be obeyed.

6. I intended that I come back the next year.

習　題　257

依照例句回答下列問句。

Example: I think he just left. (an hour ago)

> *No, it was an hour ago that he left.*

1. I think he went to the library. (the museum)

2. I think he went with his brother. (his sister)

3. I think they went to the museum by bus. (by taxi)

4. I think George told you to come here. (George's brother)

5. I think Bob wants you to take care of his business. (his children)

6. I think you are working hard for your boss. (my boss's daughter)

14-5. 相互代名詞

英語的 **相 互 代 名 詞**（reciprocal pronouns） 只 有 兩 個：each other 與 one another。雖然一般的文法書上都說：each other 用在兩個人之間，而 one another 則用在三個以上的人之間，但是實際上兩者常常可以交互使用。比較：

> John knows Bob; Bob knows John.
> John and Bob know *each other* / *one another*.

> Alice won't talk to Mary; Mary won't talk to Alice.
> Alice and Mary wont talk to *each other* / *one another*.

> Dick has been to Julie's home; Julie has been to Dick's home.
> Dick and Julie have been to *each other's* / *one another's* home.

> They love *each other*.
> *Each* of them loves *the other*.

> They give presents to *one another* at Christmas.
> *Each* gives presents to *the others* at Christmas.

> They are washing *each other's* clothes.
> *Each* of them is washing *the other's* clothes.

習 題 258

依照例句改寫下列各句。

Example: Charles loves Susan; Susan loves Charles.

　　　Charles and Susan love each other.

1. Bob helped Dick; Dick helped Bob.

2. Mr. Smith respects Mrs. Smith; Mrs. Smith respects Mr. Smith.

3. The mother depends on the daughter; the daughter depends on the mother.

4. Jane gave Mary a present; Mary gave Jane a present.

5. He knows her name; she knows his name.

6. I kept a picture of you; you kept a picture of me.

7. Jack woke Bob up; Bob woke Jack up.

8. She didn't call him up last night; he didn't call her up last night.

習　題　259

依照例句改寫下列各句。

Examples: Each one served himself

　　　　　They served themselves.

　　　　Each one helped the other to pass.

　　　　　They helped each other to pass.

1. Each one gave a present to the other.

2. Each one looked at himself in the mirror.

3. Each one corrected the other's paper.

4. Each one supports himself with a part-time job.

5. Each one reminded himself to report his address.

6. Each one trained himself to protect the other.

7. Each one told the other not to forget to bring his I.D. card.

8. Each one expected the other to buy himself a drink.

習　題　260

依照例句改寫下列各句。

Examples: They help themselves. → *It's self-help.*

　　　　They help each other. → *It's mutual help.*

1. They respect themselves.　　　　2. They respect each other.

3. They defend themselves.　　　　4. They defend each other.

5. They criticize themselves.

6. They support each other.

7. They serve themselves.

8. They admire each other.

9. They discipline themselves.

10. They destroy each other.

14-6. 不定代考詞

不定代名詞（indefinite pronouns）由 some-「某」、any-「任何」、every-「每」、no-「沒」與 -body「人」、-thing「東西」、-where「地方」、-place「地方」-time「時間」、-how「方法」連合而成：

	-body	-one	-thing	-where	-place	-time	-how
some-	somebody	someone	something	somewhere	someplace	sometime	somehow
any-	anybody	anyone	anything	anywhere	anyplace	any time	anyhow
every-	everybody	everyone	everything	everywhere	everyplace	everytime	
no-	nobody	no one	nothing	nowhere	no place	no time	

這些代名詞有下列幾種共同的特點。

(1) 不定代名詞只有單數形，沒有複數形：

There *is something* on the table.

Someone must have forgotten *his* job.

Anyone can bring *his* sister with *him*.

No one is allowed to bring *his* dog with *him*.

Everybody should love *his* country.

但是在口語中 everybody 與 everyone 常常當做複數看待：

Everyone was there, *weren't they?*

(2) 含有 some- 的不定代名詞用在肯定敘述句；含有 any- 的不定代名詞用在否定句、問句、條件句；含有 no- 的不定代名詞用在否定句。比較：

There is *somebody* in the room.

There isn't *anybody* in the room.

There is *nobody* in the room.

Is there *anybody* in the room?

If there is *anybody* in the room, I want to see him.

$$\left\{\begin{array}{l}\text{I can tell you } \textit{something}.\\ \text{I can't tell you } \textit{anything}.\\ \text{I can tell you } \textit{nothing}.\\ \text{Can you tell me } \textit{anything}?\\ \text{If you have } \textit{anything} \text{ to tell me, tell it right now.}\end{array}\right.$$

$$\left\{\begin{array}{l}\text{I have seen him } \textit{somewhere}.\\ \text{I haven't seen him } \textit{anywhere}.\\ \text{I have see him } \textit{nowhere}.\\ \text{Have I seen him } \textit{anywhere}?\\ \text{If I have seen him } \textit{anywhere}, \text{ I must be able to remember his face.}\end{array}\right.$$

(3) 含有 some- 的不定代名詞，如果用在問句裡即表示說話者希望獲得肯定的回答。

I think somebody there? (I think somebody is there.)

Is *somebody* there? (I think somebody is there.)

May I tell you *something*? (= I want to tell you something.)

含有 any- 的不定代名詞，如果用在肯定敘述句裡表示「任何」。

比較：

$$\left\{\begin{array}{l}\textit{Somebody} \text{ must do this.}\\ \textit{Anybody} \text{ can do that.}\end{array}\right.$$

$$\left\{\begin{array}{l}\text{I will do } \textit{something} \text{ for him.}\\ \text{I would do } \textit{anything} \text{ for her.}\end{array}\right.$$

(4) 不定代名詞的修飾語，只能放在不定代名詞的後面不能放在前面。比較：

$$\left\{\begin{array}{l}\text{Show me something } \textit{new}.\\ \text{Show me some } \textit{new} \text{ dresses.}\end{array}\right.$$

$$\left\{\begin{array}{l}\text{I can't imagine anything } \textit{more beautiful}.\\ \text{I can't imagine any } \textit{more beautiful} \text{ scene.}\end{array}\right.$$

$$\left\{\begin{array}{l}\text{She wants to marry someone } \textit{rich and handsome}.\\ \text{She wants to marry a } \textit{rich and handsome} \text{ husband.}\end{array}\right.$$

$$\left\{\begin{array}{l}\text{He has nothing } \textit{else} \text{ to do.}\\ \text{He has no } \textit{other} \text{ thing to do.}\end{array}\right.$$

習 題 261

依照例句改寫下列語組。

Examples: a later time → *sometime* later

a good thing → *something good*

an important person → *someone / somebody* important

by some means → *somehow*

1. a useful thing
2. a famous person
3. an earlier time
4. a quiet place
5. a very interesting thing
6. a well-known person
7. a more suitable time
8. a very near place
9. by some method
10. in some way

習 題 262

依照例句改寫下列各句。

Example: Somebody important is coming.

Do you think anybody important is coming?

No, nobody important is coming.

1. He lives somewhere near.
2. They could meet sometime earlier.
3. She can buy something interesting to read on the train.
4. He can find someplace convenient to park his car.
5. Something good is bound to come out of it.
6. You can find someone able and willing.

習 題 263

依照例句改寫下列語組。

Examples: some other person → *somebody else*

what other person → *who else*

some other time → *some other time*

1. some other thing	2. some other place	3. what other thing
4. every other thing	5. every other person	6. Some other way
7. what other place	8. some other reason	9. What other time
10. any other thing	11. no other person	12. What other way
13. any other place	14. no other thing	15. What other reason
16. no other time	17. every other way	18. Every other place
19. no other reason	20. no other way	

參考：else 用在不定代名詞與 wh- 疑問詞的後面；other 用在名詞的前面。

習　題　264

依照例句改寫下列各句。

Example: I can't get an answer from him. (ask)

Ask someone else.

Who else can I ask?

$$There \begin{cases} is\ nobody\ else \\ isn't\ anybody\ else \end{cases} I\ can\ ask.$$

1. I don't like this cake. (eat)　　　　　2. The restaurant is closed. (go)

3. I can't see him in the morning. (see him)

4. The manager never answered my letters. (write to)

5. This is not a good place for us to meet. (see each other)

6. This pair of trousers is too short for me. (wear)

習　題　265

在下面的空白裡填入適當的不定代名詞。

1. I think he was saying _____ very important.

2. I don't feel like saying _____ at this moment.

3. They didn't need to do _____ about it.

4. They're going to see each other _____ much later.

5. We'd like to live _____ quiet and peaceful.

6. I was told _____ very important is coming today.

7. I didn't see _____ famous at the meeting.

8. If _____ knows the truth, let him tell it.

9. They want him to come _____ more suitable.

10. _____ knows that it's wrong to tell a lie.

11. It is very simple; _____ could tell you that.

12. This is not my book; it must be _____ else's.

13. Why aren't you studying? _____ else is.

14. Let's eat here. _____ else is pretty expensive.

15. Would you care to order _____ else?

16. There was one piece by Brahms; _____ else was modern.

17. There is _____ in the next room. Is there _____ upstairs?

18. If there is _____ upstairs, tell him to come down.

19. _____ likes an honest boy; _____ likes a dishonest boy.

20. He is very kind to _____; he is _____'s friend.

14-7. 代名詞 One, Another 與 Other（s）

代名詞 one 有下列幾種用法：

(1) 代表「任何人」，包括說話者在內：所有格是 one's，反身代名詞是 oneself。
這種 one 在口語中常用 we, you, anyone 等來代替：

One (= We) cannot always find time for reading.

One has (= You have) to do *one's* (= your) best.

If *one* (= anyone) wants a thing done well, *one* (he) had best do it *oneself* (= *himself*).

(2) 代替在前文中已經出現的可數名詞：複數形是 ones。

I don't like this hat. Can you show me a better *one* (= hat)?

We have seven rooms, four large *ones* (= rooms) and three small *ones* (= rooms).

Here are two books for you to choose. Will you have this *one* (= book) or that *one* (= book)?

代名詞 another 與 other（s）的用法如下：

(1) another（＝ an + other）「另外一個，再一個」指無定的人或物（限於可數名詞），多數形是 others。

I don't like this hat; please show me *another* (one). (= a different hat)

These cakes are delicious. May I have *another* (one)? (= one more cake)

Some people say this, *others* (= other people) say that.

These cameras are not good enough. Do you have any *others*? (= any other cameras)

(2) the other「其他的一個」指特定的人或物，複數形是 the others。

There are two guests in the room; one is Mr. Smith and *the other* (= the other guest) is Mr. Johnson.

Some of these apples come from Korea, *the others* (= the other apples) from Japan.

參考一：

美國用法，在 one 之後，可以使用 he, him, his, himself 以代替 one, one's, oneself：

$$\text{One should love} \left\{ \begin{array}{l} one's \\ his \end{array} \right\} \text{country.}$$

參考二：

the one 與 the other 可以用來指 the former「前者」與 the latter「後者」：

Virtue and vice are before you; *the one* (= virtue) leads you to happiness, *the other* (= vice) to misery.

習 題 266

依照例句完成下列各句。

Examples: ⋯ earn $20,000 / rich man / poor man

Which one earns $20,000, a rich man or a poor man?

The rich one.

⋯ carry / heavy luggage / light luggage

Which will you carry, heavy luggage or light luggage?

The light luggage.

1. ⋯ drive / real cars / toy cars

2. ⋯ prefer / weak coffee / strong coffee

3. ⋯ want / a high grade / a low grade

4. ⋯ cost more / an old apartment / a new apartment

5. ⋯ like better / summer weather / winter weather

6. ⋯ smoke / cheap cigarettes / expensive cigarettes

7. ⋯ enjoy more / classical music / popular music

8. ⋯ prefer / Chinese tea / American coffee

9. ⋯ buy / black ink / blue ink

10. ⋯ must use / a black pencil / a blue pencil

習 題 267

把斜體部分的語詞用 one, ones, one's 或 oneself 來代替。

1. *We* must be loyal to *our* friends.

2. *You* should not live for *yourself* alone.

3. *Any person* does not like to have *his* word doubted.

4. Do you have a knife? Yes, I have *a knife*.

5. *A man* went this way; another *man* went that way.

6. He has three black pencils and one red *pencil*.

7. She has two long pencils and two short *pencils*.

8. We compared American universities with British *universities*.

9. Your plan is a good *plan* on paper.

10. There are right answers and wrong *answers*.

11. The chance was too good a *chance* to let pass.

12. These shoes are much more comfortable than the old *shoes*.

13. I like the hat on the shelf, not the *hat* in the closet.

14. That is the *camera* that I want to buy.

15. I never read the *books* in the library.

16. People who succeed most in business are not necessarily the *people* who were best at school.

参考：the one 與 the ones 只用在介詞、「介詞片語」或「關係子句」的前面：

    I bought the car from England and Bob bought *the one* (= the car) from Germany.

    I have read the books you have lent me the other day, but I didn't have the time to read *the ones* (= the books = those) I borrowed from the library.

習　題　268

    在下面的空白裡填 some, any, one 或 ones。

1. I want _____ new eggs; do you have _____?

2. I asked him for _____ soap, but he didn't have _____.

3. These maps are old; please give me _____ new _____.

4. I'll smoke a cigarette; will you have _____ too?

5. You have _____ interesting books; will you lend me just _____?

6. I asked him for _____ ice, and he gave me _____.

7. I've lost my pencil. Have you _____ to lend me?

8. I want _____ apples. Give me these big _____.

9. So this is your house. It's a very pretty _____.

10. You can take these oranges if you want _____, but I have better _____ inside.

11. They say the yellow _____ are best. I'll buy _____ if you have _____ left.

12. We have three rooms: one big _____ and two small _____.

13. Do you want _____ pine apples? Here are _____ nice ripe _____.

14. Are there _____ more newspapers? I've read all these old _____.

15. Here are _____ new shirts. Do you want to buy _____? This blue _____ is very nice.

参考：one 用來代替可數名詞；some 用來代替不可數名詞。

比較：   Do you want a pencil? Yes, I want *one*.
        Do you want any ink? Yes, I want *some*.

習　題　269

依照例句把下列各句裡重複出現的名詞（組），用 one 代替或刪去。

Examples:

This book is more interesting than that book.

This book is more interesting than that (one).

These dictionaries are more useful than those dictionaries.

These dictionaries are more useful than those.

1. Will you have this hat or that hat?

2. Will you have these suits or those suits?

3. Will you have this green hat or that blue hat?

4. Will you have these green shirts or those blue shirts?

5. Bob's exercise books are neater than Dick's exercise books.

6. My cheap camera is just as good as John's expensive camera.

7. This is my hat and that is my brother's hat.

8. Your old suit looks as smart as your brother's new suit.

9. Do you rent the house or is it your own house?

10. I put my right arm through Mary's left arm.

參考：these、those，數詞、名詞與代名詞的所有格後面，不能直接用 one（s）。

比較：

- this / that one（○）
- these / those ones（×）
- these / those new ones（○）

- three ones（×）
- three new ones（○）

- John's / his ones（×）
- John's / his new ones（○）

　　在比較正式的英語裡，最好刪去重複的名詞而避免使用 one（s）。

比較：

- We compared American universities with British ones.（非正式）
- We compared American with British universities.（較正式）

$$\begin{cases} \text{I prefer European-style houses to Japanese-style ones.（非正式）} \\ \text{I prefer European to Japanese-style houses.（較正式）} \end{cases}$$

習　題　270

依照例句改寫下列各句。

Examples:

One phone is in use. (out of order)

$\begin{cases} \textit{Another phone} \\ \textit{Another (one)} \end{cases}$ *is out of order.*

One of the phones is in use.

$\begin{cases} \textit{The other phone} \\ \textit{The other (one)} \end{cases}$ *is out of order.*

Some phones are in use.

$\begin{cases} \textit{Other phones} \\ \textit{Others} \end{cases}$ *are out of order.*

Some of the phones are in use.

$\begin{cases} \textit{The other phones} \\ \textit{The others} \\ \textit{The rest} \end{cases}$ *are out of order.*

Some advice was helpful. (useless)

Other advice was useless.

Some of the advice was helpful. (useless)

$\begin{cases} \textit{The other advice} \\ \textit{The rest} \end{cases}$ *was useless.*

1. One place accepts checks. (take only cash)

2. One of the places accepts checks.

3. Some places accept checks.

4. Some of the places accept checks.

5. Some food is for snacks. (for lunches and dinners)

6. Some of the food is for snacks.

7. TV fascinates some people. (It alienates)

8. There's one restaurant across the street. (on the corner)

9. There are places serving Chinese food. (Mexican food)

10. Some of the luggage was heavy. (light)

參考：the rest「其餘的」可以用來代替「the other + 複數可數名詞或單數不可數名詞」：

      The rest (of the phones) are out of order.（複數可數名詞）

      The rest (of the advice) was useless.（單數不可數名詞）

習 題 271

    在下面的空白裡填入 (the) one(s), another, (the) other(s) 或 else。

1. I don't like this ＿＿＿＿＿; are there any ＿＿＿＿＿?

2. Some played cards, some played chess, and ＿＿＿＿＿ watched television.

3. ＿＿＿＿＿ of the boys had walked out, but ＿＿＿＿＿ staved in the room.

4. I have read ＿＿＿＿＿ or two of these books, but I have never seen ＿＿＿＿＿ books.

5. ＿＿＿＿＿ student went this way; ＿＿＿＿＿ student went that way.

6. To know is ＿＿＿＿＿ thing; to do is quite ＿＿＿＿＿.

7. For ＿＿＿＿＿ thing he is too young; for ＿＿＿＿＿ he is not cautious enough.

8. Who ＿＿＿＿＿ could have done such a thing?

9. ＿＿＿＿＿ after ＿＿＿＿＿ the girls stepped inot the room.

10. We ought to see him ＿＿＿＿＿ day or ＿＿＿＿＿.

11. Taking ＿＿＿＿＿ thing with ＿＿＿＿＿, I had better go at once.

12. I have heard it from ＿＿＿＿＿ and ＿＿＿＿＿ during the week.

13. He raised ＿＿＿＿＿ of his hands after ＿＿＿＿＿.

14. We ran from ＿＿＿＿＿ end of the street to ＿＿＿＿＿.

15. When they finish ＿＿＿＿＿, they start ＿＿＿＿＿ somewhere ＿＿＿＿＿.

習 題 解 答

習題 1 解答

1. Be	2. V	3. AV V	4. Be	5. V
6. Be	7. AV V	8. V	9. Be	10. AV V

習題 2 解答

1. She could not understand everything.

2. They didn't have (had no) time to tell her.

3. We're not coming tomorrow morning.

4. He doesn't come here every morning.

5. There were not many people at the concert.

6. Our teacher doesn't want the homework now.

7. You must not (need not) look out of the window.

8. We could not see as far as the mountains.

9. She didn't come with him.

10. He will not (won't) come if he can't.

習題 3 解答

1. Is winter colder than summer?

2. Has he opened the window on your right?

3. Was Peter born and brought up in China?

4. Have you studied English for two years?

5. Are shoes made in pairs?

6. Have many old customs died out in China?

7. Did it take you a month to get rid of the cold?

8. Did his mother ask you to send for a doctor?

9. Do they have to finish their work by tomorrow?

10. Should I have prepared my lesson last night?

習題 4 解答

1. Yes, I can (speak English).

   No, I can't (speak English).

2. Yes, I'm (enjoying myself).

   No, I'm not (enjoying myself).

3. Yes, I have (met your sister Alice).

   No, I haven't (met your sister Alice).

4. Yes, I would (like another cup of tea).

   No, I wouldn't (like another cup of tea).

5. Yes, you must (be there in time).

   No, you mustn't (*or* needn't) (be there in time).

6. Yes, I met him yesterday. / Yes, I did.

   No, I didn't (meet him yesterday).

7. Yes, he plays chess. / Yes, he does.

   No, he doesn't (play chess).

8. Yes, you may (go out).

   No, you may not (orcannot) (go out).

9. Yes, I was (at the theater last night).

   No, I wasn't (at the theater last night).

10. Yes, we should (do our assignments).

    No, we shouldn't (do our assignments).

習題 5 解答

1. Is	2. am	3. does	4. Can	5. Is
6. Do	7. Shoul	8. does	9. Is	10. Do

習題 6 解答

1. Didn't you (Did you not) tell her to leave right away?

   Yes, I did. / No, I didn't.

2. Isn't the elevator out of order?

   Yes, it is. / No, it isn't.

3. Aren't there three windows in the room?

   Yes, there are. / No, there aren't.

4. Hasn't Smith put off his trip until next week?

   Yes, he has. / No, he hasn't.

5. Doesn't the class begin at 8:30 sharp?

   Yes, it does. / No, it doesn't.

6. Mustn't you write your excercises in pencil?

   Yes, I must. / No, I mustn't (needn't).

7. Won't Mary be in class tomorrow?

   Yes, she will. / No, she won't.

8. Aren't they going to the movies tonight?

   Yes, they are. / No, they aren't.

9. Isn't he going to have the radio repaired?

   Yes, he is. / No, he isn't.

10. Didn't he tell you not to come here any more?

    Yes, he did. / No, he didn't.

習題 7 解答

1. ..., isn't he?   2. ..., aren't they?

3. ..., were we?   4. ..., can't he?

5. ..., don't you?   6. ..., do you?

7. ..., has it?   8. ..., should you?

9. ..., doesn't she?   10. ..., did I?

習題 8 解答

1. did mail   2. does live   3. did take   4. did write   5. do want

6. Did call   7. did do   8. did show   9. does attend   10. do have

習題 9 解答

1. He can run fast and his brother can too.

   He can run fast and so can his brother.

2. He has gone home and she has too.

   He has gone home and so has she.

3. Mr. Smith is a doctor and Mr. Rand is too.

   Mr. Smith is a doctor and so is Mr. Rand.

4. The boy seems happy and the girl does too.

   The boy seems happy and so does the girl.

5. Tom voted Bill chairman and Robert did too.

   Tom voted Bill chairman and so did Robert.

6. He has been lazy lately and his friend has too.

   He has been lazy lately and so has his friend.

7. The teacher has read the book and his students has too.

   The teacher has read the book and so has his student.

8. He speaks English well and I do too.

   He speaks English well and so do I.

9. We would go with him and they would too.

   We would go with him and so would they.

10. I should have finished the assignment and you should too.

    I should have finished the assignment and so should you.

習題 10 解答

1. The train wasn't late, and the bus wasn't either.

   The train wasn't late, and neither was the bus.

2. The steak wasn't good, and the salad wasn't either.

   The steak wasn't good, and neither was the salad.

3. Paul didn't buy a new tie, and Bob didn't either.

   Paul didn't buy a new tie, and neither did Bob.

4. Dick doesn't have class on Friday, and Jack doesn't either.

   Dick doesn't have class on Friday, and neither does Jack.

5. This place won't cash checks, and that one won't either.

   This place won't cash checks, and neither will that one.

6. Ralph hasn't been to Japan, and Sam hasn't either.

   Ralph hasn't been to Japan, and neither has Sam.

7. Peter isn't studying architecture, and John isn't either.

   Peter isn't studying architecture, and neither is John.

8. He wasn't going to leave, and they weren't either.

   He wasn't going to leave, and neither were they.

9. Jane can't drive a car, and Betty can't either.

   Jane can't drive a car, and neither can Betty.

10. The Smiths won't be at the reception, and the Bakers won't either.

    The Smiths won't be at the reception, and neither will the Bakers.

習題 11 解答

1. This milk tastes sour, but that milk doesn't.

2. Mr. Smith didn't call today, but Mr. Brown did.

3. This pen is broken, but that pen isn't.

4. I have never met Mrs. March, but Ben and Dick have.

5. These sweaters aren't clean, but those sweaters are.

6. Ann smokes, but Margaret doesn't.

7. Ben can sing well, but Nancy, can't.

8. Ingrid passed the examination, but Roy didn't.

9. Today's cloudy, but yesterday wasn't.

10. On Thursday there won't be class, but on Friday there will.

習題 12 解答

1. Never have I appreciated my friends and family so much.

2. Rarely have we had such a great honor.

3. Seldom has this town entertained such a famous guest.

4. Rarely do students study as hard as they should.

5. Only in August is the weather very hot here.

6. Only in a big city like New York could such a thing happen.

7. Rarely do we see such beautiful dancing in our small town.

8. In no other part of the world are people interested in this problem.

9. No sooner had we arrived than all the lights went out.

10. Not only does Miss Helen dance well; she also sings beautifully.

習題 13 解答

1. This	2. that dress	3. The three men
4. the moon	5. We	6. Bob, Jack and Dick
7. That John eats cabbage (John, he)		8. It
9. You (Who)		10. I

習題 14 解答

1. (6)〔(1),(5)〕   2. (7)   3. (4)   4. (10)   5. (1)

6. (2)   7. (8)   8. (9)   9. (3)   10. (0)

習題 15 解答

1. student, boy, girl, Chinese, ...

2. friends, pens, books, ...

3. faithful animal, friendly animal, ...

4. brother, sister, cousin, friend, ...

5. American (student, boy), English boy, honest boy, ...

6. students, Chinese, ...

7. nice girl, diligent student, wonderful singer, ...

8. students, artists, musicians, ...

9. be

10. meeting, party, ...

習題 16 解答

1. happy, sad, sorry, tired, ...

2. taller, smaller, shorter, bigger, more diligent, ...

3. warm, hot, cold, cool, windy, ...

4. delicious, wonderful, splendid, excellent, ...

5. useful, interesting, expensive, ...

6. rich, poor, happy, friendly, ...

7. ill, sick, absent, ...

8. ill, sick, weak, tired, ...

9. was

10. be

習題 17 解答

1. here, there, on the desk, under the table, ...

2. here, inside, outside, over there, upstairs, ...

3. the street, the river, ...

4. home, school, the office, ...

5. the house, the country, ...

6. in Europe, in the south of Europe, on the south of France, ...

7. there, here, there in the yard, ...

8. upstairs, downstairs, to your right, at the other end of the house, ...

9. upstairs, downstairs, next to the drawing-room, ...

10. half a mile, two miles, ...

習題 18 解答

1. There is a car outside.

2. There was only a footpath here last year.

3. There is a sign over the door.

4. There is a gas station three miles away.

5. There are some letters for you on the table.

6. There was no one in the room.

7. There were a lot of people in the park yesterday.

8. There was an old friend of yours at the concert last night.

9. There will be a check in the mail next month.

10. There might have been several students in the library.

習題 19 解答

1. Thĕre's a létter for you.

2. Thére's the letter for you.

3. Thĕre's a good móvie.

4. Thére's the good movie.

5. Thĕre's a new teácher.

6. Thére's the new teacher.

7. Thĕre're some quéstions.

8. Thére're the questions.

9. Thĕre's the dictionary.

10. Thére're your friends.

習題 20 解答

1. The weather continued cold.

2. She stays faithful to him for the rest of her life.

3. Mr. Green becomes the richest man in town.

4. Mr. Higgins seems (to be) a very nice man.

5. They have stayed good friends for years.

6. He remained silent and said nothing.

7. Dick continues my best friend, despite our differences.

8. She remained a widow until death.

9. He became afraid and said nothing.

10. She will become a fine woman when she grows up.

習題 21 解答

1. smells	2. tastes	3. sounds	4. taste	5. feels
6. sounds	7. looked	8. keep	9. getting	10. turn

習題 22 解答

1. No, it isn't. It's cold.

2. No, he didn't. He got thin.

3. No, it wasn't. It looks light.

4. No, it doesn't. It looks dirty.

5. No, they didn't. They became noisy.

6. No, it wasn't. It was light.

7. No, I didn't. I felt sick.

8. No, they weren't. They were day.

9. No, he doesn't. He seems confident.

10. No, they don't. They smell awful.

習題 23 解答

1. The students listened carefully.

2. Mary speaks gently.

3. Bob works honesty.

4. Jack walked slowly.

5. They waited patiently.

6. She talked nervously.

7. He answered quickly.

8. You study diligently.

9. Miss Taylor dresses beautifully.

10. They speak loudly.

習題 24 解答

1. Please sit down, gentlemen.

2. They can't move in now.

3. Did John come over yesterday?

4. Can we start off right now?

5. What time did you wake up this morning?

6. Everybody please stand up.

7. Will you stop in later on?

8. He didn't show up yesterday.

9. Don't go away before I tell you to.

10. I can't hold on any longer.

習題 25 解答

1. SC	2. DO	3. DO	4. DO	5. SC
6. DO	7. SC	8. DO	9. SC	10. SC

習題 26 解答

1. He always answers my letter promptly.

2. The monkey climbed the tree easily.

3. They arrived safely after a long journey.

4. She waited patiently for three hours.

5. The children spent their money foolishly.

6. She makes decisions fast.

7. He walked into the room boldly.

8. The firemen climbed up the ladders rapidly.

9. The wind blew violently all afternoon.

10. They thought about the matter carefully.

習題 27 解答

1. They drove the cat out. They drove it out.

2. The soldiers blew the bridge up. The soldiers blew it up.

3. We have given our plans up. We have given them up.

4. She sent her maid away. She sent her away.

5. I will look the reports over. I will look them over.

6. Did the firemen put the fire out? Did the firemen put it out?

7. I'd like to try that yellow wool coat on. I'd like to try it on.

8. Why are you holding your decision off? Why are you holding it off?

9. The carpenter put his tools away and left the building.

   The carpenter put them away and left the building.

10. He reached down and picked the newspaper up.

　　He reached down and picked it up.

習題 28 解答

1. about (of)	2. at	3. at	4. to	5. for
6. on	7. to	8. for	9. x	10. on (upon)

習題 29 解答

1. she takes after her.

2. he picked it up.

3. you should take it off.

4. I can't turn it off.

5. he didn't think it over.

6. he looked into it.

7. he ought to try it out (before he buys it).

8. I don't care for it.

9. they have decided to put it off.

10. I'm not going to see about it.

習題 30 解答

1. Speak English to me.

2. Write him a letter. Write a letter to him.

3. Take her the money. Take the money to her.

4. Tell me your story. Tell your story to me.

5. Repeat the answer to them.

6. Explain the problem to her.

7. Send us a check. Send a check to me.

8. Give them your order. Give your order to them.

9. Lend me your car. Lend your car to me.

10. Report the accident to them.

習題 31 解答

1. Show us the pictures. Show the pictures to us / for us.
2. Close the window for him.
3. Get her a table. Get a table for her.
4. Keep these papers for them.
5. Find him a place. Find a place for him.
6. Introduce your friend to me.
7. Correct this sentence for us.
8. Cook me some dinner. Cook some dinner for me.
9. Throw them the ball. Throw the ball to them for them.
10. Call me a taxi. Call a taxi for me.

習題 32 解答

1. Did he teach her?
2. Did he sing to the children?
3. Did he feed the birds?
4. Did he give to the Red Cross?
5. Did he tell the police?
6. Did he write to his family?
7. Did he serve his guests?
8. Did he rent to a family of seven?
9. Did he pay the employees?
10. Did he contribute to charities?

習題 33 解答

1. Please give them to that lady.
2. Mrs. Harris brought them to her children.

3. Let's offer it to Bob.

4. Mother read it to us.

5. I showed them to my friends.

6. The merchant promised it to the boy.

7. Hand them to him.

8. We sold it to the Taylors.

9. I told it to the officer.

10. The reporter sent it to his paper.

習題 34 解答

1. Yes, the committee appointed him chairman.

2. They named the baby Jane.

3. Yes, the students chose him president.

4. They nominated him treasurer.

5. Yes, they appointed him manager.

6. They voted her the most popular girl in the class.

7. Yes, I (we) chose Tom spokesman for the family.

8. They are going to elect him president.

9. Yes, the company appointed him superintendent.

10. I (We) named the dog 'Snow White'.

習題 35 解答

1. She wears her hair short.

2. I (We) found the hotel delightful.

3. I (We) painted the walls white.

4. I want my coffee strong.

5. He plays his radio loud.

6. I (We) find English simple.

7. I like my steak well-done.

8. I prefer my vegetables cooked.

9. They serve fruit unpeeled in China.

10. They call him the father of his country.

習題 36 解答

1. He became a member.　　　　2. He got an offer.

3. He got (took) a taxi.　　　　4. He was a pest.

5. He was a happy person.　　　　6. He got a tip.

7. He got a promise.　　　　8. He was a success.

9. He got an audience.　　　　10. He was an unhappy person.

習題 37 解答

1. 〔Did you〕push〔the door〕open?

2. 〔They〕set〔the prisoners〕free.

3. 〔The sun〕keeps〔us〕warm.

4. 〔His words〕made〔me〕angry.

5. 〔She likes to〕cut〔her hair〕short.

6. 〔I〕believe〔him〕innocent.

7. 〔The court〕judged〔the man〕insane.

8. 〔Do you〕consider〔it〕good English?

9. 〔The boss〕found〔him〕a hard worker.

10. 〔He〕left〔his room〕a mess.

　　* 方括號裏面的語詞可以隨便代換。

習題 38 解答

1. ...am smell*ing*...　　　　2. ...*have* just heat*ed*...

3. *Did* you ever *talk*...　　　　4. ...*should* read...

5. ...*should* have finish*ed*...　　　　6. ...*must have* be*en*...

7. ...*will* you please help...　　　　8. ...*must be* go*ing*...

9. I *have been* hear*ing*...   10. ...*may* not *be able to* see...

習題 39 解答

1. present tense；present time（現在式；現在時間）

2. present tense；future time（現在式；未來時間）

3. past tense；present time（過去式；現在時間）

4. present tense；future time（現在式；未來時間）

5. past tense；past time（過去式；過去時間）

6. present tense；present time（現在式；現在時間）

7. past tense；past time（過去式；過去時間）

8. present tense；past time（現在式；過去時間）

9. past tense；past time（過去式；過去時間）

10. past tense；past time（過去式；過去時間）

習題 40 解答

1. comes〔z〕   2. listens〔z〕   3. studies〔z〕   4. paint   5. meet

6. writes〔s〕   7. strikes〔s〕   8. reads〔z〕   9. plays〔z〕   10. complains〔z〕

習題 41 解答

1. tried〔d〕   2. stayed〔d〕   3. watched〔t〕   4. helped〔t〕

5. close〔d〕   6. washed〔t〕   7. used〔d〕

8. started〔id〕   9. promised〔t〕   10. arrived〔d〕

習題 42 解答

1. will arrive, is going to arrive, is arriving, arrives, is to arrive

2. will be back, is going to be back, is to be back

3. will take, are going to take, are to take

4. will buy, are going, to buy, are to buy

5. will go, is going to go, to go

6. will eat, am going to eat, am to eat

7. will wear, is going to wear, is to wear

8. will tell, is going to tell, is to tell

9. will put, is going to put, is to put

10. will cost, is going to cost

習題 43 解答

1. You travel a lot, too.

2. They played handball last week, too.

3. I will travel by plane, too.

4. Alice studies all the time, too.

5. My brother enjoys going to concerts, too.

6. Businessmen talk a lot in their work, too.

7. Bob likes studying in the library, too.

8. Joe asked a lot of questions, too.

9. We will have a meeting tomorrow, too.

10. You will get a raise this week, too.

習題 44 解答

1. Was Ken writing on the blackboard?

2. Is he leaving today?

3. Was the man lying in the next room?

4. Is your mother baking a cake now?

5. Were the stars shining brightly?

6. Will you be taking a piano lesson?

7. Are you improving your English pronunciation?

8. Are the little boys behaving well today?

9. Was the car going at a full speed?

10. Is Miriam getting dressed up for the party?

習題 45 解答

1. He has been writing a letter.

2. They have been listening.

3. We have been hearing about that.

4. She has been thinking about that.

5. I have been riding this train.

6. They have been building a new building.

7. We have been paying taxes.

8. She has been worrying about her job.

9. It has been raining for an hour.

10. The government has been talking about it for years.

習題 46 解答

1. teaches, doesn't teach   2. knows, doesn't know

3. likes, doesn't like   4. writes, doesn't write

5. wears, doesn't wear   6. makes, doesn't make

7. eat, don't eat   8. studies, doesn't study

9. serves, doesn't serve   10. play, don't play

習題 47 解答

1. John is finishing his lessons〔now〕.

2. The wind is blowing hard〔at this moment〕.

3. Both children are dressing very quickly (right now〕.

4. He is bring flowers to her〔now〕.

5. Mr. Connor is beginning his lectures with a joke〔just now〕.

6. She is speaking with an accent〔now〕.

7. He is writing detective stories〔now〕.

8. We are putting the mail in this box〔now〕.

9. A car is stopping in front of the house〔at present〕.

10. They are saving money for their vacation.

習題 48 解答

1. Robert〔always〕tries hard.

2. They come here〔every morning〕.

3. He〔often〕makes furniture as a hobby.

4. Walter〔often〕drives much too fast.

5. Mary〔seldom〕does her shopping with her mother.

6. John walks to school with me〔every day〕.

7. We〔usually〕wait for you in the street.

8. She〔often〕helps me with my lesson.

9. He〔seldom〕lies on the bed.

10. We study in the same class〔every day〕.

習題 49 解答

1. is preparing	2. are beginning	3. is writing	4. is getting
5. is ringing	6. is lying	7. are sitting	8. are arguing
9. is dying	10. am working		

習題 50 解答

1. walk	2. learn	3. uses	4. is counting	5. snows
6. rings	7. is ringing	8. is praising；wants		
9. are blooming；smells	10. is wearing；resembles			

習題 51 解答

1. Are they in the kitchen eating?

2. Is he standing talking?

3. Is she back home watching TV?

4. Is he in his room sleeping?

5. Are they in the other room arguing?

6. Are you sitting waiting?

7. Are they at the bank cashing a check?

8. Are you busy doing your assignment?

9. Are they downtown having dinner?

10. Is he with his students answering questions?

習題 52 解答

1. have already read

2. has gone

3. has been

4. has never spoken

5. has brought

6. have not heard

7. has not bought

8. have often walked

9. have never met

10. have made

習題 53 解答

1. since 1920, for
$\begin{cases} \text{the last three years} \\ \text{a long time} \\ \text{over a year} \end{cases}$

2. since April, for
$\begin{cases} \text{more than a month} \\ \text{two months} \\ \text{many weeks} \end{cases}$

3. since then, for
$\begin{cases} \text{a week} \\ \text{ages} \\ \text{longer than I can remember} \end{cases}$

4. since $\begin{cases} \text{his childhood} \\ \text{he was a boy} \end{cases}$ for $\begin{cases} \text{over a year} \\ \text{at least a month} \end{cases}$

5. since $\begin{cases} \text{last Sunday} \\ \text{your birthday, for fifteen years} \\ \text{the beginning of the yea} \end{cases}$

習題 54 解答

| 1. since | 2. for | 3. for | 4. since | 5. for |
| 6. since | 7. for | 8. since | 9. for | 10. for |

習題 55 解答

1. have been living   2. Have you been waiting

3. has been working   4. has been standing

5. have been playing   6. has been speaking

7. has been feeling   8. has been burning

9. have been talking, have not been listening

10. have you been doing, have been sitting

習題 56 解答

1. have not seen

2. has not been here, has been living

3. has been lying, Have you not (Haven't you) read

4. has not had, has been

5. have been trying, have not succeeded

6. have been waiting, has not come

7. Have you been, have been ringing

8. has been working, has not had

9. have been living, have just decided

10. have not found, have been looking

習題 57 解答

1. I have been looking for an apartment for three months.

2. The temperature has been rising since yesterday afternoon.

3. She has been riding the train for five years.

4. He has been thinking about getting a job since last year.

5. We have been studying English for three years.

習題 58 解答

1. We went to a shop〔yesterday〕.

2. He hid the key〔a few minutes ago〕.

3. He lost his bag〔last week〕.

4. They drank tea〔a few hours ago〕.

5. You lied to me〔yesterday〕.

6. She told us a story〔just now〕.

7. The hen laid five eggs〔last week〕.

8. Tom fell and hurt his arm〔two months ago〕.

9. The picture hung on the wall〔last month〕.

10. They built a house〔last year〕.

習題 59 解答

1. has not written

2. wrote

3. has not bought

4. bought

5. visited

6. have never visited

7. did not have

8. have not had

9. has not had

10. finished

11. have not finished

12. have not paid

13. paid

14. has been studying

15. has been studying, was

16. has certainly arrived

17. have you known   18. did you meet

19. did you arrive   20. has studied, has not got

習題 60 解答

1. She has been away since this morning.

2. I saw her three months ago.

3. A lot has happened since my arrival here.

4. She hasn't eaten since the day before yesterday.

5. It all began a few years ago.

6. I had a physical checkup quite a long time ago.

7. The property has been in her name since their marriage.

8. He has read three books since breakfast.

9. She has made the beds since then.

10. They have not seen each other since last summer.

習題 61 解答

1. goes   2. went   3. have been   4. is reading

5. had   6. have had   7. does not look, did

8. heard, have not heard   9. is writing, has written

10. excercise, feel   11. have been feeling/felt, came

12. have been feeling / felt, have been

習題 62 解答

1. were studying   2. Was reading

3. were eating   4. Was shining

5. was still having   6. were writing

7. was working   8. was raining

9. were not looking   10. were playing, was writing

習題 63 解答

1. He was sitting in the garden when I passed by his house.

2. They were walking home when the accident happened.

3. She was eating her dinner when I telephoned.

4. The man was leaving his home at seven o'clock this morning.

5. Mrs. Brown was drinking a cub of coffee when I came.

6. Mr. Wood was listening to the radio all this morning.

7. The teacher was explaining the grammar when the bell rang.

8. Mary was speaking English at that time.

9. We were having supper at seven o'clock last night.

10. They were going to the movie when it started raining.

習題 64 解答

1. was shining
2. was still burning
3. was resting
4. went
5. was going
6. began, ended
7. was sitting, saw
8. became; were
9. fell, was running
10. was, learned
11. was walking, blew
12. drank, were
13. jumped, was moving
14. was burning, broke
15. saw, was singing, smoking
16. was getting, fell, cut
17. spoke, was always reading, did not hear
18. was thinking, were talking
19. opened, was ringing (rang)
20. was writing, rang, was going, heard, was still ringing, was walking, opened, stopped

習題 65 解答

1. had gone	2. had had
3. had done	4. had gone
5. had already begun	6. had hurt
7. had left	8. had done
9. had taken	10. had stolen

習題 66 解答

1. He said that he had waited one hour for the bus.
2. She said that she had seen him before.
3. You said that you had read the book.
4. He said that he had been ill for a long time.
5. He said that he had gone to the movies with you.
6. She said that she had enjoyed her food.
7. You said that you had gone to the seaside for a holiday.
8. He said that a fire had broken out in the neighborhood.
9. She said that her mother had helped her with her homework.
10. He said that he had liked this picture very much.

習題 67 解答

1. arrived, had already left	2. said, had had
3. told, had seen	4. got, (had) left
5. wondered, had not visited	6. had just gone, called
7. asked, had visited	8. (had) heard, hurried
9. arrived, had already begun	
10. had gone (went), found, had taken	

習題 68 解答

1. was sleeping, telephoned

2. wrote

3. was preparing, got

4. told, had visited

5. fell, was getting

6. had lived, began

7. was, had never seen

8. rained

9. was raining, left

10. had rained, started

11. was shining, got

12. reached, (had) left

13. was writing, entered

14. were driving, happened

15. (had) spread, arrived

16. (had) worried, heard, was

17. was, had thought

18. had seen (saw), told, had never seen

19. had gone (went), felt, had hurt

20. was walking, snatched, ran

習題 69 解答

1. had been studying

2. had been waiting

3. had been living

4. had been studying

5. had been reading

6. had been sleeping

7. had been working

8. had been studying

9. had been raining

10. had been preparing

習題 70 解答

1. had been working

2. had been losing

3. had been raining

4. had been having

5. had been having

6. had been playing

7. had been writing

8. had been talking

9. had been studying

10. had been preparing

The Past Perfect is used to describe an action which took place before some definite point in the past time. The Past Perfect Progressive is used to describe the similar actions, only it emphasizes the continuous nature of the action.

習題 71 解答

1. Are you (we) all going to work late〔tomorrow〕, too?

2. Are they going to play football〔tomorrow morning〕, too?

3. Is she going to work nights〔next week〕, too?

4. Are they going to visit some classes〔this afternoon〕, too?

5. Are you (we) really going to work hard〔next semester〕, too?

6. Are they going to feel very hungry〔tomorrow〕, too?

7. Is he going to play it again〔next season〕, too?

8. Are they going to eat at the restaurant〔tomorrow〕, too?

9. Are they going to have it〔tomorrow〕, too?

10. Are they going to help us with it〔tomorrow night〕, too?

習題 72 解答

1. will arrive, is going to arrive, is arriving, arrives, is to arrive

2. will be back, is going to be back, is to be back

3. will take, are going to take, are to take

4. will buy, are going to buy, are to buy

5. will go, is going to go, to go

6. will eat, am going to eat, am to eat

7. will wear, is going to wear, is to wear

8. will tell, is going to tell, is to tell

9. will put, is going to put, is to put

10. will cost, is going to cost

11. will sail, is going to sail, is sailing, sails, to sail

12. will take off, is going to take off, is taking off, take off, is to take off

13. will leave, is going to leave, is to leave

14. will leave, is going to leave, is leaving, leaves, is to leave

15. will go...and visit, is going to go...and visit, is going...and Visiting, go...and visit, am to go...and visit

習題 73 解答

1. will be studying	2. will be eating
3. will be taking	4. Will be taking
5. will probably be sleeping	6. will be working
7. will probably be raining	8. will be traveling
9. will you be staying	10. will probably be still working

習題 74 解答

1. He will be eating his lunch when I get there.

2. They will be having a party at nine o'clock tomorrow night.

3. The sun will be shining when I get to the station.

4. He will be working hard as usual when I meet him.

5. She will be watching television when he returns.

6. He will be working in his garden when we call.

7. I wonder what he will be doing at this time tomorrow.

8. I will be getting ready to go to the movie at seven o'clock.

9. He will be having his music lesson when she telephones.

10. We will be traveling together at this time next year.

習題 75 解答

1. will have studied	2. will have fallen
3. will have finished	4. will have left
5. will have been	6. will have seen
7. will also have visited	8. will have left
9. will have been	10. will have finished

習題 76 解答

1. The party will have begun when we get there.

2. He will have finished the work when we see him.

3. She will have gone away when he arrive.

4. When we get there, the guests will have already left.

5. The leaves will have fallen from the trees when we visit the park.

6. He will have spent all his money before he begins his vacation.

7. He will have forgotten all about it when you speak with him.

8. She will have told her mother before I see her.

9. He will have already written the letter when she telephones him.

10. He will have come and (will have) left when she arrived.

習題 77 解答

1. ...... will have been working ....

2. ...... will have been staying ......

3. ...... will have been driving ......

4. ...... will have been correcting ......

5. ...... will have been blowing ......

6. ...... will have been living ......

7. ...... will have been waiting......

8. ...... will have been teaching......

9. ...... will have been discussing ......

10. ...... will have been burning ......

習題 78 解答

1. He said they could learn a lot in a few weeks.

2. We expected that you'd (= you would) have enough to keep you busy.

3. He knew that he would be happy there.

4. She imagined she might have to take examinations again.

5. They hoped he could spend a little more time with them.

6. Did you feel you'd (= you would) know well enough to perform?

7. He thought they might not want to help him any more.

8. We saw that we could go ahead with our plans.

9. They told me you'd (= you would) soon be having a new job to do.

10. I noticed that they wouldn't be allowed to smoke in this room.

習題 79 解答

1. B: What did he (she) say?

   C: He (She) said he (she) was going to town with his (her) sister.

2. B: What did he (she) say?

   C: He (She) said he (she) was reading the newspaper.

3. B: What did he (she) say?

   C: He said his name was (is) Bob.

4. B: What did he (she) say?

   C: He (She) said he (she) would answer the phone.

5. B: What did he (she) say?

   C: He (She) said he (she) had finished his (her) work.

6. B: What did he (she) say?

   C: He (She) said he (she) had been to the museum many times.

7. B: What did he (she) say?

   C: He (She) said he (she) had been studying too much.

8. B: What did he (she) say?

   C: He (She) said he (she) wanted to speak to me (us).

9. B: What did he (she) say?

   C: He (She) said they (we) were very late.

10. B: What did he (she) say?

   C: He (She) said he was ready to come with them (us).

習題 80 解答

1. He told me that she hadn't prepared her lessons.

2. He told me that they would be here (there) soon.

3. He told me that he was going to London the next (following) day (is...tomorrow).

4. He told me that he had just been to the barber's.

5. He told me that he could come the next (following) week (can...next week).

6. He told me that they had gone away the day before (the previous day, yesterday).

7. He told me that he had been very ill the day before (the previous day, yesterday).

8. He told me that he had lost his temper the morning before (the previous morning, yesterday morning).

9. He told me that he had never been there (here) before.

10. He told me that I had done my homework well.

習題 81 解答

1. The students asked Miss Hopkins if / whether (or not) there was any work.

2. The tourist asked if / whether (or not) there was any road to the museum.

3. Dick asked his fried if / whether (or not) Bob was good at music.

4. He asked me if / whether (or not) I enjoyed swimming.

5. She asked the boy if / whether (or not) he knew how to dance.

6. I asked my friend if / whether (or not) his picture had been in the newspaper.

7. He asked me if / whether (or not) I had heard about the accident.

8. Mr. Smith asked her daughter if / whether (or not) she had studied her lesson carefully.

9. Mrs. Taylor asked her husband if / whether (or not) he would be staying at the Grand Hotel.

10. The children asked their mother if / whether (or not)

習題 82 解答

1. He asked me whether the train had been very full.

2. He asked me whether it was time to go.

3. He asked me whether his shoes were cleaned yet.

4. He asked me whether I could hear a noise.

5. He asked me whether he might use my telephone.

6. He asked me whether I slept in the afternoons.

7. He asked me whether he looked all right.

8. He asked me whether it was raining very heavily.

9. He asked me whether I thought it greedy to eat more than two at a time.

10. He asked me whether I knew why Dick had run away when he saw a policeman.

習題 83 解答

1. have lost, saw

2. will never forget, have just told

3. met, have already decided

4. goes, spends

5. have just decided, will take

6. was playing, arrived

7. has just come, will see

8. was walking, met

9. will (shall) meet, have finished

10. did not know, had left, came

11. was, have not forgotten, will (shall) never forget

12. is sleeping, does not understand, are saying, will wake, speak

13. do not eat, come, call

14. will (shall) go, am (went, was)

15. will go, gets (has got)

16. visited, found, was

17. had sold, got (will have sold, get)

18. had worked (had been working, worked), decided

19. will have finished, can

20. have told (will tell), need, will find, has never visited (visited)

21. strikes, will (shall) have been waiting (will (shall) have waited)

22. won't be raining, leaves (wasn't raining, left)

23. intended (had intended), find, do not have

24. were you doing (did you do), was washing

25. read, had stolen, (had) sold, were looking, have not found

26. thought, had done, was

27. (have) never read, (has) interested, read

28. went, were playing, said, had been playing

29. had read, will have read, have not seen, believe, is writing

30. have broken, broke, never broke, have broken

31. has just gone (just went), saw, was coming

32. always tell (have always told), do, say

33. rang, had finished, rang, (had) finished

34. met, had not yet heard, met, (had) heard

35. do not write, will wonder, has happend

36. forever misunderstand, explain, don't you listen, am speaking

習題 **84** 解答

1. Bob should *have been* work*ing*.

2. You ought to *have* do*ne* better.

3. Could you hold these books for me?

4. The secretary may *have* ma*de* a mistake.

5. Those words must be justifi*ed*.

6. They could *have* com*e* by plane.

7. You might *have* see*n* him before.

8. They should *be* study*ing* now.

9. Would you please sit down?

10. Can she do a good job?

習題 **85** 解答

1. Will they, they will

2. Will she, she will

3. Will he, he will

4. Will it (they), it (they) will

5. Will he (she), he (she) will

習題 **86** 解答

1. request（請求）

2. refusal（拒絕）

3. simple future（單純未來）

4. willingness（願意）

5. refusal（拒絕）

6. simple future（單純未來）

7. request（請求）

8. request（請求）

9. simple future（單純未來）

10. refusal（拒絕）

習題 **87** 解答

1. Will   2. shall   3. will   4. shall   5. will

6. will   7. will   8. Shall   9. Will   10. will

習題 **88** 解答

1. preference（選擇）

2. polite request（客氣的請求）

3. polite request（客氣的請求）

4. willingness（願意）

5. past habit（過去的習慣）

6. polite request（客氣的請求）

7. preference（選擇）

8. polite request（客氣的請求）

9. polite request（客氣的請求）

10. preference（選擇）

習題 89 解答

1. would	2. would	3. should	4. should	5. should
6. Would	7. should	8. would	9. would	10. should

習題 90 解答

1. John should have practiced English.

2. Jane shouldn't have told you about the accident.

3. I should have spoken English in class.

4. Mr. Brown shouldn't have smoked in the theater.

5. Bob shouldn't have gone to the movies last night

6. They shouldn't have borrowed the money yesterday.

7. We should have written that exercise last week.

8. You shouldn't have written your composition in pencil.

9. James should have delivered newspapers yesterday.

10. Miss Brown should have visited her aunt last week.

習題 91 解答

1. She said I could go if my father agreed.

2. He was able to play football before he broke his leg.

3. His son was able to do arithmetic when he was only four.

4. He could borrow the money if he promised to repay.

5. He agreed that they could drive the car if they were seventeen.

6. I was sure they were not able to understand because it was too difficult.

7. Mother said we could play in the garden.

8. They couldn't talk to each other because her father had forbidden it.

9. They were not able to talk to each other because the telephone was out of order.

10. My father says we could buy some sweets because we have been good.

習題 92 解答

1. should	2. can't	3. can	4. can	5. shouldn't
6. shouldn't	7. can	8. should	9. shouldn't	10. should

習題 93 解答

1. will (would)	2. shall	3. can	4. could	5. may	6. could
7. may (might)	8. may (can)	9. May (Can, Could)	10. may (might)		

習題 94 解答

1. couldn't	2. can't	3. must	4. must	5.must
6. can	7. could	8. must	9. couldn't	10. must

習題 95 解答

1. You must be mistaken.

2. It must be going to rain.

3. John must have been working late at the office.

4. Mr. Smith must be a rich man nowadays.

5. Those children over there must be playing football.

6. He must have been very busy if he couldn't come to the party.

7. That must be Mrs. Smith I can see over there.

8. I must have been dreaming when I saw her walk in.

9. You must be mad to do that.

10. The phickens must have been stolen by a fox.

習題 96 解答

1. must	2. must, ought to	3. ought to	4. must	5. must
6. ought to	7. must	8. ought to	9. must	
10. ought to, must	11. must	12. must, ought to		
13. must	14. ought to	15. ought to, ought to	16. must	

習題 97 解答

1. study	2. answer	3. have practiced	4. finish	5. have written
6. drive	7. have returned	8. love	9. have told	10. have stayed

習題 98 解答

1. will	2. would	3. won't
4. must	5. may	6. must (should, ought to)
7. Does, have	8. had	9. Did, have
10. had	11. had, hadn't	12. would, wouldn't
13. got	14. Had	15. don't, to

習題 99 解答

1. would	2. must	3. would	4. couldn't	5. used
6. used	7. able	8. Will, be	9. used, to	10. have, been

習題 100 解答

1. mustn't	2. needn't	3. mustn't	4. needn't	5. mustn't
6. needn't	7. mustn't	8. needn't	9. mustn't	10. mustn't

習題 101 解答

1. Yes, you may. No, you may not (can't, mustn't).

2. Yes, I can. No, I can't.   3. Yes, we will. No. we won't.

4. Yes, it may (would) be. No, it can't be.

5. Yes, you must. No, you needn't.

6. Yes, he must. No, he needn't.

7. Yes, I must. (I'm sorry but I have to.)

   No, I needn't. (I'm sorry. I shouldn't.)

8. Yes, it must. No, it needn't.

9. Yes, please. No, thank you.

10. Certainly (, be my guest). I'm sorry but you can't.

習題 102 解答

1. I didn't need to put on a coat.

2. You needn't have brought a coat.

3. He needn't have telephoned Mary.

4. We needn't have visited our aunt.

5. He didn't need to turn (needn't have turned) on the light.

6. The children didn't need to go to bed early.

7. I didn't need to wear my glasses.

8. He didn't need to speak to her.

習題 103 解答

1. He daren't touch the wire with his finger.

2. I needn't tell you how sorry I am.

3. Need you really be so rude to her?

4. Dare he show himself in front of them?

5. Why daren't you keep a big dog?

6. Need I bring my raincoat with me?

7. How dare you say such things?

8. Tell the children that they needn't do their homework.

9. I bet you daren't pull his beard.

10. We needn't explain it all again, need we?

11. You daren't challenge me, dare you?

12. She needn't finish the work today, need she?

習題 104 解答

1. shouldn't have stayed   2. must have eater.

3. would have helped

4. wouldn't have liked

5. might have been

6. ought to have taken

7. should have asked

8. mustn't have heard

9. needn't have bought

10. can't (couldn't) have been

習題 105 解答

1. will be working

2. could be studying

3. may not be coming

4. should be saving

5. must be losing

6. ought to be getting

7. won't be playing

8. may be looking

9. must be wearing

10. could be playing

習題 106 解答

1. should have been paying

2. will have been working

3. should have been wearing

4. might have been helping

5. may have been waiting

6. can't (couldn't) have been listening

7. could have been studying

8. must have been sleeping

習題 107 解答

1. Will (Would)

2. won't

3. would

4. should (ought to)

5. needn't

6. ought

7. should

8. should

9. Can (Could)

10. can't (couldn't)

11. may (can)

12. may not (can't, mustn't)

13. would

14. won't

15. Would

16. used

17. should

18. may, can

19. should

20. may (can, will)

21. ought

22. dare

23. used

24. May

25. must

26. needn't

27. should (ought to)

28. daren't

29. do, did   30. Did (were)   31. may

32. might   33. may   34. ought, might

習題 108 解答

2. 4. 6. 8. 9.

習題 109 解答

1. They did it by radio.   2. A radio announcer did it.

3. They did it by machine.   4. Workers did it.

5. A mailman did it.   6. They did it by mail.

7. A kind old woman did it.   8. They did it by special delivery.

習題 110 解答

1. This gun was made in England.

2. The dog was left in the garden.

3. The book was beautifully written.

4. This picture is always admired.

5. English is spoken all over the world.

6. His leg was hurt in an accident.

7. I was punished for something I didn't do.

8. Milk is used for making butter and cheese.

9. Were you told how to get in touch with him?

10. Weren't you tcld to be here by six o'clock?

習題 111 解答

1. This must be done right away.

2. It ought to be done right away.

3. It can be done right away.

4. The letter should be sent today.

5. That work used to be done by them.

6. This has to be done today.

7. A bridge is going to be built next year.

8. The letter cannot be written unless he has all the information.

9. You can be assured (that) everything will be arranged in time.

10. It will be forgotten in a few year's time, won't it?

11. It was supposed to be done yesterday.

12. What ought to be done about this?

習題 112 解答

1. Some ink has been spilt on the carpet.

2. The door has already been shut.

3. The money must have been stolen.

4. The house has been built of stone and cement.

5. This letter should have been mailed yesterday.

6. My question has not been properly answered.

7. By the time you come back, my letter will have been finished.

8. Have your questions been answered?

9. Has all the work been done?

10. What has been done about this?

習題 113 解答

1. He was being tested at the time.

2. The horse is being put in a stable.

3. That case is being argued about now.

4. A new subway is being built in that town.

5. The letter was being written when I was here.

6. The road in front of our house is being torn up.

7. The letter is being written now, isn't it?

8. Those reports are being prepared today, aren't they?

9. Why is the street being torn up?

10. It is going to be delivered tomorrow, isn't it?

習題 114 解答

1. She was given a new watch.

2. You will be asked several questions.

3. She has been shown the new buildings.

4. He was denied his right (by the officials).

5. We were asked to be there at eight o'clock.

6. She is being shown how to do it.

7. He has been made a captain.

8. I was recommended another doctor last week.

9. You will be told what time the train leaves.

10. He was taught French and (was) given a dictionary.

習題 115 解答

1. The matter must be looked into.

2. He is well spoken of.

3. You will be well looked after.

4. The old lady is read to every morning.

5. That book is often asked for.

6. That room hasn't been slept in for years.

7. Our dog was run over by a car.

8. You will be simply laughed at for your trouble.

9. She is being talked about.

10. The children who are failing will be spoken to by the principal.

習題 116 解答

1. It is hoped that everything will be all right.

2. It is suggested that we take a break before going on.

3. It was announced that there won't be any class tomorrow.

4. It is agreed that no action will be taken until next week.

5. It was found that they didn't give their right address.

6. It was assumed that there was no chance to succeed.

7. It cannot be denied that his handwriting has improved.

8. It has been decided that a new branch will be opened next year.

9. It must never be said that he was selfish.

10. It must be clearly understood that this is your last chance.

習題 117 解答

1. Dick got defeated by Peter in the contest.

2. The man got shot in the arm.

3. Mary got punished by the teacher for not being punctual.

4. The poor boy got hit every day by the master.

5. The missing boy got found by the police.

6. I have got disappointed by Bill before.

7. A new hotel is getting built now.

8. The dog has been getting whipped by the man for more than an hour.

9. He got blamed by his friends for the mistake he made.

10. That poor animal used to get beaten every day.

習題 118 解答

1. It was grabbed from his hand.

2. The horse will be put in a stable.

3. The letter has already been written.

4. It is going to be delivered tomorrow.

5. He was asked a very difficult question.

6. Such things ought not to be spoken about in publir.

7. The box has been locked and (it) can't be opened.

8. I was deeply struck by her beauty.

9. You needn't think I was taken in by your joke.

10. You were told to be here by six oclock, weren't you?

11. Were you frightened by the noise?

12. He had to be operated on (by the doctor) to find out what was wrong.

13. Weren't you ever taught how to swim?

14. Nothing was done until he came.

15. The dam would be broken by a sudden increase in water pressure.

16. Cities can be shelled from a distance of several miles.

17. By whom can that be finished?

18. I hate being looked at.

19. It is time for the children to be put to bed.

20. I won't be spoken to as if I were a child.

21. Don't let yourself be seen.

22. You are sure to be asked that question by the police.

23. I should love to be taken out to dinner.

24. You can be assured (that) everything will be arranged in time.

25. An orange cannot be eaten if it hasn't been peeled.

26. I am told your uncle has been shot.

27. Naturally you are expected to be interested in the job you have been offered.

28. He must have been terribly disappointed to be told he was not wanted.

29. Nothing has been moved since you were sent away to be cured.

30. He would not have been stared at if he had been told beforehand what clothes had to be worn in such a place.

31. The question of how to be released without being brought to trial would have to be looked into.

32. The moon is no longer said to be inhabited any more than Mars is.

    It is no longer said that the moon is inhabited any more than Mars is.

習題 119 解答

1. If you study hard, you will get a scholarship.

   Unless you study hard, you won't get a scholarship.

2. If you don't keep your promises, you'll lose your friends.

   Unless you keep your promises, you'll lose your friends.

3. If you tell me what you want, I can get it for you.

   Unless you tell me what you want, I can't get it for you.

4. If he doesn't know the way, he might get lost.

   Unless he knows the way, he might get lost.

5. If it's very cold, we'll probably have snow.

   Unless it's very cold, we propably won't have snow.

6. If I am not mistaken, that is Mr. Jones.

   Unless I am mistaken, that is Mr. Jones.

7. If the weather was warm, I would swim.

   Unless the weather was warm, I wouldn't swim.

8. If he had a good book to read, he didn't go to bed early.

   Unless he had a good book to read, he went to bed early.

9. If she didn't know the answer, she wouldn't give the information.

   Unless she knew the answer, she wouldn't give the information.

10. If Mr. Miller didn't have a newspaper to read, he didn't (wouldn't) enjoy his breakfast.

    Unless Mr. Miller had a newspaper to read, he didn't (wouldn't) enjoy his breakfast.

<h2 align="center">習題 120 解答</h2>

1. will go   2. invites   3. is   4. arrives   5. get   6. see

7. don't arrive   8. will play   9. won't find   10. have rested

<h2 align="center">習題 121 解答</h2>

1. If I have enough money, I will go boating.

  If I should have enough money, I would (/ will) go boating.

2. If I find a bicycle, I will go riding.

  If I should find a bicycle, I would (/ will) go riding.

3. If I buy a pole, I will go fishing.

  If I should buy a pole, I would (/ will) go fishing.

4. If I have the time, I will go hiking.

  If I should have the time, I would (/ will) go hiking.

5. If I stay near a lake, I will go swimming.

  If I should stay near a lake, I would (/ will) go swimming.

6. If I stay near a lake, I will go boating.

  If I should stay near a lake, I would (/ will) go boating.

7. If I buy a bicycle, I will go riding.

  If I should buy a bicycle, I would (/ will) go riding.

8. If I see a high mountain, I will go hiking.

  If I should see a high mountain, I would (/ will) go hiking.

9. If I see a river, I will go fishing.

  If I should see a river, I would (/ will) go fishing.

10. If I get a boat, I will go boating.

  If I should get a boat, I would (/ will) go boating.

<h2 align="center">習題 122 解答</h2>

1. If he makes an appointment, he can see the doctor.

If he made an appointment, he could see the doctor.

2. If he slips on the ice, he may break his leg.

   If he slipped on the ice, he might break his leg.

3. If he doesn't get sick, he won't need a doctor.

   If he didn't get sick, he wouldn't need a doctor.

4. If he hasn't enough money, he can't, buy a new car.

   If he hadn't (didn't have) enough money, he couldn't buy a new car.

5. If he studies hard, he will get good marks.

   If he studied hard, he would get good marks.

習題 123 解答

1. would show	2. could	3. would be	4. were	5. had
6. were	7. wanted	8. would have	9. read	10. wouid

習題 124 解答

1. If you studied hard, you would pass.

   If you had studied hard, you would have passed.

2. If he had enough money, he would buy a new suit.

   If he had had enough money, he would have bought a new suit.

3. If he hadn't enough money, he couldn't buy a new car.

   If he hadn't had enough money, he couldn't have bought a new car.

4. I would want to go if Joe went (did).

   I would have wanted to go if Joe had gone.

5. I wouldn't get lost if I took the map.

   I wouldn't have got lost if I had taken the map.

6. If the news spread, everyone would come to see the boy.

   If the news had spread, everyone would have come to see the boy.

7. My wife wouldn't mind if I brought a friend home to dinner.

   My wife wouldn't have minded if I had brought a friend home to dinner.

8. If we got there in time, we could see the circus pass by.

   If we had got there in time, we could have seen the circus pass by.

9. If the troops advanced, they might soon meet the enemy.

   If the troops had advanced, they might have soon met the enemy.

10. I would pay for supper tomorrow if you would pay tonight.

    I would pay for supper tomorrow if you had paid tonight.

習題 125 解答

1. would have gone
2. would (could) never have heard
3. would have bit (ten)
4. might have been killed
5. had had
6. had not been
7. had known
8. had not answered
9. would have been
10. might have been drowned

習題 126 解答

1. If I had a bicyle, I could go riding.

2. If I didn't have a bicyle, I couldn't go riding.

3. If I had had heavy shoes, I could have gone hiking.

4. If I hadn't had heavy shoes, I couldn't have gone hiking.

5. If we had enough rain, we could grow rice.

6. If we had grown grapes, we could have made wine.

7. If I had known you were there, I would have telephoned.

8. If Betty hadn't got up on time, she wouldn't have caught the bus.

9. If she didn't speak English perfectly, she would have to be in this class.

10. If he had started earlier, he would have caught the train.

習題 127 解答

1. He would not have been driving too fast if he had not needed to get home quickly.

2. He would not have needed to get home quickly if his family had not been in danger.

3. His family would not have been in dangre if his house had not been on fire.

4. His house would not have been on fire if there had not not been many cans of paint in his basement.

5. There would not been many cans of paint in his basement if he had not been planning to paint his kitchen.

6. He would not have been planning to paint his kitchen if he had had enough money to pay someone else high wages for painting it.

7. The fire would not have started if the cans of paint had not been too near the furnace.

8. His car would not have hit that taxi if he had been driving carefully.

9. He would have been driving carefully if he had not been worrying about the fire.

10. He would not have to go to court next Wednesday if his car had not hit that taxi last night.

習題 128 解答

1. Should it stop raining, I would go for a walk.

2. Were they stronger, they could lift the table.

3. Had they been stronger, they could have lifted the table.

4. Were he to listen more carefully, he couldn't make so many mistakes.

5. Were I accepted, I would go to the university.

6. Had I had time, I would have taken music lessons last year.

7. Had I known the answer, I would have told it.

8. Should I become a great artist, you would be as surprised as I.

9. Were Shakespeare alive, he would have been very surprised at our actors.

10. Hadn't the policeman shown me the way, I would have got lost.

習題 129 解答

1. were	2. weren't	3. could	4. were	5. did
6. did (lived)	7. hadn't	8. had	9. hadn't (been)	10. hadn't

習題 130 解答

1. I wish it were not time to leave now.

2. I wish I had taken some money with me.

3. I wish I didn't have to study now.

4. I wish I had not failed the examination.

5. I wish I were not living in a big city.

6. I wish he knew how to speak French.

7. I wish it hadn't been raining all weekend.

8. I wish we didn't have to go home quickly.

9. I wish I could have helped you with you problem.

10. I wish my friend wouldn't be working all day tomorrow.

習題 131 解答

1. I wish they were here.

2. If only I had gone to the movies with you last night!

3. If only I could speak English as well as you!

4. She wishes she had a handsome husband.

5. O that today were a holiday!

6. He wishes that he had been invited to the party.

7. If only I had known it yesterday!

8. O that my parents were here with me!

9. If only he would tell me the whole story!

10. Don't you wish we were living in a dreamland?

習題 132 解答

1. were	2. had spent	3. were	4. had lived
5. had never seen	6. were	7. had been	8. had been
9. were	10. had stopped		

習題 133 解答

1. went　　2. paid　　　3. hadn't gone　　　4. would try　　5. got

6. knew　7. came　　8. were　　　　　9. wrote　　10. stayed

習題 134 解答

1. go　　2. be　　　3. take　　4. wait　　　5. not stand

6. be　　7. answer　8. have　　9. not quarrel　10. write

習題 135 解答

1. meet　　　2. not discuss　　　3. come, join　　4. be　　　5. stop

6. take　　　7. sign, return　　　8. be　　　　　9. write　　10. be

習題 136 解答

1. It is imperative that he return the book promptly.

2. He demanded that I come back a little later.

3. He suggested that she take the money.

4. He insisted that you not mention this to your brother.

5. It is essential that everyone practice English constantly.

6. It is important that you not make the same mistake again.

7. The law requires that all people be treated equal.

8. It is imperative that no smoking be allowed.

9. The principal urged that every student work harder.

10. They prefer that I not serve them Japanese food.

習題 137 解答

1. eat　　　　　　　　2. would have gone　　3. hadn't broken

4. read　　　　　　　5. are　　　　　　　　6. would have found

7. would have enjoyed　8. had seen　　　　　9. goes

10. asked   11. will go   12. go

13. had been   14. don't turn   15. were

16. were   17. invested   18. is

19. had had   20. would have been

習題 138 解答

1. knew   2. went   3. went   4. got

5. had come (could come)   6. didn't go   7. knew

8. didn't eat   9. hadn't drunk   10. paid, asked (should ask)

11. got (should)   12. didn't come (wouldn't come, hadn't come)

13. had   14. were   15. refused   16. had never seen

17. could   18. were (had been, if divorced or a widow!)

19. open   20. Would   21. gave (had given)

22. had known   23. had been pulled   24. had not broken

25. had seen   26. set, did   27. were, were   28. be done

29. come   30. go   31. get   32. take

33. make   34. be informed   35. be   36. be discovered

37. not borrow   38. start   39. had   40. have

習題 139 解答

1. I learn slowly.   2. He paints badly.

3. She sings fine.   4. You think clearly.

5. Bob drives fast.   6. Mr. Taylor shoots straight.

7. Mrs. Smith listens patiently.   8. My uncle works steadily.

9. Jane reads carefully   10. Jack speaks wonderfully.

習題 140 解答

1. He is a fine swimmer; he swims fine.

2. He is a hard worker; he works hard.

3. She is a fast typist; she types fast.

4. I'm a careful driver; I drive carefully.

5. I'm a bad dancer; I dance badly.

6. She's a nice cook; she cooks nicely.

7. They're diligent students; they study diligenthy.

8. He is an excellent English teacher. He teaches English excellently.

9. I'm a poor tennis player. I play tennis poorly.

10. He's a fast and clear speaker. He speaks fast and clearly.

11. He is a slow but careful reader. He reads slowly but carefully.

12. He's a nervous and not very good story teller. He tells stories nervously and not very well.

習題 141 解答

1. sweet   2. delightfully   3. cold   4. coldly   5. suddenly

6. uneasy   7. strong   8. strongly   9. uneasily   10. safe

習題 142 解答

1. The boy walked boldly into the room.

2. The wind blew violently all afternoon.

3. Please answer my letter promptly.

4. The arrived safely after their long journey.

5. The fireman climbed their ladders rapidly.

6. She agreed willingly to our proposal (willingly).

7. She carefully put the dishes away.

   (She put away the dishes carefully.)

8. The children are playing happily in the park.

9. He eats breakfast quickly early in the morning.

10. The package was attractively wrapped.

習題 143 解答

1. The children are playing happily outside.

2. They are arguing violenthy upstairs.

3. I met him at the station yesterday.

4. He has lived here for three years.

5. They are discussing in the other room now.

6. We are staying here for a few days.

7. He took a walk in the park in the morning.

8. Is there a telephone here?

9. Is she waiting downstairs?

10. Shall we go inside or stay outside?

習題 144 解答

1. I read the newspaper every day.

   I read the newspaper yesterday.

   I'll read the newspaper tomorrow.

2. Dick has lunch with me every day.

   Dick had lunch with me yesterday.

   Dick will have lunch with me tomorrow.

3. My brother doesn't go swimming every summer.

   My brother didn't go swimming last summer.

   My brother hasn't gone swimming lately.

4. Did you see Jane last week?

   Have you seen Jane since she returned from Europe?

   Will you see Jane next month?

5. I will have finished my coffee before he leaves the house

   I finished my coffee a little while ago.

   I had finished my coffee by the time you arrived.

習題 145 解答

1. Everyone went outside after class.

2. The manager will be here soon.

3. I saw Julie at the party last night.

4. I've been waiting in the hall for a long time.

5. She left here a long time ago.

6. The guest arrived from Taipei at 6 oclock.

7. We listened to records at Bob's house in the evening.

8. The guard passes here every ten minutes.

9. People in big cities spend most of their time indoors.

10. The sun will go down behind the mountains in a little while.

習題 146 解答

1. this morning

2. tonight (/ this evening)

3. tomorrow

4. tomorrow night (/ tomorrow evening)

5. yesterday

6. last night

7. this week

8. next week

9. last week

10. two weeks ago

11. (the) day after tomorrow

12. (the) day before yesterdary

13. the month before last

14. the month after next

15. the next day (/ the following day).

16. the day before (/ the previous day)

17. one morning in May (/ one May morning)

18. one afternoon in July (/ one July afternoon)

19. not long ago (/ a short time ago)

20. a few weeks ago (/ several weeks ago)

21. all day long

22. all the night through (/ all the night long)

23. all the year round

24. once a week (/ every week)

25. three times a month

26. every other day (/ every second day / every two days)

27. every three days (/ every third day)

28. every five months (every fifth month)

習題 147 解答

1. It all happened one morning in May.

2. School will be over by four in the afternoon.

3. They had a fight on Sunday afternoon last week.

4. They see each other at three on Sunday afternoon.

5. The game will start at nine o'clock tomorrow morning.

6. We'll discuss the matter again this day week.

7. He worked all day long yesterday.

8. I saw Mrs. Wilson shortly afte lunch yesterday.

習題 148 解答

1. We often to the museum.

   We go to the museum often.

   Often we go to the museum.

2. Have you ever been to the zoo?

3. She occasionally comes to the office on Saturdays.

   She comes to the office on Saturdays occasionally.

   (Occasionally she comes to the office on Saturdays.)

4. I always do.   5. Are you still working there?

6. He has never been abroad.

7. They often are. (Often they are.)

8. She is frequently absent from school.

   She is absent from school frequently.

   (*Frequently* she is absent from school.)

9. I have seldom seen him downtown.

   (Seldom have I seen him downtown.)

10. Do they still live in England?

11. They are sometimes in high mountains.

    They are found in high mountains sometimes.

    (Sometimes they are found in high mountains.)

12. Father often has to work in the evening.

    Father has to work in the evening often.

    (Often Father has to work in the evening.)

13. He will probably come. Probably he will come.

    He will come probably.

14. She was perhaps sick. Perhaps she was sick.

    She was sick perhaps.

習題 149 解答

1. I have alread finished my homework

   I have finished my homework already.

2. The letter hasn't arrived yet.

   The letter hasn't yet arrived.

3. He already knew the answer.

   He knew the answer already.

4. She hasn't made progress in learning English yet.

   She hasn't yet made progress in learning English.

5. Her sister has already made great progress.

   Her sister has made great progress already.

6. We can't get together yet.

We can't yet get together.

7. Has he already (yet) joined the army?

   Has he joined the army already (/ yet) ?

8. They were already there when you came in.

   They were there already when you came in.

9. We already know why he is absent.

   We know already why he is absent.

10. I don't know yet whethey they have or not.

   I don't yet know whether they have or not.

習題 150 解答

1. We don't have the solution yet.

2. Bob doesn't speak English, either.

3. He still is not teaching English.

   He is not teaching English any more / longer.

   He is no longer teaching Englih.

4. She still cannot sing.

   She cannot sing any more / longer.

   She can no longer sing.

5. He didn't always work hard.

   He never worked hard.

6. They dont't often (=seldom) go to church on Sunday.

   They often don't go to church on Sunday.

7. He sometimes doesn't get here on time.

8. We usually don't have a meeting on Monday morning.

   We don't usually have a meeting on Monday morning.

9. They occasionally don't see each other on weekends.

10. We won't go on a picnic this weekend, either.

習題 151 解答

1. No, they seldom do.
2. No, he never does.
3. Yes, she usually is.
4. No, she rarely is.
5. Yes, I often do.
6. Yes, I sometime do.
7. No, I rarely do.
8. Yes, they still do.
9. No, he no longer does.
10. No, I am often not.

習題 152 解答

1. Never was she so angry before.
2. Seldom do I hear such beautiful music.
3. Never have I seen so much rain.
4. Rarely do we see such beautiful scenery in our country.
5. Never has the train been so late.
6. Never did I read such a dull book.
7. Seldom is the weather hot here in Augiust.
8. Rarely was he seen with his wife.
9. Never did Jane seem so beautiful.
10. Little do I care what he thinks of my plan.
11. Only by hard work can you succeed.
12. In no other part of the world will you find such nice people.
13. Only in a big city like New York could such a thing happen.
14. Little did we see that we hadn't seen before.
15. Nowhere else in the world is there such delicious fruits.

習題 153 解答

1. He has always prepared his lessons.
2. I never go for a walk on Sunday.
3. Do you ever go for a walk on Sunday?

4. He prepares his lessons carefully.

   He carefully prepares his lessons.

5. I saw Mr. Li in the cafeteria yesterday.

6. I have repeatedly spoken to him about his lessons.

   (I have spoken to him repeatedly about his lessons.)

7. He alway does his work cheerfully.

8. We rarely go to the theater in the summer.

9. Nobody ever has a bad word to say about Jane.

10. I saw Mr. Jones on the twentieth floor shortly after breakfast.

習題 154 解答

1. Helen went to school at eight o'clock.

2. I was born at 6 a.m. on July 29th in the year 1931.

3. Your brother spoke to us very rudely in class this morning.

4. I drink coffee at home every morning.

5. Father likes tea very much in the morning.

6. Charles loved his wife passionately all his life.

7. They stayed there quietly all day.

8. The letter was sent to New York by air mail last week.

9. She walked quietly into the room because her husband was sleeping.

10. Get up early tomorrow morning if you don't want to miss the train.

11. They are arguing in the next room in a loud voice right now.

12. We went to a movie once a week last year.

13. Dr. Hill graduated from our university with high honors in 1950.

14. We unexpectedly met the Taylors at the club once in a while. (We met the Taylors unexpectedly...)

    Once in a while we met the Taylors unexpectedly at the club.

15. We were discussing the project seriously in the office at that time.

    We were seriously discussing the project in the office at that time.

16. I still plan to go to Japan with my wife next year.

17. He seldom comes home from work after 6 o'clock unless there is an emergency.

18. The president often comes with his secretary at 9 o'clock in the morning.

19. They probably learned the news through your friend before I told them last night.

20. You possibly cannot do it sucessfully by yourself unless you follow the directions carefully.

習題 155 解答

1. How big that house is!

2. What a big house that is!

   How big a house that is!

3. How interesting this story is!

4. How intelligent your brother is!

5. How expensive these cameras are!

6. How foolish he has been!

7. How gracefully she dances!

   What a graceful dancer she is!

8. How sweetly she is singing!

   What a sweet singer she is!

9. How well he teaches!

   What a good teacher he is!

10. How fond of the dog she is!

11. How afraid of his father he is!

12. What a pretty doll she made! (How petty a doll...)

13. What a long letter he wrote! (How long a letter...)

14. How nicely he wrote a letter! (What a nice letter...)

15. How strange our life here on earth is!

16. How strangely he behaved when he heard the news!

17. How lonely this world would be if you were away!

18. You will easily imagine how happy I am!

19. How I wish to succeed!

20. What nonesense he talked!

習題 156 解答

1. Come back later.

2. Be careful.

3. Wait for me on the corner.

4. Be here by ten.

5. Remove the stone from the road.

6. Girls, sit on these chairs.

7. Boys, study in the next room.

8. Let me try once.

9. Pay attention to me while I am talking.

10. Ask her to go to the movies with us this morning.

習題 157 解答

1. Please come back a little later.

   Come back a little later, will you?

   Will (Won't / Would) you come back a little later?

   Will (Won't / Would) you please (kindly, be so kind as to, etc.) come back a little later?

   Would (Do) you mind coming back a little later?

   其他習題（2-10），可以照第一題的解答改為客氣的請求。

習題 158 解答

1. Drink your tea up!	2. Cover your legs up!
3. Clear this mess up!	4. Do your buttons up!
5. Eat your dinner up!	6. Pick that book up!
7. Pull all the weeds up!	8. Wake your brother up!

9. Read the message out aloud!   10. Take your friend out to lunch!

11. Put your tonge out!   12. Pour the tea out!

13. Turn the light out!   14. Put your coat on!

15. Take your shoes off!   16. Take these dishes away!

17. Write these sentences down in pencil!

18. Put the clock back one hour!

19. Switch the light on!   20. Turn the radio off!

習題 159 解答

1. Don't fold the paper.

2. Please don't leave the room.

3. Let's not forget our homework.

4. Don't listen to what he says.

5. Don't lay hands on the desk, please.

6. Let's not play in class.

7. Don't be kind to me.

8. Don't put down your pens.

9. Don't let us wait.

10. Don't read out the letter aloud, please.

習題 160 解答

1. let's not, Let's

2. let's not, Let's speak

3. let's, Let's meet at noon.

4. Yes, let's. Let's go to the library.

5. No, let's not. Let's ask John instead.

6. Yes, let's. Let's invite the Taylors.

7. No, let's not. Let's ride John's car instead.

8. No, let's not. Let's go to a Japanese restaurant instead.

習題 161 解答

1. shall we   2. Do not   3. Do   4. not

5. will you   6. shall   7. Don't ever   8. Never

9. What a   10. How difficult   11. Let's   12. Let us

習題 162 解答

1. 6   2. 0   3. 9   4. 8   5. 5

6. 7   7. 10   8. 4   9. 2   10. 1

習題 163 解答

1. I asked her to come here.

2. He ordered me to pick it up.

3. Tell him to do it again.

4. She told me to wash my face.

5. Ask them to give me another.

6. She told me not to put it on the desk.

7. Tell them to get your hair cut.

8. She told us not to wait for her.

9. He begged them not to go away before he comes / came

10. She advised her not to speak to a stranger. back.

習題 164 解答

1. I told her to write quickly.

2. He invites me to have another cup of tea.

3. He told me not to sit on his bed.

4. She told him to take a look at himself in the mirror.

5. Mother told me not to put my elbow on the table.

6. Father advised us never to borrow money from our friends.

7. He ovdered her not to speak until she was spoken to.

8. Mrs. Taylor told her daughter to be a good girl and (to) sit quietly.

9. He advised them not to spend all their money and (to) save some for the future.

10. He ordered me to go to bed and not to get up till I was called.

注意：解答中所用「報告動詞」可以根據句義做適當的更改。

習題 165 解答

1. He cried out what a fool he had been.

   He cried out that he had been very foolish (a big fool).

2. She said to me what a dirty face I had

   She said to me that I had a very dirty face.

3. She exclaimed how happay she was.

   She exclaimed that she was very happy.

4. She said to Mrs. Smith what a charming daughter she had.

   She said to Mrs. Smith that she had a very charming daughter.

5. She accused her husband how cruel he had been.

   She accused her husband that he had been very cruel.

習題 166 解答

1. What is this? It is a gold watch.

2. What are they? They are plans for the house.

3. What caused the flood? The rain caused it.

4. What did the thief steal? He stole a diamond ring.

5. What is this book about? It is about English.

6. What is the artist paintng? He is painting a picture.

7. What did the driver run over? He ran over a yellow dog.

8. What are the students going to discuss? They are going to discuss their plans for the summer.

9. What has the farmer planted? He has planted a row of corn.

10. What's Jane been copying? She's been copying a letter.

11. What is there on the kitchen table? There's a birthday cake on it.

12. What'll there be in the envelope for him? There'll be some money in it for him.

習題 167 解答

1. Who made the announcement? The teacher made it.

2. Who broke the window? The boys broke it.

3. Who (m) did Charles invite to the dance?

   Charles invited Susan to it.

4. Who (m) did you give the money to?

   To whom did you give the money?

   I gave it to his sister.

5. Who did you speak to about the picnic?

   To whom did you speak about the picnic?

   I spoke to Mrs. Taylor about the picnic.

6. Who is Mr. Johnson? The tall man over there is.

7. Who is the girl with a book? She is my sister.

8. To whom is your sister engaged?

   Who (m) is your sister engaged to?

   She is engaged to Bill Newman.

9. Who is going to type the book?

   Mr. Jones is going to type it.

10. Who (m) are you going to borrow the dress from?

    From whom are you going to borrow the dress?

    I'm going to borrow it from Jane.

習題 168 解答

1. Which (advice) is useful?

2. Which (magazine) is cheap?

3. Which (books) are useful?

4. Which (book) have you read?

5. Which (phone) is out of order?

6. Which (eggs) are fresh?

7. Which (books) are they going to read?

8. Which (art museum) did you visit?

9. Which (dress) did she borrow from Jane?

10. Which (clerk) did he talk to?

注意：括號內的名詞可以做適當的更改。

習題 169 解答

1. Who talked to the teacher about it?

2. What did the hunter shoot?

3. Who did you meet?

4. Which (books) did you borrow from the library?

5. What is Jane going to do?

6. Who did he give the book to?

7. To whom should I speak?

8. Who made a birthday cake for Johnny?

9. What did Mother make for Johnny?

10. Who did Mother make a birthday cake for?

11. What did Mather do today?

12. Whom did you visit Sunday?

13. Who visited Uncle Joe Sunday?

14. What did you do Sunday?

15. Which (chairs) are comfortable?

16. Who is a student?

17. Who (which) is the new student?

18. Who is George?

19. What is the trouble with the car?

20. What is a truant?

21. What did the the teacher announce?

22. What did Betty borrow from Alice?

23. Who did Betty borrow the green coat from?

24. Which (coat) did Bety borrow from Alice?

25. Who borrowed the green coat from Alice last week?

26. What did Betty do last week?

習題 170 解答

1. Are you going today or tomorrow?

2. Do we pay you or the cashier?

3. Is she playing or studying?

4. Did he or didn't he say "yes"？

5. Do they usually eat here or in a restaurant?

6. Is John or his father buying a new car?

7. Do you eat with chopsticks or (with) knife and fork?

8. Do you have a radio or a TV?

9. Will you drop me a line or give me a ring?

10. Can you or can't you speak English?

11. Is your brother studying at a college or a university?

12. Can you write or speak English?

習題 171 解答

1. Whose (hat) is this? It's the teacher's (hat).

2. Whose (car) is that? It's Mr. Smith's (car).

3. Whose (gloves) are these? They're Jone's (gloves).

4. Whose (letters) are those? They're my sister's (letters).

5. Whose (book) did Alice find? She found John's (book).

6. Whose (dress) is Betty going to borrow? She is going to borrow Mary's (dress).

7. Whose (plays) will Professor Jones lecture on? He will lecture on Shakespeare's (plays).

8. Whose (name) did they leave out of the list? They left out my brother's (name).

習題 172 解答

1. What (kind of) ring did the thief steal?

2. Which luggage will you carry?

3. What (kind of) medal did Bob win?

4. Which chemical is dangerous?

5. Which bananas did you eat?

6. What (kind of) plans is he drowing?

7. Which plans did they discuss?

8. Which book did you borrow from the library?

9. Which hat did she lose?

10. What (kind of) dog did the driver run over?

11. What (kind of) cigarettes did Mr. Jones use to smoke?

12. Which sweater did Jane lend to Mary?

習題 173 解答

1. Who	2. What	3. Which	4. What	5. What
6. Which	7. Which	8. Who	9. Which	10. Who
11. What	12. Who	13. Which	14. What	15. Which
16. Who	17. Who	18. Who	19. What	20. What
21. What	22. What	23. Which	24. Which	25. Which

習題 174 解答

1. When was your birthday?

2. When does spring begin?

3. When are visiting hours?

4. When does the airplane leave?

5. When is she going shopping for a new suit?

6. When does the museum open?

7. When is Jane going to take French and Germam?

8. When did they arrive?

9. When will Mr. Jones see me?

10. When did you take dancing lessons?

習題 175 解答

1. Where do you play tennis?

2. Where are they going?

3. Where did you see the story?

4. Where did she put the watch?

5. Where is his house?

6. Where can I find a postoffice?

7. Where are you studying English?

8. Where does Mr. Jones plan to go?

9. Where did she find the book?

10. Where did the truck run over the little boy?

習題 176 解答

1. How is the weather?

2. How do I look?

3. How does the cake taste?

4. How did the team play?

5. How do you always travel?

6. How did they get there?

7. How can you tell?

8. How did he become a good speaker?

9. How are you enjoying your visit?

10. How did she get interested in art?

習題 177 解答

1. How much does this dress cost?

2. How much (money) do you have?

3. How much pork do you want?

4. How long does the movie last?

5. How many times did he try?

6. How many boxes of typewriter paper does she need?

7. How many students are there in your class?

8. How many children do you have?

9. How long did the discussion last?

10. How far is New York from Washington?

11. How often does the bus run?

12. How tall are you?

13. How deep is the lake?

14. How old is the school?

15. How wide are the windous?

16. How long is the pool?

17. How much does she weigh?

18. How soon will the doctor come?

19. How fast does the plane fly?

20. How high is the building?

21. How often do you go to the movies?

22. How fast was the wind blowing?

23. How long have you known him?

24. How fast can you run?

25. How thick is the dictionary?

26. How far is the station?

27. How many people died in traffic accidents last year?

28. How many people were there at the meeting?

29. How much money do you need to go shopping?

30. How much did the new library cost to build?

習題 178 解答

1. What	2. Whose	3. Who	4. Who (m)	5. Which
6. What	7. What	8. What	9. Which	10. Which
11. Who	12. Which	13. Whose	14. What	15. What
16. Which	17. Which (What)	18. Which	19. What	20. Whose
21. Where	22. When	23. Why	24. How	25. How old
26. How long	27. How far	28. How many	29. What time	30. What date
31. Who	32. What	33. What	34. How soon	35. How long

習題 179 解答

1. (Mr. So-and-so) does.

2. Shakespeare did.

3. Eating does.

4. Most of us do.

5. None of us can.

6. All of us ought to / should.

7. We all do.

8. All is.

9. These do (did).

10. None did

11. Nobody does (do).

12. Elizabeth II is.

13. Your brother has.

14. My great-grandfather did.

15. Jim does.

習題 180 解答

1. What is it used for?

2. Where is it kept?

3. When is it taken away?

4. How is it written?

5. What is it eaten with?

6. How is it sold?

7. How often is it turned?

8. Who is it sent to? (To whom is it sent?)

9. How is it pronounced?

10. By whom was the window broken?

習題 181 解答

1. He asked me how many languages I can speak.

2. He asked me what I have been studying.

3. He asked me when I had eaten lunch.

4. He asked me when I would return his book.

5. He asked me how well I could (/ can) speak English.

6. He asked me where I had been the night before.(/ the previous night / last night

7. He asked me how long I had been waiting.

8. He asked me who (m) I had invited to the party.

9. He asked me why I hadn't come that (/ this) morning.

10. He asked me what kind of work I did.

11. He asked me whose plays I had read.

12. He asked me how much sugar I had used (/ use) in my coffee.

13. He asked me why I hadn't eaten anything.

14. He asked me how I (had) liked that cake.

15. He asked me which book I had been reading.

16. He asked me what time it was.

17. He asked me what the matter was.

18. He asked me what was wrong with me.

19. He asked me what the English for " 花 " is.

20. He asked me who had called while I was out.

習題 182 解答

1. She told me that she was going to move to Taipei.

2. She asked me why I was angry.

3. She asked me whether / if I had heard from my brother.

4. She asked me where I was going to spend my vacation.

5. She asked me whether / if the library had opened all day.

6. She told me that she would graduate in June.

7. She asked me when I would graduate from high school.

8. She asked me whether / if I knew the way to the station.

9. She asked me whether / if I could tell her where she could find a rest room.

10. She asked me how far it is to the National Museum.

11. She asked me who I thought is China's greatest scientist.

12. She told me that she hoped (that) I had a letter for her.

習題 183 解答

Bill, Sally White, father, mother, friends, Bill's' Uncle George,

seashore, Uncle George, Bill's, father's, brother, house, sailboat,

Bill, Salley, times, seashore, August, air, water, (swimming,)

Uncle George, hours, picnic, island, bay.

習題 184 解答

1. X	2. X	3. The	4. X	5. the, X
6. The, the	7. The, X	8. The, X	9. the, the	10. The, the
11. the, the	12. The	13. the	14. The, the	15. X, X, the

習題 185 解答

1. cooks〔s〕　　　2. parts〔s〕　　　3. eggs〔z〕

4. sounds [z]　　　5. skies [z]　　　6. keys [z]

7. roofs [s]　　　8. loaves [z]　　　9. races [iz]

10. mosses [iz]　　11. games [z]　　12. lines [z]

13. balls [z]　　　14. doors [z]　　15. months [s]

16. baths [z]　　　17. potatoes [z]　18. radios [z]

19. horses [iz]　　20. houses [iz]　21. matches [iz]

22. stomacks [s]　23. knives [z]　　24. safes [s]

25. pages [iz]　　26. garages [iz]　27. 1's [z]

28. 8's [s]　　　29. Ph. D's [z]　　30. 1970's [z]

習題 186 解答

1. banks　　　　2. guests　　　　3. teeth　　　　4. judges

5. echoes　　　6. editors in chief　7. sky　　　　8. sheep

9. taxes　　　10. spoonfuls　　　11. geese　　　12. fish

13. sons-in-law　14. passers by　　15. feet, legs

16. Ox carts　　　　　17. servants

18. Englishmen, Germans　　19. Mouse traps, mice

20. dozen, eggs, loaves, bread

習題 187 解答

1. crises　　　　　　2. bases　　　　　3. criteria

4. phenomena　　　　5. data　　　　　6. curricula, curriculums

7. stimuli, stimuluses　8. foci, focuses　9. indexes, indice

10. madames, mesdames　11. alumni　　　12. alumnae

習題 188 解答

1. deer　　　　2. series　　　　3. scissors　　　4. trousers

5. compasses　6. glasses　　　7. a spectacle　8. spectacles

9. savings　　10. means　　　11. is　　　　12. Many thanks

13. Thanks	14. is	15. has	16. is	17. is
18. are	19. is	20. are	21. is	22. are
23. is	24. spend	25. want		

習題 189 解答

1. He is a three-month-old baby.

2. It is a ten-foot-long rope.

3. It is a four-door car.

4. It is a five-story-high buildings.

5. It was a eight-cent stamp.

6. It was a six-man committee.

7. It was a twenty-year-old house.

8. It was a two-week vacation.

9. It was a six-dollar ticket.

10. It was a fifteen-minute walk.

習題 190 解答

1. a	2. some	3. some	4. a	5. some
6. a	7. a	8. some	9. a	10. some
11. some	12. a	13. a	14. some	15. some
16. an	17. some	18. a	19. some	20. a
21. a	22. some	23. some	24. a	25. some
26. a	27. some	28. some	29. some	30. some
31. a	32. some	33. a	34. some	35. some
36. an	37. a	38. some		

習題 191 解答

1. (4)	2. (3)	3. (1)	4. (3)	5. (3)
6. (3)	7. (3)	8. (4)	9. (3)	10. (2)

習題 192 解答

1. cow	2. fields	3. money	4. fun	5. a glass

6. a piece of glass   7. sight   8. a beautiful sight

9. paper   10. papers

習題 193 解答

1. **The** girl lives with **her** family in a big house.

2. **That** boy has spent all his money on **these** toys.

3. Get me ø tea instead of ø milk.

4. I live with **my** grandmother, **my** parents, **my** elder brother and a younger sister.

5. **This** house is famous for its garden.

6. ø People got off **their** train at the station.

7. Is he **your father's** brother or your **mother's** ?

8. Why did **John's** bicycle cost more than **Mary's** camera?

9. I want a pencil, **an** eraser and **some** paper.

10. **Any** stranger will get lost in ø London if he doesn't know **the** city well.

習題 194 解答

1. some	2. some	3. a	4. any	5. any	6. some
7. some	8. an	9. some	10. any	11. some	12. any

習題 195 解答

1. The engineers didn't make any plans.

   Did the engineers make any plans?

2. The factory didn't hire any workers.

   Did the factory hire any workers?

3. The boys aren't eating any candy.

   Are the boys eating any candy?

4. The secretary wasn't writing any letters.

   Was the secrectary writing any letters?

5. She hasn't got any money.

   Hasn't she got any money?

6. You won't need any help.

   Will you need any help?

7. They didn't receive any good advice.

   Did they receive any good advice?

8. John hasn't made any wonderful suggestions.

   Has John made any wonderful suggestions?

9. Betty didn't have any strange ideas.

   Did Betty have any strange ideas?

10. I can't eat any ice-cream.

    Can I eat any ice-cream?

習題 196 解答

1. He knows some English, doesn't he?

   Doesn't he know some English?

2. He doesn't know any English, does he?

   Doesn't he know any English?

3. She needed some money, didn't she?

   Didn't she need some money?

4. She didn't need any money, did she?

   Didn't she need any money?

5. They can borrow some books, can't they?

   Can't they borrow some books?

6. They can't borrow any books, can they?

   Can't they borrow any books?

7. She is making some sandwiches for us, isn't she?

Isn't she making some sandwiches for us?

8. She isn't making any sandwiches for us, is she?

    Isn't she making any sandwiches for us?

9. You have done some studying, haven't you?

    Haven't you done some studying?

10. You haven't done any studying, have you?

    Haven't you done any studying?

習題 197 解答

1. No, it didn't hire any men. It didn't hire any.

2. Yes, she invited some friends. She invited some.

3. Yes, there are some mail for you. There are some.

4. No, I don't have any questions. I don't have any.

5. No, there aren't any matches left. There aren't any.

6. No, I won't have any more tea. I won't have any.

7. Yes, I will have some more cake. I will have some.

8. Yes, I can eat some more potatoes. I can eat some.

9. No, I think there isn't any money in the purse. I think there isn't any.

10. Yes, I believe that he will lend me some books. I believe that he will lend me some.

習題 198 解答

1. any	2. some, any	3. any, some
4. some, any	5. any, some	6. some, some
7. any, some	8. any, some	9. some, any
10. any, some, any	11. some, any (/some)	12. some, some, some
13. some, some, any	14. any, any, some	15. some, some

習題 199 解答

1. ø, a   2. A, ø   3. ø, a   4. An, a   5. ø, a, ø

6. A, ø, ø   7. A, ø, ø   8. ø, a, ø   9. a, ø, a   10. ø, ø, ø, ø

習題 200 解答

1. A, some   2. A, some   3. some, a   4. ø, some   5. a, ø, some

6. ø, a   7. A, ø, ø   8. A, ø, a   9. some, a, a   10. a, some.

習題 201 解答

1. metal	2. Iron, a metal	3. an iron
4. tea	5. an excellent tea	6. a tea
7. fire	8. a fire	9. cold meat
10. a cold meat	11. a lace	12. old lace
13. kindness	14. a great kindness	
15. an excusable error	16. Error	17. education
18. an education	19. pity	20. a pity
21. a mercy	22. mercy	23. Sight
24. a sight	25. a pain	26. Death
27. a new happiness	28. a virtue	29. good
30. an amusing endurance		

習題 202 解答

1. There is no sugar.

   There isn't any sugar.

2. I can see no hat on the shelf.

   I can't see any hat on the shelf.

3. He likes no girls with red hair.

   He doesn't like any girls with red hair.

4. She has got no money to lend you.

   She hasn't got any money to lend you.

5. I have no more money.

   I don't have any more money.

6. There are no apples on the tree.

   There aren't any apples on the tree.

7. The hen has laid no eggs today.

   The hen hasn't laid ang eggs today.

8. No ink spilled on the carpet.

   Not any ink spilled on the carpet.

9. No people called last night.

   Not any people called last night.

10. He gave me no ink, so I could write no more.

    He didn't give me any ink, so I couldn't write any more.

習題 203 解答

1. a, The, a, The, ø, The 2. the   3. The (A), the

4. a   5. the   6. The   7. A

8. the   9. an   10. The   11. a

12. The   13. The   14. the   15. a

16. The   17. The, the   18. a, the   19. ø, ø

20. The, the   21. the   22. ø, the   23. ø, a

24. The, ø   25. the   26. the, the   27. the

28. ø, ø   29. the, the   30. the

習題 204 解答

1. the   2. the   3. the   4. the   5. The

6. the   7. an   8. the, the 9. the, the   10. the, the

11. the, a   12. the   13. a   14. the, the 15. a

16. the   17. the, the   18. the   19. the, the   20. the, the

21. the, ø   22. the, the   23. the   24. the   25. the

習題 205 解答

答案係指該劃掉的部分。

1. The milk   2. The foxes   3. A owl, Owl

4. The bees, Bee   5. The blood; the water

6. The man; the woman   7. A sentence, Sentence; the words, word

8. The friend; the friend   9. the church mouse

10. a telephone   11. The cow; the horse

12. A dinosaur   13. A panda   14. A bee   15. A dinosaur

習題 206 解答

1. ø, a, ø   2. ø, a, ø   3. ø, the   4. ø, (the), the, a

5. ø, ø, ø   6. a, ø   7. ø, ø   8. a, ø, the

9. A (/ The), ø   10. ø, the, a   11. a, ø   12. a, ø, ø

13. ø, the   14. ø, ø, ø   15. ø, ø, ø, ø   16. the, ø, ø

17. ø, ø   18. ø, ø   19. ø, ø   20. ø, ø

21. ø, ø, the, the   22. an, ø   23. A, a, the   24. The, ø

25. a, ø   26. a, a   27. ø, ø   28. The, ø, an

29. The, ø   30. The, the

習題 207 解答

1. the   2. the   3. the   4. ø   5. A (/ ø)

5. the   7. the   8. an   9. the   10. The, the

習題 208 解答

1. A, the   2. the   3. A (/ The), ø   4. some, a, ø

5. a, the   6. The a, the   7. a, ø   8. Some, the

9. ø, ø, ø	10. some, the	11. a, the	12. ø, the
13. a, ø, a	14. The, the, ø	15. A, a, ø	16. a, ø, some a, ø
17. a, a, ø	18. A, a, a, ø	19. The, an, ø	20. The, the, the, a
21. ø, a	22. ø, the	23. The, the	24. ø, a
25. ø	26. a	27. The, the	28. ø
29. the	30. ø, ø	31. the	32. ø
33. ø, ø	34. the	35. ø, a	36. a, the
37. the	38. a	39. a, the	40. a, the
41. ø, ø	42. ø, a	43. a, a	44. ø, a
45. an, the	46. The, a, ø	47. ø	48. an
49. The, ø, a	50. The, ø, the, ø		

習題 209 解答

1. (a) This one is.　　(b) That one is short.

2. (a) These are.　　(b) Those are wrong.

3. (a) This one is.　　(b) That one is small.

4. (a) These are.　　(b) Those are light.

5. (a) This one is.　　(b) That one is all right. (/ in good order).

6. (a) These are.　　(b) Those are old (/ rotten).

習題 210 解答

1. this	2. That	3. Those	4. those
5. those	6. this	7. that	8. This
9. that	10. this	11. This	12. that
13. that	14. that	15. those	16. that
17. those	18. that	19. those	20. those
21. Those	22. Those		

習題 211 解答

1. These magazines are theirs.

2. Those pencils aren't his.

3. I am sure these desks are ours.

4. Are those dresses hers?

5. Is this fountain pen yours?

6. This pencil is mine, but that knife is his.

7. This coat is mine, but the other coat is yours.

8. How many of these books are yours?

習題 212 解答

1. A friend of yours came to see you.

2. May I borrow this book of yours?

3. I don't know any sister of his.

4. It is no fault of hers.

5. You should not repeat these mistakes of yours.

6. That is no business of mine.

7. The Smiths are paying a visit to a relative of theirs in town.

8. They went to the park with some friends of theirs.

9. I forget where I left those magazines of yours.

10. Where did you put that new pen of mine?

11. We can show another sample of ours.

12. Which friend of yours gave this to you?

13. Which picture of hers do you like best?

14. I can't remember which book of mine has interested you.

15. I have some reasons of my own for not going there.

習題 213 解答

1. I have my own trouble.

2. They have their own plans.

3. I saw it with my own eyes.

4. This house is my own.

5. I have a watch and my brother has his own, too.

6. She makes all her own clothes.

7. I cook my own breakfast, but usually have my own dinner in town.

8. She wrote her own name, and did I mine, too.

9. I've lost my own knife. Would you lend me yours?

10. Tell Jane not to forget her own appointment; you mustn't forget yours, either.

習題 214 解答

1. his, hers	2. your, mine	3. her, mine	4. my, yours, etc.
5. mine, yours, etc.	6. my, hers	7. Mine, yours, etc.	
8. your, mine, etc.	9. mine, yours, etc.	10. your, mine, her	

習題 215 解答

1. rabbit's 〔s〕   2. teachers' 〔ø〕   3. women's 〔z〕

4. bird's 〔z〕   5. students' 〔ø〕   6. James' 〔ø〕, James's〔iz〕

7. Confucius' 〔ø〕   8. Jesus' 〔ø〕   9. PTA's 〔z〕

10. grandmother's 〔z〕   11. father-in-law's 〔z〕

12. menservants' 〔ø〕   13. Queen Elzabeth's 〔s〕

14. Mary's 〔z〕   15. no one else's 〔iz〕

16. king's 〔z〕   17. baker's 〔z〕   18. you know who's 〔z〕

19. Alice's 〔iz〕 school   20. Mary's 〔z〕 and Alice's 〔iz〕

習題 216 解答

1. a cat's paws, the paws of a cat

2. the leaves of a tree

3. birds'eggs, the eggs of birds

4. the roof of the house

5. the moon's light, the light of the moon

6. the top of a mountain

7. the president's duties, duties of the president

8. the cost of a trip   9. the taste of tea

10. the driver's seat, the seat of the driver

11. the doctor's degree   12. men's room

13. the date of his birth

14. the doctor's office, the office of the doctor

15. the price of meat   16. five dollars' worth of tea

17. a night's rest   18. ten yards' distance

19. the sale of cars   20. a month's salary

21. the joys and sorrows of life, life's joys and sorrows

22. the daughter of John's boss

23. John and Dick's parents

24. your and John's duty; the duty of you and John

25. a friend of my father's

26. that girl friend of your brother's

習題 217 解答

1. It belongs to Alice.

   It is Alice's.

2. It belongs to my brother.

   It is my brother's.

3. It belongs to her.

   It is hers.

4. They belong to her sisters.

   They are her sisters'.

5. They belong to Bob's uncle.

   They are Bob's uncle's.

6. It belongs to a friend of mine.

   It is a friend of mine's.

習題 218 解答

1. The car belongs to Mary.

2. Edison invented the electric light.

3. The licence belongs to the driver.

4. Bob was dead.

5. The bus arrived (will arrive).

6. The milk is (was) obtained from the cow.

7. Someone loves music.

8. The lion was (will be) hunted.

9. The peacock has (had) a beautiful feather.

10. The vacation takes (took) two months.

11. The tea is (was) worth ten dollars.

12. Men love God.

13. Columbus discovered America.

14. John was (will be) taken a picture.

15. A picture belongs to John.

習題 219 解答

1. three of the girls

2. five of these pencils; five pencils of these

3. one-half of the cake

4. many of those students; many students of those

5. four of her mistakes; four mistakes of hers

6. six of his ten answers

7. several of my teachers; several teachers of mine

8. these three sons of yours

9. three of my ten friends

10. even some of your students; even some students of yours

習題 220 解答

1. Two of the books are interesting.

   Two of them are interesting.

   Two are interesting.

2. Three of the girls could answer the questions.

   Three of them could answer the questions.

   Three could answer the questions.

3. One of these boys wants to go with you.

   One of them wants to go with you.

   One wants to go with you.

4. Some of the guests are in the garden.

   Some of them are in the garden.

   Some are in the garden.

5. One of the suspects has disappeared.

   One of them has disappeared.

   One has disappeared.

6. Half of the money is in the purse.

   Half of them is in the purse.

   Half is in the purse.

7. He bought two of my paintings.

He bought two of them.

He bought two.

8. One of the pictures was left on the table.

One of them was left on the table.

One was left on the table.

習題 221 解答

1. The ten books are on the shelf.

2. Ten of the books are on the shelf.

3. There are two pictures on the wall.

4. Two of his pictures are on the wall.

5. There are several signs over the door.

6. Many of your friends are in the park.

7. Every student is in the classroom.

8. All the guests are in the lobby.

9. There are five other books in the library.

10. The other five books are in the library.

習題 222 解答

1. one hundred and eighty-two.

2. four hundred and seven.

3. one thousand five hundred and forty.

4. three thousand and twenty-six.

5. twenty-one thousand nine hundred and six.

6. five hundred sixty-four thousand seven hundred and nineteen.

7. eight hundred three thousand eight hundred and ninety-two.

8. five million three hundred seventy-two thousand six hundred and ninety-four.

9. six million seventy-three thousand five hundred and forty.

10. two hundred thirty-six million five hundred sixty-seven thousand nine hundred and

ninety-four.

習題 223 解答

1. nineteen, sixty-eight
2. nineteen, O, eight
3. eighteen, seventy-four
4. ten, O, nine
5. eight hundred and forty-two
6. six hundred and five
7. fourteen, seventy-two.
8. ten, fifty-six
9. five B. C. (=Before Chris)
10. three hundred and one (three, O, one) B. C.

習題 224 解答

1. five (minutes) past (or after) one.
2. a quarter (or fifteen minutes) to (or before) five.
3. twenty-five (minutes) to (or before) eleven.
4. twenty-seven (minutes) past (or after) three.
5. twelve (o'clock).
6. ten (minutes) to (or before) three.
7. (a) quarter past (or after) eight.
8. half past (or after) seven.
9. four (minutes) to (or before) six.
10. nine (minutes) past (or after) six.

習題 225 解答

1. first; 1st	2. second; 2nd	3. third; 3rd
4. fourth; 4th	5. fifth; 5th	6. eleventh; 11th

7. twelfth; 12th   8. thirteenth;13th   9. ninth; 9th

10. twentieth; 20th   11. twenty-first; 21th

12. twenty-second; 22nd   13. twenty-third; 23rd

14. ninety-ninth; 99th   15. one hundredth; 100th

習題 226 解答

1. World War One; the First World War

2. page three; the third page   3. Charles the Fifth

4. Henry the Eighth   5. Louis the Sixteenth

6. room two hundred and four; the two hundred and fourth room

7. number thirty-five

8. lesson (s) nine and ten; the ninth and the tenth lesson (s)

習題 227 解答

1. January the first   2. February the twenty-eighth

3. March the twenty-ninth   4. April the fifth

5. May the fifth   6. June the twenty-fourth

7. July the seventh   8. August the seventeenth

9. September the twenty-eighth   10. October the twenty-fifth

11. November the fifteenth   12. December the thirty-first

習題 228 解答

1. one (or a) half   2. one third

3. two thirds   4. one fourth (or a quarter)

5. three fourths (or three quarters)   6. one fifth

7. two fifths   8. one and three fifths

9. three and four fifths   10. eleven over fifty-eight

習題 229 解答（略）

習題 230 解答

1. Five plus (and) three is (equals) eight.

2. Nine minus two is (equals) seven.

3. Seven times (multipled by) three is (equals) twenty-one.

4. Twelve divided by four is (equals) three.

5. Two thirds plus (and) three quarters is (equals) one and five over twelve.

習題 231 解答

1. cup	2. glass	3. Pair	4. loaf	5. bars
6. cake	7. piece	8. slices	9. articles	10. sheet
11. piece	12. spoonfuls	13. lumps	14. tube	15. gallon

習題 232 解答

1. handful	2. bar	3. lump	4. head	5. flash
6. blade	7. slice	8. ear	9. ear	10. drop
11. handful	12. mouthful	13. handful	14. suit	15. piece
16. pair	17. flock	18. flock	19. swarm	20. school

習題 233 解答

1. Some of the names are unfamiliar.

   Some names are unfamiliar.

   Some of them are unfamiliar.

2. Did any one of the guests stay late?

   Did any guest stay late?

   Did any one of them stay late?

3. Half (of) the news was incorrect

Half of it was incorrect.

4. A couple of my books were missing.

   A couple of books were missing.

   A couple of them were missing.

5. A few of the questions were rather silly.

   A few of questions were rather silly.

   A few of them were rather silly.

6. Not much of the talk was interesting.

   Not much talk was interesting.

   Not much of it was interesting.

7. Each of these students has a dictionary.

   Each student has a dictionary.

   Each of them has a dictionary.

8. Enough of the members have attended the meeting.

   Enough members have attended the meeting.

   Enough of them have attended the meeting.

9. Most of themoney is still in the bank.

   Most money is still in the bank.

   Most of it is still in the bank.

10. None of the rooms are (is) empty.

   No rooms are empty.

   None of them are (is) empty.

11. Both (of) the girls need glasses.

   Both girls need glasses.

   Both of them need glasses.

12. Not all (of) the guests left early.

   Not all guests left early.

   Not all of them left early.

13. I need plenty of the milk.

I need plenty of milk.

I need plenty of it.

14. Either one of the boys is good at mathematics.

Either boy is good at mathematics.

Either one of them is good at mathematics.

15. Neither one of the girls knows the answer.

Neither girl knows the answer.

Neither one of them knows the answer.

16. Not every one of the teachers was here.

Not every teacher was here.

Not every one of them was here.

習題 234 解答

1. many, few	2. a few	3. much, little	4. a little
5. little	6. a little	7. few	8. many
9. many, few	10. a little	11. many	12. many, many
13. many	14. little	15. much, little	

習題 235 解答

1. Do you have much time to study English?

Yes, I have $\begin{Bmatrix} \text{a great deal of} \\ \text{lots of} \\ \text{a lot of} \end{Bmatrix}$ time to study English.

No, I don't have much time to study English.

2. Do you have many opportunities to speak English?

Yes, I have $\begin{Bmatrix} \text{many} \\ \text{a lot of} \\ \text{lots of} \end{Bmatrix}$ opportunities to speak English.

No, I don't have many opportunities to speak English.

3. Don't you have much work to do now?

Yes, I have $\begin{cases} \text{a great deal of} \\ \text{lots of} \\ \text{a lot of} \end{cases}$ work to do now.

No, I don't have much work to do now.

4. Does Betty have much social life?

Yes, he has $\begin{cases} \text{a great deal of} \\ \text{lots of} \\ \text{a lot of} \end{cases}$ social life.

No, he doesn't have much social life.

5. Do Americans drink much coffee?

Yes, they drink $\begin{cases} \text{a great deal of} \\ \text{lots of} \\ \text{a lot of} \end{cases}$ coffee.

No, they don't drink much coffee.

6. Doesn't she know many people here?

Yes, she knows $\begin{cases} \text{many} \\ \text{a lot of} \\ \text{lots of} \end{cases}$ people here.

No, she doesn't know many people here.

習題 236 解答

1. A little   2. A few   3. A little   4. A few

5. The little   6. The few   7. A few   8. The few

9. A little   10. The little

習題 237 解答

1. Each	2. Every	3. each	4. every	5. every
6. every	7. every	8. every	9. each	10. every
11. every, each	12. Every	13. each	14. Each	15. every, any

習題 238 解答

1. Both   2. both, one   3. either

4. Either   5. Either   6. either (/ both), either

7. either, neither   8. either (one)   9. neither

10. either (one)   11. hoth   12. Neither

習題 239 解答

1. All	2. all, some	3. any	4. Any	5. Any
6. any, none	7. none	8. All, all	9. all, some	10. all, some

習題 240 解答

1. I have done none today.   2. I have read neither (of them).

3. You have given me none.   4. None (of them) are yours.

5. I want neither (of them).   6. I have hurt neither (of them).

7. I broke none at the party.   8. Neither (of them) has a hole.

9. Neither (of them) is my sister.   10. None (of them) belong to me.

習題 241 解答

1. Some of the questions are not very easy.

   None of the questions are very easy.

2. None of my friends will help me.

   Not any of my friends will help me.

3. Neither of the two sisters is very pretty.

Not either of the two sisters is very pretty.

4. Not all the students are present.

   None of the students are present.

5. None of the members was (were) interested in the program.

   Not every one of the members was interested in the program.

6. None of the brothers have (has) a new watch.

   Not each one of the brothers has a new watch.

7. Neither of them went to movies.

   Not both of them went to movies.

8. I know none of these girls.

   I don't know any of these girls.

9. Some of my friends don't speak French.

   None of my friends speak (s) French.

10. One of these tourists has not been here.

    No one of these tourists has been here.

11. I have seen no one of those gentlemen.

    I haven't seen one of those gentlemen.

12. Many of the books are not John's.

    Not many of the books are John's.

習題 242 解答

1. The children are both playing in the yard.

2. The guests each bought a gift.

3. The money has all disappeared.

4. The students have both failed the examination.

5. The boy each owns a bicycle.

6. She gave us all a present.

7. They should each at least try.

8. We took them all to the museum.

9. It all came originally from China.

10. The members each receive a card.

11. The mayor and the governor both have influence.

12. Do you each get a haircut?

習題 243 解答

1. Some of them are taking music lessons, aren't they?

2. All of us will be there, won't we?

3. Each of them has a watch, $\left\{ \begin{array}{l} \text{doesn't he} \\ \text{don't they} \end{array} \right\}$?

4. Three of them haven't arrived yet, have they?

5. Each of us like our milk cold, don't we?

6. Each of us likes his milk cold, doesn't he?

7. Either of us can do it, $\left\{ \begin{array}{l} \text{can't he} \\ \text{can't we} \end{array} \right\}$?

8. None of them are here right now, are they?

9. No one of them watches TV any more, $\left\{ \begin{array}{l} \text{does he} \\ \text{do they} \end{array} \right\}$?

10. Every one of you must have finished your assignment, haven't you?

習題 244 解答

1. **I** want no girls, **just** boys.

2. **Even** the cleverest students can't solve the question.

3. $\left\{ \begin{array}{l} \textbf{Only} \text{ the judge} \\ \text{The judge } \textbf{only} \end{array} \right\}$ can decide on the case.

4. The witness **alone** knows what happened.

5. John is $\left\{ \begin{array}{l} \textbf{rather} \text{ a} \\ \text{a } \textbf{rather} \end{array} \right\}$ nice fellow.

6. This is **quite** an expensive watch.

7. **Almost** all the students attended the party.

8. He spends **quite** a little time on the project.

9. I wonder whether there is **such** a thing.

10. They don't think there is any **such** thing.

11. Ten students mill make up such a strong team.

12. We need ten **more** students.

13. There are three **other** students in the room.

14. Where are the **other** three students?

15. **Another such** disaster will ruin the country.

16. Not a **single** person was to be seen in the street.

17. His remark has a **double** meaning.

18. Have you **any other** books?

19. I don't go there every day, only **every other** day.

20. Don't write on every line, wite on **every two** lines.

21. A **certain** friend of mine wants to buy the house.

22. **All such** possibilities must be considered.

23. I have met **many such** people.

24. The manager is too busy to spare $\begin{Bmatrix} \textbf{even a half} \\ \textbf{even half an} \end{Bmatrix}$ hour.

25. **Even all the** money in the world can't buy happiness.

26. What he needs is **just a little** sympathy.

27. This is **just another** example of your son's improvement.

28. He is **just another** fool.

29. I saw **only his first** model / **his first** model only.

30. Many a time did I warn him, but he paid **no** attention.

習題 245 解答

1. any other book

2. some other time

3. another three of these

4. every other boy

5. all the other girls

6. any more questions

7. $\begin{Bmatrix} \text{half a dozen eggs} \\ \text{a half dozen eggs} \end{Bmatrix}$

8. Almost every friend of his

9. such a diffcult question

10. quite an interesting story

11. Even some of the members

12. just a few friends of ours

13. rather an (/ a rather) astonishing piece of news

14. only the first few chapters of your book

15. Only a few of my best friends

16. almost double my salary

17. especially the first two acts of his play

18. only a few examples of his many stupid mistakes

19. only a few readers, but few merits

20. qnite a few interesting stories, very few people

習題 246 解答

1. She	2. his	3. they
4. They	5. it (/ she / he)	6. it (/ her)
7. its	8. its (/ his / her)	
9. him (/ her), his (/ her)	10. it (/ she)	11. she
12. her (/ its)	13. They	14. Its (/ His)
15. he, hers	16. theirs	17. He, its
18. mine, hers	19. It, ours	20. They, it

習題 247 解答

1. count (he), countess (she)

2. hen (she), cock (he)

3. heir (he), heiress (she)

4. bachelor (he), spinster (she)

5. mistress (she), master (he)

6. heroine (she), hero (he)

7. sir (he), madam (she)

8. witch (she), wizard (he)

9. bride (she), bridegroom (he)

10. hostess (she), host (he)

11. ewe (she), ram (he)

12. duchess (she), duke (he)

13. steward (he), stewardess (she)

14. nun (she), monk (he)

15. mare (she), horse (he)

16. lady (she), gentleman (he)

17. bull (he), cow (she)

18. grandfather (he), grandmother (she)

19. niece (she), nephew (he)

20. landlord (he), landlady (she)

21. king (he), queen (she)

22. prince (he), princess (she)

23. manservant (he), maidservant (she)

24. daughter (she), son (he)

25. widow (she), widower (he)

習題 248 解答

1. He likes me.

2. They need her.

3. It takes care of us.

4. She ran after you.

5. We understand them.

6. You are watching him carefully.

習題 249 解答

1. He bought them for her.

2. He (She) explained it to him (her).

3. She and I told him a story.

4. They came to see them.

5. We told him about it last month.

6. He will find it for her.

7. He gave a lot of them to him and her.

8. They went into the garden, where they saw it.

9. Very soon it noticed her as she went hunting about, and called out to her in an angry tone.

10. He had taken it out of his pocket, and was looking at it uneasily, shaking it every now and then, and holding it to his ear.

習題 250 解答

1. We, them	2. him	3. him
4. me	5. me	6. they
7. I	8. me	9. he (/ him)
10. us, her, she	11. he, I (/ me)	12. she
13. her	14. I (/ me), us	15. me, me
16. her, she	17. he, him	18. I (/ me), him
19. you, him and me.	20. she (/ her), I (/ me), her, me	

習題 251 解答

1. Jane is going to write a letter herself.

   Jane herself is going to write a letter.

   Jane is going to write herself a letter.

   Jane is going to write a letter to herself.

2. Jack has gone to buy a coat himself.

   Jack himself has gone to buy a coat.

   Jack has gone to buy himself a coat.

   Jack has gone to buy a coat for himself.

3. Miss Wood taught the lesson herself.

Miss Wood herself taught the lesson.

Miss Wood taught herself the lesson.

Miss Wood taught the lesson to herself.

4. James made a big sandwich himself.

James himself made a big sandwich.

James made himself a big sandwich.

James made a big sandwich for himself.

5. You told a lie yourself.

You yourself told a lie.

You told yourself a lie.

You told a lie to yourself.

6. The students asked a question themselves.

The students themselves asked a question.

The students asked themselves a question.

The students asked a question of themselves.

7. I am going to find a job myself.

I myself am going to find a job.

I am going to find myself a job.

I am going to find a job for myself.

8. Mrs. White cut a slice of bread herself.

Mrs. White herself cut a slice of bread.

Mrs. White cut herself a slice of bread.

Mrs. White cut a slice of bread for herself.

9. We are going to bake cake ourselves.

We ourselves are going to bake cake.

We are going to bake ourselves cake.

We are going to bake cake for ourselves.

10. Charles and Susan will build a new house themselves.

Charles and Susan themselves will build a new house.

Charles and Susan will build themselves a new house.

Charles and Susan will build a new house for themselves.

習題 252 解答

1. her, herself

2. mine, my, myself

3. mine, his, himself

4. ourselves, our (etc.)

5. herself, her

6. theirs, themselves

7. his, himself

8. yourself (/ yourselves), your

9. yourself, mine, yours, yourself, your

10. oneself (/ himself), one's (/ his)

習題 253 解答

1. Why doesn't he do it himself?

2. Yes, but you are a pretty good one yourself.

3. No, they'll have to go by themselves.

4. Why doesn't she get it herself?

5. Yes, but you have a pretty good one youself.

6. No, they'll finish by themselves.

7. Why don't they write him a letter themselves?

8. Yes, but you know an awful lot yourself.

9. No, she'll walk downtown by herself.

10. Why don't you look for it yourselves?

11. Yes, but you need to spend some time in the lab yourself.

12. No they'll practice English by themselves.

習題 254 解答

1. It, cold today

2. It, a lot

3. What, it is

4. How, it is

5. It is, way

6. It's, only, minutes'

7. Who, it

8. who it is

9. It, to

10. It, no, trying

11. It, that

12. It, saying

13. it, to

14. It, whether

15. it, that

16. It, is, since

17. It, that

18. Whose, is it

19. it, that

20. It, going

習題 255 解答

1. It is I that / who am fortunate.

2. It was an hour ago that / when he left.

3. It was New York that / where she wanted to go (to).

4. It was in May that / when they got married.

5. It was the president that / who proposed the bill.

6. It was his work during the weekend that / which exhausted him.

7. It is the red book, not the green one, that / which I want.

8. It was John, not Dick, that / who(m) I gave the book to.

9. It was on Sunday, not on Saturday, that / when I saw him.

10. It is the people, not the dollars, that I am concerned about.

11. It is money that / which he doesn't have much of.

12. It is whether I can go or not that I'm not sure of.

13. It was he that / who (m) we heard playing the piano.

14. It is experience that / which the young man doesn't have much of.

15. It was she that / who (m) they watched walking across the street.

習題 256 解答

1. It was her request that we help her.

2. It was their recommendation that he not follow the order.

3. It was our proposition that they change the subject.

4. It was your advice that I not buy the car.

5. It was his order that his instructions be obeyed.

6. It was my intention that I come back the next year.

習題 257 解答

1. No, it is the museum that he went to.

2. No, it is his sister that / who (m) he went with.

3. No, it is by taxi that they went to the museum.

4. No, it is George's brother that / who told me to come here.

5. No, it is his children that / who (m) Bob wants me to take care of.

6. No, it is my boss's daughter that / who (m) I am working hard for.

習題 258 解答

1. Bob and Dick helped each other.

2. Mr. Smith and Mrs. Smith respect each other.

3. The mother and the daughter depend on each other.

4. Jane and Mary gave a present each other.

5. He and she know each other's name.

6. I and you kept a picture of each other.

7. Jack and Bob woke up each other.

8. She and he didn't call up each other last night.

習題 259 解答

1. They gave a present to each other.

2. They looked at themselves in the mirror.

3. They corrected each other's paper.

4. They support themselves with a part-time job.

5. They reminded themselves to report their addresses.

6. They trained themselves to protect each other.

7. They told each other not to forget to bring their I. D. card.

8. They expected each other to buy themselves a drink.

習題 260 解答

1. It's self-respect.   2. It's mutual respect.

3. It's self-defense.   4. It's mutual defense.

5. It's self-criticism.   6. It's mutual support.

7. It's self-service.   8. It's mutual admiration.

9. It's self-discipline.   10. It's mutual destruction.

習題 261 解答

1. something useful   2. someone / somebody famous

3. sometime earlier   4. somewhere quiet

5. something very interesting   6. someone / somebody well-known

7. sometime more suitable   8. somewhere very near

9. somehow   10. somewhat

習題 262 解答

1. Do you think he lives anywhere near?

   No, he lives nowhere near.

2. Do you think they can meet anytime earlier?

   No, they could meet no time earlier.

3. Do you think she can buy anything interesting to read on the train?

   No, she can buy nothing interesting to read on the train.

4. Do you think he can find anyplace convenient to park his car?

   No, he can find no place convenient to park his car.

5. Do you think anything good bound to come out of it?

   No, nothing good is bound to come out of it.

6. Do you think you can find anyone able and willing?

No, I can find no one able and willing.

習題 263 解答

1. something else	2. someplace else
3. what else	4. everything else
5. everyone/everybody else	6. some other way
7. where else	8. some other reason
9. when else	10. anything else
11. no one else	12. what other way
13. any other place	14. nothing else
15. what other reason	16. no other time
17. every other way	18. everyplace else
19. no other reason	20. no other way

習題 264 解答

1. Eat something else.

What else can I eat?

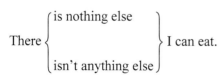

There {is nothing else / isn't anything else} I can eat.

2. Go somewhere else.

Where else can I go?

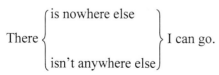

There {is nowhere else / isn't anywhere else} I can go.

3. See him some other time.

When else can I see him?

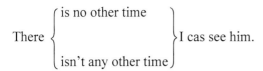

There $\left\{ \begin{array}{l} \text{is no other time} \\ \text{isn't any other time} \end{array} \right\}$ I cas see him.

4. Write to someone else.

Who(m) can I write to?

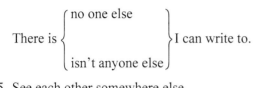

There is $\left\{ \begin{array}{l} \text{no one else} \\ \text{isn't anyone else} \end{array} \right\}$ I can write to.

5. See each other somewhere else.

Where else can we see each other?

There $\left\{ \begin{array}{l} \text{is nowhere else} \\ \text{isn't anywhere else} \end{array} \right\}$ we can see each other.

6. Wear something else.

What else can I wear?

There $\left\{ \begin{array}{l} \text{is nothing else} \\ \text{isn't anything else} \end{array} \right\}$ I can wear.

習題 265 解答

1. something   2. anything   3. anything

4. sometime   5. someplace / somewhere   6. someone

7. anyone   8. anyone   9. sometime

10. Everybody / Everyone   11. Everyone / Everybody / Anyone / Anybody

12. someone / somebody   13. Everyone / Everybody

14. Everywhere   15. anything   16. Everything

17. someone / some body; anyone / anybody   18. anyone

19. Everyone / Everybody; no one / nobody

20. everybody / everyone; everybody / everyone

習題 266 解答

1. Which will you drive, real cars or toy cars?

   The real ones.

2. Which do you prefer, weak coffee or strong coffee?

   The strong coffee.

3. Which do you want, a high grade or a low grade?

   The high one.

4. Which costs more, an old apartment or a new apartment?

   The new one does.

5. Which do you like better, summer weather or winter weather?

   The winter weather.

6. Which do you usually smoke, cheap cigarettes or expensive cigarettes?

   The cheap ones.

7. Which do you enjoy more, classical music or popular music?

   The classical music.

8. Which do you prefer, Chinese tea or American coffee?

   The Chinese tea.

9. Which did you buy, black ink or blue ink?

   The blue ink.

10. Which must I use, a black pencil or a blue pencil?

    The black one.

習題 267 解答

1. **One** must be loyal to **one's** (/ his) friends.

2. **One** should not live for **oneself** (/ himself) alone.

3. **One** does not like to have **one's** (/ his) word doubted.

4. Do you have a knife? yes, I have **one**.

5. **One** went this way; another **one** went that way.

6. He has three black pencils and one red **one**.

7. She has two long pencils and two short **ones**.

8. We compared American Universities with British **ones**.

9. Your plan is a good **one** on paper.

10. There are right answers and wrong **ones**.

11. The chance was too good a **one** to let pass.

12. These shoes are more comfortable than the old **ones**.

13. I like the hat on the shelf, not the **one** in the closet.

14. That is the **one** that I want to buy.

15. I never read the **ones** in the library.

16. People who succeed most in business are not necessarily the **ones** who were best at school.

習題 268 解答

1. some, any	2. some, any	3. some, ones
4. one	5. some, one	6. some, some
7. one	8. some, ones	9. one
10. any, ones	11. ones, some, any	12. one, ones
13. any, some, ones	14. any, ones	15. some, one, one

習題 269 解答

1. Will you have this hat or that (one)?

2. Will you have these suits or those?

3. Will you have this green hat or that blue one?

4. Will you have these green shirts or those blue ones?

5. Bob's exercise books are neater than Dick's.

6. My cheap camera is just as good as John's expensive one.

7. This is my hat and that is my brother's.

8. Your old suit looks as smart as your brother's new one.

9. Do you rent the house or is it your own?

10. I put my right arm through Mary's left one.

習題 270 解答

1. $\left\{\begin{array}{l}\text{Another place}\\\text{Another (one)}\end{array}\right\}$ takes only cash.

2. $\left\{\begin{array}{l}\text{The other Place}\\\text{The other (one)}\end{array}\right\}$ takes only cash.

3. $\left\{\begin{array}{l}\text{Other places}\\\text{Others}\end{array}\right\}$ take only cash.

4. $\left\{\begin{array}{l}\text{The other places}\\\text{The others}\\\text{The rest}\end{array}\right\}$ take only cash.

5. Other food is for snacks.

6. $\left\{\begin{array}{l}\text{The other food}\\\text{The rest}\end{array}\right\}$ is for snacks.

7. It alienates $\left\{\begin{array}{l}\text{other people}\\\text{others}\end{array}\right\}$.

8. There's $\left\{\begin{array}{l}\text{another restaurant}\\\text{another (one)}\end{array}\right\}$ on the corner.

9. There are $\left\{\begin{array}{l}\text{other places}\\\text{others}\end{array}\right\}$ serving Mexican food.

10. $\left\{\begin{array}{l}\text{The other luggage}\\\text{The rest}\end{array}\right\}$ was light.

習題 271 解答

1. one, others

2. ones, others

3. One, the other(s)

4. one, the other

5. One, another

6. one, another

7. one, another

8. else

9. One, another

10. one, another (some, other)   11. one, another

12. one, another   13. one, the other   14. one, the other

15. one, another else

參　考　書　目

　　本書的編成得力於下列參考書之處甚多，特列於後，不在書內另做詳註。

Allen, W. Stannard. *Living English Structure*

Bach, Emmon Werner. *An Introduction to Transformational,*

　　　　　　Grammar

Chomsky, Noam Avram. *Syntactic Structures*

Chomsky, Noam Avram. *A Transformational Approach to Syntax*

Crowell, Thomas Lee Jr. *A Glossary of Phrases with Prepositions*

Curme, George O. *Principles and Practice of English Grammar*

Dixson, Robert J. *Complete Course in English*

Dixson, Robert J. *Graded Exercises in English*

Francis, W. Nelson. *The Structure of American English*

Gleason, H. Allan Jr. *An Introduction to Descriptive Linguistics*

Gleason, H. Allan Jr. *Linguistics and English Grammar*

English Language Services. *The Key to English Series*

English Language Services. *English Grammar Exercises*

Fraser, Bruce. *The Verb-Particle Combination in English*

Hill, A. Archibald. *Introduction to Linguistic Structures*

Hill, A. Archibald. *The New Linguistic Method*

Hayden, Rebecca E., *et al Mastering American English*

Hornby, Albert S. *A Guide to Patterns and Usage in English*

Hornby, Albert S., *et al. The Advanced Learner's Dictionary of*

　　　　　　Current English

Jespersen, Otto. *Essentials of English Grammar*

Lado, Robert & Fries. Charles C. *English Sentence Patterns*

Langendoen, D. Terence. *The Study of Syntax*

Langendoen, D. Terence. *Essentials of English Grammar*

Lees, Robert B. *The Grammar of English Nominalizations*

Nichols, Ann E. *English Syntax*

Myers, Louis McCorry. *American English*

Rand, Earl. *Oral Approach Drills*

Roberts, Paul. *Uuderstanding Grammar*

Roberts, Paul. *Understanding English*

Roberts, Paul. *Patterns of English*

Roberts, Paul. *English Sentences*

Roberts, Paul. *English Syntax*

Roberts, Paul. *The Roberts English Series*

Rosenbaum &Jacobits. *English Transformational Grammar*

Ross, Janet & Doty, Gladys. *Writing English*

Rutherford, William E. *Modern English*

Stageberg, Norman C. *An Introductory English Grammar*

Stockwell, Robert P., *et al. Integration of Transformational Theories on English Syntax*

Whitford, Harold C. & Dixon, Robert J. *Handbook of American Idioms and Idiomatic Usage*

Corder S. Pit. *An Intermediate English Practice Book*

Virginia & Robert Allen. *Review Exercises for English as a Foreign Language*

The National Council of Teachers of English. *English for Today*

國家圖書館出版品預行編目(CIP) 資料

觀察・類推・條理化：分析性的英語語法 / 湯廷池編
著. -- 初版. -- 臺北市：元華文創股份有限公司,
2022.12

面； 公分

ISBN 978-957-711-285-9 (上冊:平裝)

1.CST: 英語教學 2.CST: 語法 3.CST: 中等教育

524.38 111016748

觀察・類推・條理化：分析性的英語語法(上冊)

湯廷池 編著　許淑慎 監修

發 行 人：賴洋助
出 版 者：元華文創股份有限公司
聯絡地址：100 臺北市中正區重慶南路二段 51 號 5 樓
公司地址：新竹縣竹北市台元一街 8 號 5 樓之 7
電　　話：(02) 2351-1607　傳　　真：(02) 2351-1549
網　　址：www.eculture.com.tw
E-mail：service@eculture.com.tw
主　　編：李欣芳
責任編輯：立欣
行銷業務：林宜葶
出版年月：2022 年 12 月 初版
定　　價：新臺幣 600 元

ISBN：978-957-711-285-9 (平裝)

總經銷：聯合發行股份有限公司
地　址：231 新北市新店區寶橋路 235 巷 6 弄 6 號 4F
電　話：(02)2917-8022　　　傳　真：(02)2915-6275